To: Robert Morris, Reviewer Pa

Business Basics

Prepare Yourself,
Add Customers,
Cut Costs, and
Eliminate Investments
for You and Your Stakeholders

Donald Mitchell

Donald Mitchell
**Coauthor of *The 2,000 Percent Solution*,
The 2,000 Percent Squared Solution,
The Irresistible Growth Enterprise, and
*The Ultimate Competitive Advantage***

400 Year Project Press
Weston, Massachusetts
United States of America

Other Business Books by Donald Mitchell

The 2,000 Percent Solution (with Carol Coles and Robert Metz)

The Portable 2,000 Percent Solution (with Carol Coles)

The 2,000 Percent Solution Workbook (with Carol Coles)

The 2,000 Percent Squared Solution (with Carol Coles)

The Irresistible Growth Enterprise (with Carol Coles)

The Ultimate Competitive Advantage (with Carol Coles)

Other 400 Year Project Books by Donald Mitchell

Adventures of an Optimist

Witnessing Made Easy (with Bishop Dale P. Combs, Lisa Combs, Jim Barbarossa, and Carla Barbarossa)

Ways You Can Witness (with Cherie Hill, Roger de Brabant, Drew Dickens, Gael Torcise, Wendy Lobos, Herpha Jane Obod, and Gisele Umugiraneza)

2,000 Percent Living

Help Wanted

Business Basics
Prepare Yourself, Add Customers, Cut Costs, and
Eliminate Investments for You and Your Stakeholders

ISBN: 978-1-470-01278-6
1470012782

For information, contact:

Donald W. Mitchell
400 Year Project Press
P.O. Box 302
Weston, Massachusetts 02493
781-647-4211

Published in the United States of America

3 3474 05128 4501

This book is dedicated to:

The 2,000 percent solution entrepreneurs
who have created complementary breakthrough solutions.

May adding many more complementary 2,000 percent solutions
always be ahead of them!

Contents

Acknowledgments

Oh, give thanks to the LORD!
Call upon His name;
Make known His deeds among the peoples!

— 1 Chronicles 16:8 (NKJV)

I thank Almighty God, our Heavenly Father, for creating the universe and all the people on the Earth; our Lord and Savior, Jesus Christ, for providing the way for us to gain Salvation; and the Holy Spirit for guiding our daily paths towards repentance and righteousness. I also humbly acknowledge the perfect guidance I received from God through His Holy Spirit and His Word to write this book.

I am grateful to Peter Drucker for encouraging me to write about 2,000 percent solutions and to continually seek simpler ways to help people learn how to employ them. His faith in this method for solving problems caused me to take the opportunity to share what I had been doing much more seriously than I otherwise would.

I owe a special note of thanks to the members of the Billionaire Entrepreneurs' Master Mind who sponsored the research and writing that led to the lessons in *Business Basics* being selected from six years of thought-provoking collaborations and implementations.

I appreciate all those who have permitted me to share 2,000 percent solution methods with them. I thank them for all the insights I have gained into teaching these methods from observing their wonderful work.

I would like to express gratitude to the members of my family for allowing me the time and peace to work on such a huge and awe-inspiring project for God. They made many sacrifices without complaining and were a continual inspiration.

I appreciate my many clients who held off on their demands for my help so that this project could receive the attention it required over the past seventeen years. Their financial support also made it possible for me to give this time to the Lord and to invest in the expenses required to make this book available.

Finally, I am most appreciative of the many fine improvements that the editor, Bernice Pettinato, made in the text. This is the twelfth book where she has helped me to make the messages clearer and more pleasant to read. As always, she was a delight to work with. Her kindness made the writing much easier. I value all she has taught me about writing.

I accept sole responsibility for any remaining errors and apologize to my readers for any difficulties and inconvenience that they encounter as a consequence.

Introduction

There are four things which *are little on the earth,*
But they are *exceedingly wise:*
The ants are *a people not strong,*
Yet they prepare their food in the summer;
The rock badgers are a feeble folk,
Yet they make their homes in the crags;
The locusts have no king,
Yet they all advance in ranks;
The spider skillfully grasps with its hands,
And it is in kings' palaces.

— Proverbs 30:24-28 (NKJV)

Business Basics will provide you with wisdom and directions that will take you beyond what you know today so that you can accomplish far more than what you have ever dreamed was possible. You will learn *what* to work on differently as well as *how* to do your most important new tasks.

The book is valuable for would-be entrepreneurs who are planning to start up a first business, entrepreneurs with experience in creating new businesses who are preparing to do so again, and leaders of existing businesses who want to expand faster and more profitably. The prescriptions are described in ways that bring helpful new insights and advanced techniques to the most successful business leaders while also giving business newcomers valuable perspectives and information they lack. Whether you have little education or a great deal, explanations are written to be easy to access, to understand, and to apply.

The contents are based on the most extensive investigations of how to achieve business breakthroughs that have ever been conducted, conveniently summarized in one volume. Unlike most business books today that look at only small aspects of business leadership responsibilities, *Business Basics* provides a holistic approach to leadership success that both simplifies and multiplies the effectiveness of leaders' work.

Let me describe how the book is organized. *Business Basics* is divided into four parts, each of which takes a fundamental look at how to develop and to implement answers to breakthrough-creating questions that are seldom addressed by business leaders. Here are those parts and the questions each one addresses:

Part One: Prepare Yourself
How should I prepare to lead an extraordinarily successful enterprise?

Part Two: Add Customers
How can my company expand a market's size by twenty times and profitably gain market share while doing so?

Part Three: Cut Costs
How can my company's costs (and those of my stakeholders) for providing and using an offering be reduced by 96 percent?

Part Four: Eliminate Investments
How can my company and its stakeholders decrease the investment needed to provide and use an offering by 96 percent?

Why focus on these particular questions? The benefits of preparing for and accomplishing such complementary results have been spectacular and are achievable for many businesses, their leaders, and their owners. Revenues grow by much more than twenty times as the business gains the bulk of the newly stimulated market growth. Profits expand by more than 400 times as revenues soar, while unit costs plunge. Cash flow is much more than 8,000 times larger because growth requires so little new investment that cash flow is always positive … and rapidly growing. An important benefit of having so much more cash flow is that the value of the business also expands by more than 8,000 times.

Other stakeholders receive exponential benefit gains as well. The dramatic decline in the costs of acquiring and using much more helpful offerings provides customers with vastly greater value. Their increased purchases allow these offering benefits to improve the lives and financial health of many more end users, employees and their families, suppliers, distributors, lenders, suppliers, and the communities in which the company operates.

These large, sustainable benefits are created because three complementary 2,000 percent solutions (ways of accomplishing at least 8,000 times as much with the same time, money, and effort because each solution enhances the value of the other solutions, something I call a 2,000 percent cubed solution) are combined. In Chapter 11 of *Adventures of an Optimist* (Mitchell and Company Press, 2007) and Appendix B of *Help Wanted* (2,000 Percent Living Press, 2011), I explain in detail the concept of complementary 2,000 percent solutions.

To produce such complementary breakthrough solutions for businesses, many people need no more guidance than can be found in books about 2,000 percent solutions (such as *The 2,000 Percent Solution*, AMACOM, 1999; *The 2,000 Percent Solution Workbook*, iUniverse, 2005; *The Irresistible Growth Enterprise*, Stylus, 2000; *The 2,000 Percent Squared Solution*, Mitchell and Company Press, 2007; and *2,000 Percent Living*, Salvation Press, 2010) to answer the breakthrough questions posed for each part of *Business Basics*.

From experience, however, I have found that more people will implement such a valuable concept after having more detailed directions and examples. In that sense, *Business Basics* can serve as a workbook, in much the same way that *The 2,000 Percent Squared Solution* shows how to apply the concepts in *The Ultimate Competitive Advantage* (Berrett-Koehler, 2003) to for-profit and nonprofit organizations by creating 2,000 percent solutions for rapidly growing how many people are served while dramatically cutting unit costs.

In contrast to its title, *Business Basics* is also an advanced book that assumes knowledge of and facility in several of the books developed by the 400 Year Project (founded in 1995 to demonstrate how to accomplish improvements in less than one year that normally take at least twenty years to achieve: see at www.fastforward400.com) including *The 2,000 Percent Solution*, *The 2,000 Percent Solution Workbook*, *The Irresistible Growth Enterprise*, *The Ultimate Competitive Advantage*, *The 2,000 Percent Squared Solution*, and *2,000 Percent Living*. Your time and attention in reading and applying those books will be well repaid by upgrading your knowledge, skills, and resources for breakthroughs you want to accomplish.

Business Basics is designed to be read and applied over at least a year. The book's messages are captured in fifty-two lessons presented in the four parts that correspond to the four breakthrough questions listed earlier. Each lesson contains assignments for you. Some of the assignments can be done in a few hours. Completing other assignments may well extend over several months. Think of *Business Basics* as a book that combines theory, advanced practices, and directions for applied work.

Each lesson has been tested by members of The Billionaire Entrepreneurs' Master Mind, a group of entrepreneurs around the world that was founded in 2006. I serve as the research coordinator for the group, and I authored all of the lessons developed so far (exceeding 300 and growing). The fifty-two lessons you find in the book are the ones that were most valuable to the study group's members in recent years for answering the four breakthrough questions.

Many people incorrectly doubt that businesses can make such exponential gains. I invite such skeptics to read and apply the book with a critical eye to see if what is shared makes sense. What do such skeptics have to lose except a little time, some money, and some false beliefs?

I am confident that readers will want to employ what they learn because each step is filled with compelling common sense that is all too often ignored in business. Part of my confidence is based on having seen businesses of all sizes successfully apply these fifty-two lessons to their operations.

You might wonder why I created this book rather than just teaching these lessons to my clients and students. *Business Basics* isn't designed just to help those who read and apply its lessons and their stakeholders. It's also intended to help business leaders who either copy or just slightly improve on the new business models that are created by the book's readers. As a result of such efforts, my goal is to encourage and to assist a million entrepreneurs to succeed in establishing 2,000 percent cubed solution businesses for the first time. From the resulting business models, I estimate that over a hundred million vastly improved businesses will eventually emerge.

The offerings and benefits for stakeholders from such new business models will improve global prosperity in an unprecedented way, one of the goals of the 400 Year Project (to help everyone on Earth improve twenty times faster than normal from 2015 through 2035). I thank you for helping humanity by reading the book and applying its lessons. You will probably never know all of the good that you are doing.

Let me leave you with one last thought: Choose the right partners and you can accomplish even more. My work on business improvement is always done in partnership with Almighty God, the Father; the Lord Jesus Christ, my Savior; and the Holy Spirit, Who guide my daily steps. I advise and encourage you, as well, to work with these three Partners. They want to and can give you all the help you need to succeed far beyond what you can ask or think (Ephesians 3:20, NKJV). If you select a purpose for your business that advances the Kingdom of God, you'll find that these wonderful Partners will provide supernatural support for what you do that will cause far greater results to occur. May God bless you as you do!

Part One

Prepare Yourself

You prepare a table before me in the presence of my enemies;
You anoint my head with oil;
My cup runs over.
Surely goodness and mercy shall follow me
All the days of my life;
And I will dwell in the house of the LORD
Forever.

Psalm 23:5-6 (NKJV)

Just before I wrote this introduction to Part One, I watched a televised interview with John Scully, the CEO Steve Jobs recruited from PepsiCo in 1983 to lead Apple when Jobs was twenty-eight. Reflecting on what happened to Apple over the subsequent twenty-seven years, Scully commented that Apple's board made a mistake in hiring him. Scully observed that Apple's board of directors should have, instead, found a way to work with the immensely talented Jobs, despite his difficult personality. The interview occurred shortly after Apple under Jobs as CEO became the most valuable corporation in the United States in 2010. By contrast, Apple barely survived mistakes under Scully's leadership after he removed Jobs as head of the Macintosh division in 1985.

Jobs chose Scully to lead Apple because of Scully's success in profitably gaining market share for Pepsi-Cola against Coca-Cola. What went wrong for Scully at Apple? While many people believe that any good business leader can successfully head any other business, history teaches otherwise. All but a few business leaders have done much better in operating some types of businesses than in any others.

Each business leader has different skills, experience, and knowledge. In some cases, the fit with what the business needs to prosper is almost perfect, much like a custom-made suit or a designer-created dress complements its wearer. In most cases, however, the leadership fit with the business is poor, creating the wrong results much as when someone wears clothes that are much too large or small, and feature colors and designs that accentuate undesirable aspects of the wearer's body shape.

Part One is designed to help you focus your business activities where your and your organization's unique skills, experiences, perspectives and knowledge will help you to be more successful. Lesson One examines the importance of leaders thinking and reacting as customers and employees do, a level of leadership congruence that rarely occurs. Lesson Two points the way to finding market segments to serve where innovation is needed, but competitors are ignoring the opportunities and will probably continue to do so. Lesson Three explains the need for following a spiritual purpose to avoid making harmful, ego-pleasing decisions. Lesson Four encourages finding problems to solve that will bring out the best in you and your business. Lesson Five helps you decide what legacy you want to leave through your business activities, a useful perspective for being a more responsible and effective leader.

If you would like to make more preparations to succeed, the lessons in *2,000 Percent Living* can equip you with many capabilities to expand the number and type of opportunities that you will be able to successfully address. As a result, you can acquire more knowledge, be more innovative, and make better decisions. After adding such capabilities, be sure to read Lesson Two in *Business Basics* before choosing a market segment to serve.

Lesson One

Think and Feel
Just Like Your Customers and Employees

Rejoice with those who rejoice, and weep with those who weep.
Be of the same mind toward one another.
Do not set your mind on high things, but associate with the humble.
Do not be wise in your own opinion.
Repay no one evil for evil.
Have regard for good things in the sight of all men.
If it is possible, as much as depends on you,
live peaceably with all men.

— Romans 12:15-18 (NKJV)

When I teach aspiring entrepreneurs about how to succeed, I emphasize one lesson above all others: *Pick a market to serve where your every thought and feeling is already identical to what current and prospective customers and employees think and feel or will think and feel.* I think of such congruence as being a gift provided by humble empathy.

Why do I provide such advice? It's simple: The most successful entrepreneurs I've met and studied thought and felt just like their customers and employees. Such entrepreneurs also displayed vastly greater imagination, desire, and determination to make improvements than did other entrepreneurs I have met and studied.

You've probably read more articles and books than you care to remember that tell you to listen to customers and to give them what they want. While it's certainly better to listen to customers than to ignore them, there are two problems with such advice:

1. If you think and feel differently than customers do about the benefits and drawbacks of your offerings, you'll often miss the point of what they are telling you.

2. Customers have a hard time imagining their future reactions to what doesn't yet exist.

As an intelligent person who has confidence in your abilities, you may be thinking, "How hard can it be to learn to think and feel like my customers do?" Becoming fluent in Hebrew (for those who aren't) will probably be an easier task.

Why? Thoughts and emotions are deeply rooted in our minds to experiences, assumptions, context, and culture. Without having the same roots as your customers you may not fully appreciate what their thoughts and feelings mean, even when you can grasp what those thoughts and feelings are.

But if you have such roots in place and think and feel like current and prospective customers, then it's a no-brainer to get it right in growing the market to a larger size.

So what's a good market for you to expand by twenty times while gaining a high percentage of the growth for your business? It's any market with large potential where you already think and feel exactly like the typical and prospective customers.

Let me give you a few examples of how this approach works. Steve Jobs is a legend in consumer electronics for having helped to develop and to market the first mass desktop computer, the Apple II. Later, he led the development of the more innovative Macintosh computer. After being ousted from Apple, he led the animation business, Pixar, which has created so many movie hits. More recently, Jobs amazed almost everyone by creating the iPod and the iTunes store that made it practical, legal, and cool to accumulate and to enjoy portable, low-cost music. Since Jobs' death, Apple is in the process of accomplishing the same result for portable communications through the iPhone and iPad.

How could one person be so inventive and so successful? It's easy: He just developed markets by creating businesses that provided offerings that he would have liked to use. Jobs was gifted with a feel for what demanding consumers wanted from cutting-edge personal electronics and electronic-based entertainment and tools. When his new offerings came out, these trend-setting buyers were quick to snap up what Jobs provided. Customers enjoyed greater access to benefits, felt smart while doing so, and loved the look and feel of the products they operated.

In that very resonance, however, was an Achilles' heel for Jobs: He had less sense of or interest in what the average (as opposed to trend-setting) consumer electronics user wanted. Consequently, competitors may eventually scoop up most of the benefit from his innovations by making a popular version that better fits what most people want. As a result, Jobs missed many of the largest related business opportunities of all time including selling operating system software (the core of Microsoft's success) despite having the best one for desktop applications, designing "cool" high-definition televisions, and providing a full line of computer products and access to software that larger companies need. Why did Jobs miss those areas? The answer is based in his perspective. Jobs was reportedly proud to be uninterested in such areas and spent millions of Apple's dollars on advertisements making fun of people who were.

Let's consider Mattel, the toy maker, as another example of how empathy affects business leadership and success in market expansions. The company prospered for many years under the leadership of Ruth Handler who developed the Barbie doll, which was until recent years the world's most popular doll. In its early days, Barbie and her accessories greatly increased overall doll sales. While Ms. Handler was at the company, the Barbie franchise soared. Why? She understood exactly what moms wanted to buy for their daughters because she was a mom who cared about dolls. In fact, the doll's name was inspired by Ms. Handler's daughter's name, Barbara.

After Ms. Handler left the company, Mattel floundered. Barbie's sales were stagnant for many years following that parting of the ways until Jill Barad began developing marketing plans for the iconic doll line. Ms. Barad displayed a wonderful touch and feel for what Barbie's customers were thinking and feeling. Riding on that success, Ms. Barad became CEO … but soon mishandled acquisitions and operating the other parts of Mattel's toy line.

As Ms. Barad's successor, the board chose to bring in a tough-talking, no-nonsense CEO, Robert Eckert, who had done well at Kraft by being a great cost-cutter who simply copied whatever the best practice was for spending little. At Mattel Eckert quickly arranged for as many toys as possible to be made inexpensively in China. Profits grew, even if new products did poorly during this time. Even worse, a new line of dolls,

Bratz, came along from a competitor that expanded the market and threatened to outpace the venerable Barbie.

Then, a new disaster struck. Mattel was accused of selling tens of millions of toys covered with lead-based paint which, if consumed, could harm the mental development of small children. In its cost-cutting program, Mattel forgot that parents want safe toys for their children more than they want less costly toys. To an outside observer it seems as though Eckert may not have been primarily thinking and feeling like a toy customer but, rather, more like a cost accountant working on commission.

Sir Richard Branson is the best-known example of someone who has been successful in dozens of new businesses. Sir Richard is an inquisitive high-school dropout who likes a good time, cannot read very well (suffering from dyslexia), and is easily distracted. That combination makes him think and feel a lot like most customers in any mass market. As a result, he's been able to succeed in almost 100 different industries, all marketed under the Virgin brand, by simply providing better offerings that he, as an ordinary consumer, would like to have.

By contrast, most people are excited about serving a market for reasons other than because they think and feel as customers do. Such motivations can keep anyone who follows those instincts from gaining success.

Here, then, are directions to help you identify places where you will be most successful in expanding the market and gaining market share:

1. Write down what's most important to you about the offerings in each market that interests you and then compare your answers to survey results from current and potential customers.

   Many organizations regularly sponsor such surveys. If they don't, you can easily conduct one by using online survey tools (such as are available for free at SurveyMonkey.com) and inexpensive click-based advertising to attract respondents (such as Google's AdWords provide). For more details on conducting a survey, read Appendix A. It's important that you write down your own answers to the survey questions before finding out how others think and feel. Otherwise, you may fool yourself into believing their answers are the same as your own … when all that has happened is that their answers merely seem to be understandable to you (as the current CEO of Mattel probably now appreciates that lead paint should be more effectively avoided).

2. Imagine innovations you might use to improve such offerings. Then simulate providing such improvements for current and potential customers, check out customer reactions, and compare their reactions to your own views.

   If you find significant differences in such customer reactions from your personal views, it's the wrong market for you.

3. If you find that your thinking doesn't match well with any of the markets that originally interested you, sit back and consider where you may have a better sense of what's wanted.

   Consider conversations you've had with customers for other markets. Where have you begun laments about what needs to be changed that everyone quickly agreed with? Once you have such an industry in mind, repeat the steps in points one and two for that industry.

4. If you find you have a good sense of more than one industry, check to see how easy it is to find people to work with you who think and feel similarly to current and potential customers.

It's not enough for you to be a good thinker about your industry: It's much better to be able to field a team who will all be able to do so. So investigate how hard it will be to find others who are already well-tuned in their thinking and feelings with this market's customers and prospects.

Assignments

1. Check how congruent your thinking is with current and potential customers and employees in markets you may want to grow by twenty times.

2. Select the market (or market segment) to focus on with which you are most congruent with current and potential customers and you can find the most congruent thinkers to become colleagues.

Lesson Two

Choose Your Market Segment
as if Your Life (and Livelihood)
Depended on Your Choice

*"Go and tell David,
'Thus says the LORD: "I offer you three things;
choose one of them for yourself, that I may do it to you."'"*

— 2 Samuel 24:12 (NKJV)

If you are the best in the world at whatever you do, market segment selection isn't all that important. You'll shine anyway. Steven Spielberg has extraordinary success in the motion picture industry due to his uncanny talent despite long odds and lots of gifted competition.

But most of us have already met someone who is much more talented than we are. *To create a highly successful enterprise, we will need to create advantages that mere talent cannot surmount.*

That's where market-segment selection can help. Most entrepreneurs haven't had much experience with market-segment selection. They usually focus on a segment based on knowing more about that segment than any others. But picking a segment in which no one is interested right now can give you more time to develop and to hone new advantages that others will find it hard to duplicate, no matter how talented they are.

The size of opportunities also varies by market segment. Luxury food sales are never going to be as big as for commodity foods. Pick a bigger segment, and you are likely to build a bigger business.

Profit potential also differs from one market segment to another. Commercial airlines in the United States almost always lose money because there are too many of them and lots of excess capacity. Life insurance companies in the United States almost always make money because most people cancel policies before they die.

Over the past fifty years a lot has been learned about why some market segments are more attractive to entrepreneurs than others … and why other market segments should be highly sought after, but aren't. It's those latter market segments that we should be looking for.

Let's consider some of the key points in identifying market segments with high potential for success, keeping in mind the admonitions in Lesson One.

Use the Unattractiveness Stall
as a Guiding Star

How long, you simple ones, will you love simplicity?
For scorners delight in their scorning,
And fools hate knowledge.

— Proverbs 1:22 (NKJV)

Every person finds some situations and activities appalling. For some this reaction might include processing sewage. For others, it might be touching an ill person who is dying. Some people don't like to go to parties because they find it hard to make small talk.

People vary in their reactions to such circumstances. Sanitation engineers are usually fascinated with providing safe sewage disposal. Mother Teresa felt uplifted by holding the dying in her arms and preparing them for passing. Many people have had the most fun in their lives at parties.

With the right combination of circumstances, you can find a highly profitable opportunity: You like an activity that very few others can tolerate, and there's a lot of potential skill to learn and bring to bear.

Tom Golisano, founder of Paychex, a U.S.-based payroll processing firm, built his fortune from such an opportunity. He realized that small employers did a poor job of taking care of their payrolls and pension plans despite the costliness of their mistakes. If you don't file your government returns or pay your payroll taxes or pension contributions on time, the penalties and interest can be enormous. Yet the employers weren't really interested in such activities. Instead, most employers wanted to be selling new business or running operations. Bookkeepers found providing such services to be annoying and relatively unprofitable. Small accounting firms wanted to work for larger clients. Automated payroll processors were set up for those who had at least fifty employees and usually couldn't see how to make a profit on any smaller scale. Yet most employees work for organizations with fewer than fifty employees.

Assignment: Look for large market segments where customers and offering providers are repelled by a task, yet economic benefits are potentially large for doing the activity superbly.

Find Repeatable Services to Offer

And whoever exalts himself will be humbled,
and he who humbles himself will be exalted.

— Matthew 23:12 (NKJV)

In my studies of large companies and major nonprofits that started small, I noticed something that surprised me. The fastest growth usually occurred for those who made products. But the most sustained and largest successes were from organizations that provided services rather than products.

I wondered why. Here are some of the lessons:

- People become dependent on service providers and are less likely to change providers than they are to try new products.
- If the customer has to learn new processes or to make other changes to use a new service provider, it's difficult and expensive to change suppliers.
- Personal relationships are formed more often with service providers than with product providers.

- Service revenues are usually smaller on a per-usage basis, and the costs are less visible to customers than for purchased products.
- Customized service offerings are difficult for competitors to duplicate exactly, which allows for noneconomic competitive differentiation. For instance, some customers may prefer a dry cleaning establishment that keeps clothes looking like new, even if the clothes aren't quite as clean.

Assignment: Identify opportunities in unappealing market segments to provide frequently repeated services that have high noneconomic value for customers.

Focus on Services That Can Be Happily Provided by Large Numbers of People

"Then came the first, saying,
'Master, your mina has earned ten minas.'
And he said to him,
'Well done, good servant;
because you were faithful in a very little,
have authority over ten cities.'"

— Luke 19:16-17 (NKJV)

Many service businesses peak at a small size because there are inadequate numbers of people who can provide the service. A good example can be found in Chinese restaurants. High quality Chinese cooking requires heating the food to extraordinarily high temperatures in a wok. Chains that want to offer Chinese food must either eliminate wok cooking (affecting quality) or slow their expansions until enough chefs with the right talents can be attracted or trained. As a result, don't expect to see fast food chains outside of China adding tens of thousands of units that provide wok-based Chinese food.

The most successful fast-food restaurant chains, by contrast, employ simple food preparation and service processes that almost anyone (regardless of skills, knowledge, education, and experience) can quickly learn to do well. It's not surprising that such chains frequently grow to exceed a billion dollars in revenues by focusing on being able to train low-wage employees to provide acceptable food and service.

Paychex dealt with this potential limitation by automating the hard parts of accounting and pension processing for small companies and eliminating unnecessary steps that required lots of people. All of the remaining simple tasks can be performed well by service-oriented people who are willing to undergo up to six weeks of training.

Assignment: Identify opportunities in unattractive market segments to provide frequently repeatable services that have high noneconomic value to customers and can be redesigned to be happily provided by large numbers of people at affordable labor costs.

Lesson Three

Engage in Spiritual Purposes
to Avoid Arrogance and Narcissism

I know that You can do everything,
And that no purpose of Yours *can be withheld from You.*

— Job 42:2 (NKJV)

As background for this lesson, I read *The Rise of the Rogue Executive* (Wharton School Publishing, 2005) by Dr. Leonard R. Sayles and Dr. Cynthia J. Smith. As you are probably aware, many of the world's biggest business frauds have been conducted in recent years by senior officers of major American corporations. In the book, I was impressed by how well the authors captured the greed mentality: Success was often considered such a right by those in charge that they felt justified in doing anything to pile up more millions for themselves. Large companies such as Adelphia, Enron, and WorldCom were operated like private piggy banks to fill the leaders' pockets while the companies were actually insolvent.

In addition to such criminal behavior, I have all too often seen extremely smart, honest, and hard-working people, especially entrepreneurs, be seduced into creating business disasters after experiencing too much financial success. As a result, leaders develop such a high opinion of themselves that everyone else becomes merely an object to be manipulated. Naturally, that psychology is a leading indicator that the company is about to have severe problems created by bad leadership decisions.

As you implement the strategies described in *Business Basics*, you could find yourself becoming vulnerable to acting based on more wrong temptations than you ever thought possible. Once you give in to such temptations, your reputation will be so tarnished that it will be hard to improve matters except by retiring.

I'm assuming that you would prefer to stay at the leadership helm until your organization reaches your goals. If so, now is the time to inoculate yourself and your current and future colleagues from arrogance and narcissism.

How can you do that? *From the beginning, establish a spiritual purpose for your enterprise.*

This may be a relatively new idea for you. Perhaps you don't even feel especially spiritual. That's okay. In that case, a spiritual purpose will be even more helpful for you.

How can you get started in establishing a spiritual purpose? Draw on any spiritual experiences you've had, your religious beliefs, your personal philosophy of life, and your subjective reactions to what needs to be done to enhance spirituality. If none of those sources work for you, I suggest taking a spiritual retreat to think through your life's purpose. Many people report great results from silent retreats where they are truly alone with God and their thoughts for a few days.

How can you tell when you've developed an appropriate spiritual purpose? If you are a Christian, you should pray that the Holy Spirit guide you to the proper purposes. You should also test any potential purposes to see if they agree with what the Bible says.

If you aren't a follower of Jesus, here's a test that may help: Imagine that the spiritual purpose you are considering is fulfilled, but you lost all your personal wealth in the process. How do you feel about that result? If you feel great, you probably have a powerful spiritual purpose. If you feel mixed or negative emotions, you need a much stronger spiritual purpose.

A spiritual purpose for your enterprise can provide you with other benefits, including:

- God's intercession to support your work
- Increased confidence that you will succeed
- A greater ability to attract and inspire others as stakeholders
- More creativity
- Increased openness to others' good suggestions
- Better balance in your life

Let me share a personal example. Through direction from God's Holy Spirit, I became convinced that the world could experience 400 years' worth of normal Godly, economic, and social improvement in only twenty years if people would simply demonstrate how such a result could occur. I came to feel this conviction so deeply that it became a spiritual quest for me both through exercising my faith and reorienting all other aspects of my life. I began sharing that spiritual purpose with other people in 1995 when I launched the 400 Year Project.

Sharing the purpose then helped me attract great supporters such as members of my learning organizations, management guru Peter Drucker, people who improved my writing, readers, students, and clients. Almost all of what has been accomplished since 1995 by this project has been as a result of guidance from the Holy Spirit and sharing my spiritual purpose with others. Considering the magnitude of the challenge and the enormous tasks that remain to be accomplished has continually succeeded in keeping me humble. I see the same effect in those who have joined me in this spiritual quest.

In the following sections, you'll find principles to consider while you search for the right spiritual purposes for your enterprise.

Serve in Ways That Are Ennobling
for Those Who Serve and Those Who Are Served

For you, brethren, have been called to liberty;
only do not use *liberty as an opportunity for the flesh,*
but through love serve one another.
For all the law is fulfilled in one word, even *in this:*
"You shall love your neighbor as yourself."

— Galatians 5:13-14 (NKJV)

Peter Drucker's career provides a good example of applying this principle of ennobling service. He wanted to divide his consulting practice evenly between serving for-profit and nonprofit organizations. He knew that only the for-profit organizations could afford to pay. How could he obtain enough nonprofit clients? He would have to work for free.

But Peter wanted the nonprofit leaders to feel good about seeking his advice and to take it seriously. He instructed such leaders to come to the meeting check in hand for the full consulting fee. At the end of the day, Peter would thank them for giving him the opportunity to serve, and he would endorse the check to the organization and hand it back to the leader.

Peter's approach ensured that the nonprofit leaders felt that they could press for his best because they expected to receive value for the thousands of dollars they thought they were paying. The nonprofit client paid for lunch and could feel that Peter had received some compensation. Peter was delighted by the fun he had in springing his surprise.

On subsequent visits no nonprofit leader could be sure that Peter wouldn't just take the check and keep it. So the relationships remained ennobling. The nonprofit leader could imagine that he or she had done such a good job of paying attention that day that Peter was rewarding him or her for being a good student. And there was certainly an element of that. Peter wouldn't work with just anyone who asked. He wanted to help the brightest stars to shine more brightly.

Assignment: Redesign your business's offerings to make receiving them feel more like obtaining a lifetime honor and providing them to be as much fun as giving gifts to poor children at a holiday gathering.

Provide Offerings That Leave You Feeling Humbler
Rather Than More Satisfied

When pride comes, then comes shame;
But with the humble is *wisdom.*

— Proverbs 11:2 (NKJV)

Habitat for Humanity International cofounders Millard and Linda Fuller often recounted that whenever the couple rejoiced from having helped a poor family to gain a home, the duo would also feel humbled. They realized that while such a celebration was happening, more families were becoming homeless for the first time than all those who Habitat for Humanity was serving. Now, that's humility!

Assignment: Serve purposes with your business's offerings where the unmet needs are important and ever increasing. If you pick an area where the gap between where we are today and where we should be is enormous, such as in educating those with learning disabilities, you'll find yourself continually wondering how you can do better and feeling humbled that you haven't accomplished more.

Create an Organization and Offerings
That Allow You to Nurture
the Spiritual Lives of Stakeholders

For no one ever hated his own flesh,
but nourishes and cherishes it,
just as the Lord does *the church.*
For we are members of His body,
of His flesh and of His bones.

— Ephesians 5:29-30 (NKJV)

Habitat for Humanity International uplifts all aspects of peoples' lives through supplying poor families with high-quality, low-cost homes and no down-payment, no-interest mortgages. When your organization and its offerings uplift important aspects of peoples' lives as well, pay attention to the spiritual opportunities that your offerings open in order to find ways to provide more of them for stakeholders. A for-profit home-building company might, for instance, conduct its training for new employees at Habitat building sites and encourage Habitat homeowners to apply for jobs. You can read more about how Habitat for Humanity International accomplishes its work at www.habitat.org.

Assignment: **Look for and supply transformational offerings and experiences that will more deeply touch the spirits of all stakeholders.**

Make Room for Spiritual Expression in What You Do for All Stakeholders

"God is Spirit, and those who worship Him
must worship in spirit and truth."

— John 4:24 (NKJV)

Ansel Adams was a pioneering American wilderness photographer and environmentalist. Do you suppose he would have been willing to carry his heavy box camera and glass plates on his back up long, dangerous rock climbs in Yosemite and the Sierra Nevada mountains during winter storms if he hadn't been spiritually energized by what he would see and how his images would create transcendence in the lives of those who would never reach those spots at such moments? How can you provide for such spiritual expressions for you, your organization, and your other stakeholders?

Assignment: **Create offerings that affect stakeholders when received with feelings similar to providing or to receiving a prayer of thanks while being among those who are being spiritually uplifted by the offering.**

Lesson Four

Choose Problems to Solve
That Ignite Your Passion,
Fire Your Curiosity,
and Warm Your Heart

"You did not choose Me, but I chose you
and appointed you that you should go and bear fruit
and that *your fruit should remain,*
that whatever you ask the Father in My name
He may give you.
These things I command you,
that you love one another."

— John 15:16-17 (NKJV)

Business focus is immeasurably helped by finding engaging problems — ones to which you and others are irresistibly drawn.

Many people make a mistake by instead picking problems to solve that are of interest only because of the potential financial gain that might result from solutions. Others make a different mistake: picking problems that bore them.

Make either mistake and you'll find yourself losing interest, not paying enough attention, and becoming complacent. You'll soon be doing the minimum to get by rather than driving forward to create the best … and then outdoing yourself. It's the latter approach that creates the healthiest enterprises.

In fact, if you don't feel more passion for what you are doing than anyone else, you are vulnerable to someone who is more passionate.

Consider great runners. At the end of world-class races, the differences between the winner and the also-rans are often measured in fractions of a second. No matter how talented someone is as a runner, those with less talent, but more passion, can do more training than the most talented person and overcome the talent disadvantage to improve past such a narrow gap.

Keep in mind that in business your own passion goes only so far in creating and delivering superior solutions. *You also need to be able to inflame such passion in millions of others who become your devoted stakeholders* (including customers, beneficiaries, end users, partners, colleagues, suppliers, distributors, lenders, owners, and the communities you serve).

Otherwise, you will be acting like Don Quixote while he was off with Sancho Panza on imaginary knightly quests in Cervantes' novel, rather than making good time moving along the road to accomplishing your goals.

Passion starts the process. Curiosity opens new doors to accomplishment through continually identifying more of what's possible. After you help open your stakeholders' hearts and minds to the excitement of solving the problem, they need to become as curious as you are.

Inspiration from the heart then binds everyone's actions together in satisfying ways to serve others. Without coming from the heart, solutions may be delivered in inauthentic, uncaring ways that undercut their benefits. I'm often reminded of that when a service person recites a memorized response that they want to be of service, but do so with averted eyes and a grimace that indicate the opposite intent.

Start your search for gaining the passion, curiosity, and heart-felt inspiration you need by examining three themes that have awakened and harnessed such qualities among many of those who have built successful enterprises from scratch: uplift the underdog, help families rear children more successfully, and add resources and knowledge that allow people to help themselves.

Uplift the Underdog

Defend the poor and fatherless;
Do justice to the afflicted and needy.

— Psalm 82:3 (NKJV)

This theme works best as a source of inspiration when you have been one of such underdogs and deeply identify with overcoming their challenging circumstances. In terms of inspiration and opportunity, the more underdogs there are that urgently need help, the better!

Here's an example that will probably be familiar to you. Let's say that you are in or have been part of a minority group in a culture and believe that you have had fewer opportunities as a result. After such experiences, helping people like you to succeed better than those who are in the majority can be particularly satisfying.

Ethnic Chinese people outside of China, for instance, have found others' preferences for Chinese food can provide large, financially rewarding opportunities to develop businesses that provide good incomes, employ lots of family members, and attract positive interest from the majority groups in the communities where they live. In such businesses, entrepreneurs have built substantial enterprises based on providing more authentic access to Chinese cuisine, a passion they shared with other Chinese people.

Poor people, the less educated, and small business owners are examples of other underdogs. Many people write them off, believing that they have few opportunities and even fewer resources. Yet profitable, billion-dollar enterprises have been built from serving the needs of such often-scorned underdogs. Examples include furniture- and appliance-rental companies, proprietary schools providing vocational training, and specialized services such as buying cooperatives.

Some people who seek to serve underdogs have combined public and private purposes to make faster progress. In India, for instance, the Aravind Eye Care System (www.aravind.org) has created the world standard for eliminating causes of blindness both in terms of quality and cost. Consider that the British health-care system regularly flies patients from the UK to India to be treated at Aravind where they receive better and less costly care than what is available in the UK. Aravind's costs are so low that the organization can use the profits from being paid $45 to $331 for cataract surgeries to cover all the costs for treating millions of indigent patients. The passion, curiosity, and heart-warming aspects of such care are driving Aravind's people forward to achieve still more astonishing levels of excellence and success. For more information about the organization's inspirational beginnings, read pages 265-286 of *The Fortune at the Bottom of the Pyramid* (Wharton School Publishing, 2005) by C.K. Prahalad and *Infinite Vision* (Berrett-Koehler, 2011) by Pavrithma K. Mehta and Suchitra Shenoy.

Assignment: Look for large groups of underdogs who are not receiving offerings that people would passionately like to provide today because it is too difficult or too expensive to make such offerings available.

Help Families Rear Children More Successfully

All your children shall be *taught by the LORD,*
And great shall be *the peace of your children.*

— Isaiah 54:13 (NKJV)

It's hard to find people who don't care about helping families. Habitat for Humanity International cofounders, Millard and Linda Fuller, felt that every family deserved to live in a decent home in a safe neighborhood. While many people agreed with them, the Fullers did something about their feelings. In the process they helped to create one of the world's largest homebuilders (www.habitat.org).

Such family-related needs can easily be identified. Many poor families still need homes. Other families need decent schools. Still other families lack clean, low-cost water. In other locales, immunizations are needed. Elsewhere, because information about HIV/AIDS is lacking, millions are likely to experience untimely, unpleasant deaths while leaving behind stunned orphans.

Provide for such basics in higher-quality, lower-cost ways, and the pent-up demand will cause your business to prosper. Consider two examples: Cemex (www.cemex.com) and the Grameen Bank (www.grameen-info.org) have made important strides by finding ways for poor people to use small amounts of savings to build homes one room at a time, to start profitable small businesses, and to improve subsistence farms. Similar opportunities for profitable growth lie fallow in many other parts of the world that Cemex and the Grameen Bank don't serve.

Assignment: Identify opportunities to provide high-quality "basics" to families everywhere by applying proven breakthroughs in low-cost, high-quality solutions.

Add Knowledge and Resources
That Allow People to Help Themselves

Teach me good judgment and knowledge,
For I believe Your commandments.

— Psalm 119:66 (NKJV)

Many of those who are not prospering up to their potential don't know what they need to know to accomplish more. When you fill such information gaps and coach people about what to do next, you will ignite enormous energies and improvements among those who aren't yet performing up to their potential.

Many people are surprised to learn that venture capital investing is concentrated in just a few industries based in the most developed countries. Such investments have proven to be an enormous source of profits. It's not unusual for long-term portfolio gains to exceed 20 percent a year.

Yet in the majority of industries in most countries, new enterprises can neither borrow nor attract risk-oriented capital at a reasonable cost. Create a way to provide such funds to those who are deserving and capable of succeeding, and you will have established win-win relationships that could build trillions in value and greatly expand employment. All that's missing now is an effective business model for providing such venture-capital investing on a broad scale for small enterprises.

Most entry-level entrepreneurs also need education in basics such as how to engage in entrepreneurship, eliminate stalls, and create and apply 2,000 percent solutions. Consider Bangladesh. The Grameen Bank has found it pays well to provide some of such educational basics to its borrowers, along with the bank's small, reasonably priced loans.

Those who want to help poorly prepared and indigent entrepreneurs can often find all the missing knowledge and financial resources among successful entrepreneurs in the same communities who already want to help others. Take a look in your community to see what untapped people and resources you can find.

<u>Assignment:</u> Look for ways to provide focused information, education, experience, and access to low-cost financial resources to enable successfully creating and expanding more small businesses.

Lesson Five

Determine Your Legacy

The wise shall inherit glory,
But shame shall be the legacy of fools.

— Proverbs 3:35 (NKJV)

I selected this lesson because of an experience I had while teaching an entrepreneurship class. I had directed the students to set their business goals by shifting perspective, looking backward from the future as though they had already attained their goals. (I asked them to imagine, in part, that they had already developed an equity stake of $400 million, as one of my entrepreneur clients had done.) To perform the assignment, I asked the fledgling entrepreneurs to pick five goals that would lead to the success they would most enjoy in the future.

The second most popular goal the students chose was to have a positive effect on their communities as a result of being entrepreneurs. They believed that they would be more fulfilled by accomplishing something meaningful in addition to making money for themselves.

Their selections of such altruistic goals reminded me of goal-setting exercises that I did with Tony Robbins and Jack Canfield that greatly influenced my day-to-day thinking. The two exercises I engaged in were somewhat similar. I was directed to see myself objectively after my death in light of what I did during my life, as Ebenezer Scrooge did during *A Christmas Carol* when the third ghost showed Scrooge the future where Tiny Tim and Scrooge would be dead, and no one would mourn Scrooge.

It occurred to me that you may not have done such an exercise. It's wonderful for helping to focus on what you want your legacy to be.

But perhaps you have done the same (or a similar) assignment. To avoid duplication, I designed a different version of the exercise for this lesson. I pray you will learn important insights from doing the assignments.

The following sections pose a series of questions you should consider in terms of selecting your entrepreneurial goals. As you prepare to answer these questions, feel free to pray for spiritual guidance, to discuss your ideas and feelings with family and friends, and to read about business leaders who were important more than a hundred years ago.

What Will People Say about You at Your Funeral?

"A certain nobleman went into a far country
to receive for himself a kingdom and to return.
So he called ten of his servants, delivered to them ten minas,
and said to them, 'Do business till I come.'
But his citizens hated him, and sent a delegation after him, saying,
'We will not have this man *to reign over us.'"*

— Luke 19:12-14 (NKJV)

Begin by imagining who will attend your funeral. Why will they decide to come? While they are waiting for the funeral to begin, what will they say when they mention you?

Assignment: Write the eulogy for your funeral as you would like it to be given by the person of your choosing.

What Will Be Said about Your Business
on the Day after You Die?

"Do not lay up for yourselves treasures on earth,
where moth and rust destroy and where thieves break in and steal;"

— Matthew 6:19 (NKJV)

Since you will have been very successful in establishing an organization, the subject of what you accomplished will undoubtedly come up. Obviously, you will be recognized for the scale of your business. But what will be said about the importance of the enterprise itself?

Assignment: Write a news story about the significance of your business as it might appear in the obituary printed by your hometown newspaper.

One Hundred Years after You Die,
What Difference Will Your Business Have Made?

Shall Your wonders be known in the dark?
And Your righteousness in the land of forgetfulness?

— Psalm 88:12 (NKJV)

Imagine that it is the centennial of your death. A news story is being written to describe your business's influence, both good and bad. What will be written then? What will people who read the story say?

Assignment: Write versions of the news story as it might appear in various publications that you respect.

What Will Your Relatives Say about the Significance of What You Accomplished during Your Family's Reunion 100 Years from Now?

As drought and heat consume the snow waters,
So the grave consumes those who have sinned.
The womb should forget him,
The worm should feed sweetly on him;
He should be remembered no more,
And wickedness should be broken like a tree.
For he preys on the barren who do not bear,
And does no good for the widow.

— Job 24:19-21 (NKJV)

Most family reunions inevitably bring up the subject of those who have passed on, commenting about what made them memorable. The oldsters share what they remember with the young sprouts, seeking to impart what should be emulated and what should be avoided.

Assignment: **Write what you would like your great-great-grandchildren to say about you at that reunion.**

Part Two

Add Customers

You have increased the nation, O LORD,
You have increased the nation;
You are glorified;
You have expanded all the borders of the land.

— Isaiah 26:15 (NKJV)

What's even better than profitably growing a company's revenues by twenty times? Expanding a market's size by twenty times while profitably gaining market share.

I first documented and analyzed the influences on and effects of profitable market-share gains in 1973, and I added to those insights through my exhaustive study of the Strategic Planning Institute's PIMS (Profit Impact of Market Strategy) database in 1977 and 1978. Since then, I've examined the sources and benefits of profitable market-share gains so often that I no longer remember how many projects I have led or when.

One conclusion stands out from these investigations: The most successful and profitable market-share gains occur when an organization greatly expands the market and is alone prepared to supply most of the increased customer demand. After learning of the benefits from this kind of market-share gain, I also began studying how businesses have more rapidly and profitably expanded their markets.

Many people associate any explosive market growth occurring while a firm profitably expands market share with providing new offerings that deliver more value for whatever price is paid (such as when cellular telephones came out to compete with traditional mobile telephones). However, my research has shown that many other types of business activities can trigger such profitable market expansions. You'll learn about many of such activities by reading the lessons contained in Part Two of *Business Basics*.

These market-expanding activities are often more helpful for the innovating firm because existing competitors rarely respond effectively. Instead, challenges to market-expanding changes will usually come (if at all) from new competitors, organizations that often struggle with the twin challenges of improving beyond the changes an effective company has just made while also creating substantial capacity to deliver enormous quantities of the new offerings.

In such circumstances customers soon become accustomed to whatever improvements an innovating firm has provided, building preferences for the improvements. Lasting competitive advantages are built in just these ways, advantages that can improve profitability at least until the next round of business model innovation occurs.

Unless your organization is already enormous, the effect of such rapid growth is to create substantial reductions in per-unit costs of an offering without much special effort, due to many fixed costs being spread over volume that may be 200 to 300 times larger than before. Unless your organization is operationally weak, rapid learning also occurs so that operational errors are reduced and unneeded activities are eliminated. Improved, lower-cost methods also become advantageous to install due to increased scale.

More stakeholders will rally to your cause, seeking to help you improve still more through sharing their insights into other valuable sales-increasing and cost-reducing options. Highly talented people will likewise seek to join with your organization in a variety of stakeholder roles.

The value of your enterprise will greatly increase, permitting your company either to sell equity at a much lower cost or to borrow money more easily and less expensively. Growth becomes much easier when it costs less.

When you make and experience these sorts of changes, you will launch a dynamic relationship that can be turned into a virtuous cycle of continually expanding benefits for all involved. In parts three and four of *Business Basics*, you will learn more about the potential to further expand and to extend such a positive sequence of events.

Lesson Six

Expand Your Market by Twenty Times
through One Big, Perfect Event

Though your beginning was small,
Yet your latter end would increase abundantly.

— Job 8:7 (NKJV)

Here's a helpful thought experiment for growing markets to much larger sizes: Imagine how you can create one big, perfect event where almost all prospects will be persuaded either to begin using your type of offering or to increase their use. Assume that you can arrange for anyone who is alive to attend the event, that you have an unlimited financial budget, that the event can be held anywhere, and that your can engage in any legal activity you wish at the event.

To help you understand what I have in mind for the thought experiment, here's an example of how such an event might be designed for a new type of online course:

- The most popular and admired celebrities and musical groups in the world are continually performing to put everyone in a good mood.
- The best teachers and professors in the world are there, trying out the various online courses and answering questions about why this new type of online course is highly beneficial for learners.
- The authors of each course are present to lead discussions about the advantages of taking their courses.
- Thousands of students who have become millionaires as a result of taking the trial versions of the courses are on hand to describe their experiences.
- There are enough online computers available so that anyone can look at any course during the event and select three courses to take.
- Purchases of the courses are guaranteed by an insurance policy from Lloyds of London so that customers who enroll in three courses and are not completely satisfied will receive double their money back.
- Free drawings for hundreds of thousands of cash prizes worth in total over $100,000,000 are held every five seconds for those who have bought three courses.
- For those who cannot attend, there is a live television show beaming the event to an audience of billions around the world who can log on or make a toll-free telephone call to buy their three courses.

- During the event, the World Cup soccer finals are played live at the event site. However, if sales drop below ten million dollars a minute during that part of the telecast, television coverage of the World Cup match will be stopped.

I'm sure this example gives you some sense of what one big attention-getting event might accomplish. I'm sure you can do better.

Now create an unlimited resources version of how to kick-start your type of offering on the most effective scale through one event.

After you finish with that intriguing assignment, next assume that you have no money to do the same event … and see how you might execute it.

While recreating something so effective at no cost may, at first, seem impossible, consider that in many cases people help others for wholly nonfinancial reasons. Chances are good that you can attract many of the same people and resources by simply earmarking a substantial percentage of the revenues generated by the event to various popular charities that the prospective customers and resource providers routinely support. Since your online courses cost very little to provide, you have the ability to raise tens of millions of dollars for each of those charities if enough people buy. Such a great event will also be attractive to many of those who would substantially benefit by gaining access to a large audience.

How can you create one big event while using few resources to expand your market by twenty times? I use helping charities as the example to suggest some possible answers in the following sections.

How Can You Increase
the Perceived Importance of Attending the Event?

In that day the Branch of the LORD shall be beautiful and glorious;
And the fruit of the earth shall be excellent and appealing ….

— Isaiah 4:2 (NKJV)

Highly regarded causes often draw celebrities and their fans alike. Start by learning what causes and activities are most attractive to the prospective customers you want to attend. Next, design better incentives to attend than prospective customers usually receive.

Few serious fans of anything can resist the lure of seeing their favorite celebrities, exciting publicity about a fun occasion, being well treated, receiving something for nothing, joining the excitement of an energized crowd, and contributing to doing good. You can also be sure most celebrities will do whatever they can to turn out those they influence. If the celebrities agree to do cause-related fund-raising through encouraging purchases of your offerings, many more people will want to buy. In addition, the charities will work overtime to turn up friends and relatives of their existing supporters for your event.

Assignment: Determine what benefits are most appealing for attracting to your event the best prospects for your offerings. Consider how such benefits can be made available inexpensively at your event.

Who Needs to Be at the Event
to Attract Maximum Attention?

"And I, if I am lifted up from the earth,
will draw all peoples to Myself."

— John 12:32 (NKJV)

If the attention-grabbing celebrities who attend are somehow connected to or credible concerning the offerings you want to encourage, your publicity will work even better.

Note that you can draw attention both by attracting appealing people to the event and by attracting reporters and other media types to cover your event in high-profile ways that will intrigue still more people. Sir Richard Branson, for instance, often helps attract such attention for his new business launches by simply being there as the organization's owner and leader. As a result of attracting appealing people and the media, tens of millions more people will see coverage of your event, including many potential customers.

Assignment: **Identify the ten people who could draw the most potential buyers to your event. Research what would most likely motivate each of these ten people to attend.**

What Needs to Happen at the Event to Create Boundless Interest?

Now Peter and John went up together to the temple
at the hour of prayer, the ninth hour.
And a certain man lame from his mother's womb was carried,
whom they laid daily at the gate of the temple which is called Beautiful,
to ask alms from those who entered the temple;
who, seeing Peter and John about to go into the temple, asked for alms.
And fixing his eyes on him, with John, Peter said, "Look at us."
So he gave them his attention, expecting to receive something from them.
Then Peter said, "Silver and gold I do not have, but what I do have I give you:
In the name of Jesus Christ of Nazareth, rise up and walk."
And he took him by the right hand and lifted him up,
and immediately his feet and ankle bones received strength.
So he, leaping up, stood and walked and entered the temple with them —
walking, leaping, and praising God.
And all the people saw him walking and praising God.
Then they knew that it was he who sat begging alms
at the Beautiful Gate of the temple;
and they were filled with wonder and amazement
at what had happened to him.

— Acts 3:1-10 (NKJV)

Doing something dramatic that's totally unexpected attracts great interest. Sir Richard Branson, for instance, launches new businesses with stunts that people talk about for years. For the launch of Virgin Bridal, he wore a white wedding dress. If you aren't a celebrity, other unexpected methods can still work well. For example, the Web site, Half.com, persuaded a town in Oregon to change its name to Half.com, Oregon, creating headline news around the world.

Christo, the famous artist, may take over a major part of a town with a jaw-dropping display as he did in 2005 when he built temporary fabric-draped gates all over New York's Central Park, drawing millions of visitors to walk under the openings (most of whom would normally avoid Central Park like the plague). Christo funds such public displays by selling drawings and small mock-ups in advance to collectors who usually turn a tidy profit from their purchases.

Jordan's Furniture, a retailer in the Boston area, provided so many appealing customer promotions during its Avon, Massachusetts store opening that the police closed the roads to the store in the interest of public safety and stopped people from entering the store. The company's owners went on the radio with a quickly concocted advertisement pleading with people to stay home and to visit instead on another occasion. And millions of people eventually did visit, drawn, in part, by wondering what all the fuss could be about.

Assignment: **Consider unexpected, low-cost promotional activities that could attract interest in your event and your offerings, both for those who attend and for those who simply hear about the activities and don't attend.**

How Can You Turn the Initial Attention into Repeat Purchases?

*So all countries came to Joseph in Egypt to buy grain,
because the famine was severe in all lands.*

— Genesis 41:57 (NKJV)

Begin rapid market expansion by educating potential customers to encourage trying and purchasing your offerings during the event. Be sure that people can access whatever samples, mock-ups, and other try-outs they might need before they buy. Car dealers often accomplish such exposure by having hundreds of brand-new vehicles available for test drives at special events authorized by organizations whose members and guests can easily afford the vehicles. After driving a brand-new vehicle with its appealing new smell and great feel, few people are going to feel satisfied with the vehicle they came in.

Have special offers available that people would be foolish to pass up. If you are pretty sure that people will like what they experience, be aggressive. Consider the potential benefits and costs of making the offer seem to be essentially free . . . and immensely desirable.

A car dealer, for instance, might make an offer of no payments for two years to anyone who signs up for a five-year lease. This offer could be made affordable by simply shifting the payments (plus a little interest cost) that would normally be made in the first two years to the lease payments for years three, four, and five. The resulting leases could be sold to a vehicle-manufacturer's financing unit for cash so that the dealer's finances would not be strained.

Assignment: **Develop ways for prospective customers to try your offerings and to begin using them that make it irresistible to purchase now ... as well as in the future.**

When you combine more ways to make your event appealing and effective, you will gain added benefits. The following event-planning assignments will assist you in achieving even more market growth and greater market-share gains.

Event-Planning Assignments

1. Locate at least twenty-five ways you can attract almost all current and potential large purchasers of your type of offering to an event and motivate them to buy and make long-term commitments that will expand some or all of your market by at least twenty times.

2. Identify what permanent competitive advantages you can gain in adopting such big-event methods.

3. Determine the best ways you could operate the same or an even better event with no up-front expenditures by you or your organization.

Lesson Seven

Turn Your Customers
into Eager Business Evangelists

Hear this, you elders,
And give ear, all you inhabitants of the land!
Has anything like *this happened in your days,*
Or even in the days of your fathers?
Tell your children about it,
Let *your children* tell *their children,*
And their children another generation.

— Joel 1:2-3 (NKJV)

Why should you turn your customers into eager business evangelists? *Eager business-evangelist customers are always telling others how wonderful your business is and encouraging potential customers to try your offerings.*

Most network marketing businesses are based on word-of-mouth promotion. You learn about a great product or service from a relative, friend, or neighbor who then helps you to experience the offering's benefits. Soon, you can't wait to share your happiness with others to improve their lives, too!

I was reminded of this approach to gaining customers while rereading *Raving Fans: A Revolutionary Approach to Customer Service* (William Morrow, 1993) by Ken Blanchard and Sheldon Bowles. Blanchard and Bowles use a parable to introduce the idea of superior, "shout-about-it" service through examples of a department store where greeters pin a flower on you when you walk in the door and employees eagerly head off to competitors' stores to obtain out-of-stock items for you, a gas station that delivers impressive full service at self-service prices, and a grocery store where you enjoy free valet parking and are aided by a no-cost personal shopper to organize your visit and to help you save money.

The key principles outlined in the book are:

- Develop a vision of what you think would be perfect service for your customers.
- Test that vision by asking customers what service benefits they want increased.
- Start consistently delivering the service you can provide effectively that fits with what customers want, and then improve service performance by 1 percent a week. To accomplish such results, you should install a process to measure and to manage the effectiveness of your improvements.

When asked about their experience, the authors argue that customers who respond that service is "fine" or are silent are often, in fact, quite unhappy with the service they are receiving. I've certainly hidden my dissatisfactions in such ways. I suspect that you have, too. Blanchard and Bowles argue that until you are inundated with unsolicited customer testimonials, your service isn't good enough to establish a highly effective corps of business evangelist customers.

They also recommend quality of service measurements that are solely based on customer experiences, rather than employing so-called mystery shoppers, so you more accurately know how consistent your service is and how effective and appreciated your service improvements are.

While those kinds of observations are valuable perspectives to act on, I believe that the principle of providing such great service that customers cannot resist becoming business evangelists goes well beyond Blanchard's and Bowles' concepts. Here's what I mean: *Business-evangelist-creating organizations convince customers that all service providers are sincerely and deeply interested in being helpful ... rather than just trying to keep a job or make a sale.* Here are seven examples of this principle that are drawn from my personal experiences:

1. When my wife and I brought our two-year-old daughter for an early dinner at La Tour d'Argent, a famous restaurant in Paris, we were a little nervous about whether her behavior would be up-to-snuff, but we didn't feel that we should leave her with a babysitter. The restaurant's legendary owner, Claude Terrail, soon came up to our table smiling, carrying a coloring book and some crayons. He introduced himself and asked if he could entertain our daughter for awhile. When we quickly agreed, he gently got down on his knees in his elegant designer suit and spent over a half hour coloring in the book with our daughter. He had a huge grin on his face while he did this, which made it clear that he was having a fine time. Naturally, the service was pretty spectacular, too, as his staff hustled to make a good impression on the owner. Our daughter continued to color happily after he left, and the meal was a great success.

2. After lunching at a modest, family-style restaurant in Maine, I discovered that I had stupidly locked my only set of keys in the car. I went back inside the restaurant to see if someone knew of a local garage that could help. Instead, the whole restaurant staff immediately filed out, unasked, to help me break in with a wire coat hanger. They had me into the car within five minutes and pleasantly refused my offer of payment while wishing me a good trip.

3. While on vacation with my parents, we visited a Nordstrom department store at Mall of America in Minneapolis. As I considered some shirts that were on sale, one of the sales associates introduced himself to my parents and, unasked, spent the next hour helping them plan the remainder of their visit to Minneapolis. None of us bought anything, but the sales associate couldn't have been any more helpful if he had been a professional guide being paid by us.

4. At a private club I belonged to, the waitresses knew that I loved a certain type of ice-cream sundae. For fifteen years after the chef took the item off the "official" menu, they kept a stock of the topping that made the sundae so good for me and a few others who craved it. I always made a point of encouraging my guests to order this sundae, and many said that it was the best they had ever eaten.

5. This same club suffered a total loss of electricity during a citywide power failure just thirty minutes before an important event that my family was hosting for over a hundred people. Without missing a beat, the staff lit candles for illumination and cooked the food over wood fires on barbeque grills

outside on a cold, blustery November day. Only afterward did we even learn that anything unusual had to be done to prepare the food.

6. My wife and I stayed at a famous hillside resort on the Riviera when our daughter was six months old. We usually took her around the resort in a fold-up stroller, and getting up and down the many hillside stairs was a little awkward. One of us would take her out of the stroller and carry her while the other parent folded and lifted the stroller. The staff decided this wouldn't do. Whenever anyone on the staff saw us near a stairway with the stroller, four strong men would rush up to carry her safely up and down the stairs while she sat comfortably in the stroller. Our little girl ate with us in a high chair. While dining, someone would come by, unasked, about every minute or two, clean her face and hands with a fresh cloth and wipe the drool and food mess from her tray. This cleaning was done so gently and pleasantly that she laughed happily while it was going on.

7. Before our daughter was born, my wife and I went to Tahiti on vacation. The people who worked at the resort learned that my wife's birthday was coming up when I asked where I could find a florist to buy her some flowers. They thought that was a funny way to obtain flowers. Orchids grow wild in Tahiti so they don't have any need for florists. People just grow their own or pick wildflowers. A woman on the front desk staff spent several hours of her personal time in the jungle picking and later arranging the most amazing bouquet we had ever seen. When I offered to pay her, she wouldn't take any money for the bouquet. The memory of the staff person's happy smile still warms my heart.

In the following sections, you will find questions you should answer to help turn your customers into eager evangelists for your business.

How Should You Improve
Your Performance and Reliability?

He gives them security, and they rely on it;

— Job 24:23 (NKJV)

Customers count on businesses to do things they cannot easily do … or don't want to do … for themselves. There is some core benefit from any offering that customers need to receive; otherwise, buying the offering is just a waste. Here's an example. In many cases Mitchell and Company client executives have wanted us to share any bad news discovered during consulting assignments with their irascible CEOs so that any wrath fell on us, rather than on the executives. Delivering the unpleasant news to such people is not much fun for us; but if we duck that duty or don't succeed in getting the message across, the client company will gain little benefit from our work. So we learned how to be quite adept at making socially challenged CEOs feel good while receiving painful news … by describing the bad news in terms of providing opportunities to create spectacular personal accomplishments and public recognition. CEOs love this way of learning about their personal and organizational needs to improve. Hearing the news from us just makes the experience seem even more desirable to them.

Assignment: Ask customers where they absolutely count on you meeting a certain standard … or they will be profoundly disappointed. Find ways to pleasantly exceed their expectations and to make them feel secure while trusting that you will continue to do so.

29

How Can You Treat Your Customers as if They Were Honored Guests in Your Home?

Jesus, knowing that the Father had given all things into His hands,
and that He had come from God and was going to God,
rose from supper and laid aside His garments,
took a towel and girded Himself.
After that, He poured water into a basin
and began to wash the disciples' feet,
and to wipe them *with the towel with which He was girded.*

— John 13:3-5 (NKJV)

People we invite into our homes for meals or to stay with us often need extra attention. We may have picked them up at the airport (or driven them to the airport) in the middle of the night, located some special food or badly needed medicine at an odd hour, rearranged furniture, or found a local expert to help them with something. We happily provide assistance because we want our guests to have just what they need and to enjoy their visit with us. While such occasions may make a lot of extra work, it's just part of the pleasure of enjoying their company.

Assignment: Learn about any special needs that customers have a hard time obtaining, but which you could supply. Consider how you can most thoughtfully provide for or generously serve such needs.

What Memorable Experiences Can You Create for Your Customers to Enjoy Sharing with Others?

Now I praise you, brethren,
that you remember me in all things
and keep the traditions just as I delivered them *to you.*

— 1 Corinthians 11:2 (NKJV)

As you can tell from the earlier examples of great service, one reason that I am such a Francophile is because French people have treated my family and me so well. Long after I cannot remember very much about a trip or location, I can remember everything about the most wonderful treatment we received. And I enjoy telling others those stories, just as I have enjoyed sharing them with you.

Assignment: Think about the most amazingly wonderful treatment you have experienced. Consider how you can provide a comparably fine experience for your customers that they will delight in telling others about.

How Can You Help Turn Your Customer into a Hero or Heroine?

Benaiah was *the son of Jehoiada,*
the son of a valiant man from Kabzeel,
who had done many deeds.
He had killed two lion-like heroes of Moab.
He also had gone down and killed a lion
in the midst of a pit on a snowy day.

— 2 Samuel 23:20 (NKJV)

We all have feet of clay. Our intentions are often better than our accomplishments due to having too little time and too few resources. Even when engaged in something important, we may struggle to complete the task. Helping customers to avoid missing such opportunities can present excellent ways to turn customers into heroes and heroines.

Remember that what's hard for a customer is often easy for someone in your organization who has different talents, knowledge, and interests. Here's an example. People want their children to do well, but they may not be able to help the youngsters to gain access or to achieve in the ways the parent and child want. In such a case, you or a colleague might be able to make an introduction, to provide a summer job, or to be a persuasive reference for one of your customer's youngsters. The gratitude you create will last for a lifetime whenever your customer gains credit for success through obtaining your meaningful help. If you can do something similar for boosting someone's career, or to enhance a business, those are powerful ways to help and gain gratitude, as well.

Assignment: Identify doors that you can open that your customers cannot open for themselves.

How Can You Make It Fun for Customers to Help You Acquire New Customers?

The Jews had light and gladness, joy and honor.

— Esther 8:16 (NKJV)

Many of Mitchell and Company's clients are enthusiastic golfers who enjoy fine meals and good wines. We have often invited clients and prospective clients to join us as our guests for events where such great activities were enjoyed in connection with a helpful business program. During those occasions, our clients have great fun describing to the prospective clients how well we treat them and what a great thing it is to be a Mitchell and Company client. Many of our clients first learned about us through such experiences and later served the same business evangelist role for other prospective clients.

Assignment: Learn more about what your customers and prospective customers like to do when they aren't working. Find ways for them to engage in such activities together as your guests while they benefit from trying out some of your new offerings.

Lesson Eight

Add Distribution

And sow fields and plant vineyards,
That they may yield a fruitful harvest.

— Psalm 107:37 (NKJV)

For success in real estate, brokers and investors are fond of emphasizing that old adage that only three things count: "Location, Location, Location." Despite awareness of this well-known saying, even those who put no spending limits on purchasing and renting top-quality real estate usually fail to understand how similarly important adding distribution is for successful development of a market.

Let's start with a simple example. Nantucket Nectars, the fruit-juice maker, was established in 1990 by two college friends who wanted to stay close to their Nantucket roots after graduating. Nantucket is a beautiful small island off Cape Cod in Massachusetts where the New England whaling industry was originally based. The friends' first business was a small store that sold and delivered groceries to boats docked in Nantucket harbor. After becoming intrigued by a peach-based beverage they enjoyed while vacationing in Spain, they decided to concoct a tasty local version in their blender by using some fresh fruit.

Initially, their only distribution was to sell fresh gallons of the beverage in used containers to boat owners in Nantucket harbor. Demand from other Nantucket islanders led the owners, Tom First and Tom Scott, to eventually produce a few hundred cases of pasteurized juice in new bottles.

The two men were soon inundated with requests to distribute the product beyond Nantucket, beginning with the ice distributor on Cape Cod who stored their pasteurized product. As a result, you could buy the product on the Cape and the islands of Nantucket and Martha's Vineyard.

Eventually, bottles became available across eastern Massachusetts … then in other eastern states … and by 1995 in thirty states. Annual revenues rose in six years from less than $25,000 to over $20,000,000, as tasting these high-quality juices stirred up consumer interest. Rapid growth in distribution since then boosted annual sales to hundreds of millions of dollars.

Obviously, not very many people keep boats in Nantucket harbor. If the two founders had not added other forms of distribution and locations, the market might still be just as small as it was when they started.

I often see a similar effect with adding more restaurants. You can draw different travel-time lines around a restaurant and predict how likely people who live or work within or drive through the various travel-time areas will be to frequent the restaurant.

Let's consider frequency just in terms of distance as a partial substitute for travel time. In the United States those who live, work, or travel within one-half mile of a restaurant are about ten times more likely to dine there than those who live, work, or travel from one-half mile to a mile away. Those who fall in that further-away band are about ten times more likely to be customers than those who live, work, or travel from one to two miles away. And on it goes, with consumption usually declining exponentially as distance increases.

The market-expansion implications are obvious: Since the appeal of a restaurant is primarily a function of how far away it is from customers in time and distance, you can expand the market and brand by putting in restaurants that are closer to potential customers.

Why do people respond this way? Few customers will drive or walk past one competitive restaurant to reach another one. So if there are a Wendy's, a Burger King, and a McDonald's (all fast-food hamburger restaurants) on a street, most people will normally go to the closest one ... unless they are located virtually next to each other. When they are almost equally close, most people will go to the one that's least crowded (especially at lunch when lines and wait times can be long). Except for a special occasion, hardly anyone will make a special trip to eat at any particular restaurant that's further than two miles away. Instead, people will most often raid the refrigerator, grab a snack from the cupboard, or order some take-out food to be delivered.

Interestingly, even high-value professional services show similar distribution elasticity. Local presence causes behavior changes among customers. When a consulting firm first locates an office in a geographical area, local revenues will usually rise by at least tenfold even if the firm has been marketing with the same staff to the same potential clients all along.

While the Internet provides the opportunity to drive lots of traffic to a single global site, those who do best find that creating local versions of their sites can greatly expand revenues, as well. For example, Amazon.com has Canadian and British sites even though the English used is mostly common to what is found on the U.S. site. Savvy marketers have also learned to stimulate more demand by creating dozens of online sites with each presenting different reasons to buy, another example of how more distribution expands purchasing.

With the exception of a few large, long-established retail industries, such as supermarkets, Mitchell and Company research continues to validate the opportunity to expand most markets by several hundred percent simply through increasing distribution in terms of locations and other access points. If you think about how the availability of vending machines containing snacks and soda affect your personal consumption of such items, I'm sure you'll appreciate how big a role convenient access plays in influencing purchases.

When you combine a unique and preferred offering (as Nantucket Nectars did with establishing the new premium-juice category) with expanded distribution, market growth can be explosive.

What benefits come from adding more distribution or access points?

1. You are noticed more often by potential customers.
2. If they need or want what you offer, they will probably buy more often.
3. If you fulfill your offer in an acceptable way, they will probably keep buying (as needed) and tell others to work with you.
4. If demand is stimulated enough, you can also grow revenues faster than costs and assets, increasing your profits and cash flow as a percentage of revenues.
5. If you purchase or rent a uniquely valuable location (such as in a high-traffic, high-visibility site with exclusivity rights), you will have eliminated some competition.
6. With distribution advantages, your pricing power will increase due to facing less competition in serving those customers for whom you are the most convenient.
7. The affordability of mass-marketing methods is improved. With enough of a distribution advantage, marketing-cost advantages and any scarcity of good locations can limit future challenges from existing and new competitors.

What's the strategic lesson of expanding your market by twenty times through adding distribution? Fully develop the market first ... or you will be leaving the door open to expansion by current competitors and a continuing supply of new entrants who can develop and use distribution advantages against you. Applying this lesson often means that a multibrand strategy with each concept operating in different locations will work best. Compete with yourself rather than with other firms. Few people ever realize the potential value of this strategy ... and miss most of the potential growth and profits they could enjoy.

If McDonald's had also developed something like Burger King and Wendy's, there would be no significant hamburger competitors in most world markets for the three McDonald's-owned hamburger brands.

The following sections address questions you should consider to locate and to obtain advantages from distribution elasticity in expanding your market.

How Can Added Distribution Become Valuable to Customers?

But he who gathers by labor will increase.

— Proverbs 13:11 (NKJV)

In most instances, there's a customer benefit from making it easier to obtain the product or service. This benefit may come in the form of less time spent on travel, faster service being received to deal with a pressing need, or reduced costs for customers.

Most companies make the mistake of having distribution that reflects their convenience, rather than that of customers. Unless carefully evaluated and controlled, most organizations will simply place their locations where leaders like to be.

Assignment: Look for new ways to provide customer benefits from expanded distribution. Through testing in small geographical markets, measure the revenue and profit effects from providing different combinations of such benefits.

How Far Can You Profitably Expand Distribution?

*And Joshua conquered them
from Kadesh Barnea as far as Gaza,
and all the country of Goshen, even as far as Gibeon.*

— Joshua 10:41 (NKJV)

There are two important dimensions to profitably expanding distribution:

1. The amount of increased purchasing that occurs
2. The amount of cost reductions for adding and operating with more distribution

A coffee-and-doughnut chain originally based in the Boston area, Dunkin' Donuts, learned how to become more effective in both dimensions. The original stores mostly served those who dined in while seated at a counter. Waitresses constantly circled, refilling coffee cups at no additional charge to encourage tips. The waitresses ignored for as long as possible the relatively few take-out customers because they didn't tip, and many such potential customers left in disgust without buying. Each store also had its own bakery and grill. Stores were located about two miles apart.

Today, each store emphasizes take-out business … with usually only eight to fifteen seats. There are no special servers and no free coffee refills for those who choose to eat in. Almost all locations have drive-through windows. None have bakeries. Doughnuts are delivered fresh to the stores several times a day, as are many other food items such as bagels, muffins, flatbread, fillings for sandwiches, and pizzas. Stores are located as close together as every two blocks (often less than one-quarter mile) in high-traffic and high-density areas. To further lower costs of adding distribution, many gasoline filling stations now offer a limited selection of Dunkin's coffee and doughnuts in their convenience-food markets. The chain has grown by more than twenty times in the Boston area alone due to such changes and has greatly increased its market share there while substantially expanding the total market. The same approach has made Dunkin' a powerhouse in many other parts of the United States and around the world.

Assignment: Take a small geographical area and saturate it with lower-cost distribution points until no more profitable sales can be added. Be sure that customers are equally delighted with any new methods of providing or delivering your products or services as they have been with current methods.

How Can You Identify and Develop the Best Areas First?

Also do not be concerned about your goods,
for the best of all the land of Egypt is yours.

— Genesis 45:20 (NKJV)

Domino's Pizza, a delivery-focused chain, demonstrates many good lessons about focusing first on the highest-potential distribution locations. Domino's owner soon recognized that areas near college and university dormitories filled with unmarried students are the best places to locate because school cafeterias rarely offer good pizzas, many students don't have kitchens, and late-night snacks are a predictable part of any living-away-from-home school experience. Domino's built first in such locations, and later expanded into densely populated areas filled with apartments where young, unmarried college graduates (who had been its customers while in college) usually lived during their first few jobs.

Assignment: Put your operations in locations where your best customers want to find you and do so in ways that block competitors from establishing equally good distribution and credibility.

How Can You Change Your Business Model to Permit Faster Distribution Expansion?

And he wrote in the name of King Ahasuerus,
sealed it with the king's signet ring,
and sent letters by couriers on horseback,
riding on royal horses bred from swift steeds.

— Esther 8:10 (NKJV)

Many businesses choose to franchise their offerings, in part because this strategy permits faster distribution expansion. Can you franchise what you do in order to make your offerings more conveniently available? If not, can you license some aspects of what you do to expand distribution more rapidly in that way?

Assignment: Reexamine all parts of your business model to see how you could accelerate adding distribution. Test your better ideas to see how well they work before making major commitments.

How Can You Locate
Undiscovered, High-Potential Markets to Develop?

I, wisdom, dwell with prudence,
And find out knowledge and discretion.

— Proverbs 8:12 (NKJV)

A friend told me a fascinating story about seeking and finding undiscovered, high-potential markets after attending his fifth reunion from Harvard Business School. While at the reunion, my friend was surprised to learn that the fellow who finished with the lowest grades while earning his MBA had become the class's first millionaire. Naturally, everyone wanted to know the millionaire classmate's secret.

Since the man hadn't been able to attract any job offers before he graduated, he decided to go into business for himself. With little experience, and even less money, he had to start a business that no one else wanted.

He acquired the exclusive rights to distribute Pong, the first arcade video game, in Africa for about $1,000 ... and the rest is history. He was able to purchase the rights easily and cheaply because no one else wanted these rights. Undoubtedly, many people discounted the opportunity because they weren't sure how well such a game with do in arcades, how reliable the electronics were, and associated Africa with poor people who couldn't afford to play games in an arcade.

This entrepreneur correctly appreciated that this new form of entertainment would go over very well in places where few alternative forms of low-cost entertainment were available. He also knew that electronic products were generally more reliable than electromechanical ones such as the pinball machines that filled many arcades. In addition, he was convinced that there were bound to be at least a few people with enough money to go to arcades among so many Africans. He was well compensated for being right.

Assignment: Consider large distribution alternatives that are different from where the bulk of the market is now. For example, the Nantucket Nectars founders eventually enjoyed great success with young people attending colleges. Yacht owners in harbors, their original focus, were a small market by comparison. These entrepreneurs had started at the narrow end of the market in distributing their products. If they had continued to emphasize yacht harbors for their expanded distribution, we probably wouldn't know about Nantucket Nectars or the founders today.

Lesson Nine

Gain Awareness

And when a violent attempt was made by both the Gentiles and Jews,
with their rulers, to abuse and stone them,
they became aware of it
and fled to Lystra and Derbe, cities of Lycaonia,
and to the surrounding region.
And they were preaching the gospel there.

— Acts 14:5-7 (NKJV)

Unless you receive an offering as a gift and try it out, ignorance will keep you from using a superior choice. When such ignorance is widespread, the market will not develop to its full potential.

Let's explore back surgery as an example. Until a few decades ago, patients who underwent back surgery were as likely to be worse off after the surgery as they were to enjoy any improvement. Harmful outcomes included increased pain, reduced mobility, and serious infections.

Then, some outstanding surgeons specialized just in back surgery, and major improvements were made in diagnostic, operating, and care practices. But even today, if you ask the wrong surgeon to operate on your back, you can still find your condition made worse by surgery.

Most people can find no reliable public records describing back-surgery outcomes from a patient's perspective. If you think you need back surgery, it's all but impossible to identify the best surgeon to use. As a result, most patients visit a few surgeons and pick the one with the best personality who can operate sooner than any of the others. Why? Patients have usually put off surgery for so long that their symptoms are highly aggravated, and they don't want to wait any longer to do something about their pain or disability.

Is such a method an effective way to find a surgeon? No! Pleasing personalities and surgical skills have little correlation. A surgeon who is immediately available may also be one who is in less demand, perhaps because of poor outcomes ... or inexperience.

As a result, most difficult back surgeries are still performed by physicians who are far from being the best qualified for the task. The dampening effect on demand due to poor results is substantial in influencing people not to have elective surgeries done: Patients hear many people report that they didn't like the results, and such reports also discourage choosing back surgery from the most capable surgeons who might be able to help.

Assuming that those with back problems could accurately determine which surgeons could probably eliminate or ameliorate their symptoms, such better-informed patients would expand the demand for back surgeries until growth was eventually limited by the availability of capable surgeons.

What benefits come from more awareness of superior offerings?

1. Your offerings will be noticed more often by potential customers.
2. If they need or want what you offer, they will consider your offerings.
3. If you fulfill your offer in an acceptable way, they will probably keep buying (as needed) and tell others to work with you.
4. If demand is stimulated enough, you will also grow revenues faster than costs and assets, increasing your profits and cash flow as a percentage of revenues.
5. If you grasp a unique way of being remembered (such as with a brand name that sticks in the mind), you will have reduced the number of effective competitors by keeping them from gaining awareness among most customers. As an example of this point, few people can name all of the many overnight-delivery couriers in their country. Since most couriers lack broad awareness, they aren't even considered when a purchase is made.
6. Your pricing power will increase because you face less competition in serving those customers who are most likely to remember your offerings.
7. The effectiveness of mass-marketing methods will be improved. With enough of an awareness advantage, competitors' marketing will be remembered by most potential customers as having come from you.

What's the strategic lesson of expanding your market by twenty times with added awareness? Fully develop the right kind of awareness in markets you can serve … or you will be leaving the door wide open to entry by new competitors who can create awareness advantages over you. Acting on this strategic lesson often means that a multibrand strategy will work best. Compete, then, with yourself rather than with competitors. Few people ever realize the value of this strategy … and miss most of the potential growth and profits they could enjoy.

Here's an example. If the Coca-Cola Company had also developed Pepsi-Cola and Dr. Pepper instead of competitor companies having done so, the Coca-Cola Company would control over 90 percent of a much larger market, and profits would be substantially higher. Just imagine the cost advantages and efficiencies of driving all of that increased volume through one bottler network!

The following sections address questions you should consider to determine how to use more awareness to profitably expand your market.

How Can Increasing Awareness Be Valuable to Customers?

But where can wisdom be found?
And where is the place of understanding?
Man does not know its value,
Nor is it found in the land of the living.

— Job 28:12-13 (NKJV)

In most instances, there's a specific customer benefit gained from using a preferred product or service. Such a benefit may come in the form of a better-performing offering, faster delivery or service being received, or in less cost for customers.

Company leaders may incorrectly assume that customers are as well informed about the industry and its offerings as the executives are. Because of such assumptions, marketing activities will often emphasize some misleading or obscure benefit … totally leaving out the primary reasons why most customers should select an offering. For instance, physicians who offer eye surgery to improve vision usually stress not needing to wear glasses any more. But many people who have such surgery will still need to wear reading glasses after age forty. Someone who has to wear bifocals now, however, will be able to eliminate wearing bifocals … only needing reading glasses. That's a big improvement and a large cost saving for many nearsighted people! Yet I have never seen nor heard an advertisement that specifies getting rid of bifocals as a primary benefit.

When I was considering such surgery, I used eye drops for glaucoma (excess eye pressure that unless relieved can cause blindness). The eye drops irritated and dried out my eyes, making it hard for me to wear contact lenses … and I needed to use reading glasses in addition to the contacts. The eye surgery ads also never addressed whether those with glaucoma could benefit from the surgery (which isn't obvious because the eye shape changes daily due to fluctuations in internal pressure with glaucoma). If I had known that such surgery would have let me get rid of my contacts and need only reading glasses, I would have lined up for the first available time.

I used to see my ophthalmologist every four months, yet for years I forgot to ask her about whether I was a prospect for this vision-improving surgery. If benefit could have been available to me, I wasn't aware of it.

After several years of occasionally wondering about the usefulness of such surgery for me, I finally remembered to ask my physician, and she referred me to a surgeon who specialized in such operations. He examined my eyes, tested me for cataracts, and pronounced me ready for cataract surgery, something my regular physician had never mentioned. In the process, the surgeon commented that most nearsighted people (the reason I needed contacts) gain improved distance vision from having cataracts removed, and I might not need any vision-improving eye surgery. Glaucoma didn't come up in the discussion.

After the cataract surgery, I found that my vision stabilized at a pretty good level for distance. I only needed a little help from glasses or contacts to improve my vision for night driving. I bought a set of glasses for that purpose, and I still use reading glasses for some close work. But miracle of miracles, my glaucoma went away for four years. When I asked about that, my surgeon casually mentioned that cataract surgery usually eliminates glaucoma. As you can clearly see (which I didn't), awareness of potential eye-surgery benefits is pretty limited among many prospective patients. I'm back using drops to control glaucoma, but I appreciate the "holiday" I enjoyed for those years.

Assignment: Look for the most important new and existing benefits potential customers value, but which they don't realize that you can deliver.

How Far Can You Go in Profitably Expanding Awareness?

What profit has the worker from that in which he labors?

— Ecclesiastes 3:9 (NKJV)

There are two aspects to answering this question:

1. The amount of increased purchasing that occurs
2. The amount of cost reductions for gaining more awareness

Many companies inexpensively enlist their customers to expand awareness. For instance, some cellular telephone plans have allowed unlimited free calling among family members. A family member who joins such a calling plan will soon make other family members aware of the benefit, and more cellular-telephone use may follow. On the Internet, marketers offer affiliate commissions to those who will help lead potential customers to their Web sites. This method of creating awareness is potentially so effective that seminar guru T. Harv Eker has found it to be financially attractive to provide free three-day seminars simply to attract customers who will become affiliates and then send their friends and relatives invitations to still other free seminars where some will decide to pay for receiving other products and services.

Assignment: Take a small geographical area and see how much awareness you can create through a variety of means. As you do, measure to determine which methods created the most awareness at the least cost. Then experiment again emphasizing what worked best in a different small geographical area. Continue to test and measure in this way. As soon as you find a combination of low-cost awareness-creating methods that work very effectively in more than one small geographical area, start expanding the most effective combination to the places you are well prepared to serve.

How Can You Make the Most Attractive Potential Customers Aware First?

And do not turn aside;
for then you would go after empty things
which cannot profit or deliver,
for they are nothing.

— 1 Samuel 12:21 (NKJV)

The 2,000 Percent Solution describes more fully how Grey Poupon mustard became well-known in the United States. Let me share just part of the story in this lesson.

Marketers at Heublein found that those who tried this mustard almost always liked it better than their usual mustard. If the person who tried Grey Poupon was college educated and had an income over $30,000 a year (in the early 1970s), she or he would almost always think the product was well worth its premium price and, due to the preferred taste, would greatly increase how much mustard he or she ate. Whenever such mustard customers became aware of the product's advantages, the profits gained from serving them were over ten times greater than for serving an average mustard customer.

Assignment: See what common characteristics your most profitable customers have now and then direct your marketing towards making similar potential customers aware of your offering.

How Can You Change Your Business Model to Permit Faster Awareness Expansion?

A wise man is strong,
Yes, a man of knowledge increases strength;

— Proverbs 24:5 (NKJV)

Grey Poupon's marketing staff determined that, at the time, airline travelers pretty well fit the high-profit-potential profile. The brand's business model was changed to start selling single-portion mustard packages to airlines at cost in order to provide such potential customers with an opportunity to try the product and to become aware of its advantages. As a result, Grey Poupon's sales soared.

Assignment: **Reexamine all parts of your business model to see how you could accelerate acquiring awareness among the most potentially profitable customers. Test your better ideas to see how they work before any making major commitments.**

How Can You Locate and Attract
Undiscovered High-Potential Customers?

" ... seek, and you will find;
knock, and it will be opened to you."

— Luke ll:9 (NKJV)

Offerings may provide benefits that have much broader appeal than marketers realize. Such untapped potential existed for Grey Poupon. As levels of education and income expanded during the 1970s in the United States, many people began to look for inexpensive lifestyle choices that made them feel as if they were living a cut above the rest. Drinking Starbucks coffee often delivers a similar type of satisfaction from consuming a small, affordable luxury. To help fulfill this increasing psychological desire, Grey Poupon ran advertisements showing people in limousines stopping one another to ask if the other limousine's passenger could spare some Grey Poupon. Soon, it became trendy to put Grey Poupon bottles on fine restaurant tables and to display the bottle at social occasions where guests served themselves with condiments. Appealing to those who wanted to make this kind of personal statement further expanded the market for Grey Poupon mustard among high-profit customers, well past those who simply craved its spicy, wine-smoothed flavor.

Assignment: **Consider appealing benefits to emphasize that are different from what the bulk of high-profit customers respond to now. For example, Dell initially sold its computers to students and small businesses. The company realized that individuals at many large companies also wanted to buy the products. The busy IT departments in many companies wanted to standardize hardware, replacing parts, software, installation, and service. Dell pointed out to the IT departments that they could accomplish such standardization best by having Dell play that role for the entire company's personal computers. With the awareness of such advantages, purchasing of PCs soared in large companies ... vastly increasing market growth and Dell's overall market share. Dell was later able to use this foundation to gain a large chunk of such firms' server purchases as well.**

Lesson Ten

Improve Your Offering's Image

*And I went out by night through the Valley Gate
to the Serpent Well and the Refuse Gate,
and viewed the walls of Jerusalem
which were broken down
and its gates which were burned with fire.*

— Nehemiah 2:13 (NKJV)

Something can have highly desirable qualities ... but if potential customers don't understand why it's desirable, they may not buy it. Consider rapeseed. In 1972, Canadian farmers had great difficulty making money selling any of their rapeseed crops for human consumption. Few wanted to buy any foods made out of rapeseed ... and the prices were accordingly quite low.

Today, the rapeseed market is far larger, and profits are fat for farmers and rapeseed processors. What happened? Rapeseed was crossbred to establish a new strain with a nicer appearance and better taste due to having less acid, and the new strain was referred to by another name, Canola (for "Canadian oil, low acid"). Canola oil was soon praised by experts as a very healthy form of fat.

The very same women who wouldn't have bought rapeseed oil to save their lives (no matter how nice looking, tasty, and healthy the product was) because of its name, now couldn't buy too much Canola oil. Although Shakespeare told us that a rose by any other name would smell as sweet, a name can certainly get in the way of helping us find useful products.

The connotations of a product's name can be important. Here's an example. Many women regularly suffer from urinary-tract infections. Gynecologists often recommend that such patients drink cranberry juice. When such advice first became common, sales soared for tasty, sweet cranberry juice cocktail, which contained only 10 percent cranberry juice. Many women didn't realize that the product they were drinking didn't have much cranberry juice in it. Three decades later, diet authorities began warning people against drinking juice that is mixed with sugar-based extenders, especially cranberry-flavored cocktails. After that, cranberry juice cocktail sales dived while sales of beverages containing a high percentage of cranberry juice boomed.

An older example of how connotations affect behavior comes from the U.S. vodka market. During the 1930s those who drank vodka were often assumed to be members of the Communist Party ... not an attractive image. This kind of alcohol also had the reputation of being very powerful — some thought it would lead a hangover where it felt as if your head was about to blow off. Gradually, vodka marketers focused alcohol drinkers on other attributes of vodka: It mixed well with nonalcoholic beverages such as orange and tomato juices, and it left less bad breath than whiskey and many other alcoholic beverages. Within four decades after the end of Prohibition, the U.S. vodka market grew by more than 1,000 times.

What benefits come from an improved image for offerings?

1. You will be noticed more often and more positively by potential customers.
2. If they need or want the benefits you provide, they will consider your offerings.
3. If you fulfill the promises of your offer in an acceptable way, they will probably keep buying and tell others to work with you.
4. If demand is stimulated enough, you will also grow revenues faster than costs and assets, increasing your profit and cash flow as a percentage of revenues.
5. If you grasp a uniquely desirable image (such as with an offering that has more attributes of the most positive association), you will reduce the impact of competitors against you by making their offerings seem inferior. As an example of this point, Smirnoff, the U.S. vodka market leader, made a virtue of its product being filtered through charcoal several times so that it was perceived as purer (suggesting fewer hangovers, less breath pollution, and better blending with juices and mixes).
6. Your pricing power will increase because you now face less competition for the customers you are most likely to attract.
7. The effectiveness of mass-marketing methods will be improved. With enough of an image advantage, competitors' marketing will be remembered by most potential customers as having come from you.

What's the strategic lesson of expanding your market by twenty times with an improved image? Fully develop the optimum image in a market you can serve … or you will be leaving the door open to continuing new entrants who can create image advantages against you. This lesson often means a multibrand strategy will work best built around the strongest image positions. Compete, then, with yourself rather than with competitors. Few people ever realize the value of this strategy … and miss most of the potential growth and profits they could enjoy.

Let's return to the example I introduced in Lesson Nine. If the Coca-Cola Company had developed Pepsi-Cola and Dr. Pepper instead of competitors having done so, the Coca-Cola Company would control over 90 percent of a much larger cola market, and profits would be substantially higher due to the power of having such combined distribution. Coca-Cola's image is of being the original and the most genuine. Pepsi's image is of being the "coolest" and most in line with young people. Dr. Pepper's image is of being for those who are most energetic and active. No other important images have yet emerged except in terms of low-calorie benefits (Diet Coke, Coke Zero, Diet Pepsi, and Diet Dr. Pepper).

The following sections address questions you should consider to locate and to gain advantages from image-building activities that will help expand your market.

What Benefits Can You Offer That Customers Don't Yet Appreciate?

Now a certain man found him,
and there he was, wandering in the field.
And the man asked him, saying,
"What are you seeking?"

— Genesis 37:15 (NKJV)

Everyone who makes extensive use of an offering will eventually appreciate most of its pros and cons. But those who haven't tried such an offering or who use it infrequently will often be confused about what benefits the offering actually delivers.

When Viagra (a prescription medicine that increases blood flow in male genitals) first came on the market, it was viewed as a product for old men and men who experienced severe sexual dysfunction. Most men avoided the product like the plague because they didn't want to think about themselves as being in either category.

Some men with minor sexual dysfunctions discovered through experimentation that Viagra could help them engage in sexual activity more often, as well as more easily, particularly when impaired by alcohol and fatigue. As a result, the product came to be seen as a potential resource for any man who wanted to be more sexually active. Sales took off after online prescribing became common, providing a benefit by eliminating the cost of a potentially embarrassing visit to the doctor's office.

Press reports suggest that the testimony of Hugh Hefner, publisher of *Playboy*, persuaded some men without sexual dysfunctions to start using Viagra. Although Mr. Hefner is far from a young man, he has a reputation for always having one or more young girl friends. Suddenly, there was a common perception that the cosmopolitan "playboy" who wanted a great sex life was smart to use Viagra.

Concerned that sexually faithful people might not want to be associated with such "swinging" uses, the product's advertising was changed to suggest enriching life with a loved one. Couples wearing wedding rings were shown while engaged in affectionate behavior. As a result, some wives encouraged their husbands to try the product. Husbands who wanted to experiment with the product also didn't have to feel as concerned that their wives would wonder what their "real" agendas were.

Some men still felt embarrassed to ask their personal physicians for a prescription. New advertisements were prepared to suggest how to speak more comfortably with a physician about any sexual dysfunctions.

Assignment: Look for highly valued benefits that current and potential customers don't realize you can deliver.

What False Beliefs
Do Current and Potential Customers Have
about Your Offering?

Who is wise and understanding among you?
Let him show by good conduct
that *his works* are done *in the meekness of wisdom.*
But if you have bitter envy and self-seeking in your hearts,
do not boast and lie against the truth.

— James 3:13-14 (NKJV)

False beliefs can be based on many sources. Here are a few of the more common origins:

- name (such as rapeseed)
- appearance (dark-colored cranberry-juice cocktail looks to many as if it is almost all cranberry juice)
- true associations (such as vodka and Russia)
- regulations concerning use (prescribed medicines are presumed by many to be more potent than over-the-counter medications, even when that's not the case)
- imaginary associations (people assume that clear beverages have fewer calories than those with dark colors)
- distribution (an item sold in a beautiful store will usually be considered to be more desirable than the same item when it is sold by a street vendor)

<u>**Assignment:**</u> **Learn what negative associations and images your offerings have.**

How Much Can You Profitably Improve Image?

Now in all Israel there was no one who was praised
as much as Absalom for his good looks.
From the sole of his foot to the crown of his head
there was no blemish in him.

— 2 Samuel 14:25 (NKJV)

There are two sides to this question:

1. The amount of increased purchasing that occurs
2. The amount of cost reductions for improving an offering's image

A number of tools can help improve image. Inexpensive publicity in the right context can make many offerings seem much more desirable. For instance, during the O. J. Simpson murder trial in Los Angeles, authors Jack Canfield and Mark Victor Hansen sent a box of their Chicken Soup for the Soul books to Judge Ito, requesting that he give the books to the jurors to read while they were sequestered during the trial. Every morning, the jurors would arrive at the courthouse and wade through the waiting journalists and photographers holding the books. Reporters began writing articles about the books, and their sales increased.

When admired celebrities use your offerings, sales often rise; but purchased endorsements are very expensive. Savvy marketers will instead simply send free goods to celebrities they want to be associated with … knowing that some celebrities will eventually be seen in public with the offerings.

Where credibility needs to be established, you can also sponsor inexpensive competitions to find more positive uses for your offerings … and publicize the winning solutions.

When authorities stand behind the validity of your benefits, you may be able to use press releases to interest journalists in correcting any popular misconceptions.

To understand more ways of building a positive image, read Robert B. Cialdini's classic book, *Influence* (Prentice-Hall, fifth edition, 2008). Chapters 3 through 6 in *The 2,000 Percent Squared Solution* also offer useful insights.

<u>**Assignment:**</u> **Test your best ideas for improving image in a small community. Measure the results to learn what works best. Then experiment again emphasizing the successes in another small community. Continue to test and to measure in this way. When you find a combination of image improvements that works very effectively, start expanding the combination in geographic areas you can serve well.**

How Can You Improve Image
with the Most Attractive Potential Customers First?

Now a river went out of Eden to water the garden,
and from there it parted and became four riverheads.
The name of the first is Pishon;
it is the one which skirts the whole land of Havilah,
where there is gold. And the gold of that land is good.

— Genesis 2:10-12 (NKJV)

In *Crossing the Chasm* (Harper Paperbacks, revised edition, 2002), Geoffrey Moore describes some helpful ways to develop new technology markets. At first, a company can primarily attract those who are intrigued by the new technology or who expect to gain large economic advantages. The market will never proceed beyond use by such customers unless the experience of the first triers is relevant to those with less interest in the technology and who expect smaller economic benefits.

The market's development will depend very much, then, on selecting as the first customers those who will attract the interest of many other potential customers. This advice may mean seeking business from a company with a good reputation for product quality and technical knowledge such as Procter & Gamble, or one with great perspectives on technological innovation such as Cisco.

The lesson is to select your first prospective customers for their evidentiary value in attracting other desirable customers because of the positive image their use brings to your offering as well as for their profit potential.

Assignment: Investigate what "customer proof" will do to improve your image so that you can gain the largest and most profitable buyers. Demonstrate your benefits first and most aggressively with the highest-rated customer-proof-enhancing organizations.

How Can You Change Your Business Model to Permit Faster Image Improvements?

Why do you gad about so much to change your way?

— Jeremiah 2:36 (NKJV)

If you have an offering that will greatly benefit from endorsements, consider how you can partner with those who could most help your reputation. For instance, rather than selling your offering as a stand-alone item, perhaps you could persuade your customer to bundle your offering with the customer's most preferred offering. For instance, I'm sure that Dell's hardware-service supplier received a big image boost when Dell began offering service for its PCs through that supplier. Since Dell had such an outstanding reputation for hardware service, other PC makers probably then wanted to hire the same service supplier.

Or you might form a joint venture as Corning did when it wanted to extend its glass technology into new end-markets where other companies had better images for their products and performance. This strategy led, for instance, to Corning combining with Owens-Illinois to make and to sell fiberglass insulation through Owens Corning.

Assignment: Reexamine all parts of your business model to see how you could accelerate market-expanding image improvements. Test your better ideas through surveys and market experiments to see how well they might work on a broad scale before making major commitments.

How Can You Locate Undiscovered High-Potential Customers through Having an Improved Image?

Let us search out and examine our ways, ...

— Lamentations 3:40 (NKJV)

The most positive potential image for our offerings is often much broader than we realize. Smirnoff marketers were always very careful not to dilute its image, and for many years they didn't spread the brand's wings as wide as they might have.

Vodka aficionados eventually became fascinated by vodkas made by distilling different raw materials (potatoes, various grains, etc.). After that, country of origin became important, and Stolychnaya did well based on the perceived authenticity of being produced in Russia. Next, many brands were launched from other countries of origin. Later, bottle shape and brand image became important. Absolut showed the way with its amusing ads playing on its name and distinctive packaging. More recently, flavored vodkas became the rage, permitting tastier experiences without using mixers. Had Smirnoff searched out and acted on such opportunities in the 1950s, the vodka market could have been profitably led to even greater popularity and size.

The sales leader usually creates most of the industry's image. If your industry has a leader with a poor or poorly developed image, you'll have to displace the leader in order to fully develop your industry's potential.

Assignment: **Consider potential benefits to emphasize in creating an improved image that are different from what benefits attract the bulk of sales now. For example, vodka marketers could combine vodka with other liquors and wines to provide proprietary drinks in bottled form that provide startlingly delightful taste and visual qualities, ones that many consider far more desirable than the standard mixed drinks that employ vodka such as the vodka martini, Bloody Mary, screwdriver, and so forth.**

Lesson Eleven

Use Social Proof

Therefore we must give the more earnest heed
to the things we have heard, lest we drift away.
For if the word spoken through angels proved steadfast,
and every transgression and disobedience received a just reward,
how shall we escape if we neglect so great a salvation,
which at the first began to be spoken by the Lord,
and was confirmed to us by those who heard Him,
God also bearing witness both with signs and wonders,
with various miracles, and gifts of the Holy Spirit,
according to His own will?

— Hebrews 2:1-4 (NKJV)

When people are unsure what to do, they may look around and copy what others do. I've often seen this occur at meals when the number and location of utensils exceeded the usual fork on the left and a knife and spoon to the right of a dinner plate. In such a situation among strangers, people wait until someone grasps a utensil before digging into the food. The results can be unintentionally quite humorous if the person who acts first is a leader more by instinct than by knowledge. I've seen many appetizers eaten by whole tables of people with dessert forks as a result of such impetuous mistakes and copying.

I began to appreciate the power of social proof after a most unusual experience. When I was ten, my family had driven to Yellowstone Park in Wyoming, which is famous for its geysers of hot, sulfurous water that erupt in impressive vertical streams. One geyser is called Old Faithful because its eruptions occur about every 91 minutes. Naturally, we wanted to see this natural wonder. The park was filled with signs pointing the way to Old Faithful.

Arriving at the indicated location, we pulled into a parking lot and began looking for the geyser. Another sign pointed past some buildings. As we walked near the buildings, we heard an enormous roar and saw a plume of water vapor exploding upwards. I ran to see what it was and found an enormous pipe that was producing the water vapor. Every two or three minutes, another jet would come out. It was wonderful. My family crowded around.

Soon, we were joined by over fifty curious people who marveled at this phenomenon. After watching for about twenty minutes, I began to wander around between eruptions. I happened to notice a sign on the building that said "Laundry". Oops! I quickly gathered my family, and we continued down the pathway to Old Faithful.

We had been admiring the exhaust from a steam vent for the industrial washing machines! When we left, the crowd marveling at this highly productive "geyser" was still growing.

The same behavior can be observed in any major city with tall buildings. Stop and look up, and pretty soon the sidewalk will be full of people doing the same. It doesn't matter that there's nothing special to see. People will look up anyway.

Edward Bernays, the father of public relations, was aware of many people being quick to follow the crowd. A fabric manufacturer once hired Bernays to do something about the company's surplus of red cloth. Red wasn't in style, and there didn't seem to be any way to sell the unwanted material. Bernays quickly invited all the top society people in New York to a ball where everyone was required to wear either a red dress or to have a red accessory. The ball was the hit of the season. Naturally, there was soon a shortage of red material, and the manufacturer had to make even more!

While I worked at Heublein, I often saw this pattern repeated in New York. Fashion changes began in Harlem (an area where many of the poorest people in Manhattan lived) in those days. Whatever the most popular people wore or did in Harlem would be big business among everyone else within a few weeks or months.

Our company was always introducing new alcoholic beverages and often concocted new mixed drinks that included our beverages. Heublein salespeople would then head to Harlem and run bar parties where they mixed free drinks where the trendsetters hung out. If the not-so-trendy people saw the "cool" people sticking with the new drinks, everyone who admired the trendsetters would follow their examples. For the next few weeks or months, those drinks would be in demand in such bars … and others frequented by the trendy people there. Sure enough, the high-fashion midtown Manhattan lounges would soon be over-whelmed by orders for the same beverages and mixed drinks. From there, the rest of the nation would follow within a few months.

Most rapidly expanding markets get a big boost at some point from social proof. Advertisers often try to cash in by paying trendsetters to endorse their products. Nike built the athletic shoe industry to its current size largely through its endorsements from high-profile athletes such as Michael Jordan, David Beckham, and Tiger Woods. Such endorsements allow purchasers to imagine that the product will help transform their performance into that of the great stars. Who wouldn't want to glide through the air as Michael Jordan did in his prime?

If you can use social proof without having to pay top dollar for it, your improved results will cost a lot less. Book authors accomplish this all the time by soliciting free quotes to put on book jackets.

If you want to learn more about social proof and how purchasing can be ethically encouraged by it, I suggest you read *Influence* by Robert B. Cialdini.

What benefits come from employing social proof to stimulate demand for industry offerings?

1. You will be noticed sooner, more often, and more positively by potential customers who want either a more interesting or a safer choice.
2. If they need or can use what you offer, they will probably decide they want to try your offering.
3. If you fulfill the promises of your offer in an acceptable way, they will probably keep buying and tell others to work with you.
4. If enough demand is stimulated, you will also grow revenues faster than costs and assets, driving up your profit and cash flow as a percentage of revenues.
5. If you grasp a unique form of social proof (for example, with an offering that is more fun to use because of its social connections, such as items branded with sports-team logos), you will have reduced the impact of competitors against you by making their offerings seem inferior. Because

Smirnoff vodka made a virtue of being run through charcoal several times so that its vodka was perceived as purer, some marketers for newer vodka brands stimulated demand for their offerings by running blind taste tests with high-profile experts to establish which brands are "purest" in tasting bland.

6. Your pricing power will increase because you face less competition for those customers who appreciate your offering the most. A Nike shoe that may cost less than $5.00 to make often retails for over $100.
7. Mass-marketing effectiveness will be improved. With enough of a social-proof advantage, competitors' marketing will be remembered by most potential customers as having come from you.

What's the strategic lesson of expanding your market by twenty times with social proof? Fully develop the optimum social proof for a market you can serve ... or you will be leaving the door open to continuing new entrants who can create social proof advantages against you. This often means a multibrand strategy will work best built around the strongest social proofs. Compete, then, with yourself rather than with competitors. Few people ever realize the value of this strategy ... and miss most of the potential growth and profits they could enjoy.

Let's further expand on the cola example that began in Lesson Nine. If Coca-Cola had developed Pepsi-Cola and Dr. Pepper instead of competitors doing so, the Coca-Cola Company would control over 90 percent of a much larger market, and profits would be substantially higher. Coca-Cola's image of being the original and the most genuine could have been reinforced with advertisements featuring celebrities who were considered to be very honorable and genuine such as former U.S. president Jimmy Carter. Pepsi's image of being the coolest and most in line with young people could have been reinforced by using a line of even more trendy young pop singers, as the brand has consistently done. Dr. Pepper's image of being for those who are most energetic and active would be helped by having athletes endorse the product and by having exclusive distribution at sports facilities favored by young people such as the major soccer venues in Europe and South America.

The following sections address questions that you should consider to locate ways to expand your market using social proof.

What Benefits Can You Offer because the Market Is Underdeveloped?

Blessed be *the Lord,*
Who *daily loads us* with benefits,
The God of our salvation!

— Psalm 68:19 (NKJV)

Trendsetters like new items because they want to be seen as being different from followers. Once something trendsetters favor comes into common use, they will move on to something newer or different.

If few people are using your offering (or using it to best advantage), the lack of popularity will be part of attracting trendsetters. To interest trendsetters, your offering must give them lots of ways to show that they are different. Obscure brands that have been around for years can benefit from such unpopularity by attracting trendsetters simply because they appear to be so different from what most people use. Keds sneakers had a brief run of increased popularity based on such appeal to trendsetters. If trendsetters' usage of your offering isn't visible enough, you may have to drum up some publicity to increase such visibility.

In other cases your offering may be more valuable if few people use it. For instance, a database that provides ways to gain new insights into how to acquire customers is more valuable to marketers if all their competitors do not have the same information. As a result you may wish to offer opportunities to purchase exclusive use of such an offering.

If there are relatively few people employing the industry's offerings, you can also reshape your offering to meet a different standard that trendsetting potential customers prefer. This happens all of the time with technical products.

After a new professional service is created, the first customers and clients often gain access to the offering's developers. When the industry is well developed, such innovators just help attract interest while other professionals supply needed services. When the market is undeveloped, consider using access to the innovators as a point of differentiation.

Assignment: Look for ways you can deliver desired "exclusivity" and other benefits to trendsetters and other desirable customers because your industry is small compared to its potential.

What New Forms of Social Proof Can You Offer that Will Impress Unconvinced Potential Customers?

Bless the LORD, O my soul,
And forget not all His benefits:

— Psalm 103:2 (NKJV)

Early trendsetters are often replaced or supplemented by less adventurous (or less wealthy) trendsetters. For instance, a new item of apparel may first be worn in public by celebrities during red-carpet arrivals at an award show. While it's great to have that visibility, sales of the same line of apparel to the high-school crowd might be more influenced by what football team captains and head cheerleaders wear.

Many offerings never provide much value other than for being unusual. If you can also demonstrate that trendsetters can gain a continuing advantage from the offering, you've accomplished a lot more. For instance, Oprah Winfrey (the most popular television host in the United States just after the turn of the 21st century) went on a diet every so often. When she did, Ms. Winfrey looked much healthier and more attractive. During the diets her talk show often featured the person who was helping her lose weight. As long as she stayed trim, that person did well. When the weight piled back on, the social proof dissipated as well. But if someone could have helped to keep her thinner, the accomplishment would have been of lasting value as social proof.

Some people are appropriately skeptical about celebrities when it comes to such social proof. They know the celebrity probably has a personal chef, a personal trainer, the ability to purchase anything that might help, a huge economic incentive to use an offering, and a band of other advisors who may be helping create some of the results. To develop the mass market, at some point you will need to use social proof involving ordinary people who share their results.

Diet and exercise books very effectively persuade with "before" and "after" photos. Some people will do well at least temporarily on any new regimen. That doesn't mean the regimen will work well for you. But if you see a person who looks like you do now who has lost weight or gotten into shape, you'll start to think it could happen for you. Based on such "slim" evidence, a purchase may follow.

At some point, there's an avalanche effect. So many people have demonstrated effectiveness that potential buyers just assume the offering is valuable. The alternative is to believe that almost all of those people are stupid or ignorant (either of which could be true, of course).

As a result, sometimes it helps to list lots of customers. A CEO told me that he would buy anything for his company after learning that ten firms with CEOs he admired used a given offering.

Assignment: Develop new forms of social proof that build on your early success with trendsetters to draw in more customers who add credibility.

How Can New Forms of Social Proof Recreate the Excitement of When the Market Was Small?

... when James, Cephas, and John, who seemed to be pillars,
perceived the grace that had been given to me,
they gave me and Barnabas the right hand of fellowship,
that we should go to the Gentiles and they to the circumcised.
They desired only that we should remember the poor,
the very thing which I also was eager to do.

— Galatians 2:9-10 (NKJV)

Companies often reenergize markets by bringing out "new" and "improved" versions of their offerings, which they make available first to the trendsetters. Companies may expand such social proof by creating other "cool" associations. For instance, an athletic-shoe company may create fantasy stores (such as Nike has done) where youngsters and youngsters at heart can daydream and have a chance to buy new items not available elsewhere. The most influential customers (such as the "hottest" retailer buyers) may be granted special access to celebrities and trendsetters at invitation-only events (for Nike, this might be a golf outing where Nike's professional golfers wear the apparel and use the company's clubs and balls). When such retailer buyers are then taken to see lots of people buying hot products in the company's fantasy stores amid images of great sports stars, such influential customers are sure to be impressed. Why wouldn't they order?

Assignment: Refresh and deepen your "cool" social proof to keep trendsetters fascinated.

By How Much Can You Profitably Improve Social Proof?

And the man said to me,
"Son of man, look with your eyes and hear with your ears,
and fix your mind on everything I show you;
for you were brought here so that I might show them to you.
Declare to the house of Israel everything you see."

— Ezekiel 40:4 (NKJV)

There are two sides to this question:

1. The amount of increased purchasing that occurs
2. The amount of cost reductions for adding more social proof

A number of tools can help to add social proof. Publicity in the right context can make an offering seem much more relevant to those in the know. Charities often provide good ways to make such connections. Many celebrities need to improve their images before they can be seen as more than just greedy people with bad habits. Otherwise, many fans will turn to someone with a more wholesome image. Putting time and attention towards helping a charity is a favored way for celebrities to spruce up their images.

Celebrity support for charities often involves fund-raising activities. When you donate some of your offerings to help raise funds for the charity, a celebrity may be seen holding or using the offering. In some cases, the celebrity will give an unsolicited testimonial for how good your offering is to encourage people to spend more for the donated offerings.

Contests where celebrities serve as judges are also a good form of gaining publicity that is rich in social proof. If an existing contest fits with what your offering provides, you can donate the offering to those who appear in the contest ... or to the judges. In the *American Idol* televised entertainer competitions, for example, cosmetics would be inexpensive to provide and could then end up gaining very valuable social proof after the contest winners become stars.

Many offering providers develop new contests just to serve this purpose. For example, Smirnoff helped launch the original world surfing championships before the event was well known and widely publicized. On the televised shows you saw lots healthy surfers against the background of the Smirnoff logo. In an era when liquor wasn't advertised on television, such visuals were very valuable for creating a "healthier" image.

As long as it doesn't involve paid endorsements from wealthy superstars, social proof is usually pretty inexpensive to generate. But creating social proof almost always takes time. Effective organizations often focus someone on this activity and develop an internal expertise, or they find a specialized agency that can do this effectively for them that is separate from the agencies that develop and buy advertising.

Assignment: Take a small community and test your best ideas for improving social proof. Measure the results to find out what works best. Then experiment again emphasizing the most effective methods in another small community. Continue to test and measure in this way. As soon as you find a combination of social-proof-enhancing methods that work very effectively, start expanding that combination to geographic areas you can serve well.

How Can You Improve Social Proof with the Best Customers First?

But earnestly desire the best gifts.

— 1 Corinthians 12:31 (NKJV)

In *Crossing the Chasm* Geoffrey A. Moore describes the way many new technology markets develop. At first, a company can most easily attract those who are intrigued by the new technology or who expect to gain large economic advantages. If someone who has a great reputation for spotting new breakthrough technologies becomes a delighted early customer of a new offering, letting others know about such success can make market development easier and faster.

The lesson is to select your first customers both for their social proof in attracting other customers because of the credibility they add to your offering and for their profit potential.

Assignment: Investigate what the social proof of your client list will gain you with those who will eventually be the largest and most profitable customers. To expand the market the most, first demonstrate your benefits with the highest-rated organizations for generating social proof.

How Can You Change Your Business Model
to Permit Faster Development of Social Proof?

And it came to pass, at the end of forty days and forty nights,
that the LORD gave me the two tablets of stone,
the tablets of the covenant.
Then the LORD said to me,
"Arise, go down quickly from here,
for your people whom you brought out of Egypt have acted corruptly;
they have quickly turned aside from the way
which I commanded them;
they have made themselves a molded image."

— Deuteronomy 9:11-12 (NKJV)

When a small vitamin distribution company was founded, the leaders decided to market their offerings primarily through social proof, providing free vitamins to high-profile professional athletes.

A lot of work was involved because the athletes needed special services. They often lost the vitamins and would request that replacements be shipped out for same-day delivery to the ball park or stadium. Or someone would ask the athlete about the vitamins, and the athlete would expect a representative to be available that night to host a dinner, to explain about the vitamins, and to hand over a free supply.

The organization adapted its business model to meet such demands, and the distributor soon attracted the bulk of the most-admired local professional athletes as endorsers at no cost other than providing free goods and great service. The athletes appreciated the caring service and realized that this small company couldn't afford to spend millions for their endorsements.

Mitchell and Company, the management consulting firm I direct, did something similar when we assembled best-practice-development organizations. After the members started to meet one another on a regular basis, they were impressed by our clientele. Clients would share stories about ways that Mitchell and Company had helped them. New assignments often resulted, and our best-practice-improvement work rapidly expanded.

Assignment: Reexamine all parts of your business model to see how you could accelerate adding social proof. Test your better ideas to see how they work before making major commitments.

How Can You Locate
Undiscovered High-Potential Customers
through Providing More Powerful Social Proofs?

"Therefore go into the highways,
and as many as you find,
invite to the wedding."

— Matthew 22:9 (NKJV)

Small social proof additions may be enough to go from making a market somewhat larger to making the same market enormous. In fact, just one additional element of social proof may be enough to serve as a tipping point, particularly if you bring in new types of customers who are active buyers.

The healing-water movement led by Masaru Emoto provides a good example. He self-published the first book he wrote, *The Hidden Messages of Water* (Atria, 2005), and sold only a few hundred copies. Then, a filmmaker happened to hear about the book and featured some of its pictorial material in *What the Bleep Do We Know?* Seeing the photographs of frozen water in the film stimulated a lot of interest.

Based on the film, the author was invited to many conferences where he showed the images. Just to see more of such ice photographs, many people bought the book.

During the conferences, he would quickly arrange to have his photograph taken with the most impressive people attending. Out on the lecture circuit, he would feature such photographs of himself with famous people. These images made him seem like a more credible authority.

After the Dalai Lama was photographed enthusiastically hugging Mr. Emoto at one of the conferences, a whole new audience became interested, those who were fascinated with Eastern religion and spirituality. As a result, the book became a runaway best seller. A series of successful books and professional services followed.

Assignment: **Consider creating social proof in areas different from where the bulk of the market is now. Think about cereal. This product is mostly eaten by young people, but in most developed countries the population of older people is larger than that of younger people. The cereal companies could locate people who live to be well over a hundred, look good on film, and eat a given cereal every day. Filming such people could offset many of the beliefs older people have about cereal being appropriate just for children. Those who wanted to live long, healthy lives might take note. Since Quaker Oatmeal is already thought to provide some health benefits, that brand might be in the best position to develop and to benefit from such social proof.**

Lesson Twelve

Add Authority

And so it was, when Jesus had ended these sayings,
that the people were astonished at His teaching,
for He taught them as one having authority, and not as the scribes.

— Matthew 7:28-29 (NKJV)

When the president of the United States meets with a prominent citizen in the Oval office and asks the person to quit her or his job, to sell or put all of his or her financial assets in a so-called blind trust, to go through a painful public-disclosure process, and to sacrifice millions of dollars in income to take a low-paying government job where it doesn't much matter who does the work, almost everyone who is asked will say "yes." Why? It's hard to turn down the leader of the world's most powerful country, even for a person who disagrees with the president's policies and has a lot to lose.

Other kinds of authority matter, as well. Research has shown that people will almost always obey a person wearing a white lab coat who tells them to turn up the dial on the electric current connected to a test subject in a "learning" experiment to a level that the equipment indicates is "lethal." Although such research only simulates sending and receiving powerful electrical shocks, the person turning up the dial doesn't know that there's no risk of harm to the person writhing in apparent agony while calling for the "shocks" to stop.

Some surgeons have performed the wrong operations despite the nurses in attendance knowing that a mistake was being made. The nurses remained silent. Why? Nurses are trained to follow doctors' orders, no matter what.

In the face of authority, most of us lack the self-confidence to follow our own perceptions and good judgment in pursuit of what's best for all concerned. It's as though giving people impressive offices, dressing them in lab coats, or hanging stethoscopes around their necks makes such people into more than mere humans. That's exactly what happens … in our perceptions. In reality, the person is no more competent or careful than before the "props" arrived.

Crest toothpaste's brand managers appreciated the psychological trait of deferring to authority and capitalized on it many years ago by acquiring an endorsement for Crest from the American Dental Association (ADA) that the toothpaste, when combined with good dental care, would reduce tooth decay. The brand's volume zoomed after Crest gained and advertised the endorsement.

When a new movie is released, producers put the hardest-hitting comments from the most positive reviews (along with the name of the reviewer and his or her affiliation) into their advertising. Moviegoers who trust a particular critic will be impressed, and many will watch the movie.

If you want to learn more about authority and how purchasing can be ethically affected by applying it, I suggest you read *Influence* by Robert B. Cialdini.

What benefits come from adding authority to stimulate demand for industry offerings?

1. Your offerings will be noticed sooner, more often, and more positively by potential customers who want more reliable choices.
2. If customers need or can use what you offer, they will probably decide they want to try your offerings.
3. If you fulfill your offers in an acceptable way, customers will probably keep buying and tell others to work with you.
4. If demand is stimulated enough, you will also grow revenues faster than costs and assets, increasing your profit and cash flow as a percentage of revenues.
5. If you grasp a powerfully unique form of authority (such as an endorsement from the world's leading expert), you will have reduced the impact of competitors on you by making their offerings seem inferior due to their sources of authority being less impressive.
6. Your pricing power will increase because you face less competition for the customers who are most likely to appreciate your offering. For instance, a pharmaceutical product that's been found to be safe and effective by the American Food and Drug Administration will probably sell for more than a hundred times the price of an effective alternative that lacks the same authority.
7. Mass-marketing effectiveness will be improved. With enough of an authority advantage, competitors' marketing will be remembered by most potential customers as having come from your offering.

What is the strategic lesson for expanding your market by twenty times through adding authority? Fully develop all sources of authority for a market you can serve … or you will be leaving the door open to continuing new entrants who can create authority advantages against you. Applying this lesson often means that a multiauthority strategy will work best when built around brand names that express or suggest superior qualities.

Crest found its authority base eroding after the ADA began to endorse other fluoride-based toothpastes. The market grew, but Crest's market share dropped. Crest should have immediately sought to maintain its early authority advantage by adding new attributes such as better whitening, enamel strengthening, reducing sensitivity to hot and cold, and killing more germs on the gums. Once such new superior attributes were added, Crest should have found authorities to endorse its approach to supplying the new benefits.

The following sections address questions you should consider to locate and to determine the potential for adding authority to help expand your market.

What Authority-Related Benefits Can You Offer because the Market Is Underdeveloped?

"And no one puts new wine into old wineskins;
or else the new wine bursts the wineskins, the wine is spilled,
and the wineskins are ruined.
But new wine must be put into new wineskins."

— Mark 2:22 (NKJV)

Cervical cancer can be almost totally eliminated by routine physical examinations and laboratory tests. Vaccines have also been developed to protect women from being infected by the virus strains that cause this type of cancer.

Despite the potential to prevent such cancers, the original Pap-smear test unfortunately provided a lot of mistaken results. Many women were told they might have cervical cancer who didn't, and some women with cervical cancer were incorrectly told that they were disease-free.

When Cytyc developed a more expensive, but more accurate, diagnostic test, few physicians used it at first because insurance companies wouldn't cover the increased cost. Few women were willing to pay for the test either, despite the obvious value of gaining more timely warnings and avoiding unnecessary fear.

Cytyc eventually solved this market-limiting problem by finding physicians with eminent reputations who persuaded health insurers to pay for the more expensive test. After that change occurred, the market for the new test geometrically expanded.

Assignment: While your industry's size is small, look for ways to deliver performance advantages and other benefits that authorities will favor.

What New Forms of Authority Can You Offer That Will Impress Unconvinced Potential Customers?

*Therefore show to them, and before the churches,
the proof of your love and of our boasting on your behalf.*

— 2 Corinthians 8:24 (NKJV)

One person's authority can be another person's humbug. To gain the most credibility for your offering, several sources of authority may be needed.

As the Crest example demonstrates, authority doesn't just come from individuals who hold positions that inspire reverence and compliance. Authority can also come from "proof" that an offering works.

A great demonstration can provide such authority. In its early days as an ADA-endorsed product, Crest ran experiments that measured the incidence of cavities where half a school or half a family used Crest and the rest used toothpaste without fluoride. Naturally, the Crest groups always had fewer cavities.

Some advertisers take providing "authority" too far by hiring actors and actresses to tout their offerings who have merely played roles of characters who have authority. An example that many older Americans remember was actor Robert Young, who played the starring role in *Marcus Welby, M.D.*, appearing in advertising for Sanka coffee. So many people associated the performer with his authority role that such advertisements may have worked better with some customers than if the same factual claim were made based on a demonstration. The ethics of such approaches are iffy at best.

Some enterprising companies have profited by persuading politicians to dedicate specific days for certain purposes, such as Mother's Day. Without such "official" recognition, do you expect that many millions of people would feel guilty if they didn't send a card, call, or purchase flowers for mom then?

Assignment: Develop new, ethical forms of authority that add credibility to your attributes and draw in more customers.

How Can You Use New Forms of Authority to Recreate the Excitement of When the Market Was Small?

Now the two of them went until they came to Bethlehem.
And it happened, when they had come to Bethlehem,
that all the city was excited because of them;
and the women said, "Is this Naomi?"

— Ruth 1:19 (NKJV)

The simplest way to recreate excitement is by finding and communicating new reasons to use an offering. For instance, fluoride-based toothpastes eventually added brighteners to make teeth look whiter.

Realizing that some people cared even more about the whiteness of their teeth than about avoiding cavities, consumer products companies began offering less-expensive substitutes for the tooth bleaching that dentists provide. In developing such substitutes, new sources of authority were tapped. Since the ADA wasn't likely to provide an endorsement based on whiteness, when Crest Whitestrips were introduced the brand instead employed "before" and "after" demonstrations and measurements to lend authority to their product's effectiveness.

Assignment: **Locate new benefits and authoritative ways to demonstrate such benefits.**

How Much Can You Profitably Benefit from Increasing Authority?

"Blessed shall be *the fruit of your body,*
the produce of your ground and the increase of your herds,
the increase of your cattle and the offspring of your flocks."

— Deuteronomy 28:4 (NKJV)

There are two sides to this question:

1. The amount of increased purchasing that occurs
2. The amount of cost reductions for adding more authority

Gaining more authority often doesn't have to be expensive, just as long as you don't have to meet tough government tests such as those for the efficacy and safety of new pharmaceuticals. You will be pleased to learn that many individual authorities are glad to provide their endorsements at little or no cost. Authors seek such advantages by asking authorities they don't know to write promotional blurbs for the dust jackets of their new books. The authorities are often honored to be asked and are usually satisfied with receiving some publicity in return.

Lack of imagination is often the only limit to adding more authority. Here's an intriguing example. When author Robert G. Allen wrote a book claiming that anyone could become rich by buying real estate despite investing no personal money, some journalists thought that Mr. Allen was making a false claim. One skeptic challenged Mr. Allen to come to the journalist's town with no money and to buy any real estate within three days.

Mr. Allen accepted the challenge, and the reporter followed Mr. Allen as he successfully demonstrated his claim. The success created an astounding increase in book and seminar sales.

Having learned an important lesson about demonstrating results, Mr. Allen followed this well-publicized event with similar demonstrations where unemployed people Mr. Allen coached made the real estate purchases with no money of their own. Press reports again provided the authenticity that made the claims resonate more powerfully.

Assignment: Test your best ideas for garnering more authority in a small community. Measure the results to find out what works best. Then experiment again emphasizing what worked best in another small community. Continue to test and measure in this way. As soon as you find an authority-expanding combination that works very effectively for increasing purchases, start employing that combination in geographic areas you can serve well.

How Can You Improve Authority with the Best Potential Customers First?

*And their father Israel said to them,
"If it must be so, then do this:
Take some of the best fruits of the land in your vessels
and carry down a present for the man —
a little balm and a little honey, spices and myrrh,
pistachio nuts and almonds.*

— Genesis 43:11 (NKJV)

Some customers are usually better connected and more highly esteemed than others. Some of such people routinely share their valued opinions with thousands of other customers through e-letters, blogs, social networks, and other mass-communications methods. Individual use by such better-networked influencers may account for less than 1 percent of total consumption … but their views may sway more than 70 percent of product users.

In the case of Crest, Procter & Gamble could have conducted a survey to locate which ordinary toothpaste users most influenced brand choices before placing any mass advertising … and invited such influencers to check out Crest's cavity-fighting qualities. If the influencers had been pleased with the results they experienced, the influencers' comments could have been even more persuasive to some of those people they influenced than the "official" tests were.

Assignment: Investigate which customers influence the most other customers. Identify what forms of authority would help to turn such influencers into "raving fans."

How Can You Change Your Business Model to Permit Faster Development of Authority?

*"And you shall give some of your authority to him,
that all the congregation of the children of Israel may be obedient."*

— Numbers 27:20 (NKJV)

Sybron Dental Specialties, a firm Carol Coles and I wrote about in *The Ultimate Competitive Advantage*, primarily grew in its earlier days by acquiring and expanding innovative products and services that were more effective than existing offerings. Almost all of such new offerings were virtually unknown when Sybron acquired them.

How did Sybron spread the word out about their new offerings? The firm's officers spent as much time as possible with the most respected dentists. Through such connections, the Sybron executives arranged for free trials of their new offerings to be conducted by such dentists who regularly attended dental conventions. At subsequent conventions, the dentists were authorized to present formal papers about their trial results to the other dentists. If the feedback from such dental trials wasn't strong enough to excite other dentists, Sybron improved its offerings and conducted new trials before making the offerings generally available.

Assignment: Reexamine all parts of your business model to see how you could accelerate adding authority. Test your better ideas to see how they work before making major commitments.

How Can You Locate Undiscovered High-Potential Customers through Providing More Powerful Forms of Authority?

For the word of God is living and powerful,
and sharper than any two-edged sword,
piercing even to the division of soul and spirit,
and of joints and marrow,
and is a discerner of the thoughts and intents of the heart.

— Hebrews 4:12 (NKJV)

There is usually only a small difference between adding just enough authority to make a market somewhat larger and providing enough more authority to make a market enormous. Just one additional source of authority may be enough to cause a huge expansion, particularly when new types of active buyers are attracted.

In the case of Crest, the ADA endorsement was so powerful, in part, because the ADA had never endorsed any toothpaste before! So this endorsement was viewed as bigger news than if the ADA had regularly endorsed toothpastes.

That unprecedented step surely suggested to many people that Crest was also big news. Had Crest's brand managers merely done all of the other work they did to establish authority for its benefits, the brand's sales would have been much smaller without the ADA endorsement.

Assignment: Look for authority in high-powered places no one in your industry has ever accessed. Although no candy maker had ever considered sending free blueberry jelly beans to a presidential inauguration before, taking this step after President Reagan was elected certainly worked well. After it became better known that former U.S. president Ronald Reagan loved jelly beans, sales of the venerable candy zoomed.

Lesson Thirteen

Encourage Reciprocity

Then the LORD appeared to him by the terebinth trees of Mamre,
as he was sitting in the tent door in the heat of the day.
So he lifted his eyes and looked, and behold,
three men were standing by him;
and when he saw them, *he ran from the tent door to meet them,*
and bowed himself to the ground, and said,
"My Lord, if I have now found favor in Your sight,
do not pass on by Your servant.
Please let a little water be brought, and wash your feet,
and rest yourselves under the tree.

— Genesis 18:1-4 (NKJV)

One of the most powerful emotional motivations is the desire to repay, in kind, what another person has previously provided. If you have ever felt an obligation to do something for someone else who helped you first, you know the strength of this psychological pressure. Sociologists call this behavior "reciprocation." You may know the behavior instead as "favor for favor," the governing principle for many political organizations.

Many entrepreneurs report having made great progress in their work by first doing favors for others … often unasked. Later, many of those the entrepreneur helped did favors in return. For instance, Alex Mandossian, the teleseminar guru, got his start by volunteering to sell CDs, books, and other information products for speakers at the back of live seminar events. Some of the speakers later allowed Mr. Mandossian to interview them, creating new information products to sell. Mr. Mandossian always provided a free copy of the finished product to the interviewees so they could sell the product as well.

I have often gained consulting clients partially as a result of doing favors for people: I have helped children to be accepted at highly regarded colleges, reviewed books that clients and prospective clients have written, provided career advice, taken people on golf outings, introduced people to reporters so they could be quoted in news articles, advised on finding jobs, and been a reference unasked for those seeking employment.

Many direct-selling businesses thrive, in part, by applying the same practices. Consider Avon as an example. Most Avon representatives primarily sell their products to friends and neighbors … or as a result of introductions from friends and neighbors. Why are the reps able to succeed? They often start with a strong positive balance of favors provided relative to favors received (such as pets fed while families were away on vacation, lawns watered under similar situations, emergency babysitting, loaning tools and equipment, covering for a colleague at work, and so forth) that made people willing to buy as a way to work off some of the perceived favor imbalance.

How strong can this desire to repay favors be? In 1985, impoverished Ethiopia's Red Cross sent $5,000 in relief aid to help the victims of Mexico City's earthquake. Certainly, Ethiopia's people needed the money more than Mexico's people did. Why was the gift made? A look at history reveals an important clue: When Ethiopia was invaded by Italy in 1935, Mexico sent aid. The Ethiopian Red Cross referenced this prior gift in its 1985 gift announcement.

I remember an example of this kind of reciprocation from my youth. My dad had been sick and couldn't work as much as usual. Money was tight, and we hadn't been able to afford our favorite foods for some time. A new supermarket opened and gave away lots of groceries that had been provided as free samples by manufacturers. On my mom's birthday, she was given several bags of groceries filled with gourmet delights we had never even thought of trying. For decades, our family would go out of its way to buy some groceries from that store … even after the ownership changed hands several times. We also bought many of those gourmet foods when we could afford them, in part because we knew that those brands had originally donated the samples we had enjoyed so much. I later did extensive consulting work for one of the brands, going way beyond what I was paid by my client to do.

There are many other ways to do favors for people so they will be more interested in helping you. For instance, if you offer valuable goods and services to someone and they repeatedly turn you down, at some point those who declined your offers may feel obliged to buy something small to make up for feeling guilty about not having bought your more expensive offerings. People who rejected proposals they had requested for a million dollars in services often turned around and bought $100,000 worth of work as a sort of consolation prize. Although receiving such "make-up" sales was not our intention, we certainly appreciated being hired.

You often see this process at work in negotiations. Two parties start by asking one another for the moon. After one party concedes a point, the other party will concede a point. Pretty soon, there's an agreement somewhere near halfway between the initial positions because they continued to reciprocate.

If you want to learn more about the sense of obligation behind reciprocity and how purchasing can be ethically affected by it, I suggest you read *Influence* by Robert B. Cialdini. I'm sure you enjoy doing helpful things for others without expecting anything in return. By focusing on being a selfless servant in accordance to what the Holy Spirit prompts you to do, you can avoid the kinds of manipulation that everyone finds so offensive. Isn't it wonderful that God has provided nice surprises for us as consequence of doing His will?

What benefits come from employing reciprocity ethically to stimulate demand for industry offerings?

1. You will be noticed sooner, more often, and more positively by potential customers who want to work off any obligations they feel.
2. If they need or can use what you offer, they will probably decide they want to try a version of your offering that sells at a low price point.
3. If you provide your offerings in an acceptable way, they will probably keep buying and tell others to work with you.
4. If demand for your offerings is stimulated enough, you will also grow revenues faster than costs and assets, increasing your profit and cash flow as a percentage of revenues.
5. If you engage in a unique form of reciprocity (such as providing a highly desired favor customers cannot obtain in any other way), you will have reduced the impact of competitors against you by making their offerings seem inferior because of their limited abilities to provide such favors.

6. Your pricing power will have increased because you now will face less competition for those customers who favor you. If they can afford to pay you more, in some cases people will even tell you to raise your prices.

7. Mass-marketing methods will work better with those who feel that they owe you a favor. With enough of a reciprocity advantage, competitors' marketing will be remembered by most potential customers as having come from you.

What's the strategic lesson of expanding your market by twenty times by relying on ethical reciprocity? Fully develop all sources of ethical obligation among current and potential customers for a market you can serve ... or you will be leaving the door open to continuing new entrants who can create reciprocity advantages against you. This lesson often means an ethical multifavor strategy will work best in providing help that's consistent with brand names that express or suggest the strongest aspects of the obligation.

Here's an example of how such a multifavor approach can work. A CFO heard about Mitchell and Company's plans for a free outing for prospective clients and their spouses at Pebble Beach. The outing was planned for the weekend of his twenty-fifth wedding anniversary. Without being asked, we arranged special entertainment for his wife and him. The CFO's wife had been ill for sometime, and she ended up enjoying this weekend more than anything else she had done for almost twenty years. The CFO was so moved by the experience that he offered to pay his own expenses. Without thinking of any future gain, we thanked him for his offer and refused, telling him it was satisfaction enough to simply bring such pleasure to him and to his wife. The CFO continually looked for ways that he could buy our services, take us on great golf outings, be our host for wonderful meals, and introduce us to others until he retired.

The following sections address questions you should consider to locate ethical opportunities to do favors that could encourage reciprocity that would help expand your market.

What Ethical Reciprocity-Related Benefits Can You Offer because the Market Is Underdeveloped?

Let not mercy and truth forsake you;
Bind them around your neck,
Write them on the tablet of your heart,
And so find favor and high esteem
In the sight of God and man.

— Proverbs 3:3-4 (NKJV)

The advantages of being among the first to use a superior offering can be enormous in an underdeveloped market. Rather than try to serve everyone in an industry, you might instead offer exclusive use of new offerings in an industry for a period of time as a favor to those who first buy. Once the benefits mount for such a favored customer organization, their competitors will be even hungrier to access what you have to offer after the exclusivity period runs out.

People may also need substantial education to make the best use of a novel offering. Provide such education for free as a favor to people who can gain career benefits as a result, and you will probably obtain some long-term advantages in selling to such people.

Most people won't know initially what they should pay for your offering. You might begin by telling people about the most expensive and valuable version (which everyone would like to have, but most cannot afford). Then, after they are intrigued and mention they cannot afford to pay that amount, have a less expensive alternative available that can serve as an initial, valuable step in helping them gain benefits so that they can eventually afford to purchase the more expensive alternative.

During negotiations with organizations, you can sometimes gain more by making your advocate in the other organization look good to his or her boss than by making an immediate sale. A word of genuine praise about the person's professionalism and knowledge can be worth millions in new business for you in the future. You will also feel good for having helped a worthy person, even if no business is ever gained.

Assignment: Look for ways you can deliver desired favors and other benefits that prospects will see as enhancing their personal situations and those of their organizations.

What New Forms of Ethical Reciprocity Can You Offer That Will Impress Unconvinced Potential Customers?

Therefore, laying aside all malice,
all deceit, hypocrisy, envy, and all evil speaking,
as newborn babes, desire the pure milk of the word,
that you may grow thereby,
if indeed you have tasted that the Lord is gracious.

— 1 Peter 2:1-3 (NKJV)

Many potential customers desperately want to meet someone they admire or to participate in a certain prestigious event. Most such potential customers have no idea how to arrange for such a meeting or for an invitation to such a special occasion. Yet such introductions can often be simple and costless to provide. If you have a wide network of influential contacts, chances are that you can find a way to make a potential customer's dream come true. Accomplishing such a result can often be as simple as hiring or arranging for a celebrity to speak at an event. With enough prospective customers present, the cost per prospect may be small. Some celebrities will be willing to come for free because a charity they favor will receive benefits. By arranging for a charitable auction to be conducted by a celebrity, you may be able to grant two favors: one to a guest and another to someone whose offering is auctioned.

When Mitchell and Company couldn't arrange for entrance into an appropriate event for clients and prospects, our firm often sponsored award dinners. We usually honored those we most highly esteemed and our most accomplished clients on one of the company's anniversaries of its founding. These memorable events impressed those who attended that we were very influential and well worth working with. Most award winners at such dinners later sought to do favors for us, as well.

Assignment: Develop new forms of reciprocity that build on your early successes to attract still more customers.

How Can You Use New Forms of Ethical Reciprocity to Recreate the Excitement of When the Market Was Small?

Therefore, brethren, having boldness to enter the Holiest
by the blood of Jesus,
by a new and living way which He consecrated for us,
through the veil, that is, His flesh,
and having a High Priest over the house of God,
let us draw near with a true heart in full assurance of faith,
having our hearts sprinkled from an evil conscience
and our bodies washed with pure water.

— Hebrews 10:19-22 (NKJV)

Do your favors in small, intimate settings. The bigger your organization becomes, the more that being treated well in intimate events will seem like a big favor. Don't hold a dinner for 10,000. Instead, hold a dinner at the most prestigious location you can access for ten highly admired people who support what you do, and treat each person so well that he or she feels like the center of attention. During such an occasion, casually invite those present to gain the first opportunities to work with your newest and most improved offerings, expert staff members, or educational programs.

Assignment: Locate valuable new advantages and provide them to those who have always returned favors.

How Far Can You Profitably Increase Sales through Encouraging Reciprocity?

As far as the east is from the west,
So far has He removed our transgressions from us.

— Psalm 103:12 (NKJV)

There are two aspects to answering this question:

1. The amount of increased purchasing that occurs
2. The amount of cost reductions in doing favors for others

What seems like providing a favor in some cases can instead actually be a highly profitable activity. Let's look at giving unpaid speeches. Neophytes see such engagements as doing favors that waste their time and resources. More experienced people bring along items to sell that listeners will find to be unusually valuable, even after they pay a serious price for them. For instance, a speaker might offer a new-customer special for some offering related to the speech's subject that's likely to lead to future purchases of related offerings.

On other occasions, you may be able to donate to charities offerings that cost little or nothing and to receive substantial free publicity in exchange. Carol Coles and I have done this with review copies of our books that our publishers have freely provided to us. When donated to the local public television station, we receive about fifteen minutes of free advertising with a large audience in exchange for providing the items.

The Internet possibilities are endless for providing electronic versions of products and services that cost very little to develop and virtually nothing to deliver. Many Internet marketers provide free information products to those who introduce friends and colleagues to their lists. Using such a favor-for-favor approach, some marketers report growing their online lists by as much as 5 percent a day.

Assignment: Test your best ideas for garnering more reciprocal behavior from those who should be ideal users of your offerings in a small community. Measure the results to find out what works best. Then experiment again, emphasizing what worked best in yet another small community. Continue to test and measure in this way. As soon as you find a combination of actions that works very effectively, expand that combination to geographic areas that you can serve well.

How Can You Improve Ethical Reciprocity with the Most Attractive Customers First?

But many who are *first will be last, and the last first.*

— Matthew 19:30 (NKJV)

Some potential customers will be more likely to reciprocate than others. You can test this possibility by looking at the results of small favors you've done to see who is most responsive and in what ways. If you have limited time and resources to do favors for potential customers, you might consider the economic potential of doing favors for the various potential customers who are most likely to reciprocate. If you create a priority list for doing favors, be sure to consider all of the favors you will receive, and not just how much business you will sell to the person who receives the favors. The favors may be more important than the initial sales.

Here's an example. One of our long-term Mitchell and Company clients seldom bought more than a minimal amount business from us, but he would scrupulously repay us for any favors we did for him. He was always willing to be an enthusiastic reference, and we gained millions of dollars in business from people to whom he spoke on our behalf.

Don't expect that every kind thing you do will provide some benefit for your business. I once courted a prospect who never reciprocated a single thing I did for him. I'm sure he just thought I was very impressed with him and the invitations I provided were his just due. After many years, I was convinced that he was never going to reciprocate. I stopped doing favors just for him … and did favors instead that his wife would enjoy as well. She loved doing kind things for others and invited our family to great events where we met delightful people we have enjoyed knowing.

Assignment: Consider determining who the most responsive customers are for reciprocating favors. Identify what forms of favors would turn these reciprocators into "raving fans" who buy more and tell everyone else to do the same.

How Can You Change Your Business Model to Permit Faster Development of Ethical Reciprocity?

*And may the Lord make you increase
and abound in love to one another and to all,
just as we* do *to you,
so that He may establish your hearts blameless in holiness
before our God and Father at the coming
of our Lord Jesus Christ with all His saints.*

— 1 Thessalonians 3:12-13 (NKJV)

Mitchell and Company originally tried to attract clients by meeting executives in their offices. That method was time consuming and paid off slowly. If you made enough visits, people would try to help you to meet others. But you could go out of business before you gained enough business to pay for all of the time and effort you had expended.

We shifted to inviting people to attend group lunches as our guests. We shared valuable information for about an hour and provided a nice meal afterward. We soon noticed that the more desirable the location, the more people who came. The better the wine we offered, the more consulting that people bought. Our meetings overlooking Central Park at the Plaza Hotel in New York City were soon legendary for the information, service, food, and wine.

We began inviting influential reporters to attend a press conference after lunch where we would read and discuss a press release. Our prospective clients were very impressed to see which journalists came… and all we had to do for the reporters was write a press release and pay for cups of coffee and dessert. The reporters were impressed by the executives we attracted and wrote favorable stories that further impressed clients and prospects.

Soon, we were selling fifty times as much business from the same amount of effort that we had formerly put into individual meetings.

Assignment: Reexamine all parts of your business model to see how you could accelerate doing favors that encourage valuable reciprocity. Test your better ideas to see how they work before making major commitments.

How Can You Locate Undiscovered High-Potential Customers through Employing Ethical Reciprocity?

And some of their brethren of the sons of the Kohathites
were in charge of preparing the showbread for every Sabbath.
These are the singers, heads of the fathers' houses of the Levites,
who lodged in the chambers, and were free from other duties;
for they were employed in that work day and night.

— 1 Chronicles 9:32-33 (NKJV)

Many people mistakenly assume that customers and prospects will only respond to receiving a certain kind of favor. Many times a person who is totally immune to a favor that's very costly to provide may be enthusiastic about reciprocating a favor that costs you little or nothing.

Keep testing new forms and types of favors with those high-potential prospects who have been immune to receiving or to reciprocating favors. You may eventually find a favor that will stimulate a helpful response. Demonstrating genuine appreciation often works best, such as occurs at our award dinners.

Assignment: Look for ethical ways to encourage reciprocity in high-powered places, even when you have no connections and experience. As an example, I was pleased to find that many authors' agents are looking for new connections. If you can make a connection for them to someone whom they cannot reach, you'll be able to receive as many other high-powered introductions as you like from the agents. Those who know lots of influential people may have a personal rule against taking you around to make introductions. Ask such a person if you may attend a small social gathering where those who you want to meet will be present. By the end of such a gathering, you may find opportunities to either introduce yourself or to find others who will. Also, donate your time to high-profile public purposes that you care about. Many influential people will be involved, and you will have a chance to meet and become acquainted with them … and possibly to do favors for them.

Lesson Fourteen

Turn Scarcity into an Advantage and
Help Reduce Customers' Risk of Loss

And David said with longing,
"Oh, that someone would give me a drink of water
from the well of Bethlehem, which is by the gate!"
So the three broke through the camp of the Philistines,
drew water from the well of Bethlehem that was by the gate,
and took it and brought it to David.
Nevertheless David would not drink it,
but poured it out to the LORD. And he said,
"Far be it from me, O my God, that I should do this!
Shall I drink the blood of these men
who have put their lives in jeopardy?
For at the risk of their lives they brought it."
Therefore he would not drink it.
These things were done by the three mighty men.

— 1 Chronicles 11:17-19 (NKJV)

Can scarcity be important to creating more sales? Researcher Robert B. Cialdini reports on how a friend described an unethical strategy that some toy companies have used to make sales in the United States through creating scarcity. Let's look at this example to begin to understand how scarcity can affect purchasing decisions.

Just after Thanksgiving (late November in the United States), some toy companies did research to determine which of that year's toys would most excite children when they saw the television ads for their products. Then, the toy companies undersupplied toy stores and other toy outlets prior to Christmas (December 25).

As the holiday approached, the toy companies and the toy stores would put out press releases about the toy shortages. Such releases hit the television news and the newspapers, stimulating even more interest in the scarce items. Excited youngsters told their parents they wanted these "hot" toys as Christmas gifts. Some youngsters negotiated a specific promise from a parent for the toy.

Many frustrated parents then could not find the toys and bought other toys as gifts to have the "right" number of packages under their Christmas tree. Almost all parents ended up buying two sets of "Christmas" toys. After facing disappointed children on Christmas day, many parents felt guilty and bought the toy when it became available in January or February … thus spending much more on toys than they had planned.

How does such psychology work from the child's and parents' points of views in terms of scarcity and risk of loss? The child will generally want whatever toy is hardest to obtain. Research with two-year-olds has shown that toys that are placed behind barriers attract children's interest much more than toys that are close at hand.

We seem to be hardwired to assume that things that are harder to obtain are more valuable and desirable. Many of us have heard the expression that the grass is always greener on the other side of the fence, which captures the same psychology. That limited availability is perceived by many as a clue to the quality of the offering. Those who are impulsive in their behavior are most likely to go against anything that restricts or appears to restrict their freedom … and thus will be attracted to whatever is hardest to obtain.

There may also be a sense of "bragging rights" involved. Others will see you as having higher status and being more desirable if you control something that's scarce. People bid up the value of items with such bragging rights whenever having the items can increase personal popularity.

Owning professional sports franchises is a good example. Most owners lose a great deal of money from operations, but the ego gratification from such ownership lures intelligent businesspeople into spending large fortunes for such franchises. Owners are often bailed out from losing money on their investments by selling their teams to a new owner with an even bigger need and greater ability to pay for bragging rights.

In the case of parents, they can impress their families and friends with their excellence and devotion as parents by doing whatever it takes to obtain a rare toy. Obtaining the item says the parents are attentive … and also have the wherewithal to play aggressively against other parents and win.

Fear of potential loss comes into play, as well. In chats with friends and school mates, children brag about what they will do when they receive the expected hot item. They plan activities with each other built around obtaining the toy. Every day that the toy is not available causes the child to feel as if he or she has lost something valuable … the chance to have fun with friends in a preferred way that day.

Research has shown that people will do three or four times as much to avoid loss as they will to achieve a gain. So if a scarce opportunity is phrased in terms of what will be lost if the purchase doesn't occur, some people will not want to lose the chance to make that purchase.

A more ethical example of this principle occurs on the Internet all the time. You are offered some item, course, or program with a limited enrollment, but you must act before a certain time. In fact, the first ten people to buy may obtain an additional bonus that's available to no one else.

There's a reason for the limited-time offer in an ethical case: There's a date when the service will be offered, and sales must be made before that date. In the case of a seminar, there may also be a limit to the available space. The limited bonus may relate to some genuinely scarce benefit such as more access to the seminar speaker by obtaining a front-row seat.

Jack Canfield has cannily used all of these techniques to pack his Breakthrough to Success programs. He once began selling one of these programs by holding free teleseminars that were attended by over 25,000 people. He used these teleseminars to explain the benefits of being one of the program's 400 participants. Can't you just feel your competitive juices rising as you think about gaining an advantage over 24,600 people?

When someone offers me a marketing service, I sometimes find myself tempted to buy something I don't need because of this principle. The salespeople may point out that only four people can have access to the service in a given month. And it always seems as if there's a waiting list for the next several months. I find myself itching to buy even before I get the facts needed to make an objective evaluation of the service's potential benefits. If it's so hard to get, it must be good. Right?

I often find that such marketing services offer few economic benefits, but may provide many ego rewards, which is the primary reason why the service is so hard to acquire. Just the other day, I saw a gorgeous video book trailer that I would love to have for one of my books. I would have to sell over 3,000 additional books to pay for the trailer, which I doubt would happen. But it sure would feel great to watch such a trailer about my book. So far I've successfully resisted, but that video trailer is clearly on my mind.

Why is scarcity treated as being so important by adults? Most people have found from experience that many of the best items and information are, in fact, restricted. Not everyone can own the nicest home in town. The best investor you know probably has access to information you don't have. Not everyone can belong to the most exclusive club. Not everyone can attend Harvard.

Just as long as the scarcity seems real to the potential buyer, even artificial or temporary scarcity can have big consequences for purchasing. I saw this psychology in action when I visited a Saturn car dealership a few years ago. I was waiting while my car's muffler was replaced, which left me plenty of time to walk around the lot to look at the new models.

I was surprised to see three sporty-looking new convertibles at the front of the lot. I was even more surprised to see that they were Saturns. I hadn't known that Saturn made such a car. The brand primarily had a good reputation for reliability and low cost.

A salesman sauntered by and started a conversation. He began by apologizing that all three cars were sold, and no more could be obtained except on eBay where people were paying $10,000 over the invoice price. He also mentioned that Saturn had only manufactured 50,000 of these cars for the 2007 model year, and he didn't know how many they would make for 2008.

If I wanted to put my name on the waiting list for 2008, he would be glad to help me. Clearly, putting my name on that list would mean I would feel committed then to act on this year's scarcity next year ... when the cars probably wouldn't be scarce at all. But I could feel a strong urge to sign, even though I had no interest in buying any convertible ... and certainly not this convertible.

If you want to learn more about how marketers can ethically employ genuine scarcity to address customers' risk of loss and increase sales, I suggest you read *Influence* by Robert B. Cialdini.

What benefits come from ethically addressing scarcity and fear of loss to stimulate demand for industry offerings?

1. You will attract much more attention as potential buyers are concerned that they may lose the opportunity to access scarce and valuable benefits from your offering.
2. If they need or can use what you offer, they'll feel compelled to consider your sales pitches and to give them a fair hearing ... even if they aren't looking to buy at that time.
3. If you provide the offering in an acceptable way, they will probably keep buying and tell others to work with you.
4. If demand is stimulated enough, you will also grow revenues faster than costs and assets, increasing your profit and cash flow as a percentage of revenues.
5. If you grasp a unique form of scarcity (such as providing customers with rare and valuable economic advantages as well as long-term bragging rights that please customers), you will have reduced the potential impact of competitors against you by making their offerings seem inferior due to the superior benefits, status, and satisfaction your offerings provide to customers.
6. Your pricing power will have increased because you will now face less competition for customers who favor your offerings.
7. Mass marketing will work better if you maintain a scarcity advantage (as American Express does with its various "elite" credit cards that are harder to obtain than comparable cards offered by others). With enough of a scarcity advantage, competitors' marketing will be remembered by most potential customers as having come from you.

What's the strategic lesson of expanding your market by twenty times through ethically addressing scarcity and fear of loss? Develop as many valuable sources of scarcity as you can among current and potential customers for a market you can serve well and encourage such people to act in ways that are consistent with their desires for scarce benefits and avoiding loss … or you will be leaving the door open to continuing new entrants who can create scarcity and fear of loss advantages against you.

Peter Drucker applied the psychology of scarcity exceptionally well to his consulting practice. He was the most famous management expert on the planet, and many people wanted to consult with him. As an active teacher, he only had a few days a year for consulting. Half of those consulting days he chose to save for nonprofit organizations. If you were any for-profit organization, you knew that you had to compete with deep-pocketed clients such as the General Electric and General Motors executives who often worked with him.

To get on his list of clients was an amazing blessing that conveyed great bragging rights to those who knew him on a first-name basis. Many people were curious about what he was like and what he did as a consultant, and I could dine out for free for the rest of my life solely on that the value of that cachet.

But Peter pushed scarcity even further. You had a maximum number of days a year he would work with you. That meant that you really paid attention at such times. In some cases you knew it would be a year before you could see him again. Naturally, you could call in between, but since he was almost stone deaf (even with hearing aids) you knew that a telephone call was agony for both of you.

Carol Coles and I scheduled days with Peter whether we needed to see him or not … just because we knew how few days we would have available while he was still alive. He was over 80 when we started working with him. Naturally, the question of price never crossed our minds. Whatever he asked for his time, we paid. He could have asked ten times the price, and we would have paid it.

The following sections address questions you should consider to appreciate how ethical forms of scarcity and helping customers avoid loss can help to expand your market.

What Scarcity- and Risk-of-Loss-Related Opportunities Are Available because the Market Is Underdeveloped?

Therefore, as we have opportunity, let us do good to all,
especially to those who are of the household of faith.

— Galatians 6:10 (NKJV)

Be careful. When a company or an industry is new, there are few people who can provide the expertise that customers and beneficiaries need. If you make scarce personnel available, such access will be considered very valuable to current and prospective customers. There's a catch: Soon your organization won't be able to grow any more because the people that customers want to access are fully occupied.

A better solution is to create access to scarce people and resources in ways that can be greatly expanded. For instance, your company might offer monthly technical conferences where your top people appear and answer questions. Another approach is to create an expert IT system that can be used by those with more limited skills and experience to help customers. Even better, have the expert system be directly available to customers. If you keep upgrading the quality of such scarce resources, you'll have more customers who appreciate and make good use of them.

You may also find that stockpiling talent will give you an advantage that will be hard to match. Talented people like to work with other talented people … and customers always prefer the best.

Carol Coles and I saw this preference for working with the best when we were young professionals at The Boston Consulting Group (BCG). At that point, the firm had fifty consultants in the United States, but many CEOs couldn't get enough of the company's offerings. Why? BCG had made itself the most preferred place to work for the top 1 percent of students at Harvard and Stanford business schools, the two top-rated business schools in those days. I remember attending a BCG-sponsored conference where the CEOs of Fortune 500 firms outnumbered the professional staff by 3 to 1 and virtually our entire staff was there!

Our leader, Bruce Henderson, played a cagey role in making himself available for unlimited free telephone conversations with potential clients. As soon as he had the CEOs intrigued and fascinated, Bruce would turn the prospects over to the rest of us with instructions for what to emphasize ... and we would close about half the leads that Bruce gave us.

Clients gained a sense from these contacts that Bruce was hovering over us twenty-somethings even though he often wasn't. BCG's strategy was a good ethical application of the principle of scarcity in another dimension. Most of our CEO clients knew that they couldn't hire the top business students ... but they believed that their companies would benefit from help provided by the most talented young people. The CEOs also liked that the firm was small and focused on strategy. They didn't have to worry that their competitors could access the same expertise, a form of scarcity that made our work more economically valuable to them.

Assignment: Look for ways you can deliver desired benefits that can only flow from scarce resources and are more valuable because the industry is underdeveloped.

What New Forms of Scarcity and Risk-of-Loss Avoidance Can You Offer That Will Impress Unconvinced Potential Customers?

Your life shall hang in doubt before you;
you shall fear day and night, and have no assurance of life.

— Deuteronomy 28:66 (NKJV)

When an industry is small, some companies make a mistake by trying to impress potential customers with how large they and the industry are. When you give the impression that customers can sign on at any time and receive optimal benefits, that approach can backfire.

A better approach may be to emphasize how small you and the industry are, and how scarce access is to your organization. Many professional-service firms use retainer agreements to convey this point. In such firms only retainer clients (who pay a regular monthly stipend) can receive any services. Someone who wants your services six months from now may well begin retainer payments after learning that she or he may not otherwise be able to hire you later.

If you avoid setting artificial deadlines and being seen as manipulative by customers, deadlines can help make scarcity clearer. For example, there was a deadline in 2006 for those who wanted to join The Billionaire Entrepreneurs' Master Mind. Unless someone came in by that deadline, they could not access the group. Those who missed that deadline fell many years behind those who joined in entrepreneurial knowledge and experience.

Assignment: Develop and communicate new forms of valuable scarcity that will encourage potential customers to act promptly to gain valuable benefits that others will not receive.

How Can You Recreate the Excitement
of a New, Small Market
with New Forms of Scarcity
and Ways of Avoiding Loss?

So it was that quails came up at evening and covered the camp,
and in the morning the dew lay all around the camp.
And when the layer of dew lifted, there, on the surface of the wilderness,
was a small round substance, as fine as frost on the ground.
So when the children of Israel saw it, they said to one another, "What is it?"
For they did not know what it was.
And Moses said to them,
"This is the bread which the LORD has given you to eat."

— Exodus 16:13-15 (NKJV)

Many success coaches understand how scarcity can create excitement among those they already coach. Such coaches continually offer new, more extensive, valuable, and expensive programs that allow clients much increased contact with the coach.

A general coaching program may provide a weekly newsletter and a monthly hour-long teleconference during which members ask questions. Those who belong to the general program may later be offered a gold program that provides daily alerts and a weekly teleconference. The platinum program could later add a one-on-one call every month and an annual two-day group session at the coach's home. And so on. Each new program excites those who are already enjoying and benefiting from what's going on by adding even more exclusivity, built around the coach's scarce time availability.

A larger organization can benefit from any preferences for scarce access by making "stars" in the field available to just the most valuable customers. Such stars may either be hired for the occasion or be part of the organization's permanent staff. The scarcity value of gaining access to the stars makes customers want to buy more. It's not unusual to dangle such opportunities before substantial customers who could buy much more … but aren't yet interested in doing so.

Avis successfully used a similar approach with me through a program that provided CEOs of companies that had exclusive Avis accounts with luxury-car rentals at no extra charge over standard rates. I enjoyed driving around in the beautiful luxury cars and my clients enjoyed riding with me … after being assured that I was just paying normal rental rates. Many of my CEO clients switched their company accounts to Avis as well.

<u>Assignment:</u> **Locate and provide scarce advantages desired by those who have proven to appreciate your offerings in exchange for increased purchases from your company.**

By How Much Can Helping Customers
Avoid Risk of Loss Due to Scarcity
Help You Profitably Increase Sales?

Our fathers sinned and are no more,
But we bear their iniquities.
Servants rule over us;
There is none to deliver us from their hand.
We get our bread at the risk of our lives,
Because of the sword in the wilderness.

— Lamentations 5:7-9 (NKJV)

There are two elements for answering this question:

1. The amount of increased purchasing that occurs
2. The amount of cost reductions in providing what is scarce or feared to be lost

Providing scarce forms of value can fall anywhere between the extremes of being either expensive or inexpensive to provide. You may be surprised to hear that providing scarce forms of value can be inexpensive. Let me share an example from research reported by Robert Cialdini showing how inexpensive valuable forms of scarcity can be.

One of his students was a successful businessman who owned a beef-importing firm. As a test, the student developed three scripts for his salespeople to use.

In the first script, buyers were offered beef by using the standard sales pitch. In a second script, some customers got the regular pitch plus information that the supply of beef was likely to be scarce in the next few months (a fact). In a third script, some other buyers were also given the standard pitch and were then told that the supply of beef was likely to be scarce in the next few months … and that this information was based on "not generally available information." The information, they were told, came from certain exclusive contacts that the company had (a fact).

Those who heard the second script bought twice as much beef as those who received the normal pitch. But those who listened to the third script bought six times as much as usual. The company soon ran out of inventory.

What accurate information about current or future scarcity can you provide to your customers that will stimulate their purchases?

Working together to take advantage of scarcity can be highly profitable for customers and their suppliers. Here's an example that I benefited from.

Xerox had been a client of Mitchell and Company's for many years. Each senior Xerox executive was required at the time to handle a few accounts just to know what was going on in the industry. We became such an executive account.

My client let me know that the first server-based computer networking systems would be available in a few months. Xerox was looking for five trial accounts in the early 1980s to run Beta tests. The White House, the Pentagon, the Library of Congress, and one other prestigious location had already signed up. Did we want to be the fifth? Naturally, I jumped at the chance.

Being part of the test gave us an inside view of the new technology, valuable knowledge that we could share with our other clients, and we gained bragging rights for years. But the cost to add us for a Beta test wasn't any greater than for any other site. I still feel grateful to and closely tied to Xerox for having made this scarce resource available to Mitchell and Company.

Assignment: Test your best ideas for supplying inexpensive scarce offerings and information to those who should be ideal users of your offerings in a small community. Measure the results to find out what is working best. Then experiment again emphasizing what worked best in another small community. Continue to test and measure in this way. As soon as you find a combination that works very effectively, start expanding what you learned with other customers you can serve well.

How Can You Attract the Best Customers First through Employing Scarcity and Reducing Fear of Loss?

Now the young woman pleased him,
and she obtained his favor;
so he readily gave beauty preparations to her,
besides her allowance.
Then seven choice maidservants were provided
for her from the king's palace,
and he moved her and her maidservants
to the best place *in the house of the women.*

— Esther 2:9 (NKJV)

Several factors should be considered:

1. The cost and availability of providing scarce offerings and information
2. The value of the scarcity for creating sales
3. The value of the scarcity for providing future influences on other prospects
4. Customers' sensitivity to gaining benefits through avoiding future scarcity

Many people make all of their offerings available to anyone. That's the Amazon.com model. But you may sell more if you limit availability of future offerings to those who commit first to you.

For example, if your offering brings a strategic advantage to either a user or distributor, you might create exclusive ventures with such parties. By making other scarce and valuable resources available in the future, you can create a situation where others bid to gain access to your scarce resource or offering.

Prior to 2000, for instance, Cisco often paid billions of dollars for very tiny businesses simply to gain unique technologies and excellent management teams. By grafting such technologies into the Cisco offerings, the company was able to expand the industry by many more billions of dollars within a short period of time. If, instead, the same businesses had been sold to anyone else, such businesses would rarely have added much to industry size or value.

Google took this approach one step further with its search-based "pay-per-click" advertising. Customers continually compete to increase the effectiveness of their advertising so they can afford to outbid other advertisers for the most valuable placements. By having its search engine work better than others, Google continually makes a virtue of there being a limited number of high-visibility advertising placements. Rather than scarcity limiting the market, scarcity instead drives online advertisers to learn how to become much more effective in conveying their messages.

If you can customize your intellectual property for different distribution channels, you'll enhance its value for each distributor as well as for the ultimate customers and end users. Translating valuable information into different languages is a simple example of this concept. If an organization gains a monopoly on selling the intellectual property in that language, it can afford to put more effort into marketing and distributing the offering. Making the translated material available instead to all comers would reduce its value to people who want to distribute such offerings. Scarcity actually accelerates access for most people to such materials by increasing the distributor's economic motivation to act.

Assignment: Determine which prospects are most responsive to scarcity benefits and concerns. Identify what actions you could take that would make the most desirable of these prospects into "raving fans" who will use their influence on your behalf.

How Can You Change Your Business Model
to Permit Faster Growth
through Supplying Productive Offsets to Scarcity?

Then justice will dwell in the wilderness,
And righteousness remain in the fruitful field.

— Isaiah 32:16 (NKJV)

Dell will custom manufacture a personal computer to meet your specifications, yet charge no more for the service … and usually ship it within a day or two. This approach provides a scarce resource, a customized computer, that better meets your needs at no extra cost or price. Your increased personal productivity from the customization will probably be so great that the computer is effectively free.

Customization can provide other kinds of benefits. For instance, some years ago it first became possible to buy customized books for children that were filled with references to a child's name, birthday, friends, and so on. Children were thrilled by such customizations that then cost just a little extra. Today, there's often no additional charge for print-on-demand publishers who do much more extensive versions of such customization.

How can you deliver highly preferred customization with low or reduced costs?

Assignment: Reexamine all parts of your business model to see how you could accelerate gaining more sales by providing more valuable forms of customization. Test your better ideas to see how they work before making major commitments to the new business model.

How Can You Locate and Attract Undiscovered Potential Customers
through Applying More Powerful Forms of Scarcity?

And he said,
"Indeed I have heard that there is grain in Egypt;
go down to that place and buy for us there,
that we may live and not die."

— Genesis 42:2 (NKJV)

Most offerings have some major problems or drawbacks. Offering providers like to avoid owning up to such problems.

Can you provide a solution to or a new way to limit such problems? Dell, for instance, knows that it's hard to obtain hardware service if you own just one computer. By partnering with the largest and most reliable network for providing hardware service, Dell became a preferred supplier for many computer customers and users who don't care whether their machines are customized.

In professional services, clients often care more about the benefits they gain than about what it costs to obtain and to apply the services. A single idea from a service provider might triple the client's value received from a professional engagement. Yet most professionals are out of contact with their clients after completing the initial engagement. By instead offering once-a-month follow-up service for 10 percent of the initial engagement's price, a professional service firm may be able to add lots of value at low cost to its clients and for itself. By making such a service unique compared to competitors for adding client value, a professional service firm may expand the market well beyond its current dimensions.

Assignment: Look for valuable, scarce offerings that you can make to customers and prospects that will greatly enhance their perceptions and estimates of the value they will receive from your kind of offering. Be particularly attentive to ways of reducing any risk of loss.

Lesson Fifteen

Sell More
through Liking People and
Encouraging Them to Like You

Then I was beside Him as *a master craftsman;*
And I was daily His *delight,*
Rejoicing always before Him,
Rejoicing in His inhabited world,
And my delight was *with the sons of men.*

— Proverbs 8:30-31 (NKJV)

Joe Girard was the champion vehicle salesman for many years in the United States, averaging more than five daily sales of cars and trucks. What were his secrets? According to Mr. Girard, it was simply due to offering a fair price and being someone customers liked to buy from. Mr. Girard made the car-buying experience pleasant; and he asked for referrals from customers to family and friends by sending out pre-printed holiday cards monthly to those who had ever bought from him that said on the front, "I Like You."

Think back to the first time one of your friends told you that a person of the opposite sex "likes you." That information was pretty heady stuff and very intriguing, wasn't it?

Today, your reaction may be more muted to learning that someone likes you, but you'll still seek out that person's company and attention.

Consider, however, the celebrities who strike you as most appealing. Have you ever seen a photograph of one of those celebrities in which the celebrity seemed to be staring into your eyes with a friendly gaze as a friend does who dotes on you? Research has shown that those who can project that they deeply like virtually everyone are much more attractive people to spend time with and to buy from. It's no wonder that celebrities who have mastered that "look" soon find themselves in the role of pitching products and services on television.

Here are some other characteristics of the people we like to buy from:

1. They are more physically attractive than their competitors.
2. They have more in common with us than competitors in terms of background and what they wear.
3. They pay us sincere compliments.
4. We know them … or they seem familiar.
5. We have successfully solved problems together.
6. They routinely bring us good news.

Many direct-selling organizations take advantage of such characteristics to involve our friends in selling to us. Tupperware (a direct-sales company known for offering its plastic containers at women's parties) has been an example of this marketing approach for many years. The hostess for a Tupperware party is usually a neighbor or a friend. The hostess receives a commission from any sales that are made at the party, and she provides the home and refreshments. Friends and neighbors who are invited often feel that they need to accept if they want to keep a good relationship with the hostess, and they also know that they are expected to buy some Tupperware when they come. American homes have been overstocked with Tupperware for decades as a result of such parties ... even though comparable containers can be bought in a store at a much lower price.

Students of neuro-linguistic programming (NLP) have also shown that you can induce liking by physically copying (mirroring) what the other person does (gestures, breathing, posture) until an unconscious rapport is established. Then, rather than copy, you begin leading the other person with your movements. Once the person follows what you do, you will probably be able to sell the person something. This persuasion method seems to be an example of people opening up to what you have to say after perceiving a similarity and familiarity at a subliminal level.

If you want to learn more about how to employ your liking for people and having them like you to ethically encourage purchases, I suggest you read *Influence* by Robert B. Cialdini.

What benefits come from employing liking to stimulate demand for industry offerings?

1. You will attract much more attention from potential buyers.
2. If they need or can use what you offer, they will feel compelled to consider your sales pitches and give them a fair hearing ... even if they aren't looking to buy at that time.
3. If you provide your offerings in an acceptable way, they will probably keep buying and tell others to work with you.
4. If enough demand is stimulated, you will also grow revenues faster than costs and assets, increasing your profit and cash flow as a percentage of revenues.
5. If you grasp a unique form of liking (such as becoming better acquainted with them than anyone else), you will have reduced the impact of competitors against you by making other offerings seem inferior because of the superior comfort customers feel towards you and your offerings.
6. Your pricing power will have increased because you now face less competition for those customers who favor you. When you make a mistake, people will let you know as a friend that you need to improve rather than simply look for a new supplier.
7. Mass-marketing effectiveness will be improved while you maintain a liking advantage (as cosmetics companies do through employing popular models and actresses). With enough of a liking advantage, competitors' marketing will be remembered by most potential customers as having come from you.

What's the strategic lesson of expanding your market by twenty times through liking? Develop as many sources of liking and familiarity as you can among current and potential customers for a market you can serve well, and encourage customers and prospects to buy more by applying these liking sources to make them feel better liked by you and to increase their liking for you ... or you will be leaving the door open to continuing new entrants who can create liking advantages against you.

Peter Drucker applied this concept exceptionally well to his consulting practice. He held the sessions in a pleasant part of his living room that overlooked a backyard pool. He began by going to great lengths to put you at ease by asking detailed questions about every member of your family, your personal plans, your travel, your hotel, your sleep, and how you were feeling that day. Peter would also share the same details about himself and his own family, and tell many wonderful stories that made you feel as if you were an old friend.

Such personal questions and comments would last for forty-five minutes if there were two people visiting Peter. Even in a one-on-one session, these personal conversations would take thirty minutes.

I once asked Peter how to persuade my clients to follow more of my recommendations. He suggested phrasing the recommendations in terms of being an extension of some great success that the person or organization had previously achieved. Peter mentioned that people have a hard time hearing anything other than praise, but everyone remembers actual praise quite well. Could it be that they also like people better who phrase recommendations in terms of honest praise? Sure they do!

The following sections address questions you should consider for employing genuine liking as a way to expand your market.

What Opportunities for Liking Can You Pursue because the Market Is Underdeveloped?

Righteous lips are *the delight of kings,*
And they love him who speaks what is *right.*

— Proverbs 16:13 (NKJV)

Liking is often more important in underdeveloped markets than in developed ones because most potential customers in an underdeveloped market have no idea whether they need an offering they haven't employed before. The easiest thing for a potential customer to do in such a case is to just ignore the industry and its offerings. But if a potential customer likes the person describing the offering, even an offering with uncertain benefits will gain advantage from receiving close attention.

I have often received positive reactions to my services during initial presentations to people who decided they liked me on the telephone and didn't realize the kinds of services we offered until we met. Someone who likes our firm or me will usually provide helpful, unsolicited advice about how to be more likeable to the organization's decision makers. I don't think they usually realize what they are doing ... but, rather, they are just reacting to a sense that people in our firm aren't yet "cuddly" enough, or in the "right" ways, for their colleagues.

When an industry is new, few potential customers will even take the time to let you come to make a sales pitch. When you have only a small number of potential selling opportunities, you should take extra time to prepare before sales presentations. You should use that extra time to find out more about the person, including what she or he likes and how he or she prefers to work with others. I've often found that two hours of such research can translate into hundreds of thousands of dollars in extra revenues. During such research, try to determine if you have any friends in common. If you succeed in identifying any, ask the mutual friends to vouch for you, ideally by everyone having an informal meal together.

The downside of developing liking can be that the person thinks you admire him or her so much that she or he need only sit there basking in your gaze to provide enough gratification for you. After a few sessions like that, pursue some other prospect. This egomaniac is headed for a large downfall! My experience has been that any company with such a leader will usually be taken over or go bankrupt within three years.

Assignment: In an underdeveloped industry, use extra preparation time to look for how to deliver desired benefits in ways that present more opportunities to build liking.

What New Forms of Liking Can You Offer
That Will Impress Potential Customers?

But the meek shall inherit the earth,
And shall delight themselves in the abundance of peace.

— Psalm 37:11 (NKJV)

The most successful organizations in new industries have often benefited by hiring people with attractive appearances and winning personalities. Such charmers fill the company's coffers by attracting those who like to spend time with attractive and delightful people.

In an earlier lesson, I mentioned Mitchell and Company's practice of presenting prestigious awards to company leaders at dinners celebrating the anniversaries of our firm's founding. Those who could not attend such occasions have often sent another senior official to accept the award. Award winners who were thrilled by the recognition often bought more consulting.

Another way to provide genuine compliments is to become the author of an annual article in a prestigious publication that recognizes outstanding achievements. Then, you can present awards to those described in the articles as gifts from your organization. We did that for many years for those who appeared in our listings of the top 100 CEOs in *Chief Executive Magazine*. After the awards arrived at such companies, the doors to the CEOs' offices were usually wide open to us. Many times, I have arrived at a company's reception desk or the CEO's office to see the award I had previously presented prominently displayed.

Assignment: Develop and communicate new forms of liking that will encourage potential customers to become acquainted and to purchase sooner.

How Can You Use New Forms of Liking
to Recreate the Excitement
of When the Market Was Small?

The steps of a good man are ordered by the LORD,
And He delights in his way.

— Psalm 37:23 (NKJV)

Many organizations hold an annual event when they recreate some important aspect of their heritage. Such an event might include rolling back prices to their original levels, providing an "old fashioned" version of the experience, offering "nostalgia" gifts, and so forth. Some organizations only invite those who are very good customers. Such events can help customers feel better liked and more appreciated.

Sometimes such special events can become the high point of the year for customers. For instance, one of our clients owns an exclusive fishing camp in Labrador near the Arctic Circle. To reach the camp, you enjoy the adventure of flying part-way by pontoon plane from Thunder Bay, the site of the big NATO base where the Luftwaffe practices dog fights. During the flight, you may even soar through an opening in an iceberg! Once at the camp, you are served wonderful meals that are prepared by a Cordon Bleu chef.

Naturally, only the biggest customers are invited. They value the experience so much that they often ask how much more they have to purchase to be sure to receive another invitation. While there, you spend a week with your salesperson. Naturally, everyone likes one another pretty well after such a week of comfortable "wilderness" fun and games.

I recommended that our client company open up more fishing camps to add capacity for entertaining potential large customers as well as to encourage good customers to buy more who are splitting their purchases with competitors.

Assignment: **Locate new liking advantages that appeal to those who have proven to appreciate your offerings, and provide new ways for such customers to increase their commitment to you to obtain such advantages.**

How Far Can You Profitably Increase Sales through Liking?

I planted, Apollos watered, but God gave the increase.

— 1 Corinthians 3:6 (NKJV)

There are two sides to answering this question:

1. The amount of increased purchasing that occurs
2. The amount of cost reductions for increasing liking

Here's where helping those in need can make a difference. As I have mentioned before, celebrities and beauty-contest winners often donate their time to raising money for worthy causes. If you host such an event featuring high-profile people at your premises, lots of potential customers will attend, and you will be better liked for being the sponsor and providing new ways for your prospects to feel liked.

Programs such as Joe Girard's monthly holiday cards can be implemented quite inexpensively. You can probably create more effective versions that will work even better with your customers and prospects.

Work on developing all the inexpensive opportunities first, before adding expensive choices.

Assignment: **Test your best ideas for building liking in a small community with those who should be ideal users of your offerings. Measure the results to find out what worked best. Then experiment again emphasizing what worked best and similar approaches in another small community. Continue to test and measure in this way. As soon as you find a combination of actions that works very effectively to increase liking and purchases, start expanding that combination to geographic areas you can serve well.**

How Can You Attract the Best Customers First through Liking?

And I will delight myself in Your commandments,
Which I love.

— Psalm 119:47 (NKJV)

Several factors should be considered:

1. The cost to develop liking
2. The value of liking for creating current sales
3. The value of liking for creating future influence with other prospects
4. Customers' sensitivity to being influenced by liking in their future purchases

You may find that the most effective approach is to combine scarcity and liking. For instance, as you make scarce, valuable information and offerings available, you can indicate that you are doing so because you like the person and organization (when that's the case).

Taking extra good care of someone also makes a powerful impression. Many hotels have found that by keeping computer files of guest preferences they can provide customized services that deliver to the guest a powerful sense of being liked. Delighted guests often reciprocate by providing unsolicited word-of-mouth praise to their families, friends, and colleagues. You can use such a prompting system to be sure you systematically respond in a desirable way to your customers and prospects.

Photographs are also good for building liking. Arrange to have photographs of top prospects taken with your leader, and provide the pictures in attractive frames. Many prospects will keep the photographs in their offices or homes. Politicians understand this practice very well, and the experience of attending a $1,000-a-plate chicken dinner is usually made more palatable by providing a photograph of a smiling handshake or hug with the politician.

Assignment: Identify the top prospects whose purchases are most influenced by liking. Find out what actions you could take that would make the most attractive of these prospects into "raving fans" who will continually use their influence on your behalf inside and outside of their organizations.

How Can You Change Your Business Model to Permit Faster Development of Liking?

Cast your burden on the LORD,
And He shall sustain you;
He shall never permit the righteous to be moved.

— Psalm 55:22 (NKJV)

Let's look at Disney for a moment. That corporation is primarily in the business of providing wholesome fun. Most employees, investors, and customers love to interact with the Disney organization. When you visit the company's headquarters, you even pass under statues of Snow White's seven dwarfs. Who can help but smile?

Showing people how to have more fun can be a great way to establish more liking. Some of my favorite business seminars have been filled with comedy, enthusiastic back rubs, dancing, and singing. Business doesn't have to be a bore.

If you can count on someone to provide fun, chances are that you can count on them to help you with more serious problems. What could be a better way to become better liked?

Assignment: Reexamine all parts of your business model to see how you could accelerate gaining more sales from customers and prospective customers by making what you do more likable. Test your better ideas to see how they work before making major commitments to the new business model.

How Can You Locate Undiscovered High-Potential Customers through Developing More Powerful Forms of Liking?

The voice of the LORD is powerful;
The voice of the LORD is full of majesty.

— Psalm 29:4 (NKJV)

One of our Mitchell and Company clients took time at his company's annual meeting to recognize every major vendor and to praise the vendor for his or her contributions to the company's success. I can assure you that being on the receiving end of such recognition is great fun. Imagine if you did the same thing for your best clients or customers … and kept their photographs in a hall of fame that was seen by everyone who came to visit.

You may remember my story in an earlier lesson about how Claude Terrail, the legendary owner the Paris restaurant, La Tour d'Argent, spent time one evening on his knees coloring with our two-year-old daughter while we dined on his restaurant's sumptuous food. There was no doubt in our minds that he liked us and our daughter. It was a very special experience. I have never stopped singing his praises.

Assignment: Look for valuable ways you can make customers and prospects feel tremendously well liked and affirmed by what you do.

Lesson Sixteen

Understand the Importance of Measuring Performance

And when they saw Him walking on the sea,
they supposed it was a ghost, and cried out;
for they all saw Him and were troubled.
But immediately He talked with them and said to them,
"Be of good cheer! It is I; do not be afraid."
Then He went up into the boat to them, and the wind ceased.
And they were greatly amazed in themselves
beyond measure, and marveled.

— Mark 6:49-51 (NKJV)

This lesson applies step one of the eight-step process for creating 2,000 percent solutions: Understand the importance of measuring performance. You will find more about this subject in *The 2,000 Percent Solution*; *The Portable 2,000 Percent Solution*; and *The 2,000 Percent Solution Workbook*.

In *The 2,000 Percent Solution Workbook*, Carol Coles and I point out that most people focus their measurements on the ways they are performing now in serving customers. Unfortunately, such data are seldom of much value for expanding an industry by twenty times.

I've been consulting with senior executives for over forty years, and I usually find that organizational leaders know little about the potential for expanding their industries. Why? The leaders weren't expected by anyone to look into such subjects, nor did they see the information as being important.

Sometimes there is no official industry measurement source. In such cases it's often possible to estimate industry size by interviewing or surveying a statistically significant sample of those who are current and potential customers (including those who serve their own needs now). I prefer to conduct such measurement research rather than rely solely on "official" statistics because I can ask questions at the same time that help locate ways to expand the market.

Before you look up official statistics or conduct interviews, you need to think about what your industry is. Many people define their industries so they have little or no competition. If I were to take that approach with my consulting practice, I might measure those who work in or near the same town I do and provide exactly the same kind of strategic services. Under that definition I have 100 percent of the market ... and the market's growth limitations seem to be the same as my organization's limitations. Wrong! Simply because we choose to see ourselves in terms of a small pond that we dominate, that perspective doesn't limit the industry or its potential.

Another misconception is that you need only compare yourself to those who receive money from customers. If you do that, you'll miss measuring what people spend to do tasks or to create solutions for themselves, activities that serve purposes that your offerings could substitute for.

Why is this broader definition important? If any time, money, or effort is being spent, that's part of what you have the opportunity to influence. Ignore such areas, and you'll usually miss the bulk of the industry-expansion potential.

As an example, let's consider services related to improving the quality of offerings. Once, very little time, money, and effort was spent for improving the quality of what was produced. The bulk of quality-related spending was applied to inspections of completed items to identify faulty ones that needed to be either junked or repaired. Services were rarely checked for quality.

Even more money was spent then on designing manufactured items than on quality improvement. Most people at the time didn't see design and quality performance as related, even though better designs are the best way to improve manufacturing quality. Few liked the inspection process, and many people could see that any alternative would be highly desirable that improved on such costly, cumbersome inspections, scrapping, and repairs. Little attention was paid to organizing services, one reason that performance quality was haphazard.

Of even greater significance for understanding industry potential is to measure what it costs customers and users because they lack the right offerings. People were always surprised when Phil Crosby showed that production and service errors cost so much that it is much less expensive to spend time, money, and effort to avoid committing errors in the first place. Or, as his book title puts it, *Quality Is Free* (McGraw-Hill, 1979).

Many times, customers and users don't realize how much of what they are spending could be avoided by employing some offering they don't use. When you measure what such unnecessary spending is, you will have a better idea of the untapped industry potential.

Let's consider poverty as an example of untapped potential that is often ignored. Governments, foundations, and donors regularly report that they cannot afford to spend more on reducing poverty. In fact, some argue that less should be done. Those making such observations don't realize that the cost of unrelieved poverty is far larger than the cost of reducing it.

Consider just the tax consequences in constant dollars. If a potentially malnourished child receives enough of the right food and nutrition to fully develop his or her mind and body, the total added cost for the first twenty years of life may be about $6,000 in a lesser developed country. If, as a result, that person can then earn $6,000 more a year for forty years and pay 10 percent of that amount in taxes, the government has the opportunity to gain at least $18,000 ($24,000 in added tax receipts less $6,000 in costs). The gain will, in fact, usually be larger than $18,000 because the person will be able to support a family that won't need any government support for food or nutrition. Any such family members who later work will each produce $18,000 in added tax receipts by avoiding a malnourished childhood. Assuming that this positive cycle continues, an expenditure of $6,000 can deliver hundreds of thousands of dollars in future government tax revenues over several generations. In addition, such higher income people will spend more with others who, in turn, will also pay higher taxes. The multiplier effect will increase the ultimate tax improvement by a factor of at least three times. It's hard to beat an investment opportunity like that. That's why successful economic development that expands poor peoples' incomes improves national wealth so rapidly.

If you then spend another $6,000 to give the person a good-enough education, beyond what is conventionally supplied, to become a successful entrepreneur who earns $20,000 more a year, you increase the income tax paid, less the cost of added education, by $74,000. In addition, the entrepreneur can probably provide the same education for his or her own children so that the higher income will be also be earned in future generations. What's more, the entrepreneur can also then employ a number of people who can also emerge from needing food and education assistance, further adding to the tax rolls. If the government can learn how to provide such useful entrepreneurial education for a reasonable cost, the multigenerational gain in tax revenues is enormous. Once again, the resulting higher incomes create more spending with others who also pay taxes, probably creating a multiplier effect of five or six times.

After seeing this quantification of the potential value of poverty-reducing programs in underdeveloped countries, you may be wondering why so many people can be making such large mistakes about what to spend their organizations' money on. I used to wonder, too.

When you find any large discrepancies, it's a good idea to dig in and look for the reasons behind such apparent irrationality. Start with Peter Drucker's observation, "Leaders have no imagination." In my experience even if you put the answers to a critical question under someone's nose, most people will miss the point.

As I'm sure you appreciate from this lesson's examples, it's important to measure the behavior and performance of current and potential customers, as well as the offerings and approaches that are current or potential substitutes for what you currently or could offer.

Here are four questions to help you apply the right focus to understand the importance of measuring performance to grow your industry by twenty times:

1. *What don't you know about the current and potential size of your industry?*

   Chances are that you are missing information about almost everything.

2. *What do you think you know that may not be accurate?*

   Particularly question assumptions and beliefs about what you compete against and in what ways.

3. *What's the best way to check your beliefs and fill any knowledge gaps?*

   Be open to spending some time, money, and effort to check out what could be done. Assume you will need more than one source to uncover what you need to learn.

4. *How can you keep your expanded view of information about performance up-to-date?*

   In most industries, circumstances are rapidly changing as markets become ever more global, competitive, and complex. You don't want to get up-to-speed once … only to fall behind right afterward, do you?

Assignments

1. Measure the size and performance of the global industry (beginning with all offerings, and including self-performed tasks by customers and users, as well as costs that stakeholders could avoid by using potential offerings).

2. Measure the untapped potential for immediate expansion of your industry.

3. Identify the largest hurdles (or stalls) to making that expansion occur immediately.

4. Measure the value of the benefits from overcoming the largest hurdles (or stalls).

Lesson Seventeen

Decide What to Measure

"Give, and it will be given to you:
good measure, pressed down, shaken together, and running over
will be put into your bosom.
For with the same measure that you use,
it will be measured back to you."

— Luke 6:38 (NKJV)

This lesson applies step two of the eight-step process for 2,000 percent solutions: Decide what to measure. You will also find material about this subject in *The 2,000 Percent Solution*; *The Portable 2,000 Percent Solution*; and *The 2,000 Percent Solution Workbook*.

Every industry has multiple choices for expanding. Before committing to a choice, it helps to quantify the costs and effects of following each one. Measurements that improve such quantifications are immensely valuable for making the right choice and monitoring performance to help make better progress during implementation.

Certain strategy questions can be applied to any industry, including:

1. How many people or organizations would benefit from using the available offerings?

2. How many of the potential beneficiaries are aware of the offerings?

3. How many of the potential beneficiaries accurately perceive the benefits, drawbacks, and costs of employing the offerings?

4. How many people who know about the offerings don't use them because of each offering's major limitations?

5. How many more people or organizations would benefit if the offerings were adjusted in various ways?

6. What is the cost of overcoming each major usage limitation in the most effective ways?

7. What is the size of the benefit for overcoming each of the usage limits?

8. What kind of industry expansion provides the most attractive opportunities for your organization and its stakeholders?

Measuring industry-expansion paths in terms of these eight strategy dimensions provides you with baseline measurements.

Thinking about such questions is one thing. Checking the soundness of your conclusions is another. I strongly favor experimentation as a way to test your evaluations. Use the experiments to define and to apply a second set of measurements based on what you learn.

After completing the eight-step process for expanding your industry by twenty times, repeat the second step described by this lesson to identify and to put in place the right measurements to direct your industry-expansion activities. If you are not yet familiar with how measurements help in implementation, I encourage you to read the following books by Robert S. Kaplan and David P. Norton in the listed sequence: *Strategy Maps* (Harvard Business School Press, 2004), *The Balanced Scorecard* (Harvard Business School Press, 1996), *Alignment* (Harvard Business School Press, 2006), and *The Strategy-Focused Organization* (Harvard Business School Press, 2000).

Questions designed to help you select measures for growing your industry by twenty times can be found in chapters 5 and 6 in *The 2,000 Percent Solution Workbook*, which also contains a publishing example of selecting measures. As you think about such questions, you may find it helpful to draw on any notes you made during your studies of the first sixteen lessons in *Business Basics*.

Focus on the most promising industry-expansion opportunities. For example, by now you should know why prospective customers who know about your offering don't buy it. In many cases, it may be impractical or very difficult to eliminate a specific usage limitation. Before giving up, develop measurements to understand more about opportunities to reduce the effects of such limitations.

Let's consider an example. For some time, I've been exploring the best ways to expand the readership of my books while spending less money and reducing the effort involved. Each time I have looked for more ways to improve, I have found a reasonably accurate way to estimate how many readers could be attracted and the likely cost in time, money, and effort to add them.

My first idea was to provide physical books for free, hoping to stimulate enough word-of-mouth interest to attract many readers. Based on the experiments I ran with *The 2,000 Percent Solution*, that method was prohibitively expensive.

The next experiment was to send out lots of review copies for another 400 Year Project book. That method worked better, but it wasn't a major opportunity.

From there, I tried writing lots of online book reviews. While this activity provided a great deal of readership for my reviews, it provided a much smaller boost for my books.

I next placed book excerpts on Amazon.com into "guides" for various subjects. This test was hugely successful. To date, such guides have been viewed over 600,000 times … probably by over 150,000 people.

Blogs were my next readership-expansion focus. I found that blogs didn't attract readers nearly as efficiently as the Amazon guides do and blogs require a lot more effort.

I subsequently began making book excerpts available in the form of articles on other people's Web sites. This method worked extremely well. A single article could attract more than 10,000 readers … over 600 times the effectiveness of an Amazon.com guide.

More recently, I started writing promotional articles for Rushmore University using an online-placement service. From this experience, I realized that with a different article approach I could gain over 100,000 readers from a single book excerpt, based on spending only a few minutes to format the material into an article and to distribute it. That experience greatly impressed me in light of Peter Drucker's observation that most best-selling nonfiction books like mine are read cover-to-cover by fewer than 500 people and partially read by fewer than another 5,000 people.

I intend to keep testing and learning, but you can see that measuring how well each limitation-removing test performed has greatly informed my progress, enabling me to uncover better opportunities to test and to implement. As a consequence, I have easily expanded the readership about 2,000 percent solutions by several hundred times over what conventional methods would have produced, while spending far less time, money, and effort to do so.

Assignment

Answer the eight strategy questions outlined in this lesson.

Lesson Eighteen

Identify and Measure the Future Best Practice

He who practices righteousness is righteous, just as He is righteous.

— 1 John 3:7 (NKJV)

This lesson employs step three of the eight-step process for creating a 2,000 percent solution: Identify the future best practice and measure it. You'll also find material about this subject in *The 2,000 Percent Solution*; *The Portable 2,000 Percent Solution*; and *The 2,000 Percent Solution Workbook*.

Identifying and measuring the future best practice begin with locating the best that is being done now and extending the current rate of improvement five years into the future. Billion-dollar industries have been established in recent years within just a few days of providing offerings. I suspect that the future best practice will be to accomplish such a result in just a few hours.

Such rapid expansions occur most often with new types of handheld electronic devices that offer expanded capabilities, such as when the Apple iPhone was launched. Let's consider that experience to demonstrate how the key principles of a future best practice can be identified and measured. Let's also draw some lessons from the iPhone success that might apply to expanding your industry by twenty times.

Begin your search for the future best practice by studying the most successful current methods. What are the most important elements of the iPhone's success?

1. *The iPhone combined features available on several other electronic items in a new, more convenient way.* Why was this benefit important? It was easy for potential customers to assess the value of a new offering that combined a graphic-user interface on a touch screen with extensive portable computing and cell-phone capabilities. The iPhone is a simpler version of a portable, Internet-connected computer that you can also use as a telephone. If you can avoid offering something totally different from what people already understand, you make industry expansion much easier.

2. *The new offering received lots of advance publicity so that most people knew quite a lot about it before the iPhone was offered.* Why was this publicity important? You aren't going to buy something that's new and different unless you understand what it is and have heard others endorse the value of what it does.

3. *The iPhone entered a market where many customers were hungry for something new and different.* In fact, it's easier to sell something new and different in electronic handheld devices than it is to make an incrementally improved version of what people are already buying. Develop your new and

different offerings for people who are already eagerly looking for something better and who like to be seen as different from what most others do.

4. *The iPhone was readily available in large numbers.* If you wanted to buy an iPhone in most countries, you could purchase it with little effort after the first day or so of its release into the marketplace. This availability was important because many people wanted to examine one before buying. Broadscale distribution led to substantial immediate sales that allowed many such purchase-oriented inspections just after the iPhone was released.

5. *The product was very visible in use.* If you were interested in an iPhone, you were likely to see someone using one and you could simply ask about its attributes. Such opportunities to speak with users made it easier to become familiar with and gain confidence in the product. Word-of-mouth referrals were quite valuable in validating this product's effectiveness.

6. *The product worked just fine.* All but a few tiny bugs were worked out in advance. Bad results after introduction could easily have killed the market expansion for this kind of portable computing.

7. *The product's manufacturer had a solid reputation for producing and delivering electronic items with superior features and reliability.* Few people probably believed that they were taking a big risk by purchasing an iPhone. Even if there were problems, purchasers probably felt confident that Apple would make appropriate fixes.

8. *The item wasn't very costly in terms of the incomes of those who were the target customers.* The initial customers didn't have to hold long debates with others in their organizations or families before purchasing. Affordability made impulse purchases more feasible.

9. *Customers had an easy and relatively quick way to deal with any problems.* They could go back to using whatever portable devices they had used before they bought the iPhone. Realizing that there wasn't much risk if major product glitches occurred helped make a purchase feel safer.

Let me extract some more universal principles that may be helpful to you in identifying and in measuring the future best practices for greatly expanding your industry:

1. Make offerings seem transparently familiar rather than strange and unusual, even when the offerings are quite new in concept and execution.

2. Create universal awareness among potential customers by obtaining validations from recognized experts.

3. Focus first on those who already know they want something new and improved that's not available elsewhere.

4. Make it very easy to see how your offering works, to try it out, and to buy one.

5. Create a lot of visible use for your offering so that those who are curious can ask a customer about it.

6. Be sure your offering works flawlessly from the beginning.

7. Either have a terrific reputation for reliability or partner with someone who does.

8. Design your offering so that someone can start by spending an amount of money that doesn't seem extravagant.

9. Be sure that customers can easily return to something that will work fine for them if they have problems with your offering. That fallback option will give them more confidence to try your offering.

Assignments

1. How could the iPhone launch have been made even more successful?

2. How could you match the success of the iPhone launch with current or potential offerings in your industry by using the methods that Apple employed?

3. How could you exceed the success of the iPhone launch with current or potential offerings in your industry by using different methods than Apple employed?

4. What measurements of the future best practice for market expansion do you think are most important for your industry?

Lesson Nineteen

Implement beyond the Future Best Practice

For we are not overextending ourselves
(as though our authority *did not extend to you),*
for it was to you that we came with the gospel of Christ;
not boasting of things beyond measure, that is, *in other men's labors,*
but having hope, that *as your faith is increased,*
we shall be greatly enlarged by you in our sphere,
to preach the gospel in the regions *beyond you,*
and *not to boast in another man's sphere of accomplishment.*

— 2 Corinthians 10:14-16 (NKJV)

This lesson is based on step four of the eight-step 2,000 percent solution process: Implement beyond the future best practice. You will also find material about this subject in *The 2,000 Percent Solution*; *The Portable 2,000 Percent Solution*; and *The 2,000 Percent Solution Workbook*. Exceeding the future best practice is often accomplished by combining more current and future best practices than anyone else has. This way of exceeding the future best practice is explained by using the iPhone example in Lesson Eighteen. If you don't remember that example, I suggest that you reread the lesson now.

To make it easier for you to keep the key information from Lesson Eighteen in mind, here are some of that lesson's more universal principles for market expansion:

1. Make offerings seem transparently familiar rather than strange and unusual, even when the offerings are quite new in concept and execution.

2. Create universal awareness among potential customers by obtaining validations from recognized experts.

3. Focus first on those who already know they want something new and improved that's not available elsewhere.

4. Make it very easy to see how your offering works, to try it out, and to buy one.

5. Create a lot of visible use of your offering so that those who are curious can ask a customer about it.

6. Be sure your offering works flawlessly from the beginning.

7. Either have a terrific reputation for reliability or partner with someone who does.

8. Design your offering so that someone can start by spending an amount of money that doesn't seem extravagant.

9. Be sure that customers can easily return to something that will work fine for them if they have problems with your offering. That will give them more confidence to try your offering.

Here are two potential dimensions for exceeding the future best practice, as measured by the iPhone's sales results:

1. Expand the market by much more than the iPhone did.

2. Achieve greater sales results than the iPhone did in its first few months by generating such sales in just a few minutes.

I advise you not to stop with considering just these two dimensions. Add several other potentially interesting dimensions, including possibly:

3. Accomplish the sales at much less expense.

4. Gain greater profits than the iPhone did.

5. Use the industry expansion breakthrough as a platform to create a second twenty-times market expansion soon thereafter.

6. Expand customer and user benefits so much that the financial ability to afford your offerings is increased by several hundred percent.

7. Extend substantial benefits to those who aren't stakeholders.

I particularly encourage you to pick dimensions to focus on that are exciting to you and to potential customers.

How might Steve Jobs have expanded his focus for expanding the industry along these seven dimensions while launching the iPhone? Here are some possible examples:

1. Sales reaching the iPhone launch totals might have been accomplished in a few minutes by offering time-sensitive incentives. For instance, Apple could have promised to provide free months of service to those who bought in the first five minutes ... with the size of the discount tied to how many people signed up during that period of time. Thus, all those who thought they might ever want the iPhone would have had an incentive to buy then and to encourage others to do the same. This possible approach is a large-scale variation on the Groupon concept.

2. A larger market expansion could have been achieved by allowing customers to swap their old cell phones and personal digital assistants along with their service contracts for an immediate 100 percent credit against the cost of the iPhone and its service. Such an offer could have been combined with a guarantee that would have made it easy for the customer to return to the old device and service contract if unhappy with the iPhone.

3. The cost of the launch could have been reduced by making the initial price lower. Apple dropped the price of the iPhone by over $100 within a few months. Early customers were outraged, and Apple eventually agreed to refund that amount of money to mollify early purchasers. This way of pricing was a mistake: A price discount of $100 when first announced would have allowed the company to achieve the same economic result with a less expensive launch … and increased sales and profits.

4. The iPhone could have been made much more profitable by adding many related features that could have been sold at a high-profit margin, such as the ability to download vast quantities of music from iTunes, the Apple music store … a capability that the initial iPhones lacked.

5. A second market expansion could have been made more possible by loading iPhones with enormous amounts of extra memory capacity. Many more software applications could then have been sold as part of the second expansion that provided new functions. Apple could have become a dominant factor with expanded capabilities in major markets such as electronic gaming, selling individual users thousands of dollars worth of games and other applications for the iPhone.

6. The iPhone obviously creates the potential for increased productivity, but such productivity gains wouldn't be enough to improve the initial affordability of buying iPhones and related services. Such a desirable social benefit might have been accomplished by providing free or low-cost education in how to earn thousands of dollars more each year by using an iPhone. After understanding how to gain such proven benefits, some people would have been willing to stretch financially (even borrowing money, if necessary, to purchase), knowing that using the iPhone would give them more than enough extra funds to offset the initial cost.

7. Social benefits for nonstakeholders could have been provided by establishing ways that iPhones could be accessed for temporary and short-term use, such as pay landline telephones are now. Making such utility available would also have expanded the market. A possible approach could have been to offer pay-as-you-use-it services to those who provided a valid credit card number or a preloaded smart card. Entrepreneurs could then have rented out the units for short-term use in areas such as airport waiting lounges and for just a few days to try out the service.

Obviously, any company that combined several of the seven dimensions I have just described could then exceed the future best practice in growing a market by a wide margin.

As you consider expanding your market by twenty times, attempt to improve on each of these seven dimensions … plus any other beneficial market-expanding dimensions that you can conceive of.

Assignments

1. How could the iPhone launch have been made even more successful than I have suggested in terms of the seven dimensions I described?

2. How could you apply Apple's methods to exceed the iPhone's launch with future offerings in your industry?

3. What methods of market expansion described in previous lessons would work better for introducing your offering(s) than what Apple applied for the iPhone launch?

4. What dimensions of exceeding the future best practice in market expansion could you employ that Apple ignored with the original iPhone?

Lesson Twenty

Identify the Ideal Best Practice

So that your trust may be in the LORD;
I have instructed you today, even you.
Have I not written to you excellent things
Of counsels and knowledge,
That I may make you know the certainty of the words of truth,
That you may answer words of truth
To those who send to you?

— Proverbs 22:19-21 (NKJV)

This lesson focuses on step five of the eight-step process for making a 2,000 percent solution: Identify the ideal best practice. You will also find material about this subject in *The 2,000 Percent Solution*; *The Portable 2,000 Percent Solution*; *The 2,000 Percent Solution Workbook*; and Appendix B of *2,000 Percent Living*.

The ideal best practice for market expansion is going to be faster, more effective, and less expensive than what you identified for exceeding the future best practice. Let's start by reviewing the market expansion future best practice described in Lesson Nineteen.

We considered the initial iPhone product launch as the current best practice in Lesson Eighteen. We then extended that success into the future by postulating that the future best practice would be to equal or to exceed the iPhone success that occurred over a few months, within just a few hours.

There are two obvious dimensions for exceeding the future best practice, as scaled to expanding beyond the iPhone's sales results:

1. Expand the market by much more than the iPhone did.

2. Achieve greater sales results than the iPhone did in its first few months by generating such sales in just a few minutes.

I advised you to continue considering past these two dimensions, by adding several other potentially interesting dimensions, including possibly:

3. Accomplish the sales at much less expense.

4. Gain greater profits than the iPhone did.

5. Use the industry-expansion breakthrough as a platform to soon thereafter create a second twenty-times market expansion.

6. Expand customer and end-user benefits so much that the overall financial abilities of people and organizations to afford your offerings are increased by several hundred percent.

7. Extend substantial benefits to those who aren't stakeholders.

That's enough review. Let's now look more broadly to see what the ideal best practice is for launching a multibillion dollar market very rapidly.

I draw on boosting sales of the Harry Potter books to sketch out key elements of the ideal best practice for industry expansion.

Each of J. K. Rowling's books about Harry Potter hit the book publishing, wholesaling, and retailing industries like a record-breaking storm. Stores stayed open past midnight to host special launch parties, package delivery companies lined up extra fleets of trucks to deliver millions of copies on the first morning of release, and millions of households saw normal routines disrupted while the latest book was devoured by one eager member of the family after another. If everyone could have gotten a copy at 12:01 a.m. of the first day of release, most eager readers would have opted for that choice. If the delivery companies had infinite numbers of trucks and drivers, such performance would have been possible. And clearly there should have also been an earlier-than-usual morning delivery option offered for early risers.

The books didn't retail for as much as a billion dollars, and Rowling says she's done with Harry Potter. But I suspect that she'll eventually begin writing another series. If she succeeds, the books and related offerings may eventually retail for over a billion dollars within one minute after midnight.

How might such a result be accomplished?

There's an obvious lesson to apply that book publishers don't appear to understand: Automatic renewals work better than individual sales for creating massive, instant market growth. If people are satisfied with what you offer, almost all will prefer the convenience of automatically receiving the next offering by allowing you to place a charge on a credit card they have authorized you to use. Many software upgrades work this way. So do subscriptions to some magazines.

By offering automatic renewals, it's likely that Harry Potter could have concentrated more sales into a briefer time period.

But people don't just read about Harry Potter, they also buy Harry Potter costumes and clothing, go to Harry Potter movies, and visit Harry Potter Web sites. What about tying in book renewals to package deals that include such other offerings? By bundling more elements together, you could sell more and make life easier for consumers. You also make it more likely that you'll receive a billion dollars in sales in the one minute after a new book is released.

Let's consider another rapid consumption thread: limited editions of offerings. J.K. Rowling could offer all kinds of memorabilia in limited editions that could increase in value as scarce collectibles. Such items would be sold only in the first one minute to those who bought the packaged deal that included several offerings.

But don't stop there, let's consider experiences. Let's have Harry Potter theme events more elaborate than a book store can hold that are only available to those who have bought the package and some of the limited-edition memorabilia. She could rent the world's major theme parks and resort areas (in addition to making good use of the Wizarding World of Harry Potter in Orlando, Florida) for such purposes and gain a piece of the vacation and travel part of the expanded revenue stream.

There's also a big market of people who like to buy through eBay auctions. Rowling could put together lots of high-value items related to her newest book and hold auctions ending exactly at 12:01 a.m. on the morning of book release. If she could provide enough sets, costumes, scripts, and other items from the movies and her book-writing activities, she could undoubtedly add tens of millions of dollars in sales.

Rowling's intellectual property is very valuable as well. She could hold simultaneous auctions ending at 12:01 to license any unlicensed intellectual property associated with the new book.

I could go on by adding more opportunities to concentrate sales, but I'm sure you have gotten the concept by now.

What are the key elements of the ideal best practice I've been describing?

1. Sell something new related to past successes such that almost every prior customer and user will want the new offering.

2. Build a base of awareness and preference such that little expenditure is required to gain massive publicity.

3. Maximize the attention and excitement by cramming as much activity and opportunity into one minute as possible.

4. Presell through contracts or subscriptions.

5. Bundle a bigger batch of offerings together that include items that most customers and end users will eventually consider purchasing.

6. Add scarcity appeal by providing limited versions only available at that moment.

7. Conduct auctions that end at the same moment for anything else you want to sell for which there is a very limited supply and huge demand.

8. Provide experience-based services that are enhanced by the excitement of the one-minute event.

9. Create an event that everyone will want to talk about having participated in. As a possible model, consider the Super Bowl in the United States where two teams play for the National Football League Championship. The average price paid for a seat in the stadium is probably over $2,000 and there are over 60,000 people present. Yet you can watch the game for no added event charge on any television set. Perhaps broadcasting a live theatrical performance of the new book to movie theaters with J.K. Rowling serving as host could provide part of such a draw.

Assignments

1. Other than my suggestions, how could a Harry Potter book launch have been made much more successful?

2. What other high-value methods of market expansion could be added to the list of key elements I have described?

3. What are the lessons for expanding your market?

Lesson Twenty-One

Approach the Ideal Best Practice

*And this I pray, that your love may abound still more and more
in knowledge and all discernment,
that you may approve the things that are excellent,
that you may be sincere and without offense till the day of Christ,
being filled with the fruits of righteousness
which are by Jesus Christ, to the glory and praise of God.*

— Philippians 1:9-11 (NKJV)

This lesson considers step six of the eight-step process for making 2,000 percent solutions: Approach the ideal best practice. You will also find helpful material about this subject in *The 2,000 Percent Solution*; *The Portable 2,000 Percent Solution*; and *The 2,000 Percent Solution Workbook*.

This lesson builds on Lesson Twenty. If you haven't just read it, I encourage you to reread that lesson now.

To make it easier to keep that lesson's information in mind, here are the key elements of the ideal best practice for rapid market expansion that are described in Lesson Twenty:

1. Sell something new related to past successes such that almost every prior customer and user will want the new offering.

2. Build a base of awareness and preference such that little expenditure is required to gain massive publicity.

3. Maximize the attention and excitement by cramming as much activity and opportunity into one minute as possible.

4. Presell through contracts or subscriptions.

5. Bundle a bigger batch of offerings together that include items that most customers and end users will eventually consider purchasing.

6. Add scarcity appeal by providing limited versions only available at that moment.

7. Conduct auctions that end at the same moment for anything else you want to sell for which there is a very limited supply and huge demand.

8. Provide experience-based services that are enhanced by the excitement of the one-minute event.

9. Create an event that everyone will want to talk about having participated in. As a possible model, consider the Super Bowl in the United States where two teams play for the National Football League Championship. The average price paid for a seat in the stadium is probably over $2,000 and there are over 60,000 people present. Yet you can watch the game for no added event charge on any television set. Perhaps broadcasting a live theatrical performance of the new book (referring to the Harry Potter series) to movie theaters with J. K. Rowling serving as host could provide part of such a draw.

To better understand this sixth step in the 2,000 percent solution process, let's consider how to approach the ideal best practice for the substantial market expansion of a professional service. Let's assume the usual price for the professional service is $100,000 (U.S.). Rather than simply expanding the market, let's also find a very cost effective way to approach the ideal best practice for market expansion.

Most professional service providers spend 20 to 30 percent of one year's revenues to develop new clients and to retain those clients over the subsequent five to eight years. Let's assume the organization can afford to spend $20,000 to acquire a client for the base service. If the market now is $2 million per year, let's set as a goal to add $40 million in revenues, which permits a marketing budget of $8 million for such a successful expansion by this organization. Because we don't know how effective the marketing will be, we should emphasize marketing methods with costs that vary according to the number of new sales.

Before creating any increased demand, we need to be sure we have the capacity to supply any increased volume, up to twenty times more volume than the market already uses. If, for example, this is a service for licensed software, expansion should be no problem. If it's a personal service, then backup suppliers and appropriate systems for supervising them will be needed.

Let's look at accomplishing each of the nine elements in the ideal best practice for such an accounting service:

1. Sell something new related to past successes such that almost every prior customer and user will want the new offering.

   This result might be accomplished by developing a dramatically improved version of the existing service that is compatible with what service users have received before. For example, if the existing service is an accounting audit, this new version might be upgraded to also include finding ways to greatly reduce operating costs by putting in a simple structure for activity-based costing (ABC) that the client could develop and apply for itself.

2. Build a base of awareness and preference such that little expenditure is required to gain massive publicity.

   Robert S. Kaplan and Steven R. Anderson are considered the authorities on the subject of ABC based on their book, *Time-Driven Activity-Based Costing* (Harvard Business School Press, 2007). One possible way to create massive awareness for the new service could be to exclusively license their methods and endorsements for performing the new service. Such a license could be negotiated to be paid as a percentage of sales so that no increased costs are incurred except when added revenues are generated.

3. Maximize the attention and excitement by cramming as much activity and opportunity into one minute as possible.

   You might hold an event where potential clients and users could learn more about the new service through presentations by Robert S. Kaplan and Steven R. Anderson. The two experts undoubtedly have a more advanced, more efficient method in mind that they haven't yet written about. Your service could be based on applying such an unpublished method. At the end of the presentations, you could offer a special price and preference for receiving the service to those who sign up immediately. You could also adjust the price downward based on how many sales occur at the meeting. Such an offer would give everyone more incentive to buy before the meeting's last minute.

4. Presell through contracts or subscriptions.

   You could provide an additional discount before the meeting to those who buy a long-term contract for your regular services as well as any related new services you provide. Many sales would already be committed at the time when the new service becomes available, adding to credibility for the new service.

5. Bundle a bigger batch of offerings together that include items that most customers and end users will eventually consider purchasing.

   This opportunity has been addressed by adding the ABC-based service, but you could also offer upgrades to the new service such as for a low-cost way to perform the application work for clients. Since it would be hard to assemble enough resources to accomplish such a result simultaneously for everyone, you might give an incentive to buy right away by assigning them an earlier date for starting the work. If you also add for that day only a guarantee of beneficial results well above the cost of the service, you'll generate more interest and sell to many more people.

6. Add scarcity appeal by providing limited versions that are only available at that moment.

   Some organizations might not have the process-redesign skills to take full advantage of the ABC information. You could offer a few organizations the opportunity to have such work done for them by one of your suppliers. These contracts might be worth tens of millions of dollars each and merely selling a few of them would greatly expand the market. To make this offering practical, it would probably make sense for your organization to effectively supervise the supplier.

7. Conduct auctions that end at the same moment for anything else you want to sell for which there is a very limited supply and huge demand.

   Anyone who is interested in cost reduction might also want help with establishing and improving quality processes. If you decide to offer a new service in this area, you might offer a few client organizations the opportunity to be trained in this work and some few others to receive full implementation of quality-improvement methods that require having a good ABC system and information in place. The training and implementation would probably also be outsourced.

8. Provide experience-based services that are enhanced by the excitement of the one-minute event.

For this dimension, you might provide some software that would help those present to estimate how much the service would improve their profits and cash flow. To make this learning more fun, you could engage highly admired industry experts to demonstrate the software and then hold a reception where those who buy the new service could immediately spend informal time with the experts.

9. Create an event that everyone will want to talk about having participated in.

Financial executives are always interested in networking with those who can help them obtain board directorships. You could invite board chairmen to attend who are looking for financial executives to join their boards. You could ask the intellectual knowledge providers and outsource supplier to help you attract more chairmen and financial executive prospects. In lieu of paying a finder's fee for your help in introducing potential board members, these chairmen could be asked to make modest donations to some popular charity. You could then use the charities to help attract celebrity supporters who, in turn, would help attract the families of the chairmen and financial executives. Such a celebrity-based approach would increase your ability to draw more attendees and to make the event even more of a "don't miss" occasion.

Assignments

1. How could a professional-service launch be made much more successful than by using the methods I have suggested in this lesson?

2. How could the cost of such a professional-service launch be greatly reduced without losing any sales?

3. How can you best approach the ideal best practice for expanding the markets your offerings serve?

4. What new offerings should you introduce that will make industry expansion easier, faster, and less expensive than what I have described?

Lesson Twenty-Two

Engage the Right People and Provide the Right Encouragement

"But command Joshua, and encourage him and strengthen him;
for he shall go over before this people,
and he shall cause them to inherit the land which you will see."

— Deuteronomy 3:28 (NKJV)

This lesson investigates how to apply step seven of the eight-step process for making a 2,000 percent solution: Engage the right people and provide the right encouragement. You'll also find material about this subject in *The 2,000 Percent Solution*; *The Portable 2,000 Percent Solution*; and *The 2,000 Percent Solution Workbook*.

I recommend that you reread at least Lesson Twenty-One unless you have just finished reading it because I refer here again to the professional-service launch example in that lesson. This example shows that there's a major role for star power ... provided by people whom your current and prospective customers and clients will want to meet and to learn from. The example's foundation builds from the celebrity and reputations of Robert S. Kaplan and Steven R. Anderson. These experts provide the new offering with credibility by their involvement, presence, and implied or explicit endorsement. Other experts with some degree of star power help by explaining how to estimate the potential value of the services.

Star power can further bolster credibility by bringing in more stars from the same field. With a marketing budget of $8 million, it's affordable to engage more celebrities whose expertise is relevant to your current and potential clients.

You should also consider involving people in the launch event whose stature is unusually high from outside of the field. Admired former heads of state can be a good choice. Also consider bringing in well-liked sports coaches and athletes who have an interest in what your clients do and can bring subject-matter credibility with them.

What's the motivation for these "star-power" people to become involved? There are several:

1. They gain an opportunity to address and to mingle with a prestigious audience. Such an experience can make stars feel more important. Many people crave that feeling.

2. They have something they want to sell to the same audience: their own services as speakers and experts.

3. They will want to meet and spend time with some of the other stars.

4. Being involved with your event gives each of them credibility to obtain more engagements from those who weren't involved in the event.

5. Some of the "star-power" people will also be paid. Usually, the better the prospect group, the less you have to pay … especially if you give those with star power a chance to make "back of the room" sales of their own materials. You'll have to decide if such sales of autographed materials would add to or detract from your event. Or you could provide the materials as bonuses for those who buy from you, and potentially reduce what you pay in speaking and appearance fees.

There's another group I described that is somewhat like the "star-power" group — the attending chairmen who are looking for board members. It's hard to attract chairmen to be part of an audience for any meeting because most of them are also CEOs. Why should these chairmen want to become involved? Their potential motivations could include such factors as:

1. Their financial executives ask them to attend to help evaluate whether the company should employ the new service. Chairmen (especially the ones who are CEOs) are very dependent on their financial executives and won't annoy them without a good reason. If your new service could make the company much more successful, the chairmen will probably want to know more.

2. They will want to meet some of the stars.

3. They will want to meet some of the other chairmen.

4. They will want to recruit financial executives as board members, and this is a cheaper, faster, and easier way to see a lot of candidates than by working with a recruiter, the usual method.

5. If you hold your meeting near some place that chairmen like to visit (such as the Pebble Beach golf course), some will want to come in part to engage in another favorite activity.

There's a third set of starlike people who can be of great value to you: financial executives who are esteemed by their colleagues. Meeting such people who are satisfied clients for your offerings will give prospective clients a lot more comfort about working with you. Many prospective clients will casually check you out with your clients during coffee breaks and social events. Being able to list the names of prestigious current and former clients (with their permissions) who did not attend will also help your credibility.

Why do these people want to be your endorsers?

1. If they can raise their stature by an association with your organization, that connection can be a valuable way to increase credibility in their own companies.

2. Many of them want to gain board directorships and will be pleased to have a high-visibility role while chairmen are present.

3. They may need to impress their own chairmen that they are doing the right thing by working with you, and a successful event like this can increase credibility with their chairmen.

Having considered the stars and starlike people, let's consider the prospects. Obviously, you would like to be sure that the prospects and their major competitors from every industry you want to serve are present. Why? Observing the attention paid by their competitors will make attendees feel more incentive to buy the new service, either to gain a potential advantage over a competitor or to be sure a competitor doesn't sneak ahead of them. Competitors' presences will also boost interest among attendees in your auctions to gain priority scheduling for any implementation services that are needed.

Without prospects' competitors being present, you may run an expensive boondoggle for prospective customers that delivers few immediate sales. Because such a risk may still be present even if competitors attend, you should check prior sales contacts with the prospects so that you invite only the people who seem to have a genuine interest in buying soon. Those who wouldn't give you the time of day are likely to take up space and to reduce buying interest for the others.

Have a brief chat with each invited prospect prior to the meeting to find out what he or she most wants to learn or to gain by coming to the event. You can use what you learn to tailor your materials, program, and contacts to fit the needs of the most people and to steer prospects toward those offerings and the people who can help the most.

Are you used to planning and running such events? Few people are. It may be a good idea to hire or to engage a top professional to organize the activities for you. The ideal person is someone who already represents a large organization whose members are your prospects. You might find it beneficial to team with such an organization as a sponsor ... a step that could reduce your costs and help to increase attendance.

Unless you already have an enormous organization, you will also need lots of people at the event to complement your staff. Why? You should be involved in as many of the casual conversations as possible. If the professional organizations you plan to use as service suppliers can't provide enough people to supplement your staff for this purpose, consider hiring attractive actors and actresses and rehearsing them to play the right kind of facilitative role during breaks and social occasions. You might also find that some of the professors you want to use in future roles would also be available to mingle and to facilitate. Keep in mind that you want people who will focus on helping you ... and not seeking work for themselves. That's one reason why actors and actresses are sometimes more effective in this mingling role than are professionals. The actors and actresses usually have less-divided loyalties and are often more comfortable playing such subordinate roles.

Partnerships need to be developed with those who may provide part of your new service (or related services). Define each relationship so that your partner will be more eager for you to succeed than to work independently of you. This result is best accomplished by involving people who and organizations that lack your credibility and access to prospects but are technically and professionally capable. In working out the financial arrangements with such partners, you should provide increased rewards if the clients stick with you so that your suppliers won't be trying to win away clients from you. Start by just inviting the most ethical organizations and conclude noncompete agreements with them with regard to the services you offer.

Do you feel unsure about any aspect of how to put such an event together? Repeat the eight-step process to focus on providing such events and how to approach the ideal best practice for conducting them to gain the most new service sales.

When you are ready to make such a sales breakthrough, get going!

Assignments

1. How could selecting the right people and providing the right encouragement for a professional-service launch lead to more success than what I suggest in the Lesson Twenty-One plan?

2. How could the cost and effort of engaging the right people and providing the right encouragement for such a professional-service launch be greatly reduced without hurting sales?

3. What other valuable opportunities are unique to your industry that should be employed in your next launch of a new offering?

Lesson Twenty-Three

Repeat the Last Seven Lessons

Now the boy Samuel ministered to the LORD before Eli.
And the word of the LORD was rare in those days;
there was *no widespread revelation.*
And it came to pass at that time,
while Eli was lying down in his place,
and when his eyes had begun to grow so dim that he could not see,
and before the lamp of God went out in the tabernacle of the LORD
where the ark of God was, *and while Samuel was lying down,*
that the LORD called Samuel.
And he answered, "Here I am!"
So he ran to Eli and said, "Here I am, for you called me."
And he said, "I did not call; lie down again."
And he went and lay down.
Then the LORD called yet again, "Samuel!"
So Samuel arose and went to Eli, and said,
"Here I am, for you called me."
He answered, "I did not call, my son; lie down again."
(Now Samuel did not yet know the LORD,
nor was the word of the LORD yet revealed to him.)
And the LORD called Samuel again the third time.
So he arose and went to Eli, and said,
"Here I am, for you did call me."
Then Eli perceived that the LORD had called the boy.
Therefore Eli said to Samuel,
"Go, lie down; and it shall be, if He calls you,
that you must say, 'Speak, LORD, for Your servant hears.'"
So Samuel went and lay down in his place.
Now the LORD came and stood and called as at other times,
"Samuel! Samuel!"
And Samuel answered, "Speak, for Your servant hears."

— 1 Samuel 3:1-10 (NKJV)

This lesson considers how to apply step eight of the eight-step process for creating a 2,000 percent solution: Repeat the first seven steps. You will also find material about this subject in *The 2,000 Percent Solution*; *The Portable 2,000 Percent Solution*; and *The 2,000 Percent Solution Workbook*.

Why is it important to repeat the first seven steps? Here are the most significant reasons:

1. Each repetition presents you with the opportunity to create a much better solution.

2. By involving different people during each repetition, you can educate more people about the 2,000 percent solution process.

3. After you implement a first 2,000 percent solution for expanding industry growth and size, you can use that experience to gain insights into what else can be improved.

4. Implementing at least one 2,000 percent solution for industry expansion allows you to begin building your next market expansion from a higher and more visible base.

5. The benefits of the implemented solutions multiply times one another.

6. You will probably find less expensive ways to implement such solutions, which will make pursuing implementation easier and more valuable.

7. The gains from past implementations will provide valuable nonfinancial resources to make future solutions even more available and successful.

In considering the full dimensions of the opportunity to further expand your market, notice how the successes described in the Harry Potter and iPhone examples discussed in earlier lessons provided valuable insights into the solutions that I proposed based on benefiting from these seven influences. For instance, each book in the Harry Potter series helped to lay down a foundation for creating an even bigger splash and more sales for the next installment in the series. As a result, sales from the last launch were vastly higher than for the launch of the first book due to each launch helping to attract new readers ... many of whom then read all of the earlier and subsequent books in the series.

The initial iPhone launch similarly built on studying the successes of earlier cellular telephone devices, the Apple Newton and prior personal digital assistants by other companies, Mac computers, and the iPod and other portable music players. Apple's reputation from those earlier successes also increased its ability to attract initial iPhone customers.

In fact, the biggest reason why those who implement a 2,000 percent solution for market expansion don't obtain all of the potential results they might is due to not repeating the process to create another, even larger, market expansion. Remember that the gain from repeating the process will be at least twenty times greater than the initial expansion.

Clearly, the critical challenge for gaining the best results is to develop and implement a 2,000 percent solution for market expansion as soon as possible and then to continually repeat the process whenever the newest market-expanding solution is ready for implementation.

Otherwise, market growth opportunities will be knocking and you won't open the door to them. In that case, don't be too surprised if someone else studies your success and makes the next breakthrough in market expansion without you.

Assignments

1. Set a timetable to develop and to implement new market-expanding 2,000 percent solutions as often as you can over the next five years.

2. Evaluate why you haven't devised and implemented more 2,000 percent solutions for market expansion in the past, and change your focus and behavior to overcome the stalls that held you back.

Part Three

Cut Costs

The LORD will be *awesome to them,*
For He will reduce to nothing all the gods of the earth;
People *shall worship Him,*
Each one from his place,
Indeed all the shores of the nations.

— Zephaniah 2:11 (NKJV)

Many of the lessons contained in Part Two of *Business Basics* direct you to take market-expanding actions that will also help to reduce costs as a secondary benefit, but it is unlikely that the resulting cost cuts will be anywhere near 96 percent for you and your stakeholders. By applying breakthrough methods to gain major cost reductions, such improvements will occur more rapidly and in larger amounts. In Part Three, you can read about such methods and obtain such improvements.

If you have been following the 400 Year Project, you are well aware of the project's earlier writings about how to make substantial cost improvements such as are described in *The 2,000 Percent Solution's* examples; *The Ultimate Competitive Advantage's* cost-reducing business-model innovations; and the methods in Part Two of *The 2,000 Percent Squared Solution*. You might be wondering, "What else needs to be written that isn't already known and described?"

There's quite a lot that most people still need to learn, beginning with realizing which of their beliefs are harmful to reducing costs. You may be surprised by how much of what people do in the name of cost reduction is actually counterproductive. Let me explain by looking at a common flaw in cost-reduction methods: taking a piecemeal approach.

What do I mean by that? Here are some bit-by-bit approaches that I've often seen applied:

- Cut all budgets by a certain percentage.

- Reduce personnel levels by a targeted number of jobs.

- Freeze, or reduce, salaries and benefits for a time.

- Reformulate a product to eliminate a certain percentage of costs.

- Stop providing aspects of a service to improve profit contribution as a percentage of sales.

- Apply Six Sigma methods to reduce errors in providing offerings to very low levels and thereby cut per-unit operating costs.

- Shift to lean-manufacturing or lean-service methods.

- Reduce the quantity provided to customers while maintaining the price per package.

- Provide a much smaller offering to reduce the price point while also erasing some costs for serving customers.

Why am I critical of such efforts? Based on my research I could make quite a long list of reasons, but I'll give just a few of the most important lessons:

- Piecemeal cost reductions often substantially increase costs in areas not considered by the cost cutters. The result can be an overall cost increase.

- After making many such cost reductions, the appeal of offerings is eventually harmed in some fundamental way so that sales fall faster than costs decline and sales remain lower.

- Such approaches often discourage high-performing employees, who then look for and find jobs at other organizations.

- The productivity of those who remain after such efforts often declines.

- Even if costs decline, these solutions often make it harder to improve, adjust, and remodel offerings and processes to improve performance for customers so that future sales and profits are reduced to well below their potential.

- Even if per-unit costs decline for the organization, the effects on customers may be adverse … often increasing their costs, causing sales to fall below what would have otherwise occurred.

- Social costs may increase as more harm is done to other people and to the environment, adding new opponents and incurring future costs for litigation and remediation.

- Efforts and funds that could have gone into making fundamental improvements to expand sales, profits, and cash flow are instead devoted to the piecemeal cost-reduction activities.

Such problems arise, in part, due to mistaken purposes for cost reductions. In many cases, a cost reduction is sought solely as a so-called quick fix to fill a temporary profit shortfall from the organization's budget. In such instances, the efforts may amount to no more than simply trying to score points with the boss. Is it any wonder that some of such ad hoc and ill-conceived cost-reducing efforts go wrong?

What accomplishments should a 96 percent cost reduction seek to provide for your organization and its stakeholders? While many people feel that they know, I believe that few actually do. Since few people have either sought or achieved this objective, let me propose a set of goals for those engaging in this activity for the first time:

1. The organization's costs to serve a customer with an offering drop by 96 percent while the performance that a customer perceives that he or she receives from the offering stays the same or improves from the highest level ever experienced.

2. The customers' total costs to acquire and to use an offering go down by 96 percent.

3. Users' costs to apply or to employ the offering decline by 96 percent.

4. Social costs of an offering (net of social benefits) are reduced by 96 percent.

As a corollary to achieving such cost-performance levels, 96 percent cost-reduction goals are also accomplished when tangible benefits received by customers, users, and society greatly increase such that they will pay more money and employ more efforts to receive the increased benefits, and the ratio of everyone's costs declines by 96 percent relative to the new level of price and benefits.

Here's an example of what I mean about cutting costs in terms of providing higher value benefits: If I provide at least 400 times more absolute value for you through this book as compared to my prior writings (by showing you many ways to gain 160,000 times, rather than 400 times, more cash flow than you have now, by expanding the market by twenty times twice and also making 96 percent cost and investment reductions), and the price I charge increases by sixteen times from the price for *The 2,000 Percent Squared Solution*; even at the higher price the book delivers the equivalent of a 96 percent cost reduction compared to the benefits customers, users, and society have received in the past ($100 [1 − (16/400)] = 96$ percent), even if my publishing costs per book stay the same, due to the sixteen times higher price I charge ($100 [1 − (.5/16)] = 96.875$ percent).

I know that if I proposed this cost-reduction objective and these goals in a meeting of executives, some of them would probably argue that such results are clearly impossible. To prepare you for such a reaction among your colleagues, let me suggest a response.

Anyone who has followed the computer or electronics industries can attest that the cost to acquire and to use a computer and most electronic devices for a given task has dropped by much more than 96 percent in the last few decades. Performing a series of calculations by using a spreadsheet program is a good example. If we measure costs in constant purchasing power, it's very clear that the reductions have been well beyond even 99 percent.

Some will counter that such opportunities don't apply in areas involving scarce natural resources (such as oil, gold, platinum, and rare minerals). Some producers have, in fact, changed the way that the resources are discovered, extracted, and processed to make huge savings. Did you know, for instance, that the price and costs for aluminum were once much higher than for gold or platinum and the available aluminum supply was tiny? Since then, technical innovations turned aluminum into a resource so inexpensive that we often throw aluminum foil away after a few seconds' use without giving the action a second thought.

Anyone who bought stock in the most efficient producers of scarce resources equal to the value of their personal or organizational annual purchases of such resources would have found that the gains in value of such securities would have much more than offset the increased prices paid for the natural resources. Others have found different ways to design an offering that uses fewer scarce resources and yet provides more benefits. Some have completely stopped using scarce natural resources, relying instead on "waste" sources as the key inputs.

Other people will argue that needing highly skilled people (such as those who are involved in producing biotechnology breakthroughs) cannot be avoided in some industries, and such costs cannot be reduced. Many would have made a similar argument just twenty years ago that software programming costs could not be reduced very much, yet the cost to produce a line of software has declined quite a lot due to new software tools and the availability of more people in low-wage countries who are well trained to program and to test software.

Some people are forgetting in making such objections that cost reductions apply to more than just raw material and people costs. For instance, establishing the safety of new biotechnology products costs a lot more than developing the products. Software testing costs a vast multiple of what software writing does and software testing doesn't require rare geniuses in order to be done well. In fact, some software (such as the Linux computer operating system) is produced and tested at no cost to users.

Why can such great cost reductions be made in almost any area? It's worth remembering Pareto's Principle, as defined by Dr. Joseph M. Juran: 80 percent of the results of any human endeavor come from 20 percent of the effort. In any substantial activity within an organization, this principle means that some people are probably sixteen times more effective than the least effective people. In an even more common activity across many organizations, scaling continues to increase differences in performance so that we can presume that some people are hundreds of times more effective than the least effective person who can add enough value to cover employment costs. By simply understanding and employing the lessons of the best performers in any activity, we can reduce costs by 96 percent.

If we go further and consider how business models might be improved and what the ideal practices are, we can make even larger cost reductions. One of my favorite examples comes from the Aravind Eye Hospital in India. A cataract operation there costs less than 2 percent of what a similar operation does in England; and the clinical outcomes for patients are better at Aravind. If you can make such improvements with surgery, imagine what you can accomplish with something that's much simpler and potentially less dangerous to do incorrectly.

The remaining challenge comes, of course, in that many doubters don't know how to even begin to make such substantial improvements. After reading the lessons in this part and doing the assignments, you will know everything you need to succeed in this seemingly "impossible" dream.

Lesson Twenty-Four

Chain-Reaction 2,000 Percent Solutions

He will lift up a banner to the nations from afar,
And will whistle to them from the end of the earth;
Surely they shall come with speed, swiftly.
No one will be weary or stumble among them,
No one will slumber or sleep;
Nor will the belt on their loins be loosed,
Nor the strap of their sandals be broken;
Whose arrows are *sharp,*
And all their bows bent;
Their horses' hooves will seem like flint,
And their wheels like a whirlwind.

— Isaiah 5:26-28 (NKJV)

This lesson describes a new concept for creating and implementing 96 percent cost reductions: chain-reaction exponential solutions. This is a subject I'm very excited about, and I hope you will share my enthusiasm for and interest in this process by the time you finish reading this lesson.

When I was a youngster, controlled atomic chain reactions were being developed as a source of electricity. To help children understand the difference between an atomic blast (an uncontrolled atomic chain reaction) and an atomic power plant (a controlled atomic chain reaction), scientists designed some impressive demonstrations.

One of my favorite demonstrations of an uncontrolled atomic chain reaction was conducted in a huge room filled with spring-loaded mouse traps that were each topped by two table-tennis balls. The narrator would start the demonstration by tossing a single-table tennis ball into the room, and within a second the air would be so filled with flying table-tennis balls that you couldn't see more than a few feet ahead. Within just a few more seconds, the energy in the traps would be expended and quiet would soon return.

To me that demonstration was very powerful because it showed that you could move from no motion to universal motion almost instantly. Although I had no interest in setting off uncontrolled atomic chain reactions, I was impressed by the potential to stir actions that would create immediate, multiplied effects. Since then, I have always wondered how such effects might be encouraged for people.

I began to see examples early in life. If someone stood up on the top level of a stadium, perhaps one or two people in the vicinity would also stand up, but no other action would usually follow. If by standing up the person at top could reach a ventilation duct that created a loud noise when struck by hand, that person could induce a much larger reaction by starting a rhythmic drumming on the duct and shouting a familiar chant. Following such a beginning, the whole stadium would soon be clapping and chanting to the beat. Occasionally, I played this role of starting the drumming and chanting just to help me understand the cause and effect.

I observed a similar phenomenon a few years later: If a person stood up in the first row of a stadium or auditorium in a way that blocked the view for the people behind the standing person, most of the people who couldn't easily see would stand up immediately rather than ask the first person to sit down. Each time one person stood up in front, four to ten people behind that person would also stand. Each of those standers, in turn, led another multiple of four to ten people to stand. Within a minute or two, most people behind the original stander in that part of the stadium would be on their feet. Some people would stay standing, even if those in front sat down. Seeing that others were standing, some people in other sections would also stand either in excitement or to stretch. Whenever such reactions followed among many of those on the bottom tier, almost the whole crowd would be standing during much of the event.

I began to think about the conditions that cause such reactions. The second example was due in part to obvious self-interest: People had come to the event to see what was going on. Interfere with their views, and they would stand up to gain a better look … even if more effort was required. The first example was helped by a more subtle kind of self-interest: People enjoy feeling that they are part of an energetic crowd. To gain that feeling, many people will quickly take up chanting, dancing, and shouting slogans that connect them with the crowd. Even some normally reserved people will be seen sheepishly joining in.

Experience and habits play roles, too. Many people have been in similar situations, and they have learned to enjoy the event more by acting in such ways.

I began to think about how self-interest combined with experience and habits could be used to stand in for those two table-tennis balls sitting on each spring-loaded mousetrap to create a chain reaction by human beings. I observed a much slower, but impressive, example as a young consultant that stayed with me.

Electronic calculators in 1971 cost about $4,000 in today's buying power. Because of the expense and need for training to use them, only a few people in any organization had an electronic calculator: those who needed to make lots of calculations and who were quick with a keyboard. Yet everyone in the consulting firm I worked for spent many hours a day calculating. We mostly did it by hand. The firm had only one computer program that we could access on a mainframe, and that program allowed us to do just one sort of calculation. It didn't really save us much time over hand calculations. When I accidentally destroyed this program, no one bothered by replace it.

Fortunately, I was good at doing arithmetic in reasonably error-free fashion and was able to get my work done on time. Some of my colleagues struggled with making errors.

One day, one of our clients, Texas Instruments (TI), announced one of the first reasonably inexpensive, truly portable semiconductor-based calculators with multiple functions. The retail price in today's buying power was about $2,000. Our CEO couldn't see spending that much, but he was able to persuade TI to let us buy the calculators for the wholesale price of about $1,000 (although I noticed that our CEO never offered a wholesale price to TI for our consulting).

Not wanting to spend hundreds of thousands of dollars of the firm's money, the CEO came up with an alternative: Clients were going to save a lot of money when we used calculators because we wouldn't have to charge them for as many hours of work. He authorized each of us to buy a calculator for $1,000 by putting the purchases on a company-guaranteed credit card and then to charge our clients about $10 an hour for using the calculators. After a month or two, we had each recovered $1,000 and paid off the credit card charge. We weren't allowed to charge clients more than the recovery cost, but we each obtained a calculator at ultimately no cost to us.

The quality of our client work went up within two months, client costs went down (It was up to ten times faster to do complex calculations, and remember that we charged clients by the hour.), and we completed the work sooner. Clients liked what we did better, and we sold more consulting studies to existing clients. The firm grew, and those of us in the firm gained promotions and raises more rapidly than before.

As clients implemented what we recommended, their customers, employees, suppliers, employees' families, partners, lenders, shareholders, communities, and other stakeholders also benefited. Like throwing a rock in the middle of a pond to start a ripple, the influence of our CEO's decision kept spreading outward.

I began to realize the full effects only after we started carrying our calculators to client presentations so that we could answer more questions on the spot. Many clients had never seen the technology and what it could do: They, too, began to order calculators for their staffs and to ask more quantitative questions. Understanding of their business decisions rose. And on went the improvements and increased use of calculators.

I observed similar ripple effects when more advanced calculators became available. Some of my colleagues were soon walking through plants spotting ways to improve profits by millions after making just a few calculations. The engineers in the plants who didn't have similar calculators were astonished. The clients' engineers, too, soon acquired such calculators and uncovered still more ways to improve.

Most people find it hard to generalize what to do from studying just one example. Let me share another example: e-mail. I clearly remember the first time I heard about e-mail. A CFO of a Fortune 500 company described how he could accomplish global projects one hundred times faster and at vastly less cost. In addition, he could work on more activities and achieve much more. He didn't even mention how much less expensive e-mail was than air freight and long-distance telephone calls. Why? I suspect it's because the cost reduction was so much less important to him than the increased effectiveness.

Let me put the cost dimensions in perspective for you by discussing how e-mail affected Mitchell and Company. We expanded from our headquarters in Cambridge, Massachusetts, by opening a second office in California in the early 1980s. Because we had so much information to share between the offices, we sent a daily air-freight package from each office to the other one. In today's buying power, the daily cost was about $80. The annual cost was approximately $17,000.

Within a year, we put fax machines in both locations and simply sent most of the material that way. The fax machines, long distance tolls, and telephone line charges cost about $4,000 a year. We were delighted to save so much money even though it took some time to feed originals into the fax machines.

We were also regularly contacting clients and client prospects by regular mail. The annual cost of preparing and sending such materials was in the vicinity of $140,000.

With the advent of e-mail, we put in one position for someone just to handle e-mail, and the cost was about $45,000. We began to send most of our material by e-mail rather than regular mail. Within a year, we stopped most of our regular mail shipments and saved over $80,000 a year.

Today, we hardly ever send regular mail. We no longer have a person devoted to e-mails. Our costs to communicate with clients and prospective clients through e-mails are about $3,000 a year. Yet, we communicate with more people than ever. Their costs and ours have declined from where we started by 98 percent. The only potential losers are the people we used to employ for that work (who didn't like doing the work very much so they probably didn't mind), the post office, and our office supplies vendors. But we certainly didn't increase the costs of any of those stakeholders. My personal productivity has risen by several hundred percent as I more frequently partner with other organizations to do tasks that we formerly conducted in-house at much higher cost and with less effectiveness.

We also found that as soon as we switched to e-mail, our access to current and potential clients improved. They responded more quickly, and we found it easier to stay in touch. Their responsiveness indicated that this was a chain-reaction 2,000 percent solution.

As another example of such cost breakthroughs, let's look next at a product: computers. I'll again put the example in terms of our Mitchell and Company experiences.

Prior to the advent of the desktop computer, computing was too expensive for us to use in our consulting practice. Even the smallest minicomputers cost over $400,000 in today's dollars and programming was still more expensive. Time-sharing costs on mainframes were huge, and good programmers were hard to find and received very high compensation.

When the first Apple computers came out, they supported the first inexpensive spreadsheet programs. Having seen the programs, I realized that custom software could be written for consulting applications on Apple computers at less than 2 percent of the cost of minicomputer programs. I also found that programmers with day jobs were often interested in learning how to program microcomputers so they were willing to work on a moonlight basis (after their regular jobs) for reasonable rates and good talent was readily available.

I began to sell new types of services, ones that required lots of calculations. Our business boomed. But our costs were tiny, so the profits from this work were enormous.

When the IBM personal computers came out, I had an even wider choice of programs, and I was able to sell other new categories of assignments that required programming that clients couldn't easily and quickly do for themselves.

With each upgrade in computer processors, the scope of what we could do improved. Calculations that used to take hours were done in a few minutes.

Costs came down too. Our first Intel 486-based personal computer cost about $55,000 in today's dollars when new. But this computer allowed us to run full-fledged statistics programs for the first time, and we were able to buy software reasonably inexpensively (around $4,000 in today's dollars). Within two years, we could buy better machines that ran much faster for only $8,000 in today's dollars.

Our costs declined by much more than 96 percent every time we put in a new computer, due to a combination of more functionality and greater speed. In addition, we were able to take on new tasks. Assignments that once took as long as eight months could now be done in as few as three days, and clients would pay a huge premium for such fast results because the increased speed in some cases could save them billions. Life was good.

Eventually, we were able to do these assignments so efficiently that it became attractive to reduce prices for the work to further expand the market.

Let me describe a service that I developed as a result of this thinking to show you how a consulting service can create a chain-reaction 2,000 percent solution. Our services for diagnosing what a company should do to improve its stock price cost a client about $2 million in today's buying power. At Peter Drucker's insistence, I developed a low-cost substitute and found a way to use some proprietary calculations to diagnose many of the same opportunities for only $15,000.

The number of our clients for this new service was much larger than for the traditional services, so we gained a lot more data about what worked and what didn't. As a result, our quality went up even faster than our costs came down.

Because these new assignments could be done very quickly, we also had more frequent and higher-impact interactions with clients. They relied on us more, and they made better decisions as a result.

Let me pull out some themes from the four examples (calculators, e-mail, microcomputers, and stock-price-improvement diagnosis) and pose some questions for you to consider:

1. Communications costs are rapidly approaching zero. What doors does that open for you?

2. Computing costs are rapidly approaching zero. What can you afford to calculate and to do now that you couldn't do before?

3. Work can be redesigned now to produce higher-quality results at vastly lower costs. What can you redesign now that wasn't possible to redesign before?

4. Customers and other stakeholders are becoming used to do-it-yourself solutions where they participate more in accessing and using information. What new offerings can you provide that depend on such increased ability to perform and interest in do-it-yourself solutions?

5. Technology is advancing rapidly in creating cost-reduction potential. What cost reductions from technology should you be using that you aren't?

6. Cost-reduction opportunities open up more frequently than before. Are you studying how to develop and to apply new cost reductions often enough?

7. Noticing new low-cost methods is a critical first step for making large cost reductions. How are you monitoring what can be done?

Now let me pose a key question for you: *What one change can you make in your business model that will set off a similar set of chain reactions by employing self-interest, experience, and habits that will cut costs for your organization and for all your stakeholders by 96 percent or more?*

Here's the answer I came to for my business: Help all my stakeholders learn how to create and to teach others ways of producing cost-reducing 2,000 percent solutions.

What's the key learning from this lesson? **Find a 2,000 percent solution that will reduce your costs as well as those of all your stakeholders by 96 percent through building on what stakeholders already believe in and are excited about doing that will engage their self-interests and habits in making the necessary changes.**

Assignments

1. What are the themes for creating chain-reaction 2,000 percent solutions that you aren't yet applying?

2. How can you quickly become effective in applying such themes?

3. What kinds of 96 percent cost reductions can you make that your stakeholders are looking for that will create the most immediate, largest increases in cash flow and profits for them and benefits for others through drawing on self-interest, experience, and habits?

Lesson Twenty-Five

Apply the Themes of
Chain-Reaction 2,000 Percent Solutions

The works of His hands are *verity and justice;*
All His precepts are *sure.*
They stand fast forever and ever,
And are *done in truth and uprightness.*
He has sent redemption to His people;
He has commanded His covenant forever;
Holy and awesome is *His name.*

— Psalm 111:7-9 (NKJV)

This lesson applies the themes of chain-reaction exponential solutions that were described in Lesson Twenty-Four for creating and implementing 96 percent cost reductions for your organization and all its stakeholders. As a reminder, here are the themes:

1. Communications costs are rapidly approaching zero. What doors does that open for you?

2. Computing costs are rapidly approaching zero. What can you afford to calculate and to do now that you couldn't do before?

3. Work can be redesigned now to produce higher quality results at vastly lower costs. What can you redesign now that wasn't possible to redesign before?

4. Customers and other stakeholders are becoming used to do-it-yourself solutions where they participate more in accessing and using information. What new offerings can you provide that depend on such increased ability to perform and interest in do-it-yourself solutions?

5. Technology is advancing rapidly in creating cost-reduction potential. What cost reductions from technology should you be using that you aren't?

6. Cost-reduction opportunities open up more frequently than before. Are you studying how to develop and to apply new cost reductions often enough?

7. Noticing new low-cost methods is a critical first step for making large cost reductions. How are you monitoring what can be done?

Let me describe examples that apply to each of these themes. Then, think about where you can combine several of these potential methods to build a chain-reaction exponential cost solution for your organization.

We start with low-cost communications. Companies often design offerings assuming that customers will employ the offerings with little help. With low-cost communications you can afford to stay in contact with customers and inexpensively perform many activities that customers find to be exorbitant to hire out and difficult to do on their own.

Here's an example: I spent about $700 in 2008 to have high-speed Internet access at home. Due to various quirks in the service, I was on the telephone with a technician for about an hour each month trying to figure out how to reconnect. This service was delivered by my cable television provider. The company could have saved the cost of all these calls (and I could have saved the value of my wasted time, which was worth a lot more than $700 a year) if it had simply provided me with videos and software over a cable television channel that I could have used to solve my problems with the Internet connection. The effect of such a shift would have been to encourage more cable television customers to use the provider for high-speed Internet, thus reducing the company's marketing costs. With low-enough costs, the cable company could have charged less for Internet service and attracted still more customers. Without all the telephone interaction, the cost of adding a new subscriber would have been almost zero. With enough growth, the company's average costs would have plummeted.

Let's look next at taking advantage of near-zero computing costs. Most marketers would agree in principle that 90 percent of their marketing doesn't work. Since they aren't sure which 90 percent isn't working, marketers are reluctant to eliminate anything.

With low-cost computing you can afford to record and to analyze information about each contact with current and potential customers. When you understand the paths that are and are not working for influencing potential and current customers, you can more quickly drop marketing programs that aren't very productive and move on to develop and to test new programs that build on the successes. If as a result of making all your marketing effective you expand new sales by at least ten times, you will reduce not only your marketing costs, but also many of your operating costs for serving a customer. When that happens, you can reduce the price that you charge while still making more money and increasing your cash flow.

Redesigning work provides lots of opportunities. If you measure the process of preparing and delivering an offering, you'll find that nothing is happening over 95 percent of the time. Redesign the work to take out many of the inactive moments, and you obtain results much faster.

Let's examine upholstered furniture. Most manufacturers wait to produce a minimum number of orders because of large setup costs and wanting to buy a minimum quantity of supplies to gain discounted prices. Since it usually takes six to eight weeks to accumulate enough orders, manufacturers only produce any given item every six to eight weeks. Consequently, customers can wait as long as ten weeks after ordering to receive their new furniture.

If you develop suppliers who will deliver just in time at reasonable prices and redesign the furniture manufacturing process to be more like the way that personal computers are built to order, you could provide furniture within two weeks of receiving an order (with most of that time being needed for shipping and delivery). That approach would expand your sales, reduce your costs, and allow you to be more effective in marketing your advantages.

Do-it-yourself is a special opportunity. Let's continue in the furniture industry. Two problems often contribute to the desire to replace upholstered furniture: The fabric becomes worn and the springs sag. Upholstered furniture could instead be made so that customers could easily replace the fabric and springs themselves. Fabric replacements might be sized to fit over the old fabric and be connected to the furniture with strong, unseen Velcro strips. Springs might be contained in modular units that could be easily taken out and replaced.

As a result you could recondition your upholstered furniture with minimal effort to make it almost "good as new" for much less than half the cost of new furniture. That change could cause the furniture refurbishing market to grow faster because people could more often afford to change their colors and improve comfort. You can, of course, reupholster furniture now at low cost, but it's a big job, many people don't know how, and they often lack interest in learning.

Perhaps no activities are being affected more by technology now than transmitting, downloading, and storing videos. By adding something entertaining to your marketing message, you could quickly reach millions of people for little more than the cost of developing a traditional video. Accessing a mass market means changing the way you write, produce, and distribute such videos. As a result, YouTube may well be a better way to share the messages about your offerings than having sales people show DVDs to current and potential customers.

This last example is also good for considering the problem of not taking new methods seriously enough. I'm sure you know about the vast low-cost marketing potential of YouTube, but how much time have you spent in learning how to apply this new method? If you are like me, you know about it but haven't done anything. Shame on me! If you don't take action after reading this lesson, shame on you, too.

I've been impressed lately by how many elements of medical and dental practices are being improved to serve poor people at very low cost. My sense is that there are always thousands of successful cost-reducing experiments being conducted. If you wait to read about the results of such experiments, you'll always be years behind the best practice. But if you design and host a Web site where people who conduct medical and dental practice experiments can easily share ideas and new developments with one other, you'll gain more insights faster.

Few organizations are using such new medical and dental lessons for serving the poor to deliver diagnosis and treatment to those who can afford to pay. By drawing from such a rich source of innovations, you could earn billions by replacing expensive forms of traditional medicine and generate lots of money to pay for providing free services to poor people as the Aravind Eye Care System (www.aravind.org) does.

What's the key learning from this lesson? **You can use each of the themes to identify related ways to tap into the large potential to find and apply chain-reaction 2,000 percent solutions that will almost instantly reduce your costs by 96 percent, as well as those of your stakeholders where they believe the largest profit and cash flow potentials are.**

Assignments

1. How could you combine these themes to design new chain-reaction 2,000 percent solutions for 96 percent cost reductions for your offerings?

2. How should you organize to continually improve the new solutions with further breakthroughs?

Lesson Twenty-Six

Cut Prices and Add Benefits for
Chain-Reaction 2,000 Percent Solutions

Look at the birds of the air,
for they neither sow nor reap nor gather into barns;
yet your heavenly Father feeds them.
Are you not of more value than they?

— Matthew 6:26 (NKJV)

This lesson examines two catalysts, cutting prices and adding benefits, for stimulating chain-reaction exponential solutions (as defined and described in lessons twenty-four and twenty-five) for creating and implementing 96 percent cost reductions for your organization and all stakeholders.

Let's start with *price cutting*. Consider long-distance telephone charges as an example. If there were no charges for this service, most people would spend a lot more time on the telephone. How do we know that? A number of long-distance providers over the Internet have sliced their prices to zero if you speak with another subscriber. Measure how much talking these subscribers do for "free," and you'll be impressed. For instance, I met a New Zealand man who has increased his international calling by about eight hours a day. With many people in the world not yet calling at all, you can imagine what the impact would be if everyone else had access to equipment and services that made such calls available for free as well.

Let's next study recorded music. Until the Internet came along, many people made low-cost copies of music by duplicating cassette tapes and CDs owned by their friends. With the Internet, it became technically possible to download music for free from anyone in the world who had any kind of a copy. Naturally, the record companies and recording artists didn't like this capability, and they fought back. A few providers such as Apple iTunes offered low-priced downloads for those who wanted legal copies. The result was that the amount of music the average person plays has never been nearly as great.

Yet there are many other places where cutting the price down to near zero probably wouldn't increase the consumption all that much: Portable toilets are probably an example. Many females don't like to use them, and the facilities are often only marginally more convenient for males than more primitive alternatives. If you have any reasonably sanitary, discreet way to eliminate human waste, buying or renting portable toilets isn't going to be seen as all that attractive regardless of how inexpensive it is to do so.

It's important to determine how price elastic a given offering is. What I mean by price elasticity is by how much consumption increases when the price declines. For example, providers of a price-elastic offering might see real volume expand by 25 percent every time that the price dropped by 10 percent. Those who provide a price-insensitive offering might, instead, see real volume expand by only 3 percent every time that the price dropped by 10 percent.

As you can imagine, the strategic opportunity for chain-reaction exponential cost solutions is far better for highly price-elastic offerings.

But there's another factor you have to consider: by how much costs decline with increased volumes. Sometimes an offering is tied to a high fixed-cost base, but the incremental costs to deliver more offerings are small. An online newsletter is an example. Writing, preparing, and marketing the newsletter account for almost all costs. Once the marketing costs to acquire a subscriber are paid, adding one more subscriber is almost free.

When incremental costs to add a customer are low, average costs will rapidly decline with increased usage. As a result, when the demand is price elastic enough, it can make sense to price relative to the incremental costs rather than the average costs.

What should you be looking for? *A chain-reaction exponential cost solution can be profitably triggered by price declines whenever average unit costs decline with lower prices faster than prices are reduced.*

When that happens, a substantial business is easily developed. Naturally, this circumstance doesn't occur very often, pointing out the need for entrepreneurs to seek to provide just the right offerings in the most price-elastic industries in order to grasp the full potential for strategic growth.

Still another factor plays an important role here: competitors' costs. In weak pricing environments companies often price relative to their incremental, rather than their average, costs … even when demand won't be increased very much. If competitors' incremental costs are higher than yours, they will continually lose customers to you when you price below what they can afford to charge. When that competitive circumstance occurs, you can grow a lot solely through increasing your market share, even without much industry price sensitivity.

A proprietary business model helps for creating such an advantageous competitive opportunity. Let's look at Paychex, the small business payroll-service provider. Before Paychex developed a lower-cost way to process small employer payrolls, such employers were typically paying ten to a hundred times as much for the total of payroll processing costs plus the fines and interest charges they received from governments for errors in payroll tax reports and payments.

Because its competitors were not able to duplicate its business model and the demand for this offering is very price elastic, Paychex rapidly grew revenues to more than a billion dollars with a very high profit margin. Costs for payroll processing are very fixed-cost intensive. The incremental cost of adding one more employee to an account is quite small. Once you have an employer's payroll records, it's also much cheaper to provide related services such as pension-fund recordkeeping for which high prices are charged by those who lack this source of cost advantage.

I hope you can see from the Paychex example that the wisest entrepreneurs will choose a market to develop after assessing the strategic potentials of many attractive markets, rather than simply providing offerings for an existing or randomly chosen business.

Let's focus next on *adding benefits* that make an offering instantly worth at least twenty times more to all stakeholders. Before examining this opportunity, let me emphasize the obvious: *You can also use combinations of lower prices and adding more benefits to instantly expand the net value to all stakeholders by twenty times.*

A chain-reaction exponential cost solution can be profitably triggered by benefit expansions that require little or no cost and generate more than a twenty-times increase in the value gained by stakeholders either through increasing their incomes or reducing their costs. Adding such widespread benefits is easiest to accomplish by also increasing benefits for using some resource or activity that affects everyone.

Energy is a good example. Gasoline to propel vehicles is the biggest discretionary use for oil. If you create a solar-powered vehicle with low-enough costs (which might be quite viable in areas with a lot of direct sun such as the Middle East and north Africa), you should be able to reduce the cost to propel such a vehicle by 96 percent compared to a comparable, conventionally fueled one.

Let's look at the logic behind my observation. General Motors has designed an electric car, the Chevrolet Volt, which the auto maker estimates will cruise around town between charges at about eight percent of the cost of a conventional gasoline-powered car. The Volt gets its electricity from being plugged into an outlet, stores enough energy to travel up to forty miles, and can supplement its range by using a gasoline engine that delivers about three times the mileage of a conventional gasoline-powered car. If the car were to be redesigned to get its electricity from solar panels on its roof, hood, trunk, and sides and on the buildings where it is parked, the cost per mile would mostly be determined by the cost of the solar panels. It's probably safe to assume that if produced in large quantities, such a car would operate around town with an energy cost of less than 3 percent of what a normal car does. Because the sun would be recharging the vehicle during the day, the driving range between charges would also be much increased.

The cost-reducing effects of such a vehicle are broader than that. When one driver decreases gasoline consumption, the overall demand for gasoline and oil falls. With enough such cars being driven rather than conventional vehicles, you reduce the price that other drivers pay for gasoline as well as what homeowners pay for heating oil. When gasoline and oil prices are lower, fuels that compete with petroleum will also decline in price (such as natural gas for heating and coal for generating electricity). The net effect for reducing stakeholders' costs could be much more than the cost of such a vehicle. How's that for a chain-reaction 2,000 percent cost-cutting solution?

Here's another example. Many plants (such as corn and cotton) require lots of expensive fertilizer to replenish the soil's fertility or their yields will be low. If you can develop a new bacteria strain that enriches the soil without requiring any fertilizer (such as by fixing more nitrogen from the atmosphere), you could permanently enrich a field's production through one expenditure. Done properly, this approach could reduce the soil-related cost of producing crops while opening up relatively infertile land for cultivation. Use this bacteria strain to help grow any crop, and the price of such a crop will come down quite a lot while the yield will rise even more than the crop's price will decline. The price of other crops that could be grown on the same land will also come down to reflect the higher profitability of this way to grow a given crop. The ripple effects will proceed throughout the world so that more crops will be available, prices will be lower, more people will be well fed and have nice clothing, and other uses of the crops will become more profitable as well. Making such a change boosts the standard of living for billions of people in ways that also increase their brain power (such as by providing better nutrition for children and nursing mothers) and economic choices (by making them better able to benefit from education). Again, the multiplier effects on benefits probably greatly exceed the value of the crops themselves as well as the cost of the bacteria.

Let's look next at a service: education. Traditional education has emphasized teaching specific skills (such as reading, writing, arithmetic, etc.) separate from applications (earning a living, starting a business, servicing and repairing a car, building and maintaining a home, etc.). The often unspoken assumption is that people will receive education well into their twenties so there's plenty of time to teach people everything they can benefit from learning.

This assumption isn't a very good one: The bulk of the people in the world don't receive very much formal education.

What if we made a simple change? Combine teaching specific skills with teaching the most valuable applications of such skills. This unified teaching approach could mean finding out how to fix a water pump in arid regions where farming is important during the second or third grade while learning to read better and to perform simple arithmetic related to the task. By sixth grade, a learner would study the most advanced practices for being a farmer or starting and successfully operating a farming-related business while expanding vocabulary and reading comprehension, and adding skill in solving written math problems.

As a result, a government or a private school might spend a little more money on developing and acquiring more useful curricula and learning materials, but the result will be enabling people to earn fifty to a hundred times more at a young age. Consequently, the cost of educating learners would drop compared to their incomes, and the learners would be able to afford much more education, creating an income-expansion cycle. Such higher-income people would also be able to spend that much more, and the world's economy would be much larger. Income for everyone would be much higher, totaling millions of times the costs of developing and acquiring the new curricula and learning materials.

As you can see, when we focus on benefit areas that greatly affect virtually everyone in the world (either directly or indirectly), vast chain-reaction benefits follow.

As you consider an area to work on for your business, concentrate on wide-impact opportunities that can deliver such vast, widespread, and immediate breakthroughs.

What's the key learning from the pricing aspect of this lesson? **You can use the combination of high price elasticity, even greater cost sensitivity to volume increases, an advantage compared to competitors' costs, and proprietary business models to employ lower pricing that drives chain-reaction 2,000 percent cost-reduction solutions that almost instantly reduce your costs by 96 percent as well as those of your stakeholders where they believe that they will gain the most profit, cash flow, and benefits.**

What's the key learning from the benefit-expansion aspect of this lesson? **You can use broad-impact benefit breakthroughs to create chain-reaction 2,000 percent cost-reduction solutions that will almost instantly expand your profits by twenty times while reducing costs by more than 96 percent by increasing social benefits more than twenty times of what you will be spending for stakeholders where they believe that they will gain the most profit, cash flow, and benefits.**

Assignments

1. What are the characteristics of your current offerings in terms of price elasticity, cost sensitivity to increased volume, costs compared to competitors, and having proprietary cost advantages through your business model?

2. What offerings could you provide that would gain more growth and cost reductions from price reductions?

3. What potential do your current offerings provide in terms of the opportunity to expand benefits by twenty times in ways that will immediately translate into huge social cost reductions and benefit gains?

4. What offerings could you provide that would have more potential in terms of such social benefits?

Lesson Twenty-Seven

Get a Faster Start with
Chain-Reaction 2,000 Percent Solutions

And the servant ran to meet her and said,
"Please let me drink a little water from your pitcher."
So she said, "Drink, my lord."
Then she quickly let her pitcher down to her hand,
and gave him a drink.
And when she had finished giving him a drink, she said,
"I will draw water for your camels also,
until they have finished drinking."
Then she quickly emptied her pitcher into the trough,
ran back to the well to draw water, and drew for all his camels.
And the man, wondering at her,
remained silent so as to know whether
the LORD had made his journey prosperous or not.
So it was, when the camels had finished drinking,
that the man took a golden nose ring weighing half a shekel,
and two bracelets for her wrists weighing ten shekels of gold,
and said, "Whose daughter are you?"

— Genesis 24:17-23 (NKJV)

In this lesson, we turn our attention to gaining a faster start in designing and implementing chain-reaction 2,000 percent solutions. In my original explanation of the concept (see Lesson Twenty-Four), I described how people have demonstrated uncontrolled atomic chain reactions by filling a large room with set mousetraps carrying two table-tennis balls each. Then, by dropping a single table-tennis ball, all the traps would be sprung in a few seconds ... filling the air with the balls.

As you can imagine, the drawback of such a demonstration was setting all of those mouse traps and putting table-tennis balls on them without starting an inadvertent explosion of balls. Such mistakes occurred from time to time, and the challenge of preparing the demonstration was great. A lot of time and effort were also required to gain just a brief view. The setup time was tens of thousands of times longer than the actual demonstration.

If you were to take the same approach to your business, you might have to spend billions of dollars over decades to get to the point where the chain-reaction creation of a major business would occur. Such a result hardly seems worth the effort.

As wonderful as a chain-reaction 2,000 percent cost-reduction solution is, I'm sure you agree that it would be enormously more valuable if the solution could be developed quickly and inexpensively.

Although this point should be obvious, I have noticed that some people have been slow to focus on accelerating the development and implementation of breakthrough gains. Part of the problem seems to be that entrepreneurs tend to be overly optimistic. Another challenge is that many entrepreneurs have no idea of what's involved in making the improvements that they envision. Without a lot of knowledge about what to do, it's also easy to seek the right help from the wrong people and the wrong help from the right people.

Goals are a good starting point for overcoming such problems. Be sure you have a goal requiring that your chain-reaction solution can be identified and implemented in a short timeframe with modest amounts of resources compared to what you have available and can afford to commit.

Here are some strategies that can help you to accomplish your goals for gaining breakthroughs faster and less expensively:

- See how a highly publicized global contest conducted on the Internet might provide you with access to better ideas at little cost.

- Examine cost reductions and benefit gains that can be easily and quickly tested on a small scale.

- Consider the difficulty and expense of applying the methods that provide the cost reductions and benefit gains.

- Think about how challenging it will be to attract talented people to help you implement.

- Evaluate the natural interest that your breakthroughs will attract and how such interest can speed progress.

Here's an example of what I mean. Let's return to the idea of helping all my stakeholders learn how to create and to teach others how to define and to implement 2,000 percent solutions.

I could easily sponsor a global contest for such a purpose by spreading information through my blogs, Web sites, book reviewer profiles, press releases, and e-mail list. I could offer a prize of receiving personal tutoring from me in accomplishing the winner's choice of a 2,000 percent solution goal. The out-of-pocket cost for such a contest would be less than $500. The contest could be completed within 60 days of starting.

While the contest was going on, I could review my experiences with helping others learn how to create 2,000 percent solutions and conduct small-scale experiments with teaching in new ways to identify far more effective, lower-cost methods. Any experiment results that seemed promising could go immediately into broader-scale tests.

When the online contest results were available, I could screen the possible solutions to see which ones might be easily and quickly tested on a small scale and focus next on trying such potential solutions.

After all the small-scale tests were completed, I should next screen for the difficulty in applying the methods that worked well. Obviously, I should place a lower priority on the methods that require lots of my time and attention while emphasizing approaches involving efforts that others could do better than I could at little cost (such as creating interactive software-based versions of the materials I've prepared in the past by using existing software templates).

The difficulty of attracting the right people varies with the learning method. Ways of learning that don't need much review or supervision would be emphasized.

To check the natural interest, I could use a survey, test various ads through Google's AdWords, or tie my tests to creating solutions for topics that have high Google search rankings. None of such methods would be expensive or slow. I could then test actual demand by making offers that would result in inquiries and measure the responses to determine which offers were most appealing.

To reduce the risk of not making fast progress, I should implement at least three different initiatives that would not have to compete with one another for resources or attention.

Naturally, if you are thinking of doing something that's for a manufacturing, retail, or capital-intensive business, you won't be able to move as quickly, cheaply, or smoothly … unless, perhaps, you consider how outsourcing might give you whatever speed and flexibility you desire. Many outsourcing organizations now specialize in providing all aspects of design and implementation for breakthrough solutions. You just have to define for them what you want to achieve. It can be expensive to work in this way, but the costs may well be lower than for your own efforts.

Even if you are engaged in manufacturing, retail, or capital-intensive businesses, you can still do lots of cheap, quick testing by simulating benefits and observing stakeholder reactions. Then, you can rely on outsourcers to speed implementation of the most appealing choices.

Now that you understand about using goals and strategies to ensure that you gain a faster start with chain-reaction 2,000 percent solutions for reducing costs of all stakeholders by 96 percent, let's shift focus to making stakeholders irresistibly attracted to areas where you need help in getting a fast start. Why is such a focus valuable? Irresistible attraction brings more resources, faster, and at lower cost to improve your chain-reaction 2,000 percent cost-reduction solutions.

Here's an example. From its inception, Amazon.com rapidly developed its online selling of new books. However, this distribution channel had a big drawback for customers: You couldn't browse a book to check it out before purchasing in the way you could in a bookstore.

What could Amazon.com do instead? The company first encouraged publishers to share information online about the book, such as reviews in important publications. Such reviews, however, often didn't come out until months after a book had been published. With newspaper and magazine profits being squeezed, the space in those publications dedicated to book reviews was rapidly disappearing.

Seeking a credible alternative to such reviews, Amazon.com hired people to look at books and to write very brief reviews. A productive reviewer could take a look at and write brief comments concerning thirty new books a day. But that was expensive. Even at a cost of $15 an hour for reviewers, this process cost over $3.75 a review. The worst problem, however, was that Amazon.com could not find enough fast book reviewers to help keep up with the deluge of new books.

From its earliest days, Amazon.com had been interested in letting its customers write about books in the form of "customer comments." After just a few months of printing such comments on its Web site, some avid book readers were touting the praises of this benefit to all who would listen. The customer comments were often very candid, and sometimes brutally frank and funny. This process became like an online reality game concerning famous (and not-so-famous) authors in which everyone could play.

Amazon.com grew exponentially faster than anyone could have imagined due to the dual appeal of more easily being able to find and order books not usually carried in local bookstores and the appeal of customer comments. Since many of Amazon.com's costs were relatively fixed (such as for site design and maintenance, research and development, list updating, warehouses, and corporate overhead), adding more customers caused the average cost for such activities to plummet. Within four years, such costs were less than 4 percent of what they had been on a per-order basis.

Then, Amazon.com had a major insight: Why not make it more appealing to write customer comments? The company's solution in 2000 was to introduce a customer commentary ranking based on the "helpful" and "not helpful" votes various comment writers received from other customers. Although at first there were no tangible rewards for rankings, thousands of people who were already writing such comments scrambled to write a lot more of them. As an example, the woman who eventually became the number one Amazon reviewer in the United States went from writing one review a day to publishing as many as fifty. The number of customer reviewers soon shot up from tens of thousands to millions.

As the number and diversity of such customer comments increased, sales of books on Amazon.com also zoomed. The added growth, in turn, further reduced fixed costs as a percentage of sales.

As costs dropped, the prices that Amazon.com charged for books also declined. Before long, the site added the opportunity for others (including customers) to sell their new and used books. Prices from such sellers were even lower. By making a profit on such seller transactions, Amazon.com could then charge even less for the books it directly sold.

Notice that the fascination with finding out what others thought drove the cost reductions. By now, putting up these customer comments is probably a source of profits, rather than a net cost. Amazon.com makes profits because it sells advertising on its offering pages and those who post such comments also buy more products at the Web site. Who knew that result would be possible?

The greatest thing that any business founder can learn is how to lead millions of people into taking actions that they enjoy. After the source of public fascination is found, deliver more and more irresistible reasons to indulge that fascination. When you do so in ways that reduce your and your stakeholders' costs, you have the potential for a chain-reaction cost-reduction 2,000 percent solution.

Shortly after starting my consulting firm, I had that experience. I coined a phrase that became widely known: "value-maximizing strategy." Mitchell and Company was the only organization doing any work at the time in this discipline. Newspapers and magazines were soon writing articles about the subject. CEO speeches and company annual reports headlined the concept. I got to the point where I wouldn't tell people I met in social situations what I did because they would want to talk about my work for hours.

As a result of the increased interest, our marketing programs were highly effective. Our cost to acquire clients dropped dramatically while our ability to charge more for our services increased. Marketing costs as a percentage of sales dropped by more than 96 percent.

However, we did not become a giant consulting firm: We would have had to add a lot more kinds of services before that would have been possible. But the foundation for that opportunity arose because of the enormous fascination business leaders felt for value-maximizing strategy and the great pleasure they enjoyed from expanding stock price.

If you have located activities that fascinate millions, you are at a good starting point. If you haven't located such areas, you should start searching for them. Begin by looking at what fascinates people you want to influence about other industries, companies, and activities. Then, think about how such attributes might be added to what you do. After that, consider how your costs and those of other stakeholders could be driven to near zero (or even turned into profit centers) by triggering and harnessing irresistible fascination.

Even when dealing with an irresistible attraction, many people may hang back from acting. I was reminded of this disconnect recently when I asked my small business students if they had tasted Grey Poupon mustard, the leading premium mustard brand in the United States. Half the class said they had never tried it.

Well, that was quite an important bit of information. Why? Experience has taught that most people who try Grey Poupon mustard like the product so much that they never want to use any other mustard, despite the product being quite costly compared to its most popular competitors.

Acting on this huge taste preference, Grey Poupon's managers have done a lot to encourage people to try their mustard. A key early breakthrough was selling individual servings of the spicy concoction to airlines for use with deli sandwiches. Many other excellent sampling programs followed. Despite following this strategy for over 35 years, half my class of future entrepreneurs (classic prospects for this up-market product) hadn't tried Grey Poupon. Clearly, even more trial-oriented marketing had been needed than had been done.

Despite the brand's amazing success, one key ingredient in creating a chain-reaction 2,000 percent cost solution was missing: Stakeholders weren't given an early incentive to jump on Grey Poupon's bandwagon.

More than a billion dollars in profits were probably missed because of insufficient trial. I'm sure you'll agree that's a pretty big mistake of omission.

Grey Poupon's biggest costs are for marketing, distribution, and packaging. By developing the market faster and gaining a higher market share, such costs would have been less than half what they are today in terms of a physical unit of mustard served. As a result, the price could have been a lot lower while the company enjoyed still higher profits per bite.

What are some of the things that Grey Poupon's managers could have done that they didn't do?

- To create more visibility at lower cost than by using advertising, celebrities should have been put under contract to order and to eat the mustard at high-profile social events.

- In sandwich shops, customers should have been provided with free samples to try on their cold cuts.

- Comparison taste tests with leading mustards should have been conducted in supermarkets and the results publicized.

- Caterers who wanted to use Grey Poupon should have been provided with large discounts for bulk purchases of branded packets and table-top bottles.

- A fan club should have been founded to sponsor fun activities for using Grey Poupon in innovative ways, such as through unusual cooking contests.

- An early advertising program should have been built around the theme of "Do you know what you're missing?" to encourage people to taste the product.

- Restaurants should have been provided with advertising allowances for adding notes to menus about dishes that contained Grey Poupon.

I'm sure you have your own ideas about what else could have been beneficially added.

I was involved in the brand's early activities, and I remember well that few people believed in the product's potential as much as three of us did. As a result, minimal efforts were made to create a bandwagon effect.

A lesson for me is that I could have probably purchased the brand then for less than $500,000 and built it into a world-class brand worth over $2 billion. If you see an opportunity to create a bandwagon effect with someone else's offering, think about how you can acquire the offering or company so that you can pursue this advantaged strategy as an owner, acting on behalf of all stakeholders.

What's the key learning from this lesson? **You can use goals, common fascinations, and incentives to gain a faster start in creating and implementing chain-reaction 2,000 percent cost-reduction solutions that will almost instantly expand your profits by twenty times after implementation while reducing** costs by more than 96 percent (or increasing social benefits by more than twenty times) for stakeholders where they believe they will gain the most profits and increased cash flow.

<u>Assignments</u>

1. What methods for getting a faster start with creating and implementing chain-reaction 2,000 percent cost-reduction solutions are you not yet using?

2. What sources of mass fascination are you not yet using to help you gain a faster start with creating and implementing chain-reaction 2,000 percent cost-reduction solutions?

3. What bandwagon effects could be established by nurturing sources of mass fascination for creating and implementing chain-reaction 2,000 percent cost-reduction solutions in ways that are you not using now?

4. Which incentives for creating band-wagon effects are inexpensive, are hard for competitors to duplicate or neutralize, and supply lasting cost advantages?

5. Which of such methods are inexpensive, are unlikely to provide inaccurate information, and have low visibility so that competitors won't get wind of your ideas in advance?

6. Which of these methods can be applied at the same time without straining your resources?

7. What strategic opportunities for creating chain-reaction 2,000 percent cost-reduction solutions should you focus on to make a faster start?

Lesson Twenty-Eight

Use Zero-Based Analysis and
Create the Minimum Core Offering

Now the Angel of the LORD came and sat under the terebinth tree
which was *in Ophrah, which* belonged *to Joash the Abiezrite,*
while his son Gideon threshed wheat in the winepress,
in order to hide it *from the Midianites.*
And the Angel of the LORD appeared to him, and said to him,
"The LORD is with you, you mighty man of valor!"
Gideon said to Him,
"O my lord, if the LORD is with us,
why then has all this happened to us?
And where are *all His miracles which our fathers told us about,*
saying, 'Did not the LORD bring us up from Egypt?'
But now the LORD has forsaken us
and delivered us into the hands of the Midianites."
Then the LORD turned to him and said,
"Go in this might of yours, and you shall save Israel
from the hand of the Midianites. Have I not sent you?"
So he said to Him, "O my Lord, how can I save Israel?
Indeed my clan is *the weakest in Manasseh,*
and I am *the least in my father's house."*
And the LORD said to him,
"Surely I will be with you,
and you shall defeat the Midianites as one man."

— Judges 6:11-16 (NKJV)

We consider an older concept in this lesson, one that has often been applied to cost-reduction thinking: zero-based analysis. You may know this concept as "zero-based costing."

Zero-based analysis reverses the usual way of thinking in which many people start by looking at how to remove costs from what is already being spent. Zero-based analysis starts, instead, by assuming that no costs need to be spent and grudgingly adds costs only after being convinced that they cannot be avoided.

Imagine that most cost-reduction analysis begins with a full pail of water (representing all costs) and uses a doll's spoon to ladle out some water. Zero-based analysis starts with an empty pail and adds water (costs) one drop at a time after microscopic examination.

There's a weakness in the way the zero-based mental discipline has often been applied: Some people haven't erased enough preconceptions from their minds about how business should be conducted before starting to add costs. For instance, those who have always worked in nice offices are likely to add the cost of nice offices as essential. Yet we know that most businesses today can be conducted virtually and through outsourcers so that no nice offices are required; in fact, no offices at all may be needed.

Start by considering the ideal best practice for having low costs and high effectiveness as the zero-cost level. Making that consideration requires you to think about many different ways that offerings can be provided.

Let me give you a few examples of what I mean to start you off:

1. Assume that you now offer a product. Can you offer information instead of a product?

    Products are typically acquired by customers to obtain some desired result. Let's say that you are in the business of providing hair shampoo. It might seem strange to suggest information as an alternative to hair shampoo. Nevertheless, several potential applications come to my mind:

    a. Shampoo isn't hard to make. You could provide custom recipes for making shampoos that are more highly individualized than what can be bought in a store. Your directions might include how to test hair to identify the most beneficial ingredients and how much of each one is required. The result can be cleaner, more attractive hair than a person would accomplish by using standard shampoos.

    b. Some people might not want to make their own shampoos, but they would like to gain the benefits of using a more customized shampoo. Your information could explain how to test hair and to mix combinations of existing shampoos to gain a near-perfect individual result.

    c. Shampoos will do less damage to hair if used in conjunction with better hair-care practices. You could also describe how to test hair and scalp to identify how an individual's hair should be optimally dried, arranged, and styled to gain an optimal appearance and to have healthier hair and scalp.

    Developing such information is going to be costly, but the cost to deliver the information will be minimal. If you provide the information in such a way that each interaction requires another visit to your database, you can establish quite a good ongoing revenue stream.

2. Assume that you now offer a service. Can you offer information instead of the service?

    I remember when personal computer software first became available for analyzing the technical aspects of finding stocks for investment. The programs were slow and awkward, but impressive insights were gained. Since then, such software has become very elaborate and is still time-consuming to use. Unless you find all the details fascinating, the effort can feel excessive. The purpose of having the software is to make profitable investments. How could information be a substitute for such analytical software? Here are some possible alternatives:

a. Using technical-analysis software presumes that the analysis such software provides helps you to make better investment decisions. It could take weeks of effort to determine which technical methods have worked best for an individual security. Large institutional investors can afford to do that, but you can't. The software company could provide fast, inexpensive ways to check which technical tools have been best at predicting the prices of each security. With that information in hand, most investors could probably employ bits and pieces of free technical software from various stock brokers and never need to buy any technical software. Your information would help level the playing field for finding good opportunities between individuals and large institutions. The cost of developing the information would be similar from security to security so such an information-based business could start with the largest, most widely held securities that would attract the most customers and add on selectively from there. Serving each additional customer with the existing information for a security would add virtually no costs.

b. Another approach would be to provide unique data for making technical evaluations of securities. For instance, such data might include the percentage of institutionally owned shares that have been held continually for over five years. Such information in this case could help indicate how much increased buying and selling would affect the price of a security.

c. A third method of providing new information would be to supplement what companies report with data that can be obtained in other public sources so that the context for stock-price shifts could be easier to understand.

3. You now provide information, but you want to reduce the cost of developing that information to near zero.

This opportunity could be grasped by creating low-cost incentives to information providers for gaining status and recognition. For instance, providers might be ranked relative to one another based on visitor votes about how helpful their information has been. If costs are low enough, you could provide the information for free and make your profit from selling advertising on pages that visitors view.

4. You now provide free information, but you want to gain more profit from such information without spending any more money.

You might work with a partner to make related offerings available to your information site's visitors in exchange for a share of the partner's revenues, payments that would exceed the usual advertising rates. In order to increase profits, the cost of developing the site to add these new revenues would, of course, be borne by your partner.

Now, let's take the analysis a step further to appreciate what the "minimum core offering" is that delivers just the right value that customers, end users, and other stakeholders want and can best use. Why is that an important subject? *Whenever you provide more than the minimum that people need and desire, you add costs that often harm them and you.*

Let's look at an example. Many Americans drive a large pickup truck or sport utility vehicle that will take her or him to rugged off-road sites, carry a half ton of cargo plus six people, tow a large trailer, and drive safely at high speeds on good roads. A new vehicle of either type typically costs about $27,000 and burns gasoline as if it were free. Who needs all that? If you cut timber in remote locations, this vehicle might be a good choice. If you are part of a typical suburban family of four, the vehicle's appeal is primarily to your ego … it simply makes you look and feel more powerful. If appearance is all that counts for you, spend a lot less money by just buying a cowboy hat, great boots, and a fancy belt buckle.

A clever vehicle-leasing company might offer a program to use a variety of vehicles after just a little advance notice. You could have a truck or SUV when tasks required it, a nice sports car for high-speed jaunts on winding roads in good weather, an easy-to-park small car for shopping in places where it's hard to find a spot, and an impressive luxury car for taking your in-laws out to dinner. If the leasing company picked up and delivered the vehicle of your choice, such a lease package could leave you with somewhat similar convenience and much less cost than owning or leasing multiple vehicles. That's pretty nice!

Let's consider a more extreme example of overproviding. Many restaurants would like to earn more money per diner. Realizing that it's hard to improve food quality and service past a certain level, many restaurants instead raise prices and justify what they've done by providing you with enough food for more than one meal. But in making such offerings, they don't limit themselves to dishes that reheat well. As a result, you can't eat most of what they serve and often don't want the rest for the next day at home. All that's happened is that you've been sold a lot more food than you wanted or needed.

Food can often be only part of the reason why you choose a restaurant. You may be looking for a place to relax, a nice environment to lighten your mood, or the chance to spend time with people you care about. It would be possible to establish restaurants that only serve, but do not prepare, food. Such establishments could instead rely on sourcing food from neighboring restaurants and beautifully placing that food on attractive, properly heated or chilled dishes. With so little to do in the kitchen, the restaurant could be a lot smaller, more could be invested in appearance, and management could focus more on providing superior service. As a result, the cost of the meal might be smaller, yet the experience could be much nicer.

Let's look next at restaurants that use superior ingredients and apply great preparation methods. The cost of such meals can be astronomical. How could you provide such fine meals, but at a much lower cost? A restaurant could offer catering packages of partially prepared ingredients that could be finished in a person's home kitchen in half hour or less by following "foolproof" directions.

Before you get too excited about this idea, let's further deconstruct it. You don't really need a restaurant to accomplish that result. Instead, a gourmet grocery store could offer high-quality ingredients that are partially prepared for finishing at home. Such an approach could take about 90 percent more costs out of providing the offering.

Well, that's not the end either, is it? You could focus on making great dishes so easy to prepare that even I could create them from scratch. Then, you are simply selling someone the ingredients and the directions. By taking out any preparation cost, you could reduce costs by another 40 percent.

But that's not the ultimate. You could simply provide the information on a Web site that explains where to purchase the ingredients in your area and how to assemble the ingredients for a great meal. While the cost to deliver the information wouldn't be zero, it could be pretty close.

Why would any restaurant want to provide such information for people who like good food? If you help people to have great meals at home, they are more likely to patronize you when they want a great meal someplace else. By focusing in the restaurant on serving dishes that greatly benefit from an expert chef's touch, there's a reason for someone who appreciates superb food to eat out occasionally at such a fine-dining establishment.

Notice from this analysis that a restaurant can become more effective at its traditional roles as well as locate new roles to profitably play in lower-cost ways.

Here are questions to apply concerning your own offerings that will help you to duplicate the mental processes I've been describing:

1. Who can't use all of what you offer?

2. What aspects can't which people use?

3. How could such aspects be eliminated?

4. Of the aspects that remain, how can an offering's costs be reduced for a stakeholder?

5. How can the remaining costs be reduced even more?

6. How can offerings be tailored to be even lower cost for providing just the most important parts of customers' and stakeholders' needs?

7. How can complementary offerings provide for more of customers' and stakeholders' needs while further reducing overall costs?

What's the key learning from this lesson? **You can use zero-based analysis to create 2,000 percent cost-reduction solutions that will almost instantly expand your profits by twenty times by only supplying the minimum core offering while reducing costs by more than 96 percent or increasing social benefits by more than twenty times of what you will be spending for all stakeholders where they believe that they will gain the most profit and cash flow benefits.**

Assignments

1. What aspects of your existing offerings add unnecessary costs?

2. What costs can you totally eliminate while still providing the most desired benefits?

3. Where can you deliver offerings at virtually no incremental cost and demand will be large?

4. Do you have products or services that you could replace with low-cost information?

5. How could you eliminate almost all information-development costs?

6. How can you gain profits from providing other peoples' products and services?

7. How could the appeal of your offerings be focused into several lower-cost alternatives?

8. How could you employ other organizations to help you provide part of what customers need while improving what you do?

9. How can you add low-cost choices for those who only want one or two dimensions of your offerings' benefits?

10. How can complementary offerings with fewer optional features attract more people while reducing everyone's costs by 96 percent?

Lesson Twenty-Nine

Eliminate Overhead and Distribution Costs and Select Suppliers with Superior Business Models

Another parable He put forth to them, saying:
"The kingdom of heaven is like a mustard seed,
which a man took and sowed in his field,
which indeed is the least of all the seeds;
but when it is grown
it is greater than the herbs and becomes a tree,
so that the birds of the air come and nest in its branches."

— Matthew 13:31-32 (NKJV)

This lesson applies zero-based analysis to the minimum core offering to eliminate overhead and distribution costs, and to select suppliers with superior business models. Let's begin by considering *overhead costs*.

How Can You Eliminate More Overhead Costs?

There is *desirable treasure,*
And oil in the dwelling of the wise,
But a foolish man squanders it.

— Proverbs 21:20 (NKJV)

What is an overhead cost? Definitions vary, but most people agree that any cost not directly used to produce or to supply an offering to a customer is an overhead cost.

Why begin this lesson about zero-based analysis with eliminating overhead costs? Such costs are not only large, but overhead activities add many other unnecessary costs. Here's an example. A survey of Leading Assistants to Outstanding Chief Executive Officers members showed that following up on casual comments and questions by CEOs often occupied more than 20 percent of all working hours within a company. A similar effect also occurs among employees who are lower in the chain of command whenever any more senior person in the company (from the CFO down to the lowest-level supervisor who has people working under him or her) makes a comment or asks a question.

In addition, most people would like to have more people reporting to them. When more people report to a supervisor, most organizations will pay more to the supervising person. Any time you add a person to an organization to supervise someone else, empire building is encouraged and unnecessary costs are likely to be added.

There is also a lot of self-satisfaction among company leaders who believe that because they are at or near the organization's top, they must be good at what they do. Right? Not necessarily. Someone who has simply run healthy businesses in good economic times often rises in a company as fast as someone who has done a good job of dealing with difficult challenges.

In an organization where there are few problems, promotion mostly follows popularity. As many people describe who is promoted, it's like being back in high school trying to stand out as the coolest guy or gal.

A particularly harmful set of behaviors often occurs when company leaders think that they are well above average in performance, but they are not. When such a victory of self-confidence over reality occurs, the door is usually closed to cost cutting, outsourcing, and new strategies. A more useful belief for company leaders to hold is that everyone else knows a lot more than the leader does, but that the company's leader can find out what others know by doing the right homework.

What's the ultimate in reducing overhead costs? Not having any such costs. You won't find many companies approaching that ideal, but these days it's possible to come a lot closer than it used to be.

You might be skeptical that much can be done about reducing overhead costs because you wonder how costs of complying with government regulations can be avoided. Well, in many countries regulatory costs are inevitable. But you don't have to operate in all countries. In countries with less regulation, you may be able to restructure your operations so that many, if not all, such regulatory costs can be eliminated.

Here's an example. You might be thinking about operating in country A. If the cost of regulation is the only reason not to be there, you can approach country A's government with an offer to open an operation if the regulatory costs can be eliminated. While the law may require complying with such regulations, the government may still have the flexibility to grant you tax credits or provide other incentives that offset the regulatory costs to operate there.

Companies can also often reduce the minimum number of employees required to accomplish necessary overhead activities. As an example, you might help the most effective of your key employees to establish businesses that provide such critical activities to your organization. Through contractual arrangements, you could obtain favorable terms and also restrict such businesses from serving your competitors.

If you still have employees, you can transition from mostly fixed to variable compensation that's tied to performance that each employee can directly influence. Such a compensation switch might mean production incentives for manufacturing personnel, more emphasis on commissions for salespeople, and bonuses for cost reductions and adding customers for those who can influence those activities.

While such ways of eliminating overhead sound fine in the abstract, how practical are they? Nucor, the pioneer in producing steel from scrap materials, has been very successful with such methods. Nucor began by looking at customers' minimum requirements. For many applications, steel made by using virgin raw materials had no advantage over steel made with less-expensive recycled materials. Naturally, if you can simply melt old steel, it's a lot cheaper than if you begin with iron ore, coke, trace minerals, lots of liquid oxygen, and huge facilities.

Most steelmakers pay their employees high wages. Nucor had a different idea. Its employees would receive low wages and a big percentage of the value of any productivity gains they made. This approach meant that even a floor sweeper would earn more than half of his or her pay in the form of productivity bonuses rather than from hourly earnings.

Because Nucor was frequently adding new facilities, the company was able to negotiate for tax savings from local and state governments, providing offsets for regulatory and employee-benefit costs. Their facilities also don't pollute as much as traditional steel operations.

What if you have a marketing business? The costs of adding customers can be more than the cost of goods. Today, even marketing has become an area where performance counts. Many media today don't charge by the amount of advertising displayed but, rather, by the results gained from the advertising. In essence, more and more media are operating as sales agents you pay only when a sale is made.

Offerings that employ less overt marketing are often more successful than those that use traditional methods. Newer marketing methods might include a branded offering sponsoring a contest that most people will support while trying to gain attention for the offering. If you would like to understand more about this alternative, take a look at *Buying In* (Random House, 2008) by Rob Walker. You'll be amused to find out how often savvy customers today deliberately pick the lowest-priced offering that doesn't advertise.

What about the costs of litigation? Eliminate mistakes and you won't have nearly as many lawsuits. Buy the right insurance or self-insure for the mistakes that remain, and you can cut some of the remaining costs. It's almost always cheaper to settle legitimate claims than to contest them. There are also many alternative dispute resolution programs that can save money. If you go to trial, law firms are increasingly willing to work on a contingency basis tied to the results that are gained through settlement or litigation.

What about the corporate headquarters building? Put it on a piece of land that goes way up in value, and you'll eventually be able to pay for the building's construction through selling the underlying land.

I'm sure you appreciate the point: Aim for zero overhead. After minimizing your core offering, reducing overhead becomes a lot easier to do. You'll be amazed at how many overhead costs are required to perform activities that aren't needed for your minimum core offering.

What's the key point about eliminating overhead? **You can use zero-based analysis to create 2,000 percent cost-reduction solutions for eliminating overhead to help reduce costs by more than 96 percent or increase social benefits by more than twenty times for all stakeholders where they believe that they will gain the most profit and cash flow.**

Assignments

1. What aspects of your core offering add unnecessary overhead costs?

2. How could current overhead costs be eliminated without affecting nonemployee stakeholders?

3. How could you employ other organizations to help you provide part of your overhead activities at less cost and with greater effectiveness?

4. How can you substitute variable costs tied to performance for fixed overhead costs?

5. How you turn overhead costs into profit sources that are larger than the overhead costs?

6. How can you help employees become such effective entrepreneurial thinkers and doers that their added profit contributions more than offset their costs to the organization?

How Can You Eliminate Distribution Costs?

And the word of the Lord was being spread throughout all the region.

— Acts 13:49 (NKJV)

Next, let's turn our attention to eliminating costs that occur outside of your organization, beginning with *distribution*. By distribution cost, I mean any costs associated with taking the offering from your enterprise to the ultimate end user. Let's look at two examples to ensure that you understand what we are focusing on.

Let's first consider coffee. If I go to my local Starbucks coffee bar and order a venti (large) mocha coffee, I'll pay around $4.75 for the privilege (before consumption taxes). Of that $4.75, approximately $0.10 will go to the farmers who grew the coffee beans that provide a key ingredient for my brew. To that coffee grower, $4.65 of the $4.75 I pay will be seen as a distribution cost.

As a second example, let's consider an e-book that I download from the Internet. Many such e-books are now priced around $9.95. If the author has a standard publishing contract, about 25 percent (or $2.49) of that amount will be paid to the author. For the author, $7.46 of the price represents distribution costs.

As you can see from both examples, distribution costs to reach end users are often much larger than the price an enterprise or an individual receives for an offering, even if the rest of the distribution chain doesn't do much to improve what the enterprise originally sold.

In such circumstances, many organizations will start selling directly to end users. For instance, the author can self-publish a different e-book (eliminating the need to share revenues with a publisher and an online book seller), selling it on the author's own Web site for $5.00, cutting the price to end users by more than half, while increasing revenues per offering by over 100 percent. While there are some costs to developing and maintaining such a Web site, it doesn't take many sales per month to reduce such costs to quite a small amount per book.

If there is no way to sell directly to end users, alternative strategies require creating new, lower-cost distribution channels. For example, most individual books can be printed on demand for about $4.00 in the United States. Realizing that, some authors formed a company called BookSurge that allowed authors to self-publish and to enjoy low costs while selling through online booksellers to gain distribution. The program was so effective that Amazon.com eventually bought BookSurge and merged it with another entity Amazon.com owned, CreateSpace. More efficiencies followed. Today, the self-published author of a book retailing for $19.95 on Amazon.com will receive a royalty payment of about $6.95 per copy through CreateSpace after paying modest setup costs. If sales are substantial, the royalty is almost all profit. By comparison, a traditional publisher would usually pay a royalty of only about $2.00 per copy on the same book sale by Amazon.com or at a bricks-and-mortar book store.

As you can see, you need to understand the economics of how your offering travels through to an end user, what intermediaries do, and how costs are incurred at each stage. Then, see how you can eliminate layers of distribution, reduce the roles played by each remaining layer, and cut the prices that are charged.

A brilliant way to accomplish such streamlining is by providing a reason for eliminating the layers of distribution that will make good sense to end users. For instance, if an author offers customized books rather than copies of identical books, end users would expect to work directly with the author to make the right customization and gain added benefits such as having the books autographed.

After a minimum number of items are produced, it is often no more costly to produce custom versions than standard ones. Thus, people who hire an author to speak at a conference might like having a custom version of the author's book that contains material not available to those who attend any other conference. If the conference sponsor buys one copy for each listener, there's little more required for the custom version than inserting some unpublished material the author had previously written that is relevant for the purpose.

The coffee growers might develop a custom blend of organic coffees that they sell as a branded item through the Internet. The growers could purchase shipping, roasting, and packaging services from others to turn their beans into a product that many end users would prefer. With reduced costs and suitable marketing through online videos, the growers could sell a superior organic coffee blend direct to end users at a price that would be well below what consumers pay now for lower-quality coffee purchased in a supermarket.

With such lower-cost distribution in place, the growers could also operate their own branded coffee bars to serve superior organic offerings featuring their own beans. I believe that such a concept would have large appeal to those who care about organic products and are concerned about the low incomes that most coffee farmers and their workers receive.

What's the key point about eliminating distribution costs? **You can use zero-based analysis to create 2,000 percent cost-reduction solutions that eliminate distribution expenses to help you reduce costs by more than 96 percent or increase social benefits by more than twenty times of what you will be spending for all stakeholders where they believe that they will gain the most profit and cash flow.**

Assignments

1. **What aspects of your distribution to the ultimate end user add unnecessary costs?**

2. **How could distribution costs be eliminated without harming stakeholders?**

3. **How could you employ other organizations to help you provide part of your offering's distribution at less cost and with greater effectiveness?**

4. **How can you eliminate most of your customers' and end users' variable distribution costs?**

5. **How can you turn distribution costs into profit opportunities?**

How Can You Greatly Reduce Costs by Selecting Suppliers with Superior Business Models?

Now therefore, let Pharaoh select a discerning and wise man,
and set him over the land of Egypt.

— Genesis 41:33 (NKJV)

This section examines *choosing suppliers with superior business models* to help you provide the minimum core offering at less expense. Almost every organization has suppliers. Why? Someone else can almost always perform some of the functions you need done more effectively or less expensively than your organization can.

Let me give you an example from my Heublein days when I was a corporate planner. Our most profitable product was vodka, but we didn't make the grain neutral spirits used in our product. That critical ingredient was brought in by rail tank car from Archer Daniels Midland (ADM), a big agricultural processor. All we did was filter the spirits through charcoal to further purify it, and then fill bottles with the filtered vodka and distilled water.

My boss once asked me if Heublein should start making its own grain neutral spirits. I analyzed what was involved and concluded that we would have to produce and sell sixty times more volume than we needed for our vodka business in order to build a plant that would give us lower costs than what we paid to buy this ingredient from ADM. At that volume, the investment would be huge and the return on investment would be meager … assuming that we could sell all the volume that we didn't need. The same time and effort would yield far more profits if we instead added a few percentage points more volume in vodka sales. Because ADM had many more customers for processed grain-based products, it could afford to have such a plant and still earn a decent profit on it. The ADM approach constituted a superior business model for producing grain neutral spirits.

One of the most successful ways to reduce costs is by choosing suppliers who have such business model advantages. When that happens, your effectiveness can be higher and costs lower.

Let me give you a different example. One of the oak trees along our driveway died. It was quite a tall tree, over sixty feet high, and it leaned precariously over the electrical power lines that ran into our house. If the tree fell straight towards the house, it could potentially do over a hundred thousand dollars of damage. In addition, the house would be uninhabitable for months while repairs took place.

I decided it was wiser to remove the tree than to hope it would fall away from the house. I found that the electric company wouldn't remove the tree because it didn't threaten any power lines but ours into the house. Also knowing what tree extractions cost from doing such work with my father as a teenager, I estimated the removal cost from a standard supplier to be about $3,000.

I wanted, however, to see how much I could lower the cost without losing any performance I cared out. I remembered that my small business students had taught me that they often started new companies by moonlighting on nights and weekends while still working for their employers. Because such new small businesses had low costs, they could often charge quite low prices for experienced people providing skilled services. All such students advertised their services through an online site called craigslist.com.

I located the local tree removal companies that were listed on that Web site. There were ten of them, all of which promised free estimates. I sent ten e-mails asking for free estimates. Within a week, I had received seven estimates.

There are two primary alternatives for taking down such a tree. The safer way is to use a large crane holding a gondola in which a tree trimmer can stand and move to various places on the tree to tie ropes and to make cuts with a chain saw. The more dangerous way is to climb the tree, cut off small sections one at a time, and carefully lower such sections to the ground using ropes. If the tree breaks while using the latter method, there's a chance of injury for the person working in the tree.

The more expert tree removal people felt that they could climb the tree and cut it down in that way. They varied in price from $1,000 to $1,200.

The less experienced tree people felt that they needed a crane. Since none of them owned a crane, they would have to rent. Most added the cost of such a rental to the cost of the job and quoted from $1,300 to $1,600.

Some of the tree companies focused on business model innovation. They looked to perform several jobs during the same twenty-four hours so that the cost of the crane would be less for each job. It would take longer to get the job done due to waiting for them to accumulate enough jobs, but this approach would eliminate most of the cost for renting a crane.

Two of the tree companies also asked me about my needs. Did I want to keep the wood to burn in my fireplaces? I said, "No." Since both companies were in the firewood business, they could then take the wood, convert it into firewood, and earn an additional profit. As a result, they could discount the tree removal work for me.

Of the two that were in the firewood business, one also wanted to do four jobs during one twenty-four-hour crane rental. This company quoted me a price of $600. Naturally, I hired this organization. Their superior business model saved me 80 percent of the cost of normal tree removal.

Let's consider another alternative. I could have kept the wood, aged it, and later split it into firewood. I am physically able to do all of that work. If I had, I would have acquired about three cords of wood (worth about $1,400 at the time). If I had hired someone for $1,000 to take the tree down, I would have gotten the tree lowered for free, benefited from many hours of good exercise, gotten paid $400 for my work compared to buying firewood, and enjoyed many warm fires.

Such an alternative is often available when you put together a superior business model from a supplier and your own unique capabilities and needs: The results can cost nothing, or even yield a profit.

I want to encourage you to look at every activity that your organization might do ... or might have someone else do as a supplier ... and consider how superior business models on both sides might more than eliminate all costs. You can use the concepts and questions in *The Ultimate Competitive Advantage; The 2,000 Percent Squared Solution;* and *Adventures of an Optimist* to identify such opportunities.

In this analysis, realize that you may not find a supplier who already has the business model you need. That's okay. You simply need to help your potential supplier understand what the missing benefits are and to make the necessary improvements in its business model. When you make arrangements for such changes, be sure to tie up the supplier or suppliers so that the advantage isn't automatically transferred to a competitor who starts working with the same supplier.

What's the key point about selecting suppliers with superior business models? **You can use zero-based analysis to create 2,000 percent cost-reduction solutions to choose suppliers with superior business models that will almost instantly expand your profits after implementation by only supplying the minimum core offering while helping you reduce costs by more than 96 percent or increase social benefits by more than twenty times of what you will be spending for all stakeholders where they believe that they will gain the most profit and cash flow.**

Assignments

1. **What aspects of your potential business model add unnecessary operating or supplier costs?**

2. **How could you eliminate such costs without harming stakeholders?**

3. **How could you employ other organizations to help you provide part of your supplier-cost-reduction activities at less expense and with greater effectiveness?**

4. **How can you turn suppliers into a profit source, rather than being stakeholders that add costs?**

Lesson Thirty

Help Customers Develop
Superior Business Models,
and Change End-User Behavior

This I say, therefore, and testify in the Lord,
that you should no longer walk
as the rest of the Gentiles walk,
in the futility of their mind,
having their understanding darkened,
being alienated from the life of God,
because of the ignorance that is in them,
because of the blindness of their heart;
who, being past feeling,
have given themselves over to lewdness,
to work all uncleanness with greediness.
But you have not so learned Christ,
if indeed you have heard Him
and have been taught by Him,
as the truth is in Jesus: that you put off,
concerning your former conduct,
the old man which grows corrupt
according to the deceitful lusts,
and be renewed in the spirit of your mind,
and that you put on the new man
which was created according to God,
in true righteousness and holiness.

— Ephesians 4:17-24 (NKJV)

In this lesson, we continue applying zero-based analysis to create the minimum core offering by considering ways to help customers develop superior business models and to change end-user behavior. Let's start with *assisting customers in their development of superior business models.*

143

How Can You Eliminate More Stakeholder Costs by Helping Customers Develop Superior Business Models?

Even the youths shall faint and be weary,
And the young men shall utterly fall,
But those who wait on the LORD
Shall renew their strength;
They shall mount up with wings like eagles,
They shall run and not be weary,
They shall walk and not faint.

— Isaiah 40:30-31 (NKJV)

This section's topic will be controversial with some people. Why? Many business thinkers advocate that suppliers should simply work at making life easy and pleasant for customers so that they receive more and more benefits while only making minimal efforts of their own.

If your customer has an ideal business model, that's good advice. However, such advice doesn't apply if your customer could make great improvements: If your customer is going to lose market share, have problems, or even fail, you should clearly step in to help your customer to survive and to prosper. If you are tactful in such circumstances, your advice will be welcome.

Beyond that, the most demanding customers today expect their suppliers to add more value … including contributions to improved business models. What's more, you can't know how a customer will respond to an improved business model until you share a desirable alternative. You may even be receiving low grades as a supplier for not helping some customers in this way.

While customers are making mistakes, a supplier's silence is almost always harmful to customers. If you simply do whatever they ask without telling them the consequences, you'll end up with customers who will make many mistakes that will hurt them and your organization.

Here's an example of harmful supplier silence from my days as a strategic planner. Our company owned a winery and had contracted for large amounts of grapes to be provided over many years. We either had to turn all those grapes into wine and profitably sell the wine, or take a huge loss on the unsold portion.

Our company felt that it would help if we owned a glass-bottle-making plant based on learning that in many years the profits from making glass bottles exceeded the profits on the wine for our major competitor, Gallo. Having learned that some companies had failed to make new glass-bottle plants operate successfully, our company decided to hedge its bets by forming a joint venture with a bottle-making company. Thinking that such a structure would reduce costs, our company offered the partner a cost-plus management contract to make the bottles.

On the surface, the venture appeared to work well. Our company regularly won awards for innovative packages, we could make anything the designers specified, and the joint venture reported huge profits.

However, our joint-venture partner failed to explain to us what it was costing us to accomplish those results. Because we made so many different kinds of complicated bottles in small volumes, our costs to make many of these bottles were enormous. In fact, we were financially worse off than if we had not been making glass bottles … but bought standard bottles instead. The joint-venture partner didn't mind because our misguided approach increased the profits it earned while crushing the winery's bottom line. We were doubly hurt, by high packaging costs and by paying way too much to have the plant "managed."

As soon as we understood the economics of glass-bottle making, we were able to standardize into a very few, low-cost … but attractive … designs and to slash our costs. As a result, the plant made more bottles … and eventually our partner made more money than ever before. But I believe that partner would never have told us what to do, even if the winery had continued to struggle for profits.

In other cases, customers need a wake-up call because they are harming themselves in ways they should realize on their own. When Mitchell and Company began, one of our consulting clients kept me very busy. But I noticed that he seldom followed my advice. And not following the advice was costing him a fortune.

I invited him to lunch and told him that I quit. There was no point in him paying me if he wasn't going to follow my advice. I felt that he shouldn't have the cost of making bad decisions and the cost of acquiring unused advice. Startled, he vowed to do better ... and he did. Within five years, he turned a net worth of $200,000 into more than $25,000,000.

I am also reminded of this need to be candid, unreserved, and helpful in suggesting improvements by my experience in working with one of my MBA students. This man was taking a course intended to help him make better use of his time. After he made all the changes he learned about, it was clear that he would still be taking three times as long as he should to complete each course. Yet he was eager to race ahead and to start on a particularly difficult academic course. I felt I had no choice but to tell him that he first needed to learn to read and write better and faster. We compromised on his studying these skills on his own while starting the course he wanted to take.

There's a problem we all have. We cannot see ourselves as others see us ... which is usually closer to how we really are than our own perceptions. It's as though we have a large spot on the back of our clothes that we cannot see without first removing our clothes or looking at our backs in a mirror. Anyone who sees the back of our clothes knows that we need to change into something clean, but we don't change until someone says something to us.

Many suppliers attempt to load customers with the most offerings they can at the least marketing cost for them. Such a practice will come to an unhappy end if the customer goes out of business or cannot afford to pay for what isn't really needed.

Other suppliers are quite open about telling customers ways to obtain more benefit out of working together. But if the customer's business model is going to undermine the results, such advice isn't enough for a customer to prosper.

You may also be concerned about customers reacting negatively to your making suggestions about their business models. After all, they are the customers ... your kings and queens, as it were.

Here's a good way to begin: If your customer has any kind of supplier council, ask if you may join it. If that's not possible, ask if you may speak to that group. If that is rejected, ask if you may contact people on the council.

What if your customer doesn't have a supplier council? Well, most companies have some sort of customer council. You might ask your customer if the customer council has been helpful. If the answer is positive, then you could ask if the customer might also like to put together a supplier council. You could offer to help organize the activity. Chances are good that your suggestion would be welcomed.

Once you have access to such a supplier council, you can naturally ask the members if they have thought about evaluating the customer's business model. If you are knowledgeable in this subject (as you surely are after all these lessons), it will be natural for you to be a leading contributor to the evaluation. In the process, you can propose business-model improvements that will ultimately carry the weight of the council's recommendation. Your customer will probably pay attention, particularly if you also sit on similar councils doing parallel investigations for competitors who are also your customers.

If you don't succeed in such efforts to communicate with or to form a supplier council, invite your customer to join your customer council. Be sure that the other customer council members include those who have superior business models of the sort this customer needs. Choose agenda items at such meetings that will include your organization doing more to support improved business models for your customers.

You need only apply what you have learned from this book's lessons to help create substantial cost reductions throughout the economic system that supports and benefits from your customer. If you share information effectively, at some point you should also present this very lesson and persuade your customer to help improve the business models of your customer's customers. In this way, you'll be able to encourage improvements in organizations that you would normally not be able to access. In doing so, be sure to let your customer know that you are happy to be a resource to your customer's customers.

What's the key point about helping customers develop superior business models? **You can use zero-based analysis to create 2,000 percent cost-reduction solutions to help customers develop superior business models that will almost instantly expand stakeholders' and your profits after implementation by only supplying the minimum core offering while helping them and you reduce costs by more than 96 percent or to increase social benefits by more than twenty times of what you will be spending.**

<u>Assignments</u>

1. What aspects of your customers' business models add unnecessary operating or supplier costs?

2. How could your customer eliminate such costs through business-model improvements without harming stakeholders?

3. How could you employ and improve other organizations to help you provide part of your cost-reduction activities as a supplier at less cost and with greater effectiveness?

4. How can you help turn the activities of other suppliers into sources of profit for your customer, rather than continuing to be only a source of costs?

How Can You Reduce Stakeholder Costs by Changing End-User Behavior?

> *"What do you mean when you use this proverb*
> *concerning the land of Israel, saying:*
> *'The fathers have eaten sour grapes,*
> *And the children's teeth are set on edge'?"*
> *"As I live," says the Lord GOD,*
> *"you shall no longer use this proverb in Israel.*
> *Behold, all souls are Mine;*
> *The soul of the father*
> *As well as the soul of the son is Mine;*
> *The soul who sins shall die."*

— Ezekiel 18:2-4 (NKJV)

One morning during the fall of 2008 while energy prices were soaring, I read an article in our local newspaper, the *Boston Globe*, containing interviews with Bostonians about plans to heat their homes during the following winter. In the article, some people said they wouldn't turn on the heat until January. Others planned to keep their thermostats at 58 degrees Fahrenheit. Some were chopping wood to use for cooking fires that would also heat their homes. Many people were buying warmer clothes, putting on layers of such clothes indoors, and installing extra insulation in their homes.

As I read this story, I remembered U.S. President Jimmy Carter appearing on television during the first oil price spike in the 1970s wearing a sweater indoors and advising Americans to set their thermostats at 68 degrees Fahrenheit. I also remembered how most people complained that they couldn't possibly live at such a low interior temperature. Today, few private homes in the colder regions of the United States would have a temperature setting that high in the winter. Many people now find themselves being more active outdoors in the winter because the difference in temperatures between buildings and the outdoors is less. What a difference thirty years and much higher prices can make.

More importantly, I think this example eloquently points out how adaptable end users can be. Provide the right incentives, and end users will find a better solution that makes them feel comfortable.

When the incentive to change is also based on something that people agree with, behavior will shift more rapidly. Before deposit fees were charged on returnable bottles in the United States, hardly anyone bothered to recycle glass. When a fee of about five cents per bottle was introduced, thrifty couples and children who wanted more pocket money began recycling. In addition, homeless people could earn enough to buy three satisfying meals a day by going along the sides of roads and picking up discarded bottles. As children learned more about the environmental benefits of recycling, the rate of glass recycling went higher and higher, even though there was no increase in the amount of the bottle deposit.

Many Americans also didn't like wearing seat belts in cars when manufacturers were first required to provide them. Even after states enacted laws mandating that seat belts be used, many people did not fasten them. Responding to new regulations, manufacturers then designed seat belts that automatically fit around drivers and passengers. Without a lot of extra effort, people in such cars were using seat belts … whether or not they favored the safety feature. Deaths and serious injuries from vehicle accidents declined.

Provide the right incentives, encouragements, and redesigned offerings, and you can totally *change end-user behavior*. Why is that important? In many industries, end-user behavior accounts for a vast and unnecessary percentage of the total costs for the industry. Change behavior in ways that will eliminate or greatly reduce such costs, and you will benefit from a much more attractive business opportunity.

Let's consider the traditional MBA program in the United States as an example. Prior to World War II, hardly anyone followed such a course of study. Why? No one was sure how to teach business, and there was no significant track record of success. After World War II, many men who had served in the military and were starting their careers at an advanced age wanted to learn as quickly as possible how to be effective civilian leaders of major business enterprises. Harvard Business School offered a surrogate for that sort of training through discussing case histories of issues major American companies had faced.

Prior to World War II, college graduates were rarely found in the executive ranks of American businesses. After World War II, the new MBAs were able to leap two levels ahead of those with only high-school degrees by using their reading, math, and analytical business skills to look at problems more thoroughly. Not surprisingly, these MBAs advanced rapidly in their companies and starting salaries rose for MBAs. On a cost-effectiveness basis, these MBA graduates were a bargain for their employers: The new employees arrived with skills that normally would have had to be taught by the company or learned through long experience filled with expensive mistakes.

As the career progress and salary surveys of MBAs were publicized, many people realized they could add hundreds of thousands of dollars to their lifetime incomes by attending a business school and earning an MBA degree. As long as that advantage was true, MBA applications and enrollments zoomed. Today, the trend for more MBA education continues even though it takes many MBAs a decade or more to earn enough increased income to cover the cost of such a two-year education.

With the habit of seeking such knowledge firmly in place in the business community, MBA programs will probably continue to grow … long after they fail to provide enough added economic incentive through increased income. Such programs will simply become like seat belts that automatically fasten: People who plan to go into business management will automatically seek to enroll in and to complete such programs.

What can we conclude from these examples? Six principles apply:

1. You can expect that large shifts in behavior can occur (and quite quickly) if the incentives are large enough.

2. If you provide incentives for all stakeholders to make the change, you will get better results than if you only provide incentives for end users.

3. You should make it more difficult to resist the change than to make the change.

4. You need to avoid having competitors undercut the change.

5. If you can appeal to strongly held end-user values, the spread of change will be faster and more complete.

6. If you focus on making end users feel that their lives have been improved by the change, there will be faster and more thorough shifts in behavior.

Let's consider an example of what might be accomplished by looking at how to shift the behavior of the families buying groceries and nonfood items. The trend in supermarkets has been to offer more and more items, to be open for longer and longer hours, and to provide more and more services to customers. Why? The stores know that people don't have much time for shopping. If purchasers can get more shopping done in less time when it's convenient for them to shop, providing such expanded opportunities will help attract those who feel that food shopping is more of a pain than a pleasure.

At home, the shopper's family may not be so happy with such infrequent shopping, particularly if purchasing trips occur without notice to those who want some special item to be acquired. When the shopper brings home "the bacon" on such occasions, someone in the family who wanted Canadian bacon will complain.

Due to the purchaser not having a complete list of what the family wanted, the store sold less than it might have. The shopper may have also come into the store at a busy shopping time so that some items were missing from the shelves and high costs were incurred to have extra help on hand at the cash registers.

What could a store do to change end-user behavior in cost-reducing ways? Here are some ideas:

1. Provide a way to create password-protected lists of items that family members want purchased. The store should use such lists to plan in-store inventory levels. Such lists would then mean that special-request items would be more often purchased on the next shopping trip.

2. Make it easy for anyone in the family to use the lists for shopping and provide optional controlled access to the usual shopper's debit or credit card to pay for the purchases. These services could save the usual shopper from having to go as often.

3. Restock the most popular items just before the busiest times of the week, as well as overnight.

4. Offer time-sensitive pricing so that those who shop when there are fewer customers and excess staff capacity can enjoy lower prices for purchasing then.

5. Provide each family member with the option to receive e-mail and cell-phone alerts about price specials concerning items each person has bought in the last year so the family can stock up at lower cost.

6. Provide a free service of assembling sacks of dry packaged products on the list of desired items for those who pick up their orders at times when cashiers and shelf stockers have been least busy.

7. Offer volume discounts similar to what the warehouse clubs do so that there's a financial incentive to buy a lot more at one time.

8. Encourage local banks to put in ATMs at their own expense. Offer price discounts for cash payments so that fewer credit and debit cards fees will be incurred by the stores.

The effect of such changes should be to increase the total purchases, reduce the time shoppers spend in the store, attract more shoppers, and reduce operating costs while increasing on-shelf availability. Shoppers and family members will be happier, feeling more satisfied with what they eat and use and how easy it is for them to acquire what they want, while families will save money on what they purchase.

Are you ready to make such changes for your end users? If not, you should start getting ready.

What's the key point about changing end-user behavior? **You can use zero-based analysis to create 2,000 percent cost-reduction solutions to change end-user behavior in ways that will almost instantly expand your and your stakeholders' profits and cash flow after implementation by only supplying the minimum core offering while helping you reduce costs by more than 96 percent or increase social benefits by more than twenty times of what you will be spending.**

Assignments

1. What aspects of your end users' behaviors add unnecessary operating costs for them, for you, and for other stakeholders?

2. How could your offerings be redesigned to eliminate such costs without causing any harm to other stakeholders?

3. How could the new offerings be structured so that competitors would feel compelled to move in the same direction, but would probably lag further and further behind in the rate of implementation?

Lesson Thirty-One

Cooperate with Strangers and Volunteers and Help Unemployed People Start Complementary Businesses

Therefore love the stranger,
for you were strangers in the land of Egypt.

— Deuteronomy 10:19 (NKJV)

Your people shall be volunteers
In the day of Your power;
In the beauties of holiness, from the womb of the morning,
You have the dew of Your youth.

— Psalm 110:3 (NKJV)

And let the beauty of the LORD our God be upon us,
And establish the work of our hands for us;
Yes, establish the work of our hands.

— Psalm 90:17 (NKJV)

This lesson explores three sources of cost-reducing help that most businesses ignore: strangers, volunteers, and unemployed people. Think of the unifying themes for this lesson as helping to overcome the unattractiveness and tradition stalls. Let's begin by considering what strangers can do to help your enterprise reduce costs for all stakeholders through applying zero-based analysis to providing the minimum core offering.

How Can Strangers Contribute to Reducing Costs for all Stakeholders by 96 Percent?

Let another man praise you, and not your own mouth;
A stranger, and not your own lips.

— Proverbs 27:2 (NKJV)

How can *strangers* be most helpful in identifying and making cost reductions? If you are asking yourself that question, this section of the lesson will be quite an eye-opener.

Although there are many possible ways that strangers can help you, I want to focus on just one useful quality of strangers: Some of them already know how to reduce your costs and those of your stakeholders by 96 percent. All the answers you need are already present in the minds of some people whom you have never met (and who may have never heard of you or your enterprise).

Why do some strangers know the answers? They have backgrounds and experiences that are different from yours, but that are very relevant to your circumstances.

For example, consider that extremely difficult chemistry problems are often solved by amateur physicists. Such solutions come from this unexpected source because chemists too often limit themselves to chemistry-based solutions, which are just one part of the spectrum of potential solutions. Rather than seek another type of expertise to find possible solutions, many chemists go over the same ground … again and again.

Considerable research has been undertaken concerning how strangers help find solutions to difficult problems. If you would like to read more about what has been learned, I recommend a book that provides an overview of some highly effective practices, *Crowdsourcing* (Crown Business, 2008) by Jeff Howe.

Let me focus on just two of the newer applications from that book for working with strangers to create exponential cost savings. The first application is to hold a contest to find a solution to a significant problem in which all contestants are allowed to see details of the best proposed solutions to date and to suggest their own added improvements to those solutions. When this approach was used during a contest to find the fastest way for a salesman to make all of his sales calls, the ultimate solution was 1,000 times better than the best initial solution. Why? Many people can see ways to slightly adjust an overall solution to make it much better. As the posted solutions improve, more strangers become intrigued by the challenge of making useful improvements to the fine solutions that have already been proposed.

Such experience is consistent with what I have learned about 2,000 percent solutions. Each time you repeat the 2,000 percent solution process, you can create a twenty-times-better solution to the last twenty-times-better solution. Such a repetition creates a four-hundred-times better solution. If you are looking at costs, that means reducing costs by more than 99 percent. How's that for saving money?

You probably don't feel as if you have the time to develop 2,000 percent solutions for reducing every aspect of your organization's costs … and then to repeat the process. If that's the case, you can instead "hire" strangers to do the work for you.

Usually, such stranger-directed solutions are developed through well-publicized contests that recognize and reward those who create the best solutions during a short amount of time (usually two weeks or less). Most people who enter do so in part to learn something and in part just for the fun of it … so tangible rewards don't have to be very large. Most small businesses can afford to sponsor such a contest. It's a good idea to spread the news of your contest as widely as you can through social networking sites relevant to the people you want to reach.

The second newer approach for working with strangers to make huge cost reductions is by encouraging *amateurs* to suggest solutions. Although many organizations and people are succeeding with online contests that involve professionals, it turns out that there are hundreds of times more amateurs who can help make cost reductions than there are relevant professionals. The most capable amateurs will usually come up with better results than the professionals do. Such an advantageous result seems to occur for two reasons:

1. Solving most difficult problems requires the fresh perspective of highly intelligent people more than a narrowly expert or experienced background.

2. Diverse sources of perspective are very valuable (as I noted in describing the other new method, letting people see and improve on each others' solutions during a contest).

I can also validate such results from amateurs based on the research into innovation that I began back in the early 1970s. From that time, many organizations have found the best innovations by involving large numbers of people who were from seemingly unrelated backgrounds and who were also strangers to the organization and its offerings. I also suspect that another reason such amateur strangers do well is that they aren't limited by professional blinders that eliminate considering most alternatives.

One of the benefits of working with amateurs who are strangers is that the recognition and rewards they want to receive can be quite modest. Amusing t-shirts are often considered by amateurs to be enough reward.

To find out how well this method can work for you, take your highest cost area, write a description of how you do things now and how your process affects other stakeholders, and underwrite a contest to find a more effective, more desirable, lower-cost method. Once you've had your first success with this kind of contest, you'll be ready for more!

What's the key cost-reducing point about working with strangers? **You can use zero-based analysis to create 2,000 percent cost-reduction solutions by cooperating with strangers to provide the minimum core offering in ways that will almost instantly expand your profits after implementation by reducing your and your stakeholders' costs by more than 96 percent or increasing social benefits by more than twenty times what you will be spending.**

Assignments

1. What aspects of your costs can you find no way to reduce very much?

2. Is there any compelling reason not to share your problem and to seek solutions from strangers through an online contest?

3. If there is such a compelling reason for secrecy, can you share portions of the problem with strangers to find solutions?

4. If neither alternative seems feasible, would an anonymously sponsored contest solve your problems about sharing information with contestants who are strangers?

5. What would be appropriate rewards (credibility, recognition, and tangible benefits) to encourage strangers to participate that your organization can afford?

6. How can you gain lots of low-cost publicity for and awareness of your contest?

How Can Volunteers Contribute to Reducing Costs for all Stakeholders by 96 Percent?

*I issue a decree that all those of the people of Israel
and the priests and Levites in my realm,
who volunteer to go up to Jerusalem,
may go with you.*

— Ezra 7:13 (NKJV)

Mention the word "volunteer" and many people think of donation solicitors for nonprofit organizations. In the online world, some people think, instead, of those who contribute content to and spend time editing entries for Wikipedia.

What do volunteers and for-profit businesses have to do with one another? "Too little" is all too often the cost-reducing answer. The tradition stall causes us to accept what has always been done as arbitrary limits to what can and should be done. "If it ain't broke, don't fix it" is the well-known mantra of many stuck-in-the-mud adherents to the "wisdom" of blindly following tradition.

The potential use of volunteers to assist for-profit businesses has often been blocked by the tradition stall. To understand how big this stall is, you should realize that even many renowned management authorities such as Peter Drucker (who often talked and wrote about how much for-profit companies could learn from their nonprofit kin) never mention the idea of staffing or relying on volunteers to operate or to improve for-profit businesses.

But we should all know better now. Why? Some successful for-profit businesses are based on volunteers donating their efforts. Consider teetonic.com as an example. (Visit their site now to get a better grasp of what I'm describing.)

Designing tee-shirt images has been a favorite activity for young people since shortly after the first tee shirt was made. When teaching small-business classes, I often encounter students who want to design tee shirts for a living. They are daunted, however, by the prospect of selling what they design. Many imagine themselves traveling from one flea market to another peddling their offerings from their automobile trunks. Implementing that marketing strategy doesn't excite the would-be designers.

The managers of the site, teetonic.com, had a better idea. The organization started out by offering free contests for people who wanted to submit designs. (You can see more by visiting the following Web page: http://www.teetonic.com/submit/?sid=795d6819fe83ff013710f37842692227/.)

Many companies would have stopped there and simply sold the designs that its owners and managers liked best. The management of teetonic.com was, however, committed to involving as many volunteers as possible. They also chose to have volunteers vote to determine the best designs.

With volunteers designing the products and picking out which designs to make, what's left to do? You just have to apply the designs to tee shirts and to sell them. In the case of teetonic.com, these activities are more profitably accomplished by only offering limited editions of the winning designs. And who buys such tees? Why, the volunteers, of course!

The organizers of teetonic.com aren't abusing these volunteers as it might seem at first glance. The contest winners receive a free tee shirt in their design, a cash prize of one hundred pounds sterling, and a royalty payment of 50 pence for each tee shirt sold carrying their design (5 percent of the retail price). Runners-up each also receive a free tee shirt.

According to *Crowdsourcing*, the pretax profit contribution on sales for teetonic.com is about 80 percent (or 8 pounds out of every 10 pounds paid). The "volunteers" in total are paid only about 6 percent of the company's profit contribution from a tee-shirt sale. That's pretty nice for the company, isn't it?

Without using volunteers, other tee-shirt makers typically earn a profit margin on sales of about 6 percent before income taxes. Using volunteers handsomely pays off in slashing costs for the tee-shirt makers by adding more customers, taking the risk out of how many tee shirts to produce, and eliminating almost all marketing and distribution costs.

The company's founder decided it was time to cash out his ownership a few years ago and sold the business for about $150 million. That's not a bad profit for simply organizing a few volunteers.

As good as this approach seems, the company's business model can still be improved on. If you instead work with an information product that can be downloaded for almost no cost from the Internet, you are able to enjoy such favorable economics and slash both prices and costs by over 99 percent. That's just what www.istockphoto.com did with stock photographs.

On this photographic Web site, photographers post their images and receive credits based on payments made by others who download their work. Such credits can be used to pay for downloading other peoples' stock images. In this way, designers who are also photographers can use many photographs for no out-of-pocket cost. In addition, such photographers enjoy the pleasure of having others make more use their work.

If you don't have such credits, you can simply buy them. Before istockphoto.com became popular, downloading most photographs cost only $7.00 to $14.00 compared to several hundred dollars at other stock-photo sites. Many professional photographers were surprised to see their incomes rise by using the site, despite the low prices, due to their stock photos being selected so much more often for presentations and simple brochures.

What are some activities that you should be thinking about having volunteers do for you?

1. Determine which offerings to provide.

2. Design your offerings.

3. Create your offerings.

4. Improve the quality of your offerings.

5. Market your offerings.

6. Distribute your offerings.

7. Provide services for your offerings.

8. Develop new uses for your offerings.

What do you need to do in return for the volunteers who help you? Here are a few suggestions:

1. Improve the selection of offerings they can access.

2. Improve the quality of the offerings they can access.

3. Reduce the price of the offerings.

4. Make it easier to use the offerings.

5. Provide credibility for volunteers.

6. Give prestige to volunteers.

7. Create public recognition for volunteers.

8. Give volunteers ways to earn income for high-quality efforts.

By using inexpensive automated software on the Internet, it should be possible to develop a billion-dollar enterprise that's totally operated by volunteers. Why not? Are you ready?

What's the key cost-reducing point about working with volunteers? **You can use zero-based analysis to create 2,000 percent cost-reduction solutions by cooperating with volunteers to provide the minimum core offering to almost instantly expand profits after implementation by reducing your and your stakeholders' costs more than 96 percent or increasing social benefits by more than twenty times.**

<u>Assignments</u>

1. **What aspects of your costs can you find no way to reduce very much?**

2. **Is there any compelling reason not to recruit volunteers to help lower such costs?**

3. **If there is such a compelling reason, can you eliminate portions of the problem through involving volunteers?**

4. **If neither alternative seems feasible, would partnering with a different organization that uses volunteers solve the problem?**

5. **What would be appropriate rewards (such as credibility, recognition, and tangible benefits) that you can afford to encourage participation by volunteers?**

6. **How can you gain lots of low-cost publicity for attracting the interest of potential volunteers?**

How Can Helping Unemployed People Start Complementary New Businesses Contribute to Reducing Costs for all Stakeholders by 96 Percent?

Now he who plants and he who waters are one,
and each one will receive his own reward
according to his own labor.
For we are God's fellow workers;
you are God's field, you are God's building.
According to the grace of God which was given to me,
as a wise master builder I have laid the foundation,
and another builds on it.
But let each one take heed how he builds on it.
For no other foundation can anyone lay than that which is laid,
which is Jesus Christ.
Now if anyone builds on this foundation
with gold, silver, precious stones, wood, hay, straw,
each one's work will become clear;
for the Day will declare it,
because it will be revealed by fire;
and the fire will test each one's work, of what sort it is.
If anyone's work which he has built on it endures,
he will receive a reward.
If anyone's work is burned, he will suffer loss;
but he himself will be saved, yet so as through fire.

— 1 Corinthians 3:8-15 (NKJV)

When one of my small-business classes was filled with workers aged fifty-five and older who had lost their jobs and hadn't been able to find new ones, I became aware of the opportunity to engage unemployed people with an organization that helps them to start complementary businesses. Despite being unemployed, each person impressed me as above-average in intelligence, detail-orientation, and determination to succeed. Although all of these people wanted to find jobs, they realized that their best bet was to start a new business.

All of them immediately perceived that they should find a way to make their businesses complementary to better-established entities. For instance, one couple wanted to start an online retail business to sell quality briefcases and luggage. They did not intend to manufacture the items, but simply to market goods that others would supply on a drop-ship basis. (Orders would be sent electronically from their Web site to the manufacturers who would pack and ship the items from their own facilities.)

One woman wanted to provide custom party favors (little gifts for guests to take home). She intended to have others design and manufacture the favors; her company would help party givers select items and pick the right suppliers to serve those needs.

These business models would require limited capital for the new organizations because they would have no fixed location, no inventory, and no staff. Customers would pay for the items before they are ordered from suppliers. All the day-to-day work would be provided by the business owner, as supplemented by a few suppliers and some simple software.

I later read about a variation on such an approach. A different online tee-shirt company decided to refocus itself to become a custom manufacturer for anyone who wanted to sell tee shirts. Rather than just produce and market the top choices after an online design contest, this company would produce and market tee shirts for everyone who wanted help. This business model is a lot like what online print-on-demand publishers do for book authors. In the process, an unemployed (or underemployed) tee-shirt designer can arrange to have a few tee shirts made and offered online without having to spend much money.

As I thought about such examples, I realized that my unemployed students didn't lack energy and enthusiasm ... they simply lacked some of the knowledge needed to be successful. Since a great many organizations could use more people selling or developing the market for their products, one obvious opportunity for such organizations is to help unemployed people earn some money by offering or educating people about the organization's offerings and enterprises. To succeed, organizations should focus on filling in knowledge and experience deficiencies that might keep unemployed people from being effective on their behalf.

For instance, a luggage manufacturer could provide Web hosting and a Web-site template that would allow people who wanted to sell its merchandise to get into business at less cost with a nicer-looking and easier-to-use Web site. The manufacturer could also make it easy for the new business to attach its own brand to the offerings. A party favor provider could offer to make customizations for each of these new online vendors who purchased a minimum number of any custom item.

I also found that the unemployed people didn't know much about finance, taxes, accounting, or business processes. Manufacturers could also set up service organizations to provide such functions for the new businesses either on an inexpensive fee-for-service basis or at no cost for those who buy enough offerings.

One of my university students discovered another opportunity. Unemployed people are often eligible for government programs that can be used to establish new businesses. By lending his technical support to villagers in India, the unemployed people there were able to establish a cooperative that could borrow money inexpensively from the government as well as purchase farming and manufacturing supplies at lower prices. A supplier could have performed the role that my student did. In fact, the supplier could probably have found volunteers to do such work at no cost to the supplier.

This cooperative is interesting because the student added a lot of basic educational activities to its purposes so that all the members would be creating and applying 2,000 percent solutions to virtually all of the cooperative's business activities. Such a cooperative could probably afford to hire one person with expertise part-time to provide whatever technical knowledge the local people were lacking whenever volunteers could not fill the gap.

There are a lot of programs to help reduce unemployment. I believe there will be even more such programs. Now is a good time to investigate how you could unleash an army of highly motivated, properly trained people to advance your company's interests as owners of complementary small businesses.

While I've focused on marketing or purchasing opportunities in this section of the lesson, it may also be that you need people who will customize your offerings, provide service, train people to use the offerings, or perform a variety of other related activities. Consider how you could profitably facilitate and assist unemployed people to start businesses that will also serve such needs.

What's the key point about helping unemployed people to create complementary new businesses? **You can use zero-based analysis to create 2,000 percent cost-reduction solutions that allow you to benefit from helping unemployed people start complementary businesses that play a role in providing the minimum core offering in ways that will almost instantly expand your profits by helping reduce your and your stakeholders' costs by more than 96 percent or by increasing social benefits more than twenty times of what you will be spending.**

Assignments

1. **What aspects of your costs can you find no way to reduce very much?**

2. **Is there any compelling reason not to encourage unemployed people to start complementary businesses to help reduce such costs?**

3. **If there is such a compelling reason, can you eliminate portions of the problem through involving new businesses established by unemployed people?**

4. **If neither alternative seems feasible, would partnering with another organization that encourages start-ups by unemployed people solve the problem?**

5. **What appropriate support can you afford to encourage and to assist more unemployed people to start such new businesses and succeed?**

6. **How can you gain lots of low-cost publicity for attracting interest from unemployed people to start such businesses?**

Lesson Thirty-Two

Attract Sponsors and Advertisers

So continuing daily with one accord in the temple,
and breaking bread from house to house,
they ate their food with gladness and simplicity of heart,
praising God and having favor with all the people.
And the Lord added to the church daily
those who were being saved.

— Acts 2:46-47 (NKJV)

This lesson examines sponsorships and advertising as ways to make cost breakthroughs and to generate extra revenues. Let's start with sponsorships.

What do I mean by a *sponsorship*? It is any way to combine recognition with providing access to desirable prospects and customers for someone who, or an organization that, makes a payment or otherwise subsidizes an activity. Sponsorships are more important than ever because they help marketers avoid being lost in advertising clutter by providing higher visibility and prestige to the sponsor. When a sponsor pays you, that's income to offset costs you cannot otherwise reduce. The effect is similar to simply reducing costs.

As the primary benefit, sponsors are usually looking for access to attractive prospects for their offerings. In many cases, your prospects and customers are also highly appealing for other companies and nonprofit organizations, making them interested in sponsoring your activities.

You may have observed some of the ways such sponsorship access is provided while attending a seminar or conference. Typically, the sponsors have a chance to speak briefly to the assembled group and to have lots of marketing people present for mingling during meals and breaks. There may also be banners on the walls and notices in the printed program carrying sponsors' names and logos. On the event invitations, there are probably mentions of the sponsors. Publicity for the activity probably includes listing sponsors by name, as well.

Under such circumstances, it's not unusual for the sponsors' fees to cover more than the total costs of the conference or seminar so that all attendance fees contribute profits for the conference or seminar organizer.

You may not be holding conferences or seminars. How, then, can sponsorships cover some or all of your costs? Well, you can provide online services or material that can be downloaded for little or no cost from the Internet. Such an online site can also have sponsors whose identities are prominently displayed.

You can also develop offerings that sponsors purchase. As an example, a sponsor might provide your offering as a gift to those who buy their products or services. During times of high gasoline prices, for instance, some dealers in the United States have offered hundreds of gallons of free gas for people who bought new vehicles that didn't get very good mileage.

A sponsor might also provide marketing access for other organizations. In our community, some charities play this role by selling inexpensive books of discount coupons. The charities keep the proceeds from the book sales, after obtaining the books for free from the publishers. The companies providing the coupons pay the publisher to appear in the book. Those who buy the books save lots of money by using the discount coupons. Through the coupons, coupon providers introduce new prospects to their offerings and bring some customers back more often.

In other cases, almost all offerings will be sold to sponsors who, in turn, directly provide the offerings to their prospects and customers. For instance, golf tournaments are often staged to provide funds for charity. Sponsors are given access to special venues at the tournaments and provided with most of the tickets for the events to distribute to customers and prospects. Sponsors also receive lots of visibility in the event's promotions. The prestige of sponsorship is increased over the company conducting such an event just for itself by improving the quality of the competing golfers, the amount of media coverage, and the number of attendees.

In another variation, a sponsor may be a supplier seeking recognition that provides a lower price for its offerings in exchange for the sponsorship. An example can be found on the computer I am using to prepare this lesson. The machine has a seal on it that says "intel Core™ Duo inside™," indicating what brand and kind of microprocessor I have. In exchange for this recognition, Intel slices its microprocessor prices by about 5 percent to its computer-manufacturer customers.

Another way sponsorships are structured is through paying for "objective" measurements and rankings. Those who want to be evaluated pay a fee, which pays for the ranking process. The organization making the rankings distributes awards among those who sponsored the contest. The winners use the results to tout their superiority over competitors in press releases, interviews, and advertising.

You may not have thought much about how your marketing activities and offerings could benefit from encouraging sponsorships. Now is a good time to remove such blinders. Companies are more interested than ever before in sponsorships to replace more expensive and less productive marketing programs. You can cash in to make cost breakthroughs when you help such organizations to meet their needs through helpful sponsorships of your high-quality activities and offerings.

Now, how is *advertising* different from a sponsorship? Where a sponsor obtains recognition for making an activity or offering possible along with privileged access to prospects and customers in exchange for a payment, advertisers are solely purchasing the right to put their commercial messages in front of prospects through some form of media that you provide.

We've all seen television advertising. At regular intervals in the regular programming, short commercial messages are inserted. Companies pay large fees for such time slots in addition to covering their own costs for producing the messages. The fee paid relates to the number of people who will see the message and their potential value as customers for the advertiser.

The same concept generally applies to magazines and newspapers. All or part of a printed page offers the opportunity to attract the eyes of readers. Because the whole publication may not be read, the assumed benefit is considered to be less than the overall readership. In addition, television advertising provides the opportunity to create more emotion … which, in turn, can be translated into making a bigger and more lasting impression with more people.

Advertising is also sold on commercial vehicles such as taxis and trucks. Some companies have been paying to display advertising on personal vehicles. Such exposure is often cheaper than renting billboard space and may offend fewer people who are concerned about cluttering the sides of roads.

With the advent of the Internet, advertising possibilities expanded. Initially, advertisers were encouraged to buy so-called banner ads that took up a big space near the top of the screen and said little. Most advertisers found that such ads weren't worth much in terms of adding profitable sales.

Yahoo, Google, and others found that carrying commercial messages with some relevance to those reading the online page worked better for encouraging purchases from advertisers. Rather than advertisers paying to reach people who merely see the ad, payments for such ads are tied to how many people click on the ad to reach a site where there is a more extensive commercial message or an offering can be purchased. This media approach was intended to be similar to paying for attracting someone to a store where he or she could buy an offering. Accomplishing the latter was worth quite a lot more than simply exposing the name and offering of the advertiser to more eyeballs.

Through Web 2.0, Web sites can become communities where people spend many hours a day. On such sites, the advertising revenues can be a vast multiple of the cost of providing the site … assuming that enough visitors are attracted who post and view videos and photos, exchange opinions, share ideas, and interact in other ways. As an example, a student of mine developed a very sophisticated social networking site of this sort for families at a software cost of less than $3,000, yet the advertising potential of her site was several million dollars a year.

If you don't have such a site now, you can inexpensively develop one that can become a major source of cost-reducing advertising revenue by using software designers and programmers who are based where pay rates are inexpensive. While working on the site, you can speak with your developers at no cost over Skype or another Voice-over-Internet-Protocol service. Naturally, you can have as many sites as you want … as long as each one serves a different purpose and attracts enough visitors to more than cover its costs through advertising revenues.

If you hold gatherings of customers and prospects and don't have sponsors for such gatherings, you can also sell advertising to place on the materials that you share with attendees. In many cases, your advertisers will also market your gathering to their prospects and customers, and you may attract a lot more potential customers to attend. When that happens, you gain direct cost savings for your marketing in addition to the advertising subsidy.

You can provide videos on your Web site as well and sell time slots on such videos to advertisers. Such online advertising opportunities have become popular with truck and automobile manufacturers.

You can also put advertising on your buildings, your packages, and anyplace else where customers and prospects may see the messages. Your suppliers, for instance, may want to be recognized on your final offering in some way (even placing their logos on a Web page may be of interest) as Intel does with its "intel inside™" stickers on personal computers and laptops.

The sky's the limit for attracting advertisers. You should realize that when print media were more popular, publishers regularly earned a profit on their entire operations just from the advertising revenues. The subscription revenues, by comparison, were usually quite small … just a tiny fraction of total profits.

Can you provide both sponsorships and advertising? Yes, as long as you keep them separate. A sponsored event usually shouldn't include advertising from those who aren't sponsors, but Web sites can offer a combination of sponsor recognition and pay-per-click ads from organizations that don't compete with sponsors. Some magazines have been following this dual course for a long time. *Fortune*, *Forbes*, and *BusinessWeek*, for instance, carry lots of ads for offerings and sell sponsorships to gatherings that senior executives pay to attend. Such gatherings are potentially quite profitable.

What's the key cost-reducing point about sponsorships and advertising? **You can use zero-based analysis to create 2,000 percent cost-reduction solutions that allow you to gain new sources of revenue from sponsorships and advertising to support the minimum core offering by offsetting costs for you and your stakeholders in ways that will almost instantly expand profits after implementation to help reduce costs by more than 96 percent or increase social benefits by more than twenty times what you will be spending.**

<u>Assignments</u>

1. What aspects of your costs can you find no way to reduce very much?

2. Is there any benefit to other organizations from sponsoring some of your activities or offerings, allowing you to offset some of such costs or to help you gain customers less expensively?

3. If there is no potential benefit for sponsors from what you do now, can you design new activities and offerings that would deliver such major benefits?

4. If neither alternative seems feasible, would partnering with another organization that already has sponsors help solve the problem?

5. What is the best way to make sponsorships more appealing to sponsors, and to your customers and prospects?

6. How can you gain lots of low-cost publicity for and attract more interest in sponsorships?

7. Is there any benefit to other organizations from advertising through some of your activities or offerings to offset some of your costs or to help you gain customers less expensively?

8. If there is no such benefit for advertisers, can you design new activities and offerings that would deliver such major benefits?

9. If neither alternative seems feasible, would partnering with another organization that already has advertisers help solve the problem?

10. What is the best way to make placing advertising more appealing to advertisers and to your customers and prospects?

11. How can you gain substantial low-cost publicity for and attract interest in purchasing such advertising?

12. How can you combine offering sponsorships and advertising to lower your costs still further while helping sponsors and advertisers to reduce their costs, as well?

Lesson Thirty-Three

Minimize the Time Needed
to Manage Your Enterprise
to Develop the Minimum Business Model

"And which of you by worrying can add one cubit to his stature?
If you then are not able to do the least,
why are you anxious for the rest?
Consider the lilies, how they grow:
they neither toil nor spin; and yet I say to you,
even Solomon in all his glory was not arrayed like one of these.
If then God so clothes the grass,
which today is in the field
and tomorrow is thrown into the oven,
how much more will He clothe you,
O you of little faith?
And do not seek what you should eat
or what you should drink,
nor have an anxious mind.
For all these things the nations of the world seek after,
and your Father knows that you need these things.
But seek the kingdom of God,
and all these things shall be added to you."

— Luke 12:25-31 (NKJV)

In this lesson, we look at how simplifying management to develop the minimum business model reduces costs for an enterprise and its stakeholders. As background for simplifying management, please read the article that appeared in the January 1, 2009 issue of *Inc. Magazine* describing Plentyoffish.com and its founder, Markus Frind (http://www.inc.com/magazine/20090101/and-the-money-comes-rolling-in.html).

To wit, Markus Frind was determined to create a business that could be simply, easily, and quickly managed by him. Because staring at a computer screen gave Mr. Frind eye strain, he tried to minimize that aspect of his work. Since he wrote and maintained all the software ... as well as ran the company ... his business had to be very simple and he made it that way. As a result, he reported being done with work in just ten minutes on many days.

In most cases, *minimizing the time of the person running the business* will dramatically reduce costs for the enterprise and all stakeholders. If you focus on minimizing leadership time, I think you'll be amazed at how low your and stakeholders' costs can go.

Let me share a personal example. When I started Mitchell and Company, I was advised to devote about fifteen hours a week to seeking new consulting clients. Initially, I did more than that ... spending every waking hour that wasn't devoted to billable work on any kind of marketing I could imagine.

As the firm grew, I kept doing the same thing ... except that I also developed endless lists of marketing tasks for my colleagues to do. As a result, it wasn't unusual for the firm to devote hundreds of hours a week to marketing even when we were small.

Years after the firm was well established, I began to think in terms of how I wanted to spend my days. I developed personal goals that included lots more family activities, vacations, holidays, learning experiences, and bonding with friends. As a result, I had fewer than fifteen hours a week for all my work.

Naturally, I had to cut back a lot on the time I spent on marketing. Without any intention to do so, I also cut back on the money spent on marketing and the time that my colleagues invested. In consequence, our marketing costs declined by over 90 percent while our growth and profitability improved. I was surprised by that result.

What was the difference? We only worked on marketing activities that were very high payoff and cost little.

For instance, I would only visit a potential client if there was a large project under discussion and I was going to be within twenty miles of their offices for some other purpose. Someone in our office would telephone the CEO and CFO to ask if either wanted me to stop by to discuss the potential project. If the answer was "yes," I went. If "no," I didn't go.

I also learned to substitute technology for many marketing trips and often employed video conferences to make substantial marketing presentations. Although it cost a lot in those days to run an hour-long video conference, the expense was generally less than 20 percent of the cost to visit the people and typically involved less than 5 percent of my time.

As part of my new approach, I also redesigned our consulting processes so that they would take less of my time. In this streamlining, I often eliminated major consulting activities that formerly took a lot of my time, but didn't seem to help clients.

In other areas, I reduced my time involvement by making critical decisions early in the project rather than waiting until the end to review what my colleagues had done. As a result, the work that everyone else had to do also declined. For every hour of project time I personally saved, my staff usually saved fifty to one hundred hours.

Eventually, I designed new processes that totally replaced the need for many staff members. The new procedures speeded up the work while improving its accuracy and helpfulness. As a result, I also became more familiar with the details and provided better advice to clients.

Naturally, such simplifications are easier to do if you have a small business and are content to keep it small. A better plan is to seek ways to create a substantial business and to have it grow while keeping your personal time involvement quite limited. Otherwise, your costs will be small in absolute terms, but could be quite a large percentage of a small revenue base. A better approach is to shrink the costs while continually expanding revenues.

Here are some principles that can help:

1. Identify large, high-value needs that organizations and individuals are unable to satisfy from any existing sources.

   In my case, one such need was for a company's stock to be higher priced without improving the company's earnings and cash flow from what they would normally be. Most CEOs and CFOs thought they knew how to accomplish such a stock-price improvement by simply making optimistic promises of future performance based on all of their new activities working perfectly. Such executives were usually fired after performance badly lagged their promises or they were caught making fraudulent financial reports.

   My clients were honest people who wanted to tell investors what was likely to occur and to gain more understanding and approval for what they were accomplishing. I could help them by aligning their plans more closely with what investors were looking for and were finding hard to obtain.

2. Locate ways of getting paid that don't cause customers much pain.

   Public companies could charge my fees and expenses directly to any completed capital transactions that I had studied for them. As a result, payments to Mitchell and Company were only charged to the balance sheet rather than to the profit-and-loss statement, the primary measure used for determining their executive bonuses. Company leaders liked that!

   Wealthy individual clients usually arranged for me to draw commissions or to receive finders' fees from sponsors of any opportunities they invested in. As a result, they never had to write me a check, despite paying nothing extra for their investments.

3. Find a low-cost method of filling such a need that doesn't require much of your own time.

   In the field of corporate finance, people spin lots of theories about how financial markets work. In reality, such markets often act much differently than what the theories assert. I simply employed standard decision-making methods to cross-check at least three independent sources of data (typically the sources were answers to hypothetical questions during investor interviews, historical patterns of valuation, and case histories of results experienced by companies with similar investors in similar circumstances) and then created stock-price forecasts based on our experiences in such forecasting. Once we had the necessary data, I could make the forecasts in twenty minutes.

4. Keep your methodology secret so no competitors can duplicate or improve on it.

   I designed a stock-price forecasting methodology that included several key elements known only to me. No one else ever saw all the calculations I used, so they didn't know how I went from the data to the results. The process was complicated enough that you couldn't reverse engineer it. As a result, my method is just as proprietary today as it was when I developed the initial version in 1976.

5. Build your reputation so that you can add customers that can benefit more.

   Done properly, you may be able to charge more for doing similar work because you are delivering a lot more in total value. (If the total stock-market value of some client is larger initially, expanding value by the same percentage as for a company with a smaller market capitalization provides more financial rewards for investors.)

As a result of such thinking, you, too, can expand your business size while shrinking costs as you squeeze out the time you spend managing your business and making it better.

A good way to start is by examining the economic payoffs of how you spend your time now. Locate the most productive 1 percent of what you do and seek to make everything you do even more productive than that 1 percent, while working a lot less.

With that perspective in mind, let's go on to consider a *minimum business model*. I find that most entrepreneurs don't think much about such business models. In fact, many entrepreneurs prefer to think about how many more people they can employ and how busy those people can be kept. Actually, such a people-intensive business model will have lots of extra costs ... unless employees pay you for the opportunity to work.

I first learned about minimum business models after becoming interested in if you could have a one-person corporation bringing in more than a billion dollars in annual revenues. I expected that most people would believe that such an accomplishment was impossible. Instead, I found that virtually all experts agreed it was possible, and many provided examples of what had been done in the past ... or could be done in the present.

Peter Drucker told me about the first such business that he had found, a Swiss investment bank owned and operated by a man who spent most of each day on the telephone introducing those who needed capital to those who had money to invest. The banker's fees were about 5 percent of the sums invested, and he raised tens of billions of dollars a year. As a result, the bank's revenues (against which it had almost no expenses) were over a billion dollars a year.

Let's examine the example more closely to understand how it worked. You and I could sit in our offices and make lots of telephone calls offering to place capital and asking to access capital. Everyone who couldn't raise enough capital would be delighted to speak to us. Those who wanted to invest and already had more deals to look at than they had time would be politely unavailable. Those who could easily raise capital would not so politely ignore us. We would have no revenues by operating in that way.

Clearly the Swiss investment banker must have had access to very attractive deals that made investors substantial sums of money. Unless you once worked for a large, successful investment bank and provided lots of high quality deals while there, it takes awhile to develop such a clientele. I don't know this banker's employment history, but I suspect that he may have had such experience.

If we think about this gentleman's success, we can guess that he probably began with a more complex and expensive business model than the one we are suggesting.

How might such business success be accomplished instead by using a simple, inexpensive business model? I raise this question for two purposes:

1. To provide an idea that you may want to implement

2. To provide a template that you might apply to another business opportunity

Before reading the rest of this lesson, I encourage you to write down all your ideas for duplicating the investment banker's success with a simple, inexpensive business model. I provide that encouragement because you will gain a lot more from the lesson if you attempt to find your own solutions. The more time you spend in this way, the more valuable this lesson will be for you.

Have you written your ideas? Good. Let's now look at the subject together.

Think for a minute about what kind of successful deals would probably come to such an investment banker. If the company needing capital were well known, had a stellar balance sheet, and generated lots of cash, the company could have undoubtedly saved money by holding an auction among twenty investment banks that wanted to find investors. That's what the Tennessee Valley Authority (TVA) did in the 1990s to raise more capital. Because it was an agency of the U.S. government, owning the TVA's bonds was low risk, and the organization used that advantage to spend less for raising capital.

What else can we conclude about the client company that was looking for capital? The client probably didn't want a lot of publicity or to make much disclosure. Otherwise, the deal would have been shopped around the globe to all potentially interested parties. Swiss investment banks have an above-average reputation for secrecy, and a one-person investment bank would be in a position to keep secrets better than a large one. So we can assume that these are "hush-hush" deals for some reason.

Since such an investment bank isn't going to be able to do much on-the-ground due diligence, either the deal doesn't need that kind of examination or the company providing the capital is prepared to find its comfort in something else.

Here's an example of what I mean. If you need money to finance a project in a famously unstable country, everyone knows that it's risky doing business there. But if the project's customers agree to deposit enough money into a Swiss escrow account to cover the first ten years of their purchases, the capital provider can comfortably agree to fund such a project after placing a lien on the escrow account that puts him or her ahead of the customers' claims. If the investment bank's client and the project's customers have already agreed to such an arrangement, it's simple to raise the money. Despite this low risk in practice, the client company doing the project might not want any publicity due to potentially negative political ramifications in the famously unstable country from the financing details becoming known.

By looking at how such "hush-hush" deals might be done, it becomes clearer what role a single investment banker can play: See how he can structure deals so that they will be attractive to a wide group of confidential capital providers. You don't need a big staff to design such structures. After all, the details for putting the deal together are going to be worked out by some of the best independent international lawyers and accountants.

Who can provide such confidential capital? Well, it has to be someone or an entity that's not regulated and doesn't have to disclose where its money goes. Such investors are often high-risk managers of private capital pools that don't borrow money to leverage their deals. You can pull out a list of the world's wealthiest people from *Forbes* and begin thinking about who fits this profile. There will be about thirty names that will strike you as being a good fit.

What do you do next? You telephone such people and organizations to inquire what kind of deals they are looking for. Chances are they will send you a list of requirements by e-mail. If they don't, you can just look up any past public transactions and draw a profile from those deals. If you have detailed questions after being able to articulate what the person or organization appears to be looking for, someone will usually answer you.

Then the fun begins. You think of trustworthy industries, companies, and people needing money that would probably prefer to keep the details of the funding secret. After you identify some such prospects, think of a structure the potential investors would be glad to use (such as my theoretical example of having project customers put money into an escrow account in Switzerland to secure transactions in a risky country). Then, you contact those who probably need funds to see if they would like to hire you on a contingent-fee basis to put together deals. Most won't. Some will. Sign contracts to represent the ones who hire you and develop term sheets describing the deals they want to do.

Then, go to those whose investment criteria match what you've put together on the term sheet. Some may be interested, or none may be. Find out why some or all aren't interested. Then, either work with your client to adjust the deal to make it more appealing, or develop a totally different type of deal that capital providers like better.

Keep repeating this process, and eventually you'll have a business like the one Peter Drucker described to me.

Okay, so let's say that you don't want to establish such an investment bank. The same thought process applies to the business you do want to establish ... with one exception: Imagine that the billion-dollar one-person business already exists and then work backward to figure out under what conditions such a success could develop.

Here's an example: Let's assume that you instead want to head up a bank with fee revenues of over one billion dollars a year from providing capital to entrepreneurial start-ups in your country. Let me outline the questions this approach creates about its ideal origins:

1. Why do start-up entrepreneurs come to this bank rather than somewhere else?

2. Where does the bank get the capital to fund the start-ups?

3. Why don't the bank's competitors steal all of this lucrative business?

4. Why doesn't the bank need more than one employee?

5. Why will regulators allow this kind of capital provision?

6. How can the risk of loss be reduced to very low levels?

I encourage you to answer these questions as an exercise for developing your thinking about business models and to send the answers to me at askdonmitchell@yahoo.com. I'll share my reactions to your solutions, and I'll give you credit for any ideas I include in future books.

What is the key cost-reducing point about reducing management time to develop the minimum business model? **You can apply zero-based analysis to create 2,000 percent cost-reduction solutions that will expand your profits after implementation through reducing the amount of time you spend managing your enterprise and by revising your business model to meet just the minimum best practice while providing the minimum core offering to help you and your stakeholders to reduce costs by more than 96 percent or increase social benefits by more than twenty times of what you will be spending.**

Assignments

1. What large market where you think like its customers and employees could you serve that needs better performance?

2. How are the needs of the largest and potentially most profitable customers in that market different from the other customers?

3. How little time could you spend and still provide a much improved offering for the most attractive customers?

4. How can you keep your methods secret?

5. How can you easily expand your reputation so that potentially more profitable customers will want your offerings?

6. How can you reduce by more than 95 percent the time and expense of gaining a new customer?

7. Identify ten one-person business models that attract you.

8. Examine each alternative one-person business model to consider what the cost, profit, and cash-flow potentials are by evaluating:

    a. What you can charge

    b. How many customers will be attracted

    c. How well each business model will probably perform

    d. How large the organization's revenues can grow by using each business model

    e. What proprietary knowledge advantages you will gain and how you will be able to employ such advantages

9. Consider the difficulty of implementing these ten alternatives.

10. Look at the risk involved if any activity doesn't turn out well.

11. Select one minimum business model to develop on a part-time basis.

Lesson Thirty-Four

Operate Only on the Internet,
Add a Cost-Breakthrough Customer, and
Adopt the Minimum Business Model

There is *one body and one Spirit,*
just as you were called in one hope of your calling;
one Lord, one faith, one baptism;
one God and Father of all,
who is *above all, and through all, and in you all.*

— Ephesians 4:4-6 (NKJV)

This lesson continues our consideration of the minimum business model as a way to reduce all stakeholder costs by 96 percent. Our investigation this time considers what can be accomplished by operating only over the Internet and by adding a single customer that makes industry-best costs possible. Let's begin by looking into *Internet-only operations.*

How Can Operating Only on the Internet
Enable a Low-Cost Minimum Business Model?

For as the heavens are high above the earth,
So great is His mercy toward those who fear Him;
As far as the east is from the west,
So far has He removed our transgressions from us.

— Psalm 103:11-12 (NKJV)

I was inspired to consider this question in 2008 when the two largest newspapers in Boston featured a headline that the larger of the two, *The Boston Globe* (which was owned by the same company that published *The New York Times*), had threatened to shut down the print version of the paper and to operate online only unless employees agreed to cut their salaries and benefits by over $20 million a year.

That threat brought to mind a conversation I had when the Internet was new with a senior executive at *The Boston Globe*. The executive's view was that much classified advertising, especially for jobs, would eventually go online and that some material (such as the stock-price lists) would no longer need to be printed. Never once did he consider that online publishing would become a total replacement for holding a printed newspaper in your hands to read the news.

Having seen how things turned out, I can't help but think that the newspaper executive would have benefited from this lesson. I aim to help you avoid his myopia.

I encourage you to ponder two hypothetical cases for your business before reading further. The first case involves replacing every single thing your business does now with Internet-only activities, much like the option that the newspaper executive should have considered at some point. In the second case, identify a business that you cannot initially imagine could ever be run solely on the Internet ... and then design a business model for such a business that would be superior to what at least some customers receive today. After you've come up with your best thinking in both cases, start reading the next paragraph. If you would like to sleep on these two cases before proceeding, that's fine.

Here's an example that I initially found daunting to provide over the Internet: being a golf caddie. I picked this personal service business because it's related to a powerful example that appears on pages 5 through 8 of *The Ultimate Competitive Advantage*, describing a caddie who built an extremely successful and profitable business without the Internet. Now, I want to explore some of what he missed.

If you don't play or follow golf, let me describe a little of what golf caddies do. The golf bags and clubs that many players use are pretty heavy, and there's about four miles of walking involved in playing eighteen holes. Most older golfers don't feel up to carrying their own clubs. In addition, a good caddie will often be helpful in reading putts on the green so that strokes are saved. Great golf caddies can also give advice on club selection and help keep a golfer in such a relaxed mood that it's easier to play well. Some caddies are also good storytellers and bring a lot of enjoyment by being delightful companions.

Naturally, providing all of these benefits depends on being there with the player and carrying the bag and clubs. Well, you can't carry a bag and clubs over the Internet. What could an Internet caddie do instead?

Let's start by looking at what many golfers are interested in: having a better experience while taking fewer strokes. Otherwise, if the course allowed it, golfers could just put their clubs in a bag atop a pack animal and lead it around the course.

In practice, there's an easier solution: Buy an inexpensive pull cart for about the cost of hiring a caddie for a round or two. If pulling a cart is too much work, you can instead buy a battery-powered version to carry the clubs for the cost of about six or seven rounds of a caddie's services. Most courses will also rent you electric- or gasoline-powered riding carts for two that also carry bags. A cart rental often costs the same or less than a human caddie does.

So being there to carry the clubs and bags can be pretty easily done away with. In fact, the Internet caddie could sell pull and battery-powered carts to golfers (or arrange for rentals when golfers are traveling).

For golf purists, I am happy to agree that many of my next solutions would require changes in the rules of golf. Meanwhile, many casual golfers might be happy to use such alternatives during noncompetitive rounds.

Most caddies are pretty useless for lining up putts. If an Internet caddy developed detailed information about each green and provided directions for what to do based on where the ball lands and where the cup is, the golfer could gain such better advice electronically over the Internet through cellular telephone or wireless Internet connections.

Some golf courses already offer a variation on such advice by putting GPS devices on their riding carts that tell golfers how far it is to the pin, the front of the green, and the hazards (water and sand traps) ahead. It wouldn't be hard to supplement such electronic information with copyrighted instructions for aspects of playing a hole that aren't covered by the GPS-based information and to distribute the information along with the distance information that is provided now.

If a golfer input information about what clubs had been used throughout each round and the results, an Internet caddy could also make increasingly accurate club recommendations during the round. Receiving this information would be like having the same expert caddie helping you every time you played golf.

Most golfers enjoy being amused while playing. The Internet caddie could archive lots of stories, legends, and jokes that golfers could select depending on their circumstances and moods. For those who wanted to pay more, a knowledgeable caddie could be available for conversations using Voice-over-Internet Protocol technology. Thus, even if your favorite caddie was 3,000 miles away, you could arrange to chat with her or him while you played.

Playing a great course at the time *Business Basics* was published often cost $600 to $700 a round. Fine caddies on such courses earned $120 to $200 a round for their services. The Internet caddie could assist 72 golfers simultaneously on such a course. At a price of only $10 a round, the Internet caddie could earn revenues of over $2,000 a day … far more than any other golf caddie did except those who worked for top pros in tournaments (usually receiving 10 percent of the prize money the pro earned). Provide this kind of caddying seven days a week for a busy, expensive course, and you could receive over $700,000 a year in revenues. Naturally, there would be some set-up and operating costs. But there's no reason to stop at serving just one course. You could provide such services for the top one hundred courses in the world and potentially make $70 million a year in revenues. Is anybody interested?

Let's take the thinking process I used in the golf caddie example and describe how to develop such an Internet-based minimum business model:

1. Identify how the product or service is provided now.

2. Locate the highest value-added aspects from the customers' perspectives.

3. Construct alternative ways to deliver even higher value-added at much lower cost over the Internet.

4. Be sure that all needs are met in flexible ways that will please the customers you want to attract.

5. Build on what you already know how to do well, and find ways to accomplish even more by working with suppliers to write the software and to provide Internet interfaces.

What are you waiting for?

What's the key cost-reducing point about only operating on the Internet? **You can reduce your and stakeholders' costs by 96 percent in ways that will expand your profits after implementation through revising your business model to the minimum best practice by operating only over the Internet.**

Assignments

1. Identify three attractive Internet-only business models related to your business goals that no one else is yet doing.

2. Examine each alternative business model to consider what the cost, profit, and cash flow potentials are by evaluating:

a. What you can charge

b. How many customers will be attracted

c. **How well each alternative business model will probably perform**

d. **How large the organization's revenues can grow**

e. **What proprietary knowledge advantages you will gain and how you will be able to employ such advantages**

3. **Consider the difficulty of implementing each of these alternatives.**

4. **Look at the risk involved if any activity doesn't turn out well.**

5. **Select one business model to develop on a part-time basis.**

How Can Exclusively Serving a Single Cost-Breakthrough Customer Provide the Basis for a Minimum Business Model?

"No one can serve two masters;
for either he will hate the one and love the other,
or else he will be loyal to the one and despise the other."

— Matthew 6:24 (NKJV)

Now consider how to *obtain one customer that changes the economic potential of your enterprise* so much that it becomes practical to accomplish an overall 96 percent cost reduction after gaining just that one customer.

I chose this topic after thinking about how often the conventional wisdom about business strategy is wrong. Almost every businessperson I've ever met wanted to have as many different customers as possible and to sell them the widest possible variety of offerings. Why? The businesspeople felt very vulnerable to their organizations losing their biggest customers or the bulk of the huge volume such customers represent.

From my earliest days as a strategy consultant, I often noticed the opposite opportunity: Attract a customer whose needs were so special and whose purchase volume was so valuable that you could dominate an industry simply by gaining that customer. The Martin-Brower Company, which zoomed to national preeminence through serving McDonald's (the fast-food company) as its sole distributor of paper goods, is a good example of this focused approach.

McDonald's wanted to have a consistent image from restaurant to restaurant, and that meant using the same type of printed paper items (such as French fry containers, soft drink and milkshake cups, and hamburger wrappers) everywhere. Because there was no national paper goods supplier for restaurants at the time, McDonald's decided to create one by asking Martin-Brower to match the hamburger chain's store openings across the United States and into Canada.

McDonald's later asked Martin-Brower to increase its distribution capabilities to handle other dry (as well as frozen) items that McDonald's wanted to be uniform from restaurant to restaurant. Ultimately, Martin-Brower delivered all of the supplies to most McDonald's restaurants in the United States, Canada, and Latin America.

Today, many consumer goods manufacturers take a similar approach by seeking distribution at Wal-Mart, the world's largest retailer. When such distribution success occurs, the organization will suddenly have much larger sales and the ability to spread overhead and other fixed costs while seeing production and shipping costs plunge on a per-unit basis.

Imagine instead that you have a training product. If your country requires compulsory secondary education or military service, a similar breakthrough would be to obtain a contract to provide such training to all the young people who go through schools or the military. Then, having made a whole generation aware of what you do, you would have an opportunity, years later, to sell add-on training to the young people after they gain responsible positions in various organizations.

Here are some of the many ways that an industry-dominating strategic customer can slash your costs on a per-unit basis:

- Provides much larger volume than any other combination of customers so that your per-unit costs immediately drop below those of your competitors. The effect is to create a price umbrella that will let you set your prices relative to much higher-cost organizations that could potentially substitute for you, but can't match your costs and capabilities due to exclusively serving the strategic customer.

- Delivers credibility that makes your organization the one other customers want to work with based on knowing how fussy the strategic customer is in choosing suppliers. The incremental volume you gain from other customers often helps reduce costs almost as much as if you had instead gained all of the increased volume from the strategic customer.

- Allows your organization to access lower-cost financing. Small and unknown organizations often find themselves paying double or more the cost of larger and well-known organizations for the equity and debt capital they need to operate and to expand. While serving the strategic customer, your credit rating and attractiveness will improve toward the level enjoyed by your customer.

- By focusing in just a few offering areas, your per-unit operating costs to provide such offerings can go down even faster than overall costs. This focusing of your activities will also simplify your operations so that you will be able to streamline your processes in ways that further reduce costs. In addition, your quality should improve, allowing you to better satisfy customers and end users.

- Provides a base load of volume that permits you to increase marketing activity to higher levels than that of competitors. When that happens, customers and end users mostly remember all industry marketing activities in terms of your offerings. Thus, your marketing expenditures become two or three times more effective. Any added volume you gain then also helps to reduce overhead and fixed costs on a per-unit basis.

- With increased scale, you may find that the ratio of sales-to-net assets increases so that you can invest less capital to grow revenues. This increased asset utilization will greatly expand the cash flow generated.

- If you have a long-term relationship with the strategic customer, you have opportunities to help that customer optimize the relationship so that any alternative supplier would be much more expensive to use. The effect of drawing closer together can be to reduce your competitive risk, even though your volume is highly concentrated.

- Your customer won't need as many aspects of the offerings and related activities as you have been providing. You can then eliminate such costs unless another customer will pay enough to make such offerings and activities financially worthwhile.

173

- You may be able to shift your specifications and operating methods so that fewer items have to be scrapped, reworked, or provided again … further lowering costs.

- The customer may have unique knowledge that can help you operate more effectively and at a lower cost.

Naturally, many people will still worry about only having one customer. But if all you do is think about providing for that customer and act appropriately, isn't it likely that you won't make a mistake that will cost you that customer's business?

What's the key cost-reducing point of gaining exclusive access of the industry's most strategic customer? **You can help reduce costs by 96 percent for your organization and all stakeholders in ways that will expand your profits after implementation through revising your business model to the minimum best practice by gaining, serving, and retaining your industry's most valuable strategic customer in the most effective and efficient ways.**

Assignments

1. Identify three current or potential customers that could help you gain the lowest-cost position among your competitors.

2. Examine each of the three current or potential customers to consider what the cost, profit, and cash flow potentials are for serving each by evaluating

    a. What you can charge

    b. How many and which other customers will be attracted

    c. How well each potential customer will probably perform

    d. How large the organization's revenues can grow

    e. What proprietary-knowledge advantages you will gain and how you will be able to employ such advantages

    f. What elements of per-unit costs will decline and by how much with each current or potential customer

3. Consider the difficulty of gaining all of each one's purchases.

4. Look at the risk involved if any activity doesn't turn out well.

5. Select one customer to focus on first, and develop and implement a plan to obtain all of that customer's business.

Lesson Thirty-Five

Serve Social Purposes and
Operate in the Ideal Location

The elders who are among you I exhort,
I who am a fellow elder and a witness of the sufferings of Christ,
and also a partaker of the glory that will be revealed:
Shepherd the flock of God which is among you, serving as overseers,
not by compulsion but willingly, not for dishonest gain but eagerly;
nor as being lords over those entrusted to you,
but being examples to the flock;
and when the Chief Shepherd appears,
you will receive the crown of glory that does not fade away.

— 1 Peter 5:1-4 (NKJV)

In this lesson, we finish examining how to develop the minimum business model for reducing all stakeholder costs by 96 percent. Our investigation considers what can be accomplished by serving social purposes and by operating in the ideal location. Let's begin by understanding *how social purposes can help lower costs for all stakeholders.*

How Can Serving Social Purposes
Reduce the Costs of Your Minimum Business Model
for Your Organization and All Stakeholders?

Now some *of them were in charge of the serving vessels,*
for they brought them in and took them out by count.
Some of them were appointed over the furnishings
and over all the implements of the sanctuary,
and over the fine flour and the wine and the oil and the incense and the spices.
And some *of the sons of the priests made the ointment of the spices.*
Mattithiah of the Levites, the firstborn of Shallum the Korahite,
had the trusted office over the things that were baked in the pans.

— 1 Chronicles 9:28-31 (NKJV)

I became interested in how serving social purposes can help reduce costs while attending a lecture at the Massachusetts Institute of Technology (MIT) sponsored by the Legatum Center for Development and Entrepreneurship, which educates entrepreneurs in the least economically developed nations about how to help people leave poverty.

The lecturer was Mr. Fernando Nilo, founder and CEO of RECYCLA Chile, the first Latin American recycling company to handle electronic products (such as computers, fax machines, printers, and cell phones) in the most environmentally friendly ways. In Chile at the time, such products were 2 percent of the volume in landfills but contributed over 70 percent of all toxic waste. If you can keep electronic products out of landfills, you help avoid poisoning future generations. In addition, much of such discarded equipment was either functional or could be easily repaired. RECYCLA Chile erased the memories of any usable electronic gear and supplied them for free to organizations serving the poor.

As you can see, the company's basic work contributed to two important social purposes that no other enterprise was addressing in Chile: reducing toxic pollution and equipping organizations that served the poor. How did serving these purposes affect the firm's costs?

- Customer companies were willing to pay high prices to have their electronic gear hauled away and properly recycled in order to gain the "Green Seal" that RECYCLA Chile used to certify that its customers were responsibly disposing of all their electronic gear. Green Seal products are much more appealing to manufacturers' environmentally conscious customers.

    Other Latin American recyclers, in contrast, received no pay for disposing of electronic products because they didn't provide such certifications. As a result of receiving such pay, RECYCLA Chile's operating costs were 60 percent less than for many competitors.

- RECYCLA Chile picked suppliers that properly recycled the disassembled equipment. As a result of paying suppliers to do more extensive processing, some of RECYCLA Chile's recycling costs were higher than those of competitors. Such increased costs were more than offset by the value of receiving customer payments for recycling.

- Because of its exemplary practices, RECYCLA Chile won many environmental and entrepreneurial awards. The company's founder met the CEOs of many large, environmentally conscious companies while receiving recycling awards, and the CEO-to-CEO contacts helped lead some of the companies to hire RECYCLA Chile. Such recognition helped reduce marketing costs while allowing the firm to be much more successful in gaining customers, also reducing fixed costs as a percentage of sales.

Mr. Nilo didn't stop there in providing social benefits. He also chose to only hire ex-convicts to work in his recycling facility, as well as to pick up and to deliver recycled goods. Many such employees wouldn't otherwise have been able to find honest work in Chile. As a result, they were often highly motivated to do well and didn't require high wages. Here are the three most important ways that hiring ex-convicts reduced the firm's costs:

1. Wages were lower.

2. Productivity was higher.

3. Customers were added who liked the idea of "recycling" people by giving them another chance to become productive. Such added volume further reduced marketing and fixed costs as a percentage of sales.

In 2007, Mr. Nilo wrote a book about his company and its business model called *The New Trash of the 21st Century*, which can be downloaded in Spanish from http://www.ecoeduca.cl/casadelapaz/publicaciones _doc/residuos_electronicos.pdf.

During the MIT lecture, Mr. Nilo mentioned that he would be glad to assist entrepreneurs who wanted to set up similar operations in other underdeveloped nations. If that's of interest, you should contact him through his company's Web site (www.recycla.cl*)*.

Even if you don't intend to become an electronics recycler, what lessons does this example suggest for developing a minimum best practice? The primary lesson is to add several social purposes to your business model. To do so, apply the lens of such social purposes to help you anticipate cost-reduction opportunities that you might otherwise miss.

Here are some examples of social purposes and associated cost-reduction opportunities that might apply to your situation:

- Improve the environment.

  — Gain income from recycling.

  — Attract environmentally concerned customers more easily and less expensively.

  — Charge higher prices to offset some of any increased costs.

  — Lower operating costs by wasting fewer materials.

  — Draw the attention of more potential customers and hire a more determined work force through positive publicity.

  — Obtain grants from governments to do important tasks that no one else will pay for.

- Reduce disease.

  — Sell some offerings to public health agencies and governments with less marketing cost.

  — Receive support from government agencies when selling to physicians and hospitals to further reduce marketing costs.

  — Open doors to selling related products and reduce any shared costs of sales and distribution.

- Hire poor people who couldn't otherwise find honest work.

  — Lower the cost of wages and benefits.

  — Gain a more productive work force.

  — Increase sales to organizations and individuals that care about poor people.

  — Qualify to compete for government programs aimed at reducing poverty.

  — Receive foundation and government grants to help educate and train workers.

- Certify customer and supplier practices.

    — Acquire the most socially conscious customers and suppliers more easily, reducing marketing and operating costs.

    — Charge higher prices to customers and pay less to suppliers due to the economic benefits of certification, thus reducing total costs as a percentage of sales.

    — Obtain free positive publicity.

    — Add consulting services that make it less costly to work with customers and suppliers to reform their practices, generating extra income to subsidize costs that cannot otherwise be eliminated.

- Provide essential services to poor people who otherwise wouldn't receive them (such as potable water, electricity, waste removal, telephone, etc.).

    — Qualify for lower-cost financing from governments and foundations.

    — Potentially receive ongoing operating subsidies from governments and foundations.

    — Develop infrastructure scale that makes it possible to also provide services to those in nearby areas who can afford to pay.

    — As more people are served, lower costs due to increasing economies of scale.

    — Perform highly profitable activities that are related to the basic offering. (For example, a treadle pump seller may be able to make sales of drip-irrigation equipment to some of those whose profits rapidly expand from using treadle pumps.)

I'm sure you have your own ideas well … all of which will undoubtedly be better than mine. Please feel free to share your ideas with me!

What's the key cost-cutting lesson from serving social purposes? **You can help reduce your and stakeholders' costs as a percentage of selling prices by 96 percent in ways that will expand your organization's profits through revising your business model to serve many beneficial social purposes.**

Assignments

1. Identify ten social purposes that could help you lower costs to below your competitors.

2. Examine each of the ten social purposes to consider what the cost, profit, and cash-flow potentials are for serving each by evaluating:

   a. What you can charge

   b. Which customers will be attracted

   c. How large can the organization's revenues grow

   d. What advantages you can gain in accessing and pleasing customers

e. **What free resources you can draw on**

f. **How productivity can be enhanced**

g. **What proprietary knowledge advantages you will gain and how you will be able to employ such advantages**

h. **Which elements of cost will decline and by how much when serving each current or potential customer**

i. **What the effects on each stakeholder will be**

3. **Consider the difficulty of operating with each social purpose.**

4. **Look at the risks involved if your business model doesn't work well in providing each social purpose.**

5. **Select one social purpose to focus on first and develop a plan to adjust your business model to optimize the advantages offered by that first social purpose.**

6. **Later add other social purposes by repeating steps 1-5.**

What Locations Should Be Part of Your Minimum Business Model?

*Then the prophet Haggai and Zechariah the son of Iddo, prophets,
prophesied to the Jews who were in Judah and Jerusalem,
in the name of the God of Israel, who was over them.
So Zerubbabel the son of Shealtiel and Jeshua the son of Jozadak
rose up and began to build the house of God which is in Jerusalem;
and the prophets of God were with them, helping them.*

— Ezra 5:1-2 (NKJV)

When I teach new entrepreneurs, sometime during the very first class hour someone usually asks where to locate a business. It's good for you to ask and thoughtfully answer that question. However, I find that most people select the sites for their business based solely on where they live. To test my observation, check announcements of companies moving their headquarters. Then find out where the CEO lives, and you'll usually see that the new location is less of a commute to and from the CEO's home.

Professor Michael Porter from Harvard Business School has done research concerning how location affects costs and effectiveness. He points out that ideal locations are often far from obvious. For instance, farmers in Israel lower their costs for selling and distributing flowers to other Middle Eastern countries by first air freighting their offerings to the flower market in Holland, even though the new owners will then have to air freight the same flowers from Holland to their countries. Although the cost of transportation is obviously much higher, the total cost is much less for connecting the Israeli growers with Arab buyers and distributing the flowers than by seeking direct sales. That beneficial result occurs because the Holland flower market is so efficient in bringing buyers and sellers together.

Another example of an efficient central market may encourage you to consider alternative locations. If you want to buy or sell a hundred shares of a publicly held stock in the United States, you can probably make the transaction by paying a brokerage fee of $5.00 or less, and paying or receiving money based on a spread between the quoted buy and sell prices of 0.5 percent or less.

Now imagine that you want to buy or sell the same dollar value of stock in a privately held company of the same size. Both the buyer and the seller will probably have to employ business brokers, attorneys, accountants, and complete lots of paper work. Closing the transaction could easily cost all parties over $10,000 in total.

Although lots of people work hard to pick the best location for a business facility, they almost never look at the whole value chain to determine what the overall cost impact will be on all stakeholders. When most people think about supply chains, they often focus on just the people who supply them and the people they sell to. The complete value chain, however, is much larger, beginning with those who contribute to designing offerings and continuing through to those who purchase from salvagers for reuse or entirely different uses, until nothing from the original offering is still being employed in any form.

While considering the ideal locations for a business model, you should be open to changing the business model to reflect what you learn about the benefits and unusual characteristics of attractive locations.

Let me outline eleven of the more important factors that could affect your decision:

1. Investigate price effects.

   The lowest-cost market for producing something is seldom the highest-priced market for selling something. Look for where the spread between prices and costs will be the highest and most sustained because of the extra value you are delivering to stakeholders by being present in that market. In that way, your costs will be lower … relative to your prices.

   Yes, you can get your hair cut less expensively in the Amazon rain forest than in downtown Manhattan, but the prices for the offerings of most organizations are also very low in the Amazon rain forest.

2. Consider how base demand shifts.

   As I have mentioned before, increased revenues allow businesses to spread their fixed and semifixed costs over a larger base and reduce those costs as a percentage-of-sales and per-offering. No offering is purchased at exactly the same rate from one geographical location to another. That's because some offerings are more relevant in certain areas (such as very warm clothing in Antarctica) while customer preferences favor certain locales (listening to live Jazz in bars is much more popular in New Orleans than in most other places).

   Most people only think in terms of separating supply from demand when considering locations. In the minimum business model, you will often seek to serve and supply from the same place. Why? It gives you a greater ability to understand your market and to focus on providing what's needed very rapidly and more appropriately.

3. Quickly deliver custom offerings.

   Unless the price premium is unaffordable for custom offerings, most people prefer them to standard offerings. Many people also like custom offerings to be immediately available. As an example, some tailors in Hong Kong will fit your custom-made suit in the morning and deliver it just after lunch. If you don't like some little aspect of what was done, the change can be promptly made, and you'll be happily wearing your new suit just a few minutes later.

4. Make it painless to buy.

Imagine instead that the tailor shop for custom suits is located in the hotel where you are staying and the fittings can be done in your room. Such extra convenience would make it harder to resist having a beautiful new suit that has your name sewn on the lining in gorgeous calligraphy.

5. Be impossible to avoid.

Most people like fresh flowers, but they often don't think to buy any. Why? Nothing reminds them to do so. One florist in New York City overcame that limitation by putting astonishingly beautiful arrangements throughout one of Manhattan's most popular hotels, the Pierre, and locating its shop opposite the lobby's most impressive arrangement. After viewing such an arrangement, I have often found myself unexpectedly wandering into that shop to order flowers for my business meetings in Manhattan, my hotel room, and friends who live nearby.

6. Be where you can make people feel great.

For many years, I regularly traveled to San Francisco. For convenience, I usually stayed at the same hotel, the Hyatt on Union Square. Because of the nice weather, it was almost always pleasant to be outdoors while I was in the vicinity, and I could walk to my meetings.

The hotel's daytime doorman made it a point to remember my name. Whenever he saw me within fifty yards, he would display a big grin, shout my name, wave, and make me feel like the King of England. Naturally, my tipping was stimulated by all this extra attention.

7. Use free resources to your best advantage.

I don't know about you, but I enjoy beautiful views. As part of your business, you could supply such a view (at great expense) for stakeholders, or you could just pick a location where those who visit will enjoy such a wonderful view at no added cost. Many of our firm's offices have been located on upper floors of buildings or in buildings located atop hills where we paid no premium for enjoying spectacular vistas.

Similarly, there may be some wonderful place to visit near your place of business that will attract stakeholders. Our consulting firm was located for many years in the middle of Harvard University so that we could speedily travel to the school's libraries. During those years, we often attracted clients who were in town to visit professors or who had relatives attending the university.

8. Consider the minimum configuration.

I have often seen tutors providing lessons at quiet out-of-the-way tables in libraries, software consultants training clients in coffee-bar nooks, and venture capitalists listening to pitches from entrepreneurs at outdoor picnic tables in office parks. In most cases, using such comfortable facilities cost nothing extra.

9. Turn accessibility into lower costs.

The more accessible you are, the easier it is for prospective customers to decide to do business with you. But accessibility doesn't have to be expensive. For instance, rather than rent expensive space to sell coffee in a high-rent, warm-weather neighborhood, find a nearby public place, acquire an inexpensive municipal license to operate there, and operate from a beautiful cart where you brew and serve great coffees. If you find a public place with lots of foot traffic, it will be closer to many potential customers than would be the nearest coffee bar that's renting space.

10. Offer a specialty that customers cannot obtain elsewhere.

In this way, your business can become a destination for those who are intrigued by what you offer. Because there is no other source, you can also charge prices that optimize costs for stakeholders and you.
      The test of a desirable specialty is that people will come to your location in that city from other cities just to acquire what you offer.

11. Pick locations that greatly boost productivity.

I long ago discovered that I am much more productive in some locations than in others. As an example, I attended the Salzburg Festival in Austria for a few summers because I could get so much work done while sitting in the public gardens there. Eventually, I learned how to achieve similar levels of personal productivity in my hometown. Naturally, that learning cut expenses quite a lot!

To deepen your understanding of operating in the ideal location, I invite you to reread the golf caddie example that is on pages 5 through 8 of *The Ultimate Competitive Advantage*.
      What's the key cost-reducing point about location? **You can help reduce your and all stakeholders' costs compared to prices by 96 percent in ways that will expand your profits through revising your business model to provide just the minimum best practice in the optimal locations.**

Assignments

1. Identify three locations that could help you gain a lower cost compared to competitors than you have now.

2. Examine each of the three locations to consider what the cost, profit, and cash-flow potentials are for each by evaluating:

　a. What you can charge

　b. Which customers will be attracted

　c. How much the organization's revenues will grow

　d. What advantages you can gain in accessing and pleasing customers

　e. What free resources you can draw on

　f. How productivity can be enhanced

　g. What proprietary knowledge advantages you will gain and how you will be able to employ such advantages

　h. What elements of cost will decline and by how much with each current or potential customer

　i. What the effects are on each stakeholder

3. Consider the difficulty of operating in each location.

4. Look at the risks involved if your business model doesn't work well in each location.

5. Select one location to focus on first and develop a plan to adjust your business model to optimize the advantages and unique characteristics that location offers.

Lesson Thirty-Six

Develop Superior Solutions
to Sell to Many Others

But you, brethren, are not in darkness,
so that this Day should overtake you as a thief.
You are all sons of light and sons of the day.
We are not of the night nor of darkness.
Therefore let us not sleep, as others do,
but let us watch and be sober.
For those who sleep, sleep at night,
and those who get drunk are drunk at night.
But let us who are of the day be sober,
putting on the breastplate of faith and love,
and as a helmet the hope of salvation.
For God did not appoint us to wrath,
but to obtain salvation through our Lord Jesus Christ,
who died for us, that whether we wake or sleep,
we should live together with Him.
Therefore comfort each other and edify one another,
just as you also are doing.

— 1 Thessalonians 5:4-11 (NKJV)

In this lesson, we add to the minimum business model foundation a major new dimension of cost reductions: *developing and providing superior breakthrough solutions at low cost to many others.*

The lesson was inspired by a discussion with a business professor who was interested in changing how companies view their roles in society. At the time, he had begun to form three organizations for advancing the concept.

As the professor described his plans, it was clear to me that he knew very little about business-model innovation and the kinds of sales-expanding and cost-reducing concepts that we have been working on. As a result, he had objectives that were much too modest, a need for resources that was much too large, and a strategy that would make too little progress. Clearly, he would need hundreds of millions of dollars to do it the way he intended, and he had acquired much less than 1 percent of that amount.

I designed a new business model for him based on the successes of the 400 Year Project (see www.fastforward400.com). As I described the model, I realized that this approach could be easily shifted to become a great business model for entrepreneurs, as well.

Let me describe the solution I have in mind for you. While making outstanding breakthroughs in industry growth and cost reductions, and avoiding investments by your organization and its stakeholders, you will learn a great many things that could also benefit businesses that are similar to yours. As a result, you have opportunities to enter the business of helping others learn how to do what you have done. Because you can add much more value in total to their businesses than to yours, teaching such lessons will often be a much larger and more attractive alternative to just operating your business well.

Here's an example. A sawmill owner worked on reducing how much lumber was spoiled during drying. He experimented with new ways to dry lumber until he found one that greatly reduced wastage. The impact on his profits was impressive, adding about $100,000 a year.

After employing the solution for awhile, he took a marketing course where he was encouraged to teach other sawmill operators how to cure lumber the way he did. Over the years, the sawmill innovator kept raising his rates for seminars. At the time I met him, each attendee was paying around $25,000. Profits from running the seminars increased to several million dollars … a much larger amount than what he earned from employing the innovation in his own sawmill.

You could do something similar. Start by using the new crowd-sourcing methods for problem solving to cut your costs of locating superior solutions (as described in Lesson Thirty-One). Then, offer for-profit services demonstrating how to employ the best solutions. As a result, you would make more market-expanding, cost-reducing, and investment-eliminating improvements in your operations, as well as gain a major new source of income to offset other costs.

Here are the steps for how such a new business activity might be conducted:

1. Provide a blog on a free site that's relevant to owners and managers of businesses like yours. Attract an audience by sharing lots of valuable information that isn't widely known.

2. After you have a sufficient audience, propose a contest to make a breakthrough in some activity that many such organizations have problems with. An example of the kind of common problem that I have in mind is reducing payroll costs during a sales slump without laying people off or causing top performers to leave. To help more people become aware of your contest, you can alert user groups interested in related issues about your contest and invite people to go to the blog.

   Crowdsourcing tells us that the best way to organize such a contest is by identifying the best available solution on a daily basis and allowing entrants to incorporate elements of the current-best solution into their own proposals. In this way, solution paths are rapidly tweaked to become much better rather than staying stuck at a given improvement level until the end of the contest. You can provide such information to current and potential entrants by simply making a daily blog entry. In such a contest, it's not unusual for the best solution to be over a hundred times more valuable than the best solution from a typical, provide-only-one-solution-per-entrant contest.

   You should conduct the contest for from two to six months, depending on how valuable the answers are likely to be. The higher-value contests should be kept open longer. At the end, you would recognize, praise, and reward the winner and publicize the solution's general characteristics and benefits. Be sure to obtain the legal right to use the solution for other purposes as a condition of entering the contest.

3. Next, implement the solution in your organization and those of any stakeholders who would like to participate, carefully observing what the best practices are. Credibly document the gains your organization and any stakeholders make.

4. After you learn how to do this improvement well and document the gains, offer in-person training, seminars, teleseminars, and written materials that demonstrate how to apply what you learned to similar businesses. You can publicize such learning opportunities through the people who entered the contest, your blog, and the various places where you publicized the contest. If you don't have the time or staff to do this, you can instead work with a partner skilled in such activities and pay the partner with commissions tied to the sales of the services and products to develop the materials, to organize the offerings, to market them, and (if appropriate) to provide the offerings. With the right partner, you may at most need a video describing your experiences that can be shared with those who purchase the offerings.

As you can see, the potential income from such breakthrough solutions is endless. You can continually run new contests to find better solutions for the same issues and then provide what you most recently learned and demonstrated for a fee to the same people who bought offerings demonstrating less helpful solutions.

I hope that you are as excited about this cost-reduction concept as I am.

What's the key cost-reducing point about developing superior solutions at little cost to sell to others? **You can use zero-based analysis to create 2,000 percent cost-reduction solutions that help to eliminate more than 96 percent of your and stakeholders' costs or to increase social benefits by more than twenty times of what you and your stakeholders will be spending in ways that will expand your profits by developing superior solutions at little cost to sell to others while providing the minimum core offering to benefit all stakeholders.**

Assignments

1. Pick a high-value activity that many organizations like yours would like to improve.

2. Conduct a global contest at low cost by employing the methods described in Lesson Thirty-One and in this lesson to locate a breakthrough solution based on publishing daily updates about what the best available solution is.

3. Pick a winner and announce the results.

4. Implement what you learned and credibly document how much you gained as a result.

5. Package your experience with applying this new concept into various materials and services that many organizations like yours can easily afford to acquire and to use.

6. Make such learning-related products and services available.

7. Repeat steps 2 through 6 in the same breakthrough activity every three years.

Part Four

Eliminate Investments

The song of the terrible ones will be diminished.

— Isaiah 25:5 (NKJV)

We turn now to the third of the first three 2,000 percent solutions needed to create an outstanding enterprise — reduce by 96 percent your and your stakeholders' investments to provide and to use an offering. Before shifting into lessons about how to accomplish such a result, let's consider some of the financial effects.

Growing revenues by twenty times is obviously necessary to having a larger enterprise, one that can have a more substantial impact. Reducing costs by 96 percent makes expansion highly profitable and helps to finance growth. What does reducing stakeholder investments do for finances?

Let's start with your organization. A typical manufacturing company will have two dollars of sales for every dollar of net investment (total assets minus the total amount of accumulated depreciation and amortization). Thus, a million-dollar revenue manufacturer needs approximately $500,000 of investment capital (provided by debt and equity). Acquiring this money can be a big hurdle for an entrepreneur. As a result, most larger manufacturing companies have many investors who combine to provide the needed debt and equity.

Next, let's shrink the amount of capital needed by 96 percent. When we do that, $500,000 of investment capital becomes $20,000. That's still a lot of money, but for a low-cost enterprise that earns several hundred thousand dollars a year, it's a drop in the bucket.

In addition, your total cost of capital is a lot smaller ... no matter how much or little you pay for the amount of capital you use. For instance, at 10 percent interest borrowing $500,000 would cost $50,000 a year (before considering tax deductions to offset some of the cost). In comparison, if you only need to borrow $20,000 at 10 percent interest, your annual pretax borrowing cost is $2,000.

But an enterprise that is highly profitable and growing rapidly is going to need a lot more capital. Imagine now that you want to expand from being a $1 million a year manufacturer to becoming a $10 million a year manufacturer. Normally, that would mean adding $4,500,000 in investments.

By reducing investment needs by 96 percent, you would only require $180,000 more investment capital. If you have a good track record and well-documented business plan, many banks will finance that much investment knowing that you will earn it back in just a short amount of time. As a result, your choice of capital sources is wider, and the difficulty of gaining the capital is much reduced.

Let's now consider the typical $10 million a year manufacturing company. Let's assume that it grows revenues by 10 percent in a year. That growth means $1 million more in revenues and $500,000 more in required investment each year. Most manufacturers of that size earn about 4 percent of sales after paying income taxes. That profit margin translates into earnings of $400,000, and all of that amount (plus an additional $100,000) would be needed to pay for the growth. As a result, no money could be paid to shareholders in dividends. The value to owners would rise, but that increased value would have no cash component until the owners sold their stock in the enterprise.

Let's compare that situation with having reduced reinvestment needs by 96 percent. When that's the case, the increase of $1 million in revenues requires only $20,000 more capital. As a result, $380,000 in earnings can be paid out to shareholders after financing growth.

If the organization also employs the 96 percent lower-cost methods in Part Three, profits are twenty times larger ($8 million) and the dividends that can be paid to investors are much larger ($7.98 million). When that's the case, investors see the value of their shares rise by 10 percent and the value of their dividend payouts rise by almost as much as the earnings increase each year. It's like getting paid twice for making the same investment.

As you can see, there are huge owner benefits for reducing the cost of capital, improving cash flow, and increasing dividends.

But those aren't the most important benefits from reducing investments by 96 percent. Let's look at seven strategic advantages:

1. By requiring very little capital to grow, accessing money is never going to limit growth. Thus, during times of rapid industry expansion, you should be able to gain market share just by being more able to afford adding capacity.

2. By having very small investments in assets, you have enormous flexibility in making changes to your business model. For example, let's imagine that you decided to replace all of your assets in a ten million-dollar-a-year manufacturing business. It would only cost you $200,000, what your company earns after tax in a little over three weeks. As a result, you could afford to totally upgrade your business model as fast as you could think of an improvement you wanted to make.

3. Because your investment is so small, the value of your enterprise is much higher. You deliver lots of profits *and* cash flow. As a result, you can use less stock to make acquisitions. Then, by applying your superior low-investment business model, you can quickly increase the value of any business you buy. You have plenty of cash to change its business model all the time, too. As a result, you can quickly take over your competitors, subject only to any legal restraints. As a result, your competitive risk is very small.

4. Because your need to make new investments is so small, you free up lots of time to work on other areas of improving your operations and outperforming competitors in serving stakeholders. As a result, process improvements should be installed at least three times more frequently.

5. Without a need to be concerned about capital constraints, you can adjust much faster to changes in the market. Thus, when the world changes (as it seemed to do in 2007 when many advanced nations hit the wall economically due to housing price and banking bubbles collapsing), such a firm can adjust more rapidly to the new realities by switching to offerings that fit the changed needs of their stakeholders.

6. Reducing investment needs often leads to fewer operating costs. For example, companies with limited investments don't have as large charges for depreciation, amortization, and interest expense.

    In addition, methods of providing offerings that need fewer investment resources often don't require as many costs, either. When you visit a contract custom-manufacturing facility, for instance, the assembly station will typically receive its components just a few minutes before assembly, the assembly and testing processes will be completed in a few more minutes, and the item will be out of the facility on its way to customers in not too many more minutes. The infrastructure costs for such an activity aren't much different from what a highly efficient, low overhead garage shop could do with highly skilled, low-cost help.

7. Stakeholders gain parallel benefits from reducing their investment intensity, allowing them to improve their circumstances and to adapt to changed circumstances much more easily and rapidly.

What's the key point about reducing investment intensity? **You and your stakeholders gain important strategic advantages and ownership rewards from reducing investment needs by 96 percent compared to what is done now to provide and to use an offering.**

Assignments

1. Identify the five most important strategic benefits that your enterprise would gain through reducing by 96 percent its need for investment capital.

2. Consider what it is about your current business model that requires so much investment capital compared to your revenues.

3. Investigate how competitors operate in ways that reduce their investment needs compared to what you do.

4. Research how companies in other industries operate with less investment capital than you do.

5. Identify five ways you could improve your business model to greatly reduce your investment needs while increasing your effectiveness in serving stakeholders.

6. Consider how similar benefits could be provided to stakeholders through these five business-model improvements.

Lesson Thirty-Seven

Produce Almost Instantly

Behold, I tell you a mystery:
We shall not all sleep, but we shall all be changed —
in a moment, in the twinkling of an eye,
at the last trumpet. For the trumpet will sound,
and the dead will be raised incorruptible, and we shall be changed.
For this corruptible must put on incorruption,
and this mortal must *put on immortality.*

— 1 Corinthians 15:51-53 (NKJV)

This lesson begins considering methods that can contribute to reducing all of your and your stakeholders' investments by 96 percent by focusing on an operational discipline that provides many other advantages: producing a product or service almost instantly.

In practice, it's not possible to produce instantly … but it's certainly desirable to get as close to that result as you can. As an example, one of the closest ways anyone comes to instant production is on Wall Street, where a security purchase or sale will be executed by computers in a few milliseconds after market conditions match two trade orders.

Almost any business can do nearly as well by providing electronic access to an information product or service over the Internet that can be purchased by clicking on an icon.

In the personal computer industry, Dell has long made it a standard manufacturing practice to produce and to ship many custom-made machines within a few hours of an order being placed over the Internet.

In fast-food restaurants, most orders are delivered within a few minutes of being received.

Okay, so now you probably agree that many organizations do produce and deliver products or services almost instantly.

What are the benefits of such fast performance for reducing investment intensity?

1. *Any process that moves very quickly has to eliminate times where nothing is being done to provide and to distribute the offering.*

    As a result, work-in-process inventories for products are reduced to almost nothing.

    In addition, such a process has to be designed to be conducted with few errors (otherwise lots of mistakes reach customers' hands … causing all kinds of problems). As a result of making few errors, there's very little product inventory being reworked or returned by customers.

Further, customers aren't holding back payments because they've received faulty offerings. As a result, accounts receivable are lower.

Instant production processes for physical offerings are almost always produced by using just-in-time inventory deliveries. As a result, input inventory levels are kept to just a few hours' worth of materials.

Since the production process itself has to be very simple (or it can't be done very fast), production areas are smaller, and the equipment is often simpler and less expensive. For example, Dell assembles and tests its desktop computers in work areas that contain just a few more tools and resources than what most hobbyists have in their home shops.

2. *When providing offerings is almost instant and nearly perfect, it can be appropriate to ask customers to pay more promptly.*

   In many such circumstances, customers either pay just when they order or just after an offering is shipped. When either happens, the usual payment delay of thirty, sixty, or ninety days can be eliminated or reduced. Customers are not disadvantaged because they are receiving the value from their orders much sooner and may also be paying a lower price. Customers who would like the convenience of writing checks less often can simply use stored credit-card information for the payments, and producers can receive good funds in their accounts just a few hours later.

3. *Near-instant production can usually be combined with fast design cycles so that there is less time, money, and effort expended in developing new offerings before customer cash begins to be received.*

   Many such offerings are designed to have a very short life. For instance, if the price of pork ribs temporarily drops, a restaurant chain may design a new menu item with a low price to take advantage of a large bulk purchase, intending to eliminate the menu item whenever the inexpensive raw materials are used up. In electronic products, many upgrades based on using newer components are expected to have a market life of only a few weeks or months before being replaced by the next improvement.

   Traditionally, the length of time from starting to design an offering to making it available was several years. Because of such long durations, it was possible to tie up billions of dollars in development investment for a single item (such as a new game system). If development is going to last only three months, you simply can't spend that much … and you start receiving a return on whatever money you spend a lot faster.

4. *Near-instant production usually relies on general-purpose facilities and equipment that can have very long economic lives. As a result, capital investments are a smaller percentage of sales than for firms that produce from special-purpose facilities.*

   General-purpose facilities are often necessary when production is frequently reconfigured to supply new offerings. The special investments needed for supplying such offerings are also very limited.

5. *Organizations with near-instant production benefit when such operations are located close to customers. As a result, many investments can be avoided.*

   One of my students discovered that his organization's production could be very closely integrated into customers' production methods. In that way, his company was able to benefit from existing customer investments in power plants, land, buildings, and infrastructure. As a result, the new business model only required half the capital of the old business model to support a given level of revenues.

I'm sure you have your own observations about how near-instant production can eliminate investment needs. Please add such opportunities to your thinking, as well.

What's the point about producing almost instantly? **Near-instant production and delivery of offerings can rapidly reduce a company's and its stakeholders' investment needs by 96 percent compared to what they are now in ways that will also help make an organization and its stakeholders more successful and profitable.**

Assignments

1. Identify the five most valuable ways you could produce and deliver products and services closer to instantly than you do now and reduce your needs for investment by 96 percent.

2. Consider how such changes would affect your stakeholders.

3. Investigate how your business model could be shifted over time to be even more effective and less investment intensive by producing and delivering faster.

Lesson Thirty-Eight

Eliminate Receivables and Slash Inventories

Now for *the third time I am ready to come to you.*
And I will not be burdensome to you;
for I do not seek yours, but you.
For the children ought not to lay up for the parents,
but the parents for the children.
And I will very gladly spend and be spent for your souls;
though the more abundantly I love you, the less I am loved.
But be that as it may, *I did not burden you.*

— 2 Corinthians 12:14-16 (NKJV)

In the preceding lesson, I described a large number of advantages gained by providing offerings almost instantly. Now I would like to describe more general-purpose ways to gain some of the same advantages. We begin by considering useful ways to *eliminate receivables* (accounts receivable) and *slash inventories*. We look first at receivables.

Eliminate Your and Your Stakeholders' Receivables

To receive the instruction of wisdom,
Justice, judgment, and equity;

— Proverbs 1:3 (NKJV)

What is an *account receivable*? It's an invoice you've issued to a customer for a payment that's currently due. In essence, you have extended credit to your customer until the customer pays. How much credit you grant is determined by the likelihood that you will be paid on time, the creditworthiness of the customer, how much influence you have with the customer, and payment practices in your industry. Accounts receivable are simply the sum of all of the outstanding invoices that are due to your organization because they haven't yet been paid.

Why do customers want credit? You would have to ask each customer to know for sure, but common reasons include the following:

- They want to examine the offering to be sure it doesn't have flaws before paying in order to make it easier to persuade you to either take a defective offering back or to correct any defects.

- It's impractical for them to process and pay invoices very fast, and the credit period allows them time to do the necessary steps.

- They already owe a lot of money and don't want to pay interest costs to borrow more in order to pay you more rapidly.

- Their management bonuses are based in part on having more cash on hand. As a result, their managers earn bigger bonuses when you are paid more slowly.

- The company is in desperate need of cash to keep operating and cannot borrow any more at a reasonable cost. This reason occurs more often during deep or prolonged recessions.

- They have always gotten credit at no cost and see no reason to lose the benefit.

Now let's look at the other side of the credit issue. Why might you want to extend credit?

- You make a lot of mistakes in providing your offerings and don't want to annoy your customers even more by expecting them to pay before you correct matters.

- They aren't going to pay in the usual time because their payables processing is so inefficient, and you don't want to annoy them by sending reminder notices and calling when you know that they lack the systems to pay.

- They negotiated for lots of credit as part of the deal through which you got the order. If you ask them to pay sooner, you just increase the likelihood that they will switch suppliers.

- You have lots of extra cash and can afford to use extended credit as a way to attract business ... something your competitors cannot match.

- Your bonus isn't affected by the size of accounts receivable, but it is affected by whether or not you lose an account (as is the case with sales- or profit-based bonuses).

Next let's examine why a customer might not want to have credit.

- You offer a lower price to those who pay cash in advance or on receipt of the offering.

- The person you work with in the customer company knows that internal budget cuts might be coming and wants to spend the existing budget with you before that happens.

- The cost of your offerings doesn't negatively affect the company's investment and equity returns because the expenses are charged only to the balance sheet rather than the profit-and-loss statement, which is the case for many services associated with capital transactions such as investment-banking fees for making an acquisition or a divestiture.

- Paying you more promptly gains the customer some desired advantage in working with you and your organization such as having more access to your best people.

Finally, let's look at why you might not want to extend credit.

- If you can get paid sooner without making a price concession or annoying the customer, you can earn a return on that capital or avoid paying interest on that amount of money (if you are a borrower).

- If there is any risk that the customer will never pay you, you avoid losing money due to such a default.

- If your organization is committed to working closely with customers, not extending credit may increase your focus on providing the best possible offerings and services so that you don't annoy someone who has or will be paying you very promptly.

- If you have limited funds, the cash you have can be redirected into a more valuable use for all of your customers and stakeholders.

- If you don't have to carry very many accounts receivable, you will be able to serve more customers from the capital base that you have now.

Now that you've seen a number of different perspectives on the subject, I'm sure it's begun to occur to you that substantial accounts receivable exist mostly for good reasons that can, however, be offset by providing even more desirable reasons for customers not to receive credit. When you offer and deliver on your promises concerning what customers care the most about, you usually don't have to offer much, if any, credit, and customers feel well treated by obtaining something that's more valuable to them than credit.

Here's how my consulting firm approached this issue. Beginning a few years after we started, we provided the option to make a prepayment of one-third of the estimated professional fees for the total project. We would keep the prepayment until the other two-thirds of the project had been paid, then credit our customer's account for the prepayment. When someone took this option, we operated with advance-paid funds throughout any project. We justified this option to customers by offering lower prices that reflected the prevailing interest rates. People were always happy to take that option. In the process, most clients saved about 2 to 5 percent of the project's cost. Later, we began asking for 100 percent prepayment of professional fees on the same basis, and people were happy as long as we guaranteed our work.

Each company will have to examine its own circumstances and those of its customers to see how it might provide customer benefits that are more valuable than credit.

Obviously, it will be easiest to establish such an approach when starting a new customer relationship or launching a new company. If your alternatives to offering credit are more attractive to each customer, you'll find that they will start shifting toward your preferred credit practices once they understand the benefits.

I'm sure you have your own ideas about how to eliminate accounts receivable in ways that are desirable for all stakeholders. Please add such opportunities to your thinking, as well.

What's the key point about eliminating receivables? **By reconfiguring your relationship with customers to provide more value in different ways, you can rapidly reduce your company's need to offer credit by 96 percent compared to what you do now in ways that will also help make your organization and its stakeholders more successful, profitable, and cash rich.**

Assignments

1. Identify the five most valuable ways you could provide benefits to customers that they would prefer over receiving credit from your organization.

2. Consider how such changes would affect your other stakeholders.

3. Investigate how your business model could be shifted to be even more effective by providing even more valuable benefits than credit to customers that are helpful for other stakeholders.

Slash Your and Your Stakeholders' Inventories

"When Israel was a child, I loved him,
And out of Egypt I called My son.
As they called them,
So they went from them;
They sacrificed to the Baals,
And burned incense to carved images.
I taught Ephraim to walk,
Taking them by their arms;
But they did not know that I healed them.
I drew them with gentle cords,
With bands of love,
And I was to them as those who take the yoke from their neck.
I stooped and fed them.
He shall not return to the land of Egypt;
But the Assyrian shall be his king,
Because they refused to repent.
And the sword shall slash in his cities,
Devour his districts,
And consume them,
Because of their own counsels.
My people are bent on backsliding from Me.
Though they call to the Most High,
None at all exalt Him.

— Hosea 11:1-7 (NKJV)

What is *inventory*? It's an accounting term that applies in a big way to all manufacturing organizations, in an important way to retailers and wholesalers, and to some extent to other service organizations in terms of essential equipment that frequently wears out (such as replacement airplane parts for an airline).

Let's start with manufacturers. They usually have four kinds of inventories: raw materials, in-process goods, finished goods, and spare parts. A screw manufacturer might start by purchasing steel rods to make screws. Such rods would be raw-material inventory. Without some such inventory, the screw manufacturer couldn't start its production process. As soon as some cuts are made into the steel to reshape it into screws, the steel moves from being raw-material inventory to being in-process inventory. When the work is completed on the in-process inventory and the products are ready for use, the screws become finished-goods inventory. Until someone buys and takes legal possession of the finished screws, they are part of the manufacturer's asset base as inventory. The screw-making equipment will probably need to have some spare dies to cut the screw threads, and such dies and any replacement production components will be in the spare-parts inventory. After a purchaser takes legal possession of the finished goods, the manufacturer's finished inventory moves onto the balance sheet of the purchaser.

I won't continue the example for how inventory is treated on the customer's balance sheet. Please send any questions to askdonmitchell@yahoo.com.

For retailers and wholesalers, typically there is only one class of inventory: finished goods that they sell. Some of that inventory may be readily accessible to customers while other inventory is in backup storage, such as offsite warehouses.

For other service organizations, typically there is only one class of inventory: spare parts on hand that are needed to sustain operations when an essential part wears out.

Before looking at how inventories can be slashed, let's first list some of the reasons why there are inventories. We'll start with manufacturers:

- If you do any manufacturing for yourself (as opposed to hiring contract manufacturers), you need some raw materials, in-process goods, and spare parts.

- If your customers do not take immediate ownership of all finished items before or when you complete them, you are going to have some finished inventory.

Retailers and wholesalers usually need to have some stock on hand for people who immediately want the goods. For instance, when you go to the supermarket to buy food for dinner tonight, you don't want to wait for what you bought to be delivered tomorrow. You would, instead, buy the items from whatever stores had the food in stock or purchase different food that is in stock.

Other service organizations will have some spare parts so that critical equipment can be kept in service. Otherwise, there might be a delay of two or three days waiting for a part, causing some operations to halt. Manufacturers have a similar need for spare parts, but that need usually accounts for just a small percentage of all their inventories.

Your business model and the ways you manage your business also have large effects on your level of inventories. Let's look at a few manufacturing examples:

- If your raw-material suppliers provide large price discounts for volume purchases, you may only purchase from them every few months. In the meantime, the unused inventory simply sits at your premises until you put all of the last purchased raw materials into the manufacturing process.

- If your equipment is highly automated, it may not make sense to set it up to make certain items until you need a minimum quantity of such finished items. In that case, you may accumulate orders until you can produce a minimum batch (which may be quite a bit larger than the amount you have orders for, creating some finished goods inventory until more orders come in).

- If your customers have a seasonal use for your product, their consumption may exceed what you can produce during the busiest times of the year. In that case, you will start making extra items before the busy period starts. An example is a petroleum refiner making heating oil in the late summer.

- If you have a complex production process that is unreliable, you may keep extra raw-material and in-process inventories so that you won't run out of materials to work on during times you experience manufacturing problems.

- If your salespeople have trouble meeting their quotas until the end of the quarter and year, you may have to start building products before you have orders so that you can ship in time to get credit for a sale before the end of the accounting period.

- If your products need to age before they are ready to sell (such as fine wine and whiskey), you end up with lots of in-process inventory.

For a retailer or a wholesaler, you might operate so that you have no stock other than what is on your shelves. If customers want something else, they have to wait. This approach may cause sales to be lost, but it does keep inventory levels down.

A service organization might provide equipment maintenance for customers who require that spare parts be kept in stock that aren't billed until the parts are put into the customer's equipment.

What, then, are some of the classic techniques for slashing inventories?

- *Reduce the number of different offerings you provide.* Each physical offering requires inventory, yet 20 percent of your offerings will probably provide 80 percent of your volume and almost all of your profit. Cut back to just providing the most profitable 20 percent of your offerings, and you can probably eliminate 80 percent of your inventory. If you very lightly stock the lowest volume of the remaining items, you can further reduce inventory. But be sure you keep plenty of stock for what's highly profitable (in terms of return on investment) and produces most of your total profits.

- *Add inventory only when you receive an order and then custom manufacture or custom ship the item.* This is what Dell does for its desktop computers. They don't buy computer monitors until they have an order. The monitors are in inventory at the suppliers' warehouses. UPS draws from the suppliers' warehouses and coordinates delivery to the customer of the total computer order (some parts of which come from Dell's factories and some parts from suppliers' warehouses).

- *Have suppliers carry lots of finished inventory if you are a wholesaler or retailer and direct them to supply you just when you need to provide the items.* Gas stations that repair vehicles keep almost no parts. They simply expect wholesalers to deliver needed parts within an hour of calling for them.

- *Outsource as many activities as possible so that any necessary inventories are efficiently held by your suppliers.* This is a standard practice in working with outsourced suppliers.

In thinking about such techniques, it's clear that you should not focus solely on inventories in making such decisions. You want, instead, to have a business model that optimizes the overall opportunity to produce more sales, to cut costs, and to reduce investment for you and your stakeholders.

Consequently, your thinking shouldn't stop at the limits of your organizational boundaries. You also need to consider how you can slash inventories for suppliers, partners, customers, customers' customers, end users, and any other stakeholders. Otherwise, you are just moving the inventories around rather than actually slashing them. If you don't look out for stakeholders' inventories, expect that the costs of such investments will eventually come out of your profitability and cash flow in some indirect way.

Good business-model designs should reduce the amount of inventory throughout the supply chain for supplying consumption. In many manufacturing businesses, it's not unusual for there to be six months of inventory to support consumption. A better goal would be to have a few days of inventory in the entire supply chain to support consumption. How low can you go?

Here's where offering design can play a critical role. There are many different ways to serve the same need. Some methods of serving customers require much more working capital than others. Look hardest at the choices that don't require much working capital. For instance, design manufactured offerings to have fewer parts. When you do, you'll slash inventories as well as lower costs and reduce errors.

What's the key point about slashing inventory? **Redesign your company's offerings, breadth of product line, and business models to help slash the amount of inventory that's needed by your organization and by your stakeholders, contributing to reducing overall investment by 96 percent** compared to what it is now in ways that will also help make your organization and your stakeholders more successful and profitable, and rich in cash reserves.

<u>Assignments</u>

1. Identify the five most valuable ways you could reduce inventories that would provide the most benefits that customers and suppliers want.

2. Consider how such changes would affect your other stakeholders.

3. Investigate how your offerings, breadth of product line, and business models could be shifted over time to be even more effective by making it easier for your company and its stakeholders to operate with very little inventory.

Lesson Thirty-Nine

Reduce Investments in
Buildings, Land, and Equipment

Surely men of low degree are *a vapor,*
Men of high degree are *a lie;*
If they are weighed on the scales,
They are *altogether* lighter *than vapor.*
Do not trust in oppression,
Nor vainly hope in robbery;
If riches increase,
Do not set your *heart* on them.

— Psalm 62:9-10 (NKJV)

In the last lesson, we began looking at general-purpose ways to gain some of the same benefits that producing almost instantly provides. In this lesson, we continue that examination by considering how to constructively reduce your and your stakeholders' investments in buildings, land, and equipment. We look first at reducing building investments.

Reduce Your and Your Stakeholders' Building Investments

So the LORD scattered them abroad from there over the face of all the earth,
and they ceased building the city.
Therefore its name is called Babel,
because there the LORD confused the language of all the earth;
and from there the LORD scattered them abroad over the face of all the earth.

— Genesis 11:8-9 (NKJV)

What do I mean by *building investments*? These are funds expended for ownership of or leasehold improvements to any structure that rests on land.

While land almost always appreciates in market value over the long term, the value of buildings almost always depreciates due to wear, tear, and obsolescence. The market value of new special-purpose buildings on the open market immediately is a big discount from the cost of erecting them. Even if buildings don't depreciate in market value, the maintenance to keep them sound may cumulatively exceed the original building cost.

I am often reminded of such historical patterns when I drive on Route 128, the storied technology highway that rings Boston. Just north of my home, the road passes by the former Polaroid production facilities for cameras and film. When the buildings were completed in the 1950s, they were technological marvels. Today, they are being gutted so they can be rebuilt for some other use. The land beneath the dated structures is probably worth more than a hundred times the original purchase price. I'm sure that the only reason that the structures are being rebuilt rather than destroyed is to avoid digging up the land and possibly being required to clean up any undiscovered chemicals that may have been spilled into the ground over fifty years.

If the Polaroid Corporation had spent the same amount of money as it did on these buildings to purchase adjoining land and to erect general office space, the company would never have gone into bankruptcy and instead could be worth billions of dollars today as a commercial-property owner. But the company put its money into the wrong investments as well as spending more than was necessary.

To conduct its original photography business, Polaroid obviously needed film and cameras. Let's look at the possible alternatives today to building plants on prime commercial real estate that is more suitable for offices. How can a manufacturer avoid investing in special-purpose structures to produce its unique offerings? While there are hundreds of choices, these eight alternatives are usually among the best now:

1. Outsource production to more effective suppliers.

2. Outsource most production to more effective suppliers and simply do some final assembly and testing in your facilities.

3. Redesign the offering so that the physical aspects are minimized while the virtual aspects (such as software programs and electronic presences) are maximized.

4. Lease rather than own your buildings where that approach provides cost and investment savings for your offering's supply chain.

5. Produce in countries where facility costs are very inexpensive and transportation costs to customers' locations are low.

6. Use production methods that can be applied in low-cost, general-purpose buildings.

7. Narrow your line of offerings to just the most successful and produce them in space-saving ways.

8. Take advantage of scale effects when larger facilities can substantially lower the cost of building investments per unit of output.

If you are a service provider, how can you avoid having investments in any buildings? Again, there are many choices, but eight categories typically provide the most helpful answers today:

1. Redesign your services so that they can be provided by more effective suppliers.

2. Redesign your services so that they can be conducted by employees working at home or in public places.

3. Redesign office layouts so that multiple employees take turns sharing the same space (through something like the office-hotel concept).

4. Redesign service work so that it is more often provided through electronic automation.

5. Lease rather than own your facilities where that provides cost and investment savings for your offerings' supply chains.

6. Base your services in countries where facility costs are very inexpensive and communications costs to provide services are low.

7. Use service methods that can be applied in general-purpose buildings.

8. Narrow your line of offerings to just the most successful and produce them in space-saving ways.

If you are a retailer, how can you avoid having building investments for places to stock and to display your offerings? Here are nine suggestions:

1. Shift to direct selling online and on television.

2. Set up temporary sales sites (such as for auctions).

3. Restrict what you offer to very fast-selling, high-priced goods.

4. Arrange for customers to make long-term purchase commitments and then ship the items directly to them from the producer or wholesaler.

5. Ask suppliers to provide or to pay for facilities where such an approach can provide integrated, more effective, and lower-cost operations for other retailers and you.

6. Lease rather than own your facilities where that provides cost and investment savings for the supply chain.

7. Operate in countries where facility and transportation costs are very low compared to selling prices.

8. Use business methods that can be applied in general-purpose buildings.

9. Narrow your line of offerings to just the most successful ones and provide them in space-saving ways.

In looking at such choices, be sure to consider any trade-offs involved. For instance, you don't want to reduce building investments in ways that greatly reduce revenues. Such an unfavorable result might occur if a retailer of high-quality fur coats began selling them from card tables temporarily located on city streets. Ideally, you want to employ business-model innovations that also increase revenues, lower operating costs, and eliminate the need for other investments.

Amazon.com has been a case in point for showing the importance of making such trade-offs. The company originally planned to ask wholesalers to ship all ordered goods directly to customers so that Amazon.com wouldn't need any facilities except for its headquarters and computers. As the company added more product lines, Amazon.com learned that customers wanted to avoid shipping costs. One of the most effective ways to reduce shipping costs was to combine multiple ordered items into one package. The company eventually put in specialized warehouses that make it simpler and less costly to do such multiple-item shipping. As a result, the company gained more sales and reduced costs, but it still avoided the substantial retail building investments and costs that competitors such as Barnes & Noble, Best Buy, and Wal-Mart have.

As you can see, the ideal business solution may not be one that aims primarily at minimizing investments in buildings. Have a business model that optimizes the overall opportunity to produce more sales, to cut costs, and to reduce total investments.

Your thinking shouldn't stop at the limits of your organizational boundaries. Consider how you can slash building investments for suppliers, partners, customers, customers' customers, end users, and any other stakeholders. Otherwise, you are just moving the costs of building investments around rather than actually avoiding them. When you just try to shift the investments to others, you'll probably find your profitability and cash flow are eventually reduced in some new, indirect ways.

In many manufacturing businesses, it's not unusual for there to be one dollar spent on a company's building investments to support every six dollars in sales. A more desirable ratio would be to have one dollar of a company's building investments to support every fifty dollars in sales. How low can you go without harming sales, increasing costs, or expanding total investments in other ways?

Here's where offering design can play a role: There are many different ways to serve the same need. Some are much more investment intensive than others. Look hardest at the choices that don't require much investment in buildings.

What's the key point about reducing building investments? **Redesign your company's offerings, breadth of product line, methods of operating, business models, ownership of facilities, and use of facilities to help slash spending on building investments by you and your stakeholders so that overall investments can be reduced by 96 percent compared to what they are now in ways in ways that will also help make your organization and your stakeholders more successful and profitable, as well as better able to generate and to sustain cash flow.**

Reduce Your and Your Stakeholders' Land Investments

The LORD said to me, "Go up against this land, and destroy it."

— Isaiah 36:10 (NKJV)

In this section, we consider how to constructively avoid land investments. Having read and heard so much about the potential to make money from land investments through price appreciation, you are probably surprised to find that I'm looking for how to spend less.

So many people know about and appreciate the potential of land for value growth that the knowledge often leads to unnecessary investments. Just because you have the potential to gain from an investment doesn't mean that you should spend more than is absolutely necessary. When you invest too much, you just reduce your cash flow and raise your costs.

Most organizations spend a lot more than they need to on land. Let me give you a few examples.

A homebuilding company was very sensitive to the need to gain zoning and other regulatory approvals before it could begin constructing homes, the point in the development process where profits and positive cash flow could begin. Feeling risk-averse, this company would buy every single acre it might ever need for a housing development … even if there was no possibility that some of the land would be built on during the next seven years.

When I challenged that approach, the company discovered that it could control a piece of property just as effectively through a series of inexpensive options to purchase parts of the total acreage. As a result, land could be purchased only a few days before construction began on an individual parcel.

The company was pleasantly surprised to find that the combined costs of the options plus the purchase prices were just the same as if the company had bought the land ahead of time and paid interest costs and real estate taxes over the subsequent years. Why? The sellers were planning to sit on large investments in raw land and were accustomed to carrying such costs. Some landowners gained tax advantages by delaying the time of sale. Because landowners were confident that all the land would be purchased, they didn't mind a slower rate of actual transactions. If all the options weren't acted on, the remaining land they still owned was much more valuable .... so the landowners knew they would probably be better off by selling options to homebuilders.

In a different case, a restaurant company decided to cut investment costs by putting a warehouse and its corporate headquarters on the same land, land that was much more valuable than most organizations would use for storage. The location also wasn't very good for distributing the goods. As a result, the costs of warehousing and distribution were higher than they needed to be. Eventually, the company sold the land and moved the headquarters and warehouse to different parcels of much less expensive land. The price received for the original land was equal to the total value of all the company's public shares at the time.

In a third instance, a different company planned to add capacity for one of its business lines. Rather than adding onto existing plants where it had extra land, the company decided to buy a parcel in a different part of the country that was closer to some customers, in hopes of cutting shipping costs. Forecasting a lot of rapid growth, the firm bought three times the land it expected to need immediately in an undeveloped area. After the purchase, the company shifted its business strategy to deemphasize volume growth. As a result, the company never needed any of the new land it purchased. All of the purchase price plus the efforts and costs involved in obtaining zoning were wasted. The land was eventually resold for a pittance compared to the company's investment.

A fourth company decided to consolidate many smaller plants. In doing so, it designed a plant that was optimized for producing the product mix from those plants. Later, one of the plant's products became very unprofitable ... a product that kept two-thirds of the plant busy. If the company pulled out of that product line, it made no sense to have the plant on that site. The investment was totally wasted because the building was so special purpose, reducing the value of the land by the potential cost of demolishing the building and limited general-purpose needs for such a parcel shape. For years, the company dilly-dallied with keeping the site and all the products going, satisfying no one while losing money and tying up a lot of extra investment capital.

Another common error is to put in unnecessary site improvements. For instance, a concert operator built a facility and parking lot (which takes a lot of land) to serve 15,000 patrons, but the nearby access road could only accommodate 4,000 patrons in a reasonable amount of time. As a result, almost two-thirds of the land investment was wasted. The same entrepreneur also started building on a site in another state, investing a million dollars in improvements before finishing a business plan. After the plan was completed, it became clear that the site was a bad one for a concert venue. The site-improvement money was wasted.

Part of making money from land appreciation is being able to resell it for a wide variety of high-priced purposes. If you put a chemical plant on the land and let the chemicals leak into the ground poisoning the soil, the land won't go up in value. At some point, you will, instead, spend a fortune on digging up and carting away the old soil. The land probably won't ever be used for anything more valuable than as a landfill.

Your land and building investments will influence what else goes into that area. If you also encourage the right kind of zoning, new neighbors will lift the value of your land. And later you'll be able to sell your land for much more to your neighbors or to those who want such neighbors.

Mistakes concerning land don't end with the company's own investments: Strategies and policies may also force stakeholders to buy too much land and spend too much money in other ways. As an example, many manufacturing organizations provide big price discounts at the end of a quarter to encourage distributors, retailers, customers, and ultimate users to stock up on items that they won't need for many months. Why are such large discounts offered? Well, the people who buy the goods when they don't need them may have to incur extra interest costs on borrowed money to finance the purchases. They may also have to buy or rent extra warehouses on bigger parcels of land to protect the goods. In addition, the purchasers will experience product losses during such extended storage.

Here are six principles you should keep in mind when making land investments:

1. Don't buy until you are sure you need the land.

2. If you won't be using all of the land right away, explore purchasing options to buy the remaining land later at a price that is fixed now.

3. Design your processes to use as little land as possible.

4. Plan your work sites and warehouses to be reused twenty years later by different organizations for much higher-value purposes.

5. Add as much capacity on existing land as possible before acquiring any more land.

6. Look at your suppliers, partners, distributors, retailers, customers, and end users and consider how your strategies, policies, methods, and marketing affect how much land each of them has to use and for what purposes. Consider how you could shrink the total land usage in your value chain.

In thinking about such perspectives, it's clear that you should not focus solely on reducing land investments in making these decisions. Choose, instead, to have a business model that optimizes the overall opportunity to produce more sales, to cut costs, and to reduce total investments.

Your thinking shouldn't stop at the limits of your organizational boundaries. You also need to consider how your reduced use of land can be combined with other decisions to also slash any kind of investments for suppliers, partners, customers, customers' customers, end users, and any other stakeholders. Otherwise, you are just moving a reduced cost of your land investments around, rather than actually avoiding investments. When that happens, the costs of such increased stakeholder investments will eventually come out of your profitability and cash flow in some indirect way.

Good business-model design should have as one of its goals limiting the amount of money spent on investments throughout the supply chain that are needed to sustain consumption. In many manufacturing businesses, it's not unusual for there to be one dollar of a company's land investments to support every twelve dollars in sales. A better goal would be to have one dollar of a company's land investments to support every one hundred dollars in sales. How low can you go without harming sales, increasing costs, or expanding total investments in other ways?

Here's where offering design can play a role: There are many different ways to serve the same need. Some offering designs are much more capital intensive than others. Look hardest at the choices that don't require much land investment.

What's the key point about reducing land investments? **Redesign your company's offerings, breadth of product line, methods of operating, business models, ownership of facilities, and use of facilities to help slash the amount of money spent on land investments by you and your stakeholders so that overall investments can be reduced by 96 percent compared to what they are now in ways that will also help make your organization and your stakeholders more successful and profitable, and better able to generate and to sustain cash flow.**

Reduce Your and Your Stakeholders' Equipment Investments

And the temple, when it was being built,
was built with stone finished at the quarry,
so that no hammer or chisel or *any iron tool was heard in the temple*
while it was being built.

— 1 Kings 6:7 (NKJV)

In this section, we investigate constructive ways to avoid equipment investments. This subject reminds me of an experience while I was consulting for a major automotive supplier to General Motors (GM) in the 1980s.

At that time, one of the GM CEO's children worked for my client. I could tell that the ideas I was sharing with my client concerning business investments were reaching GM as well. However, something was lost in transmission, and GM kept doing the wrong things. From that experience, I learned that sometimes people need help to correctly apply business concepts.

At one time, it was believed by some that total automation was the appropriate goal for manufacturing and service businesses alike. That belief was stirred by the observation that Japanese companies, whose firms seemed unstoppable to Americans in the early 1980s, were headed that way. That belief was the business headline, but many people didn't realize the underlying purpose: Japan had an aging population and was headed for a future shortage of skilled workers. Pretty much every other country with an advanced economy had an oversupply of skilled manufacturing workers.

As a result of following the Japanese example, companies such as GM and Motorola sought total automation as fast as possible … even when that approach was more expensive and capital intensive, a big mistake.

Today, it's well understood that the best manufacturers and service providers use as little automation as possible. Why? Workers prefer and produce more when they experience more human interaction and interesting activities than what automation usually provides. As a result, less automation often leads to higher quality, lower costs, and higher sales.

There is an exception: Some jobs are best done by robots or automated processes because the work is very dangerous and disagreeable. An example is replacing water pipes next to an active nuclear reactor. Another example is spraying car parts with toxic chemicals.

Automation has other problems:

- It usually takes a long time to change the set-up so that a different item or service can be produced.

- It adds total investment much faster than by using more employees and less equipment.

- It makes companies more reluctant to improve business models.

- 2,000 percent solutions are seldom achieved through automation.

- It takes a long time to do well.

- It adds to fixed costs so that profits and cash flow are worse during industry downturns.

- Most people automate old processes … which usually aren't very good ones to begin with.

One of my clients coined an expression about processes that was quoted in *The 2,000 Percent Solution*: "eliminate, simplify, then automate."

Today, I think my client's concept should be applied first to a business model. After unnecessary business-model elements have been eliminated and the remainder simplified, then see how the remaining methods can be eliminated and simplified so that your offerings don't need much, if any, equipment. Lastly, consider what automation might be appropriate at that point.

Past lessons have discussed taking a product and turning it into a service that doesn't require many assets (such as by providing information rather than a product) as well as the idea of taking a service and turning it into a product that doesn't require many assets (such as an upscale restaurant providing cooking videos that can be downloaded from the Internet). Such thinking about business models is very helpful as the first step in eliminating equipment.

Also question how much of the product's or service's value-added you should provide through your own manufacturing and service operations. In many cases today, another organization can do value-added tasks much better and less expensively than you can. That's particularly true if your offering is likely to have a short market life (such as with most electronic items). In many cases, your supplier is able to reuse its equipment for other companies. By using the equipment for more customers, the total equipment investment is less than if each company made its own products or provided it own services.

In addition, consider if the customers might prefer to use some equipment for their own enjoyment. Many people, for instance, like to tinker with old cars. If you make the cars so that they require very specialized equipment to repair and tune, some car enthusiasts will be turned off. Instead, you might design the car so that customers can easily do their own work and automotive repair shops can also provide good service without making extensive equipment investments for infrequent repairs. Such a solution will probably mean that a car manufacturer would also require less equipment.

If customers already have excellent equipment, then provide offerings that make using the customer's equipment more desirable. For instance, many people would like to prepare gourmet meals at home as a source of personal satisfaction … but don't have the knowledge and skill to do so. Since some of these people have kitchens full of the equipment usually found in fine restaurants, food companies might provide offerings these people can easily employ with such sophisticated equipment to make extraordinary dishes.

Here are six principles you should keep in mind when making equipment investments:

1. Don't buy until you are sure you can't improve your business model any more during the expected life of the equipment.

2. Design your processes to use as little equipment as possible.

3. If you won't be using all of the equipment continually, explore rental and leasing options that would allow you to only employ what you need.

4. Plan for ways to create higher salvage values for your equipment when its economic life in your operations is over.

5. Increase throughput on existing equipment before acquiring any more equipment.

6. Look at your suppliers, partners, distributors, retailers, customers, and end users to see how your strategies, policies, methods, and marketing affect how much equipment each of them has to use and for what purposes. Consider how you could shrink that total equipment usage.

In thinking about these perspectives, it's clear that you should not focus solely on equipment investments in making these decisions. You want, instead, to have a business model that optimizes the overall opportunity to produce more sales, to cut costs, and to reduce total investment.

Your thinking shouldn't stop at the limits of your organizational boundaries. You also need to consider how your reduced use of equipment can be combined with other decisions to also slash total investments for suppliers, partners, customers, customers' customers, end users, and any other stakeholders. Otherwise, you are just moving the costs of equipment investments around rather than actually avoiding them. The costs of those stakeholder investments will eventually come out of your profitability and cash flow in some indirect way.

Business-model design should seek to limit the amount spent on equipment investments throughout the supply chain to sustain consumption. In many manufacturing businesses, it's not unusual for there to be one dollar of a company's equipment investments to support every eight dollars in sales. A better goal would be to have one dollar of a company's equipment investments support every fifty dollars in sales. How low can you go without harming sales, increasing costs, or expanding total investments in other ways?

Let me remind you that offering design can play a role: There are many different ways to serve the same need. Some are much more investment intensive than others. Look hardest at the choices that don't require much equipment investment.

What's the key point about reducing equipment investments? **Redesign your company's offerings, breadth of product line, methods of operating, business models, ownership of facilities, and use of facilities to slash the amount of money spent by you and your stakeholders on equipment investments so that total investments can be reduced by 96 percent compared to what they are now in ways that will also help make your organization and its stakeholders more successful and profitable, and better able to generate and to sustain cash flow.**

Assignments

1. Identify the five most valuable ways you could reduce investments in buildings, land, and equipment that would provide the most benefits that customers and suppliers want.

2. Consider how these changes would affect your other stakeholders.

3. Investigate how your business models, operating methods, breadth of product line, and offerings could be shifted over time to be even more effective and to make it easier for stakeholders and your company to operate with very little investment in buildings, land, and equipment.

Lesson Forty

Teach and Encourage Stakeholders
to Avoid Investments

*"Now when they bring you to
the synagogues and magistrates and authorities,
do not worry about how or what you should answer,
or what you should say.
For the Holy Spirit will teach you
in that very hour what you ought to say."*

— Luke 12:11-12 (NKJV)

In preceding three lessons, we look at specific ways to reduce your and your stakeholders' investments. In this lesson, we examine sharing with stakeholders what you learn about this subject and encouraging them to apply what they learn.

Sometimes a potentially helpful action is so obvious that it's easy to miss. That's one reason why I want to step back a bit and discuss teaching and encouraging all your stakeholders to avoid 96 percent of their "usual" investments.

I would normally discuss a point such as this one at the very beginning of a major topic. Unfortunately, I've found that such timing doesn't work very well with reducing investments because most people are so accustomed to making unnecessary investments that they cannot believe that it's possible and desirable not to make most investments. Hopefully, Part Four's introduction and lessons thirty-seven, thirty-eight, and thirty-nine have convinced you it's important to reduce investments, and you have already gained some valuable knowledge to share.

I believe that investing too much in a business and pushing stakeholders to do the same are based in these five influences:

1. Spending money to implement a plan makes most people feel more confident that the plan will succeed, even when the plan calls for actions that unintentionally will, in fact, make the business less likely to prosper. Why does such confidence build? It's because many people haven't developed their imaginations. As a result, they find it easier to think about how to improve a business after they make their ideas real (no matter how poor the idea or execution) than while just thinking about some possible business activity or expansion.

2. In long-established businesses, making more investments can be an apparent way to boost profits by either increasing production capacity or by reducing costs. Since profits are the metric that managers are most likely to be measured on, many businesspeople aren't very sensitive to cash flow and the value of increasing it.

3. If people don't feel cash constrained in any way while operating a business, cash flow seems like an irrelevancy. Such people often don't realize how much potential to do more is eliminated by excess investing.

4. Many businesspeople have a "win-lose" attitude (believing that "I can only win if you lose") toward stakeholders, even while paying lip service to the idea of creating "win-win" relationships (saying to stakeholders that "we can cooperate in ways that will leave us both better off").

5. Most businesspeople never think about what investments their stakeholders may or may not be making.

Independent of increasing cash flow and cash availability for all stakeholders, avoiding investments has another great benefit: reducing the barriers to continuing business-model innovation, the biggest factor in making major improvements.

Let me explain. Imagine that you've just built a huge special-purpose facility that optimizes your current business model and operating methods. Your mind will naturally focus on how to gain the most advantage from that gorgeous facility, surely taking you further down the path of what you have been doing.

When someone tells you that doing the opposite (or something quite different) from what you do now will work better than optimizing that new facility, you probably won't pay much attention. Why? You probably wouldn't receive ten cents on the dollar for any specialized investments that you made in the facility. To shift would mean looking foolish (at least in your own eyes, and possibly also in the eyes of those who evaluate you) and taking a large write-off that affects accounting profits (but not cash flow). Under such circumstances, surely you'll feel more comfortable by avoiding any new directions.

Instead you'll probably try harder to make the current direction work better, possibly investing more to do so. The consequences of such a reaction are like swimming deeper into a powerful whirlpool: You can be sucked in so that you cannot escape.

I was reminded of such lessons while teaching one of my small business classes. I had arranged for some course alumni to speak, and each had explained how she or he had started up a business with little or no investment. These testimonies were big eye openers for my students.

I always start such a course by explaining that I began my first business with a total investment of about $14, as measured in today's purchasing power. Knowing what I know today, I could have done a lot better: instead starting up the business by spending no money of my own and receiving $100,000 of clients' money for advance fee payments. This financial approach would have been ethical and comfortable for clients because I could have provided such great value that they would have immediately extracted tens of millions in return from these consulting services.

One of the alumni examples was especially arresting for the students. This man planned to keep his day job. Before taking the course, he had been raising money for nonprofit children's groups as a public service. Due to his profession, he was ethically constrained from conducting any part-time business activities. Despite his intention to make a little money through such joint ventures, he had always lost money. While taking the course, we challenged him to revise his business model to reduce investments, and he did an experiment before the last class from which he earned about $2,500. He was hooked on a lower-investment business style.

Because he had little time for this activity, we pointed out that he should outsource everything he did. He took us at our word and he now does that. He spends 98 percent less time on this part-time activity and earned a profit of $12,000 in three months from doing about five hours of work. And the best part is that his new business model doesn't require much investment by anyone. "Pretty nice," as my father would have said.

Another course graduate was asked how much money she invested before her business turned cash-flow positive. She thought for a minute and observed that she had been cash-flow positive from before she started the business: She had sold customers prepaid classes at discounted prices.

Her original plan had been to invest hundreds of thousands of dollars. When asked about the change of plans, she commented that spending so much money would have been a big mistake. Her business would have been hurt, and her services would have been less valuable to customers.

However, none of these small business owners had gone the next step and begun to teach their stakeholders to eliminate or to vastly reduce unnecessary investments. But, of course, none of them at the time had access to this book's lessons from which to construct such teachings. You do, so let's look a little further into what you could do.

If I could instruct someone in only one lesson about teaching and encouraging less investment, it would be:

Avoid any investments by you and by each of your stakeholders while gaining the ability, as a result, to improve your business model more frequently.

Following this advice is how I run my businesses. In doing so, I have found that it usually makes more sense to work first with customers and second with suppliers before moving on to assist other stakeholders. That's because customers' willingness to change limits what you, suppliers, and other stakeholders can do. But don't rule out the possibility of following the opposite order if other stakeholders are more open to your teaching and encouragement.

Here's a hypothetical example of what I mean by teaching and encouraging customers first and then suppliers. Imagine that we are providing software and software-related services to manufacturing customers. In today's world, manufacturers typically use processes that are either highly automated or labor intensive. Both types of manufacturing processes require more investments than using an optimal combination of the two.

Highly automated manufacturing processes usually involve dedicated machines. Thus, the more types of products that are made, the more machines are needed. That's because it usually makes sense to eliminate the cost of changeovers, even if the machines are often idle.

Labor-intensive processes, by comparison, don't require much investment for machines, but such processes usually require more inventories and hand tools. Some such operations may make literally tens of thousands of different offerings. As a result, raw-material and finished-goods inventories also proliferate. If offerings are sent long distances by ship rather than rapidly by air freight or local delivery, such an approach also means a higher risk of finished-inventory obsolescence.

For all but the smallest customers, the optimal manufacturing approach is a cross between highly automated lines and hand production that is performed close to the ultimate product user. Think of such solutions as providing customized products in tiny production runs that are aided by machines that improve quality and reduce costs. The parallels can be found in the team-assembly processes for custom personal computers used by Dell and for custom cars conducted by Toyota that I have described in earlier lessons.

To be effective, such combination processes require software that allows an order to be produced and shipped in just a few minutes. That's the role that our example's hypothetical supplier plays.

Now, let's move away from considering optimal manufacturing to look at an entire industry being reshaped to eliminate layers of suppliers and distributors. Perhaps the most intriguing new method involves the printers and binding equipment used in each Amazon.com warehouse to produce one book at a time in response to computer orders from individual customers.

Typically, such warehouse-produced books are printed, bound, and shipped within an hour of the customers' orders being made. This production and distribution method provides a several-day speed advantage over when Amazon.com ordered an out-of-stock book from a wholesaler that then shipped the book to Amazon.com, which, in turn, shipped it to the purchaser. Readers like the faster delivery because Amazon.com is considerably slower than a bookstore for obtaining popular, in-stock paperback books. Since Amazon.com was already much faster and cheaper for less popular paperback books that had to be special ordered, book purchasers were encouraged to do even more of such buying.

Although books can be printed for much less cost in quantities of a few thousand, Amazon.com rarely receives such a large order, or combinations of small orders amounting to nearly as much. So, instead, the company reduces the costs and investments of producing a single paperback book. One result has been to pay most self-published authors more than double per book what traditional publishers pay their authors in royalties.

A software supplier that wanted to help a distribution customer to make a similar shift would first have to persuade a customer of the advantages from such a manufacturing approach, before it would make sense to provide the software to make such a process work well. Without having a customer, there would be no point in developing the software to produce and to distribute products in this new way. Once the distribution customer decided to change, the software supplier could begin to work with equipment manufacturers to produce the right results.

Typically, such a change would mean a major adjustment in the customers' and suppliers' business models. In working on such a task, you can also improve the competitiveness of your customers and suppliers so that they will be able to gain market share, increasing your revenues while decreasing your costs.

Seldom do all such optimal changes occur at one time. Instead, one improvement leads to another one, and so on. My understanding is that Amazon.com improvements followed this twelve-step sequence:

1. Software companies greatly reduced the cost of converting an electronic manuscript into a finished electronic template from which a physical book could be printed.

2. Printing companies produced new equipment that made books one at a time at reasonably low cost with so-so quality.

3. Authors became good at working with software companies to produce electronic book templates, eliminating the need for most expensive editing, composition, and design services. As a result, authors could more easily bypass publishers.

4. Specialist software companies were established to do tiny aspects of template-preparation at still lower costs and more rapidly.

5. Amazon.com started buying software companies so that it could control the standards used in the electronic templates.

6. Once standards were set that met the needs of many authors, Amazon.com began working with equipment makers to develop low-cost, print-on-demand equipment that unskilled people could operate in its warehouses with quality comparable to that obtained during long production runs performed on offset printing equipment.

7. When the warehouse print-on-demand equipment was in place, Amazon.com increased royalty payments to authors to encourage more volume going through its specialized equipment and software. This shift reduced costs and investment intensity compared to buying finished books from traditional publishers and having substantial quantities of books on hand to ship to customers.

8. Amazon.com began providing a new type of electronic reading device called a Kindle. This reader could use the same technology for electronic templates as the paperback books did, but did not require a manufacturing process to create a book ... just some software manipulation.

9. As the Kindle volume grew, Amazon.com began cutting costs and making it simpler for authors to produce their books in Kindle format.

10. Quality of Kindle reader experiences improved, and prices declined for the devices.

11. Prices declined on Kindle-format electronic books.

12. Amazon.com increased the number of print-on-demand facilities beyond its warehouse network so that time in the mail for physical books was often reduced by several days.

This iterative process will undoubtedly continue, making it easier and more attractive for Amazon.com customers to buy print-on-demand paperbacks and Kindle-compatible electronic books. At the time of this writing, Kindle books were already outselling the combination of paperbacks and hardcover books on Amazon.com.

Future changes will be aimed at supplying reading customers with more of something they like such as lower prices, better quality, and faster delivery. All of the shifts will probably reduce investment intensity for customers, suppliers, and Amazon.com.

What's the key point about teaching and encouraging stakeholders to avoid investments? **Teach and encourage your stakeholders to avoid all investments, to do the same for their stakeholders, and to demonstrate ways to accomplish such results as part of a program to reduce investments in all activities for all stakeholders by 96 percent to generate lots of excess cash for all.**

Assignments

1. Turn your operations into a model of avoiding investments and seek lessons for doing even better from your industry and similar activities in other industries.

2. Find out what kinds of unnecessary investments your stakeholders are making.

3. Identify what information and resources stakeholders need to avoid unnecessary investments.

4. Help stakeholders to see how any existing investments could be cashed out and avoided in the future to improve their business models, rate of business-model innovation, and cash flow.

5. Repeat the process described in steps 1 through 4.

Lesson Forty-One

Work with Part-Time and Nonprofit Suppliers

For I do *not* mean *that others should be eased and you burdened;*
but by an equality, that *now at this time*
your abundance may supply *their lack,*
that their abundance also may supply *your lack*
— that there may be equality.
As it is written, "He who gathered much had nothing left over,
and he who gathered little had no lack."

— 2 Corinthians 8:13-15 (NKJV)

If for no other reason than expanding your business model to include new types of offerings, you will probably add new suppliers from time to time. In addition, sometimes suppliers go out of business or are unwilling to make necessary changes to improve their and your business models. In other instances, your rapid expansion may outstrip the quantities that current suppliers can provide.

Deciding to work with part-time and nonprofit suppliers can add breakthrough resources for reducing your and your stakeholders' investments. Let's start by looking at *part-time suppliers*

A break-even analysis I did for one of my small business classes encouraged me to describe for you the investment-reduction benefits of working with part-time suppliers. In that analysis, I compared the costs and investments of someone working part-time from home in a new business while holding a full-time job, with instead setting up separate premises and working full time for a new business. There was a large increase in investments (as well as operating costs) associated with shifting from part-time income supplementation at home to full-time work away from home in a new enterprise.

One of the cases I studied was for a computer consultant who served other small businesses. This man had a good-paying job at a local investment company, a job that kept him busy about fifty hours a week. Because he was young, and had lots of energy and ambition, the computer consultant was willing to work another ten to fifteen hours a week for his own business.

Because the young man's employer required him to work at home sometimes, he already had all the necessary equipment, Internet connections, and software for the consulting business. To serve a small business client added neither any investment nor any costs.

Because many of his benefit needs (such as health insurance, retirement plan, and so forth) were covered by his full-time employer, the computer consultant only looked for the part-time business to yield the same after-tax income per hour as did his full-time job. As a result, his small business clients could hire him at a much lower cost per hour than his full-time employer was paying. If the small business clients were located on the other side of the world, he was available during the daytime where they were, which was almost as good as having him working part time on their payrolls. In addition, his employer paid for the computer consultant to receive lots of training, something that small business clients benefited from at no additional cost to themselves.

While not all part-time suppliers will offer as low prices and lack of investments as this computer consultant did for his clients, the case for working with part-time suppliers is often not too much less attractive than this example. If the part-time suppliers operate in a low-wage country, you add that benefit to buying their time at a large discount from the full hourly cost of someone in a high-wage country.

Such cost and investment advantages become more significant when you choose a business model (either by the way you organize the work or how customers are served) so that lots of part-time suppliers can provide a substantial percentage of all the work you need done. For instance, if you wanted to use lots of part-time suppliers to automate your processes, each one could do just a few bits and pieces of the project while an independent part-time supervisor coordinated the virtual team.

Tasks such as twenty four hours a day, seven days a week customer service could be parceled out so that individuals could sign in from their computers and be paid on a piecework basis for whatever work they do.

Such an approach is obviously fine for activities that aren't very capital intensive, but you may be wondering what can be done if you need someone to use expensive equipment. The part-time supplier can have an advantage in such circumstances, as well. Most companies only operate one work shift, which means that their equipment is idle for fourteen to sixteen hours a day. A part-time supplier can often contract with his or her full-time employer to use the equipment during the evenings and early mornings. When such equipment sharing occurs, the equipment cost may be minimal compared to the full investment or lease price.

I experienced why it can be an advantage to work with part-time suppliers when I contracted to have the cover designed for *Adventures of an Optimist*. Because the quality of cover designs doesn't seem to relate to the cost but, rather, the talent and experience of the designer, I normally pay as little as possible while seeking the most capable person available. In this instance, I had met one of the best book-cover designers in the United States, and I thought it would be worthwhile seeing what he could do.

I was pleasantly surprised when the designer quoted me a fee that was only about 10 to 15 percent of the amount that top independent book-cover designers usually charge. He also made himself available to work with me on the assignment during the business day while at his full-time job with a local publisher. Where an independent cover designer will normally produce, at most, three designs to choose from, this man did more than twenty-five designs. And he produced by far the best cover that anyone had done for me. It was a pleasant surprise to find that I could access that kind of talent on a tiny budget.

I suspect that part of the reason I got such a good deal was due to his interest in the project. As a part-time supplier, he could afford to put extra time into my job because it pleased him … without risking his family's livelihood. I'm sure his employer, by comparison, expected a certain number of book covers to be completed every week or the company would have replaced him with someone who would meet their expectations. It also may have been enjoyable for him to work without any production pressure. Since I was in no hurry, he could play with things in a way that he normally could not with new books.

Part-time suppliers can become more effective through specialization without experiencing the emotional or physical fatigue that can come from doing too much of one thing. Part-time suppliers can pick assignments, as the book designer did, that are quite different from their normal tasks so that the work feels a little like recreation … for which payment is received.

The importance of part-time suppliers is so significant that I want you to be aware of its corollary: Your part-time suppliers should also use part-time suppliers. In the case of the book designer, for instance, working with a part-time photographer to shoot a special cover image cover could have helped to create an even better result from little added investment.

Let's look next at *nonprofit suppliers*. My observations are based on a case history that one of my former small business students presented. This woman had been a world-class dancer until an accident cut her career short. Not sure what to do next, she took a job working for a government agency (which bored her to tears) and began part-time teaching for various dance studios. Tired of her government job, she became a full-time nanny (taking care of youngsters in their family's home during the days) and taught dancing part-time in the evenings and on weekends. Her income was low, and her life was difficult.

In my course, she learned about growing revenues, reducing costs, and eliminating investments. A key challenge was where to hold her classes. She couldn't afford to buy a building, and rents were astronomical for space that could be used to teach dancing. Dance studios are usually quite busy serving their customers during prime hours, and they don't want to rent to a competitor. What could she do?

I suggested that she rent space in churches. These houses of worship were often the biggest and most beautiful of the older buildings in the area, and they were usually empty except on weekends. To help cover the costs of heating and upkeep, many churches rent space to reputable people for activities that benefit the local community. Teaching exercise and dance classes seemed to fit within what a church would welcome.

She was delighted to find a perfect spot about five minutes away from where I taught my class. A space like this one in Boston would have cost about $800,000 to purchase. Even the least expensive space she could find in not very convenient locations charged $5,000 a month for rent. She lacked the money to make a security deposit for such space.

The church happily offered her up to sixteen hours a week during the hours she wanted to teach. The rental rate was $25 an hour. As a result, her monthly cost for rent was only $1,700, and she didn't need to provide a security deposit or to make any investments in leasehold improvements.

The church offered another important advantage: It was filled with people taking classes from morning to night, six days a week. All of them could see that she was offering exercise and dance instruction there. If they wanted help with dance or exercise, most of those who attended other classes or church services there would find the location to be convenient. For some, it would be possible to take two unrelated classes back-to-back during the same evening.

The business model also offered another important advantage: Instead of spending money for space that would be empty most of the time, she would only have to rent what, where, and when she needed space. If she could add a class that would be highly profitable in another community, then she could rent space in a church in that community for just the hour or two a week she needed to offer such a class. A highly profitable, low-cost, minimal-investment business model was born.

Let's examine several reasons why using a nonprofit organization as your landlord may be a very low-cost and low-investment choice:

1. Nonprofits usually receive financial donations that subsidize the cost of all their operations.

2. Nonprofits receive donations of volunteer time to do most of their activities, which further reduces their operating costs. In some cases, volunteers even construct buildings ... further reducing investment costs.

3. In many countries, nonprofits are also exempt from sales, use, property, and income taxes. As a result, nonprofits can charge less for rent and receive more cash after taxes than a for-profit organization that has to pay such taxes.

4. If a nonprofit organization's leaders decide that they like what you do, they can choose to subsidize your activities and to offer you their premises or supplier resources below their own low costs.

5. Customers may favor your organization because you are operating from the site of a nonprofit organization that they approve of. As a consequence, customers may be more willing to buy and to pay higher prices when considering your organization's offerings.

Now let's look at an extreme example of the advantages that nonprofit suppliers can provide. Wealthy people often find it more attractive to donate their land, buildings, and other valuable resources to nonprofit organizations rather than to sell them. Such a decision is normally motivated in part by a weak market for selling such items, some reduced costs from obtaining income and estate tax deductions for donations, and a desire to help the nonprofit organization prosper in some new way. When such motives and circumstances exist, the nonprofit organization may experience unusually low costs for its newly acquired and mostly unused properties.

I saw many examples of such advantages while I was taking self-improvement classes. Each class was held in one mansion or another. These were not only gorgeous buildings, but some were also surrounded by beautiful grounds. Each mansion had been a gift to the organization that provided the classes. Whenever I stayed overnight at such facilities, the cost was very low … often lower than for a hostel, even though the facilities compared favorably to what you would pay many hundreds of dollars a night for in Europe. Although I never looked into it, I'm sure I could have leased some land or buildings for business purposes from this organization on a highly favorable basis. If I had tied what I was doing on the premises to something that would have greatly helped the teaching organization to add more students, there might have been no facility charges at all.

Many times for-profit organizations perceive that they would gain great strategic advantages by having a sister organization that is a nonprofit entity. The for-profit organizations often go to great lengths to establish such arrangements. It may be much more attractive for for-profit organizations to seek, instead, supplier arrangements with existing nonprofit organizations that deliver major cost and investment savings.

What is the key point of working with part-time and nonprofit suppliers? **Redesign your company's business models, methods of operating, ownership of facilities, use of facilities, breadth of product line, and offerings so you can employ part-time and nonprofit suppliers to help reduce investments by 96 percent for you and your stakeholders compared to what these investments are now in ways that will also help make your organization and your stakeholders more successful, profitable, and cash-flow positive.**

Assignments

1. Identify the ten most valuable ways you could reduce investment intensity by using part-time and nonprofit suppliers while providing more benefits that customers and suppliers want.

2. Consider how these changes would affect your other stakeholders.

3. Investigate how your business models, operating methods, breadth of product line, and offerings could be shifted over time to be even more effective by making it easier for stakeholders and your company to operate with very little investment as a result of employing part-time and nonprofit suppliers.

Lesson Forty-Two

Operate from Home

The curse of the LORD is on the house of the wicked,
But He blesses the home of the just.

— Proverbs 3:33 (NKJV)

As we explored in Lesson Forty-One, part-time suppliers often charge lower prices, in part due to lower expenses associated with having a full-time job with an employer and working at their part-time business from home. Most enterprises that operate from homes do so to reduce costs, a good reason to work from home and to have employees and suppliers who do the same.

Some businesspeople favor other advantages of being at home, such as a reduced commute, a more personal place to meet customers, and more easily being able to tend to family needs. Management guru Peter Drucker chose to operate his consulting practice from home for such reasons.

After writing that lesson, I felt that your understanding of how home-based businesses can eliminate investments would benefit from a more complete discussion. The most obvious investment advantage is that no purchases are required for land or buildings. Instead, you simply use what you have already paid for. The investment advantages don't stop there.

Chances are that any home-based organization will find itself operating in a small space, providing another investment advantage by reducing expenditures for furniture and equipment. As a result, a home-based business is more likely to purchase services as needed that require the occasional extensive use of furniture (such as for a large meeting with customers) or office equipment (such as when lots of copies need to be made).

Space limitations will cause home-based businesses to hire fewer employees, reducing needs for space, equipment, and furnishings. As a result, working capital investments for office supplies are less.

Space limitations encourage leaving frequently to visit or to work at customers' premises. Customers generally like to see you more often. The home-based business provider can use customers' investments to perform many activities without increasing the amount that customers have to invest, such as by using borrowed space in the customer's site while doing work there.

Operating a home-based organization provides insights into how an enterprise could be expanded and improved by relying on others who operate from home. In that way, a much larger enterprise may be created without the need to provide facilities, furnishings, and equipment for employees, franchisees, licensees, and suppliers.

Establishing a home-based organization can be the first step in creating a virtual enterprise, with employees and suppliers working together in cyberspace rather than in physical space. Even people without their own Internet connections and computers will usually be able to access a connected computer at a library or an Internet café. Working over Internet connections can help an organization to migrate toward more frequent and continuous activities over electronic connections. See Lesson Forty-Three for more details.

If employees (or other stakeholders) have a reason to go regularly to a library, they can perform research there that eliminates purchasing needed information sources that would require investment capital. When I first started Mitchell and Company, for instance, we located one office quite close to the library at Harvard Business School and used its materials for our research ... saving ourselves tens of thousands of dollars annually in investments and costs.

Home-based organizations can also have some valuable advantages for reducing marketing investments. Let's consider direct-selling businesses such as Avon Products whose part-time representatives sell mostly to neighbors and coworkers. Such a home-based business will be able to stay closer to the neighbors who are customers without making investments in low-payoff marketing programs. By noting when neighbors come and go, the home-based businessperson can be alert as to better times to visit. If a repeat call is needed, that call will probably occur sooner, even if the representative doesn't have access to any transportation beyond what two feet provide.

A home-based business may be able to establish a business model that includes lots of part-time, unpaid volunteers. That's the case with Amazon.com and its two million volunteer reviewers who comment on its products and help attract many customers. In addition, Amazon.com fulfills lots of its sales through individuals who sell items that they stock and ship from their homes. Amazon.com also credits much of its success in creating software-based advantages to making it easier for home-based software developers to provide custom software for the company's site.

If home-based businesses are so terrific for lowering investment costs, you might be wondering why anyone ever owns or rents a large facility. Let me describe four circumstances where concentrating work typically makes it attractive to have company-owned premises, equipment, and facilities:

1. *Costs decline from the concentration of people and resources much faster than investments increase.* Such economies-of-scale will often occur where specialized activities and equipment provide big increases in productivity. You can't make steel coils in your backyard with nearly as low cost and with as high quality as you can in a modern rolling mill.

2. *Concentration of resources can increase scale to reach the minimum effectiveness level.* For instance, using solar panels to produce enough electricity for part of your home's needs won't supply anyone else with electricity. To produce significant low-cost power for others, you need a big-enough generating station.

3. *Substantial numbers of people need to be physically present with one another on a regular basis.* You cannot teach advanced martial arts very well except by being present to demonstrate and to correct what students do as they practice with instructors and one another.

4. *Organizational learning can only take place when people are present with one another.* The effectiveness of Intel's semiconductor fabrication processes is very sensitive to nuances. Great efforts are made to be sure that each person precisely copies what every comparable person does in every other facility. Training is done by routinely shadowing teams of process workers in different facilities.

I'm sure you have your own examples of when concentration is unavoidable and desirable. But from the global trend toward smaller work units, it's clear that many such small units are more effective than larger ones. As this trend continues, more work will be done at home. This trend can help to reduce investments by your company and your stakeholders while allowing everyone to operate in highly effective ways.

What's the key point about operating from home? **Redesign your company's business models, methods of operating, ownership of facilities, use of facilities, breadth of product line, and offerings to operate as a home-based organization and to help slash the investments you and your stakeholders make by 96 percent to help make your organization and your stakeholders more successful, profitable, and cash rich.**

Assignments

1. Identify the five most valuable ways you could operate as a home-based organization to eliminate asset investments and to provide more benefits that customers and suppliers want.

2. Consider how such changes would affect your other stakeholders.

3. Investigate how your company's business models, methods of operating, ownership of facilities, use of facilities, breadth of product line, and offerings could be shifted to become even more effective by making it easier for your company and its stakeholders to operate with very little investment through functioning as a home-based organization.

Lesson Forty-Three

Operate Virtually

Therefore, brethren, we are debtors —
not to the flesh, to live according to the flesh.
For if you live according to the flesh you will die;
but if by the Spirit you put to death
the deeds of the body, you will live.
For as many as are led by the Spirit of God,
these are sons of God.
For you did not receive the spirit of bondage again to fear,
but you received the Spirit of adoption
by whom we cry out, "Abba, Father."
The Spirit Himself bears witness with our spirit
that we are children of God, and if children,
then heirs *— heirs of God and joint heirs with Christ,*
if indeed we suffer with Him,
that we may also be glorified together.

— Romans 8:12-17 (NKJV)

I began the discussion of investment-reduction methods with a description of producing almost instantly. In Lesson Thirty-Seven, I described a large number of benefits that occur when providing offerings almost instantly. In subsequent lessons, we have been drilling deeper into describing general-purpose ways to gain some of the same benefits.

In this lesson, we consider another strategic tool for reducing investments: operating virtually. So what, then, is a virtual enterprise or company? Businessdictionary.com offers this definition:

Ad hoc alliance of independent experts (consultants, designers, developers, producers, suppliers, etc.) who join to pursue a particular business opportunity. Virtual enterprises have little or no physical presence or infrastructure, rely heavily on telecommunications and networks such as internet, and usually disband when their purpose is fulfilled or the opportunity passes. Agile, flexible, and fluid, they are extremely focused and goal driven, and succeed on the basis of little investment requirements, low startup and overhead costs, and fast response time. Geographically dispersed members of a virtual enterprise collaborate on the basis of their core strengths from wherever they are and whenever they are able to do so, and may become competitors in pursuit of another opportunity. Also called virtual company or virtual corporation.

Today, traditional companies are acting more like virtual enterprises. Creating competitive advantages through increased flexibility, rather than simply to reduce investments, is the usual purpose for switching to more virtual methods. In considering flexibility, having lots of assets is often a competitive disadvantage.

With a virtual enterprise, it's possible and less expensive to change your business model much more often. When making such changes, remember that you'll have to honor your contracts with and promises to customers and suppliers. To maintain more flexibility, watch that you don't restrict yourself too much in such relationships except when you gain highly attractive advantages.

Most enterprises take a long time to become truly global due to the difficulties and expenses of creating substantial local presences in many countries. As a result, organizational leaders often choose first to strengthen their position in one country before providing the organization's original offerings globally. As a partial substitute for worldwide expansion, some smaller companies appoint distributors in a few nations. Such distributors usually don't do much more than make local sales calls on customers who are already pretty much committed to buying.

How can a virtual enterprise do better than a company adding partially global distributor networks or making country-by-country expansions of its own operations? A key step is to design offerings so that their presences are powerfully established in each locale where a customer resides. That's obviously not too difficult with an information product or software. However, I believe that any offering can develop a powerful local presence through a virtual business model.

Here's an example of what I mean. Think of Rushmore University (www.rushmore.edu), which hires online tutors who are experienced professors, consultants, and business experts to work one-on-one online with students to provide custom learning programs that are adapted to be relevant in each nation. In so doing, Rushmore offers learning benefits that no other university can improve on by merely supplying local bricks and mortar. A competitor who wanted to overcome the advantages of such distance education would probably start with a similar virtual business model, improving upon it by adding telephone conversations with well-respected tutors who speak the same first languages as the students.

By opening access to greater expertise or higher quality offerings, a virtual enterprise can also provide outstanding local excellence for its customers. With either approach, the virtual company's management will focus on adding local quality enhancements rather than just providing local distributors and company operations. Do you see how the virtual business model shifts the management focus in a helpful way?

In most cases, virtual companies can gain valuable advantages by using local specialists to produce whatever aspects of their offerings that don't travel well. You see this principle applied by the microbrewing industry in the United States. Consider Boston Beer Company, best known for its Samuel Adams brand. The company provides tasty, high-quality, prize-winning products and aggressively touts its extensive use of expensive ingredients and careful production methods in television advertisements displaying sections of its small Boston, Massachusetts, brewery.

Few customers realize that when they are more than 100 miles from Boston, the Samuel Adams beer or ale they are drinking is probably brewed, bottled, and distributed according to Boston Beer's recipe and specifications by a major local brewer whose regular beer the customer probably wouldn't touch with a ten-foot pole. Clearly, Boston Beer is operating a lot like a virtual company, while giving the impression of not being one. Your virtual company may wish to do something similar.

Since it's expensive to ship water around, international beverage companies have long done something similar either by using local high-market-share companies as suppliers and distributors, or by licensing their brands to the same kind of companies while personally directing branded marketing.

To properly coordinate their activities, most global companies require very complex computing networks tied together by dedicated communications. A smaller organization can, instead, use off-the-shelf software and networking products to create a near-equivalent over the Internet.

Keep in mind that a virtual structure also provides smaller organizations with important cost advantages that are frequently even more significant than the reduced investment requirements.

Virtual companies often have no physical premises. Employees are kept to a minimum: Quite a large company might have only ten employees working from laptop computers wherever they happen to be. Some virtual companies have no two employees working in the same city. Supplier service organizations, such as accounting and human resources firms, often play formal roles as permanent parts of virtual companies. Increasingly, even core functions (such as developing offerings and launching new products) are handled by virtual partners.

In addition, virtual companies typically find it quite easy to work with other virtual companies. When such connections occur, the entire supply chain is unburdened from investments that would hurt cash flow, slow growth, and reduce flexibility.

Linking virtual companies with customers and suppliers that have made substantial investments can also help reduce the investment intensity for such stakeholder firms by allowing them to provide more offerings from their extensive facilities without added investments.

The virtual company can use its great communications links to customers and virtual partners to provide offerings almost instantly. In fact, it will be hard to produce almost instantly without having many of the linkages that a virtual company must use.

Even if you cannot create an entirely virtual operation, you'll certainly reduce investment intensity by adopting more virtual-company characteristics, particularly when it comes to providing offerings.

What's the key point about operating virtually? **Redesign your company's business models, methods of operating, use of facilities, ownership of facilities, breadth of product line, and offerings to operate virtually in order to slash the amount of money spent on all investments by you and your stakeholders so that investments can be reduced by 96 percent compared to what is done now in ways that will also help make your organization and its stakeholders more successful, profitable, and cash rich.**

Assignments

1. Identify the five most valuable ways you could operate virtually to eliminate asset investments and to provide the added benefits that customers and suppliers eagerly want.

2. Consider how such changes would affect your other stakeholders.

3. Investigate how your company's business models, methods of operating, use of facilities, ownership of facilities, breadth of product line, and offerings could be shifted over time to be even more effective by making it easier for stakeholders and your company to operate virtually with little investment.

Lesson Forty-Four

Operate as a Marketing Organization

*"However, if you tell the dream and its interpretation,
you shall receive from me gifts, rewards, and great honor.
Therefore tell me the dream and its interpretation."*

— Daniel 2:6 (NKJV)

While operating as a marketing organization is a fine way to reduce costs and to increase effectiveness, those benefits aren't the focus here.

This lesson looks at two ways to operate as a marketing organization that reduce investments:

1. Marketing for another organization that provides its own branded offerings to customers

2. Providing offerings to the organization's own customers by outsourcing all or nearly all nonmarketing activities

Why does the first type of marketing organization require little investment? Think of independent insurance agents as an example for such an entity. Most of these organizations are started by one person who works from home. Typically, the insurance company providing the policies will promptly pay commissions and incentives. If the insurance company believes that the agency's performance will be good, a monthly retainer might also be paid to finance part of the agency's start-up costs. Many offering providers will also pay for required marketing materials in advance of any sales being made. When the offering provider makes such concessions, there are often few investment needs left for the marketing organization to make. An existing computer can usually support the marketing business. If the organization succeeds to the point that it can become a full-time job for someone who needs an away-from-home office, everything else that's required can be rented at a nominal monthly cost.

Now, let's consider marketing organizations that provide offerings to their own customers through relying on outsourced suppliers. Sara Lee is a consumer-goods company that operates this way.

If you want to provide a standard item that many people can use, most outsourced suppliers will be happy to provide what you want to order without any investment by your organization.

If, instead, you want to offer a proprietary product that not everyone can use, suppliers may seek payments for tooling and anything else they have to invest in for you that no one else can use. Such unique tooling might include a plastics mold for the exterior of an item with an unusual shape for which you hold the intellectual property rights.

If you agree to purchase a minimum quantity of any proprietary offerings that is large enough for the supplier to recoup its start-up costs, many suppliers will let you avoid making advance payments for any special tooling or equipment. In such instances, there will usually be a capital or interest charge included in the supplier's price. If well negotiated, the price you pay for the offerings should be similar to the actual cost of renting the necessary tooling or equipment by using your organization's credit.

Now that you have the two business models for marketing organizations in mind, let's consider nine potential causes of increased investments:

1. *A long sales cycle*

   While many offerings are purchased after only a few seconds of thought, larger and more expensive products and services may only be bought after many months (or even years) of evaluation and consideration. When there is a lengthy time involved and salaried staff members are actively engaged in such sales activities, working-capital investments are required to pay for the sales-people's salaries and expenses.

2. *A market that needs to be developed from scratch, beginning with basic education*

   As you can imagine, it's a lot harder to sell a new type of gizmo than it is to sell a widget that everyone already uses and finds to be very valuable. I remember meeting a salesman for a major chemical company whose job was to sell its chemicals for totally new applications. After ten years of educating customers, he had made only two small sales. Almost all of his salary, benefits, and expenses for those years represented unsuccessful investments. The same result can occur while marketing for a new industry during a time when customers aren't yet convinced of the offerings' value.

3. *Extensive investments in a proposal*

   The proposals for some U. S. government contracts may require providing a stack of information on paper that's taller than a person. In most cases, such proposals will require the expertise of engineers and others with technical skills. The salaries, benefits, and expenses of the technical people are then added to the cost of the salespeople and their expenses to increase the total working-capital investments. Such proposals also take a long time to develop, which automatically extends the sales cycle and further increases the size of investments.

4. *Creating a prototype*

   If you offer something new that's pretty unique and difficult to accomplish, potential customers can be concerned about your ability to perform. They may seek to satisfy themselves by testing a prototype. If you don't yet make such an offering, you will have start-up expenses associated with preparing the necessary prototype. For highly technical offerings, such prototypes can cost as much as tens of millions of dollars. Many times potential customers will make token payments towards the cost of prototypes, but the bulk of the expense will always rest on the seller's or marketing organization's shoulders. If you are a marketing-only organization and the potential profit benefit would mostly accrue to the offering provider, you may be able to persuade your client organization to bear almost all the investment burden. Even if your organization gains most of the benefit, suppliers may be willing to pay a substantial portion of the total prototype costs.

5. *Not attracting customers*

No matter how brief or long, easy or difficult, and inexpensive or expensive it is to gain a sale, not selling a prospect involves working-capital investments in salaries, benefits, and expenses that are not recovered. Unfortunately, many new salespeople will not succeed. The time, money, and effort that you expended to hire, to supervise, and to pay them end up simply being investments that did not pay off.

6. *Offerings being returned without receiving any offsetting contributions from your client organization or your outsourced suppliers*

Returns often happen during difficult economic conditions. A customer may buy something and later find out that the item isn't needed. If so, the item will be returned for credit. When that happens, you will have money tied up selling, producing, shipping, and storing the item until you can resell it.

7. *Customers who don't pay on time*

Customers may not pay for a variety of reasons, but not having enough cash on hand is one of the most common. When that happens, you run the risk of never being paid. Organizations that are overly eager to make sales sometimes don't do enough to check on customers' credit or to insist on prompt payment. If the customer doesn't ever pay and the offering you provided is one that has already been consumed, you may not be able to salvage any cash from the transaction. The marketing and any costs to provide the offering then become investments that will never pay off for your organization.

8. *Your client organization or its outsourced suppliers failing customers so badly that the customer cancels the purchase*

Unless you are very careful, your client organization or outsourced suppliers may not deliver what you promised the customers. When that happens, a sale may be lost along with much investment.

9. *The client organization you market for or your outsourced suppliers increasing their prices to you more rapidly than what you can raise prices to customers, shrinking your profit margin*

This is an old story in many industries that once depended on having many different layers of distribution to deliver offerings from large producers to individual users. Whenever a new distribution channel emerges that's more effective and efficient than having your marketing organization in place, there will be an inevitable profit margin squeeze on your operation. With such a margin squeeze, you will eventually incur losses, and such losses will have to be funded by investment capital. The best way to avoid this problem is by being an innovator in employing new, lower-cost marketing methods.

After reviewing these nine potential causes of investment increases, you may be doubtful about the wisdom of operating as a marketing organization. Consider, then, the following characteristics that could make a marketing-only organization more attractive:

- Proposals are simple, easy, and cheap to prepare.
- No expensive prototypes need to be developed.

- Sales success rates are high.
- Offerings are unlikely to be returned for credit.
- There is little risk that customers will not pay promptly.
- Your client organization and any outsourced suppliers will find it to be easy to meet customer requirements.
- You have a substantial cost advantage that competitors are not likely to overcome anytime soon.

You can also help ensure your own success in establishing a marketing-only organization by doing the following two things:

1. Sell offerings with short sales cycles.

2. Focus on established markets where customers continually need to purchase.

What's the key point about operating as a marketing organization? **Redesign your company's business models, methods of operating, use of facilities, ownership of facilities, breadth of product line, and offerings to be a marketing organization and slash the amount spent by you and your stakeholders on all investments by 96 percent compared to what it is done now in ways that will also help make your organization and its stakeholders more successful, profitable, and cash rich.**

Assignments

1. Identify the ten most valuable ways you could operate as a marketing-only organization to eliminate asset investments and to provide the most benefits that customers and suppliers want.

2. Consider how such changes would affect your other stakeholders.

3. Investigate how your company's business models, methods of operating, use of facilities, ownership of facilities, breadth of product line, and offerings could be shifted over time to be even more effective in helping stakeholders and your company to operate with very little investment as a result of your functioning as a marketing-only organization.

Lesson Forty-Five

More Efficiently Operate Activities
for Customers

But when the wise is instructed, he receives knowledge.

— Proverbs 21:11 (NKJV)

This lesson continues our examination of ways to gain investment-reducing benefits by looking at doing more for customers, in more efficient ways, than they can do for themselves.

Customers often make unnecessary investments due to performing too many activities for themselves. Why would customers do that? A number of potential causes can contribute:

- In times of higher-than-usual employment insecurity, employees seek to do more things in order to appear to be more indispensable to their employers.

- Employees often fail to understand how inefficient their use of investment funds is.

- Management may not appreciate by how much investments and costs could be reduced through asking suppliers to do more for the customer organization.

- Many customers make decisions based solely on what the profit impact is compared to their history, mostly ignoring whatever investments are required and their impacts on cash flow.

- Many company leaders believe that they become more secure by expanding the number of their "core competencies" into areas where they could potentially add great value for their customers.

- Many customers fail to look at ways to reduce investments once made or the organization becomes committed to making an investment.

Here's an example of such causes drawn from my consulting experiences. A client organization decided to hire Mitchell and Company instead of its usual consulting firm for stock-price improvement. Client executives were tired of having lots of young consultants hanging around the company's offices doing tasks the executives could probably do better for themselves after they learned how. The other consulting firm refused to teach the executives and to hand off any tasks, most of which related to day-to-day management.

The consultants were very highly paid by the consulting firm, which charged the client almost four times their salaries for providing services ... much more per hour than the client executives received in salaries.

In making this choice of consulting firms, the client executives failed to appreciate that the ongoing activities related to the stock-price-improvement assignment were very simple and inexpensive to do. Even if the company had hired Mitchell and Company to do all such tasks for them, the annual cost would have been minimal. The big cost was for developing the data, something that only had to be done every few years.

The client executives were determined to learn how to do as many things as possible for themselves, including things that they wouldn't have to do for several years. Wanting to gain the fullest value from their learning, they sometimes brought thirty people to the Mitchell and Company's training sessions.

A consequence of this demand for training was to increase charges for the consulting project, to add lots of internal costs by diverting time and attention from other tasks, and to discourage people from wanting to work on stock-price improvement (because it seemed so difficult, due to learning about complex data development).

The client executives had the right idea about not hiring consultants to do routine activities they should be doing for themselves ... but they were mistaken in believing that the data-development work involved in stock-price improvement was such an activity.

If, instead, they had simply asked for a five-year contract to routinely develop the necessary information and to describe the implications for them, I could have reduced the external and internal costs of the work by about two-thirds. Since they were capitalizing the cost of my work onto their balance sheet, such an alternative approach would have saved the company a tidy investment. They would have also received more benefit from the money they spent, while allocating much less time to learning about stock-price improvement and more time to employing stock-price-improvement methods in useful ways.

I see similar miscalculations in other activities in many of the companies I visit. Their facilities are often operating at a tiny fraction of their potential due to not having enough business, not knowing how to optimally run the equipment, and having offerings poorly matched to such equipment and facilities.

What could they do instead? Some company leaders realize they have such operating and facility issues and ask those who specialize in the related tasks (such as contract manufacturers and IT outsourcing firms) to buy their facilities, to hire their staffs, and to conduct the tasks for them.

In making such a decision, company leaders may not realize that even with expert leadership, existing facilities and current employees may not be able to provide much more value in performing such activities. In such circumstances, a better approach is to ask suppliers what offerings they would like to provide that would enable the customer company to operate much more efficiently in terms of costs *and* investments. Left with a free hand, customers will often be astonished by how much suppliers can help them to save.

Let me explain what I mean about operating with a free hand by elaborating on the consulting example. A very large percentage of the costs associated with stock-price-improvement consulting is potentially useful for other people in the industry. A wise client would encourage the consulting firm to make a pitch to everyone else in the industry for sharing the data development, while maintaining appropriate safeguards so that sensitive data are not disclosed to other clients. As a result, more than 80 percent of the investment cost of data development for each company in the industry could be eliminated.

Similar opportunities can probably be found elsewhere. For instance, an equipment manufacturer could create one optimal facility using its own gear to serve all the production needs of its customers within a geographical area. Costs and investments for each customer served would plummet due to the facility being operated at a higher throughput rate for more hours by experts.

In some countries, potential cooperation among competitors is limited, such as due to antitrust laws and regulations in North America and Europe. Other countries allow more cooperation, permitting suppliers to invite their customers to meet and to explore how having the supplier perform their operations could provide cost and investment breakthroughs.

In some cases, suppliers know how to design and to produce outstanding equipment but aren't nearly as good at making it run. In such instances, equipment suppliers should seek the best operators and either hire or learn from them … in ways that are acceptable to customers.

When it comes to IT, outsourcing opportunities are usually even greater. A supplier can use free open-source software as the foundation for enhancing the systems that all of its customers use. When that happens, investments by customers can be greatly reduced. In some cases, it can be helpful for the supplier to fill in what the open-source providers cannot easily do. You see that motive in IBM's extensive support of the Linux operating system: IBM wants its service customers to avoid expensive investments in Microsoft's operating systems and applications programs.

Here are five questions to guide you when seeking to do more for your customers:

1. How can you make all your customers more efficient and less investment intensive by combining and performing their activities?

2. What major activities can you do for customers that they cannot do nearly as well for themselves?

3. What resources and knowledge can you add to be even more effective in such a role?

4. Who else can you partner with to make even larger efficiency improvements and more substantial investment reductions?

5. What new offerings will most encourage customers to choose you to operate activities for them in ways that provide major efficiencies and investment reductions?

What's the key point about operating activities for customers more efficiently? **Redesign your company's business models, methods of operating, use of facilities, ownership of facilities, breadth of product line, and offerings to take on activities where you can operate more efficiently and with less investment than customers to allow them to reduce investments in such activities by 96 percent and to create lots of excess cash for all.**

Assignments

1. Identify the five most significant activities you could operate more efficiently for customers while vastly reducing their investments.

2. Consider how you can build the trust needed to encourage customers to let you operate such activities for them.

3. Investigate how such changes would affect your other stakeholders.

4. Explore how your company's business models, methods of operating, use of facilities, ownership of facilities, breadth of product line, and offerings could be shifted over time to be even more effective and to make it easier for stakeholders and your company to operate with very little investment as a result of your doing more activities for customers and other stakeholders.

Lesson Forty-Six

Add Grants and Subsidies

Then the king made a great feast, the Feast of Esther,
for all his officials and servants;
and he proclaimed a holiday in the provinces
and gave gifts according to the generosity of a king.

— Esther 2:18 (NKJV)

The cost of investments that benefit many stakeholders can unfairly fall more on one organization. Amtrak, the American government-owned passenger rail corporation, is an example of this problem.

Amtrak was formed at a time when for-profit passenger rail operations were losing lots of money, as were the railroads that owned such operations. Fearing for their financial survival, U.S. railroads petitioned the federal government for legislative relief so that they would no longer be required to transport passengers. Since citizens still needed rail service, Amtrak was chosen by Congress for the purpose.

For most of its history, Amtrak leased access to railroads' tracks. Eventually, it was able to obtain its own tracks from Washington, D.C. to Boston and the funding needed to upgrade its track so that higher-speed trains could operate on it. This higher-speed service soon became profitable and continues to be so today.

Overall, Amtrak loses lots of money, which U.S. taxpayers subsidize. As a result, the passenger rail corporation has a hard time making any new capital investments for upgrading the track it owns, for improving the stations it uses for passengers, and for adding rolling stock.

In 2009, Vice President Biden (who while in Congress daily rode Amtrak's high-speed service to and from Wilmington, Delaware and Washington, D.C.) helped Amtrak to gain $1.3 billion in investment funds to improve its services.

Normally, such a story might describe a political favor for a failing organization that gained support unfairly. Closer examination reveals, however, that this investment is an opportunity to reduce investment intensity for U.S. citizens.

Amtrak isn't the only form of passenger travel that's heavily subsidized in the United States. Airlines are subsidized through airport building and providing of air-traffic control. Roads are heavily subsidized to keep high-speed Interstate highways in good shape. Even cruise ships for vacations are subsidized through safety-related services.

Railroads provide a major opportunity to add travel capacity without taking a lot more highly desired (and expensive) urban land. You could lay ten rail lines side by side in the space that a new freeway occupies. To expand an airport usually means carving out major sections of the most densely occupied land in or near any urban center. Most rail lines, by contrast, are often lightly used and could easily handle much more passenger traffic if the requisite track maintenance and upgrades were done.

As an example of what I mean about alternative solutions being investment intensive, part of the Boston area's major roads were rebuilt over twenty years at an estimated cost of $22 billion. That's four times what was needed at the same time to add or to improve higher-speed railroad tracks over all the most congested parts of the United States.

Here are some statistics about subsidies: The average Amtrak passenger is currently subsidized to the extent of $40 per trip, mostly to pay for legally mandated services where usage is light. By comparison, travel in the average American passenger vehicle is subsidized through road building to the tune of $600 to $700 a year.

I rode Amtrak from Seattle, Washington, to Portland, Oregon, in 2009. I was delighted to find that the fare cost 80 percent less than flying, and 90 percent less than renting a car. The service was terrific, the seats were new and comfortable, the trip was quick, the scenery was outstanding, and I couldn't imagine why anyone would travel between those two cities in any other way.

Clearly, in places where it would be hard (or ridiculously expensive) to add capacity for airplanes and vehicles, it makes a lot of sense to expand higher-speed passenger rail capacity and services. Alternative ways to travel would probably require fifty to a hundred times greater investments.

Naturally, if your business has heavily subsidized competitors, you need to be prepared to obtain your own subsidies in order to compete.

If you don't have subsidized competitors, it may still make good sense to seek grants and subsidies when the alternative is for all stakeholders to incur much higher investments and costs.

Let's next consider the idea of a service that would provide comprehensive databases for tracking and delivering services to all the poor people in the United States. Because many poor people don't know what services are available to them, they often don't receive needed services that they qualify for and often, instead, consume more expensive services than they need. For instance, most poor people could qualify for subsidized or free food, housing, and job training. Most will only be getting one or two of these benefits because they are ignorant of how to obtain the others.

Some poor people don't know that most state governments will provide them with no- or low-cost health insurance so that they can receive many of the same medical services as everyone else. Lacking health insurance, these people often go to a hospital's emergency room for care because they know from experience that hospitals rarely turn them away. Through subsidies to cover the cost of such "free" services, governments may pay $600 to $1,000 for a medical visit rather than the $60 to $300 that would have been incurred for treatment at a physician's office.

By using all the comprehensive services well that governments provide, most poor people can get a job and take care of themselves within two or three years. Otherwise, they may need government help for decades.

By having a comprehensive database for poor people who are receiving government services, a social worker could be sure that someone is receiving all the needed benefits he or she is eligible for. In addition, service providers can tell if the person has access to other forms of services that are less expensive. As a result, a hospital emergency room could forward the prospective patient to a nearby clinic where a nonemergency medical condition or illness could be better treated (and often more quickly), focusing more of the emergency room's scarce resources on critical care.

It's unlikely that such a database would be built and maintained without a government subsidy. That's because although many other stakeholders would benefit from such a database, none of the stakeholders has enough financial incentive to develop and to maintain it.

In seeking grants and subsidies, it naturally helps to point out how other investments and costs are reduced as a result so that total stakeholder benefits are substantially increased well beyond the investment costs.

In a for-profit business environment, it's not usual to think in terms of how some stakeholders might receive benefits that are so substantial for reducing investments and costs that these stakeholders might be willing to provide grants and subsidies to encourage the use of the for-profit enterprise's offerings. Such opportunities are probably more common than you think.

Here's an example. Imagine that you provide new software that enables certain types of equipment to perform with fewer breakdowns. Let's further assume that such breakdowns often cause serious injuries. If the country where you sell the software normally incurs major ongoing costs for injuries, its government may be very interested in paying for software improvements that further reduce injuries or to subsidize equipment owners' purchases of the existing software.

When no other funding source is available, governments may pay for the development of technologies that reduce investments and costs for their citizens. Such grants and subsidies can be essential to making improvements available.

In examining business opportunities, you should consider where new developments, offerings, expansions, and other investment-intensive activities would yield major benefits for all stakeholders … as well as for citizens at large. When everyone benefits, you should look into applying for grants and subsidies. Whether or not the government agrees, also consider foundations and other private sources.

What's the key point about seeking grants and subsidies? **Redesign your company's business models, methods of operating, use of facilities, ownership of facilities, breadth of product line, and offerings to develop alternatives that reduce investment and costs for all stakeholders, and seek grants and subsidies from beneficiaries to help reduce investments by 96 percent and to create lots of excess cash for everyone.**

Assignments

1. Identify the five most significant activities you could provide that would reduce the investments and costs required by all stakeholders.

2. Measure what the benefits of each activity would be for all stakeholders.

3. Evaluate if it would be uneconomic to provide any of those benefits without grants and subsidies.

4. Where you need grants and subsidies to invest, determine the most likely sources.

5. Investigate how your business models, operating methods, use of facilities, ownership of facilities, breadth of product line, and offerings could be shifted to become even more effective by making it easier for stakeholders and your organization to reduce their investments and costs through obtaining grants and subsidies.

Lesson Forty-Seven

Avoid Mistakes in Extracting Cash
from the Balance Sheet

So King Solomon surpassed
all the kings of the earth in riches and wisdom.
Now all the earth sought the presence of Solomon
to hear his wisdom, which God had put in his heart.

— 1 Kings 10:23-24 (NKJV)

What happens when you increase an organization's revenues by twenty times, reduce costs per-offering by 96 percent, and eliminate 96 percent of all investments per offering? You create an organization that has a very high profit margin, large profits, little need to reinvest, and a lot of cash.

One of the most famous examples of this phenomenon occurred when Microsoft successfully rode the personal-computer industry's expansion by selling operating systems and application programs. In the year of this writing, the company generated seventeen billion dollars more in cash more than it needed to operate. Even after eliminating lots of excess cash in recent years, the organization still retained cash reserves of more than forty billion dollars.

While it's always good to be sure that you have enough cash to meet your organization's needs in good times and bad, it's not such a good idea to pile up lots of excess cash. Here are some of the potential problems from doing so:

- You may have slowed the market's growth rate by charging too-high prices and making too-few improvements so that customers' capacities to afford your offerings were less than they could have been.

- You earn only a small return from holding the cash (probably no more than 2 percent after-tax at the time of this writing) compared to the much higher returns available from wisely investing in business improvements.

- The extra cash can suggest to investors that you have too few growth and investment opportunities, reducing the value of your organization's equity and thereby harming shareholders.

- You could attract adverse attention from those who regulate your firm as well as from those who make decisions about buying from your organization.

- Stakeholders might become wary of your intentions, sensing an attitude of "all stakeholders exist to make the company disgustingly wealthy."

- You may encourage entry by new competitors and expansion by existing firms because it is so financially attractive and affordable to compete against you.

What do companies typically do with excess cash before the amount becomes an embarrassment? I didn't conduct a study — nor do I know of one — but my impressions are as follows:

- Pay larger dividends to shareholders.

- Purchase the company's own stock.

- Repay any debt.

- Make acquisitions.

- Pay for backward-and-forward integrations that make the organization more capital intensive.

Each of these cash uses may have serious problems. Here are some of the difficulties:

- Pay larger dividends to shareholders.

   In some countries (such as the United States), dividends don't receive a favorable tax treatment so that part of what you send to shareholders ends up going to the government. The net effect may be to reduce shareholder value.

   It's also hard to reduce dividend payments once started without causing a major drop in equity value. As a result, this decision could lead to a future cash drain at a time when the cash could be used more productively in some other way.

   Unless your equity is a high-yield stock (by which I mean that the ratio of the dividend per share divided by the share price is a much higher percentage than what comparable stocks yield) that attracts people who mostly want to receive a dividend, most investors just reinvest the cash you send them in some other security, incurring added brokerage costs that reduce returns for them.

   You may unintentionally signal that you lack important new activities that might ever require investing some of the cash. If your growth is slow, this perception could cause some stakeholders to give up on their hopes for growth through working with you.

- Purchase the company's own stock.

   This transaction is often viewed as a more logical alternative to paying higher dividends. Share repurchases are easier to suspend without annoying shareholders. Tax issues are usually not quite so difficult.

The effect is to boost the stock value and dividend growth for those who retain their shares for several more years.

The potential exists for sending the negative signal that you don't have any significant future opportunities for the cash.

- Repay any debt.

When interest costs associated with debt are high, such repayments can boost profits. In today's financial markets, debt costs are usually low. Also, companies with high profit margins, fast growth, and few assets probably aren't going to have much, if any, any debt to repay.

Again, the potential exists for sending a negative signal that you don't have any significant future business opportunities to use the cash.

- Make acquisitions.

If you have a high-multiple stock (as measured by price-to-earnings per share, price-to-book per share, and price-to-revenues per share compared to other companies in your industry), it's often more advantageous to use stock rather than cash to pay for such transactions. That decision may be partially driven by tax considerations (such as when a share exchange isn't taxable to shareholders, but cash payments are). The other consideration is simply the cost of one kind of capital versus another.

Most acquisitions, other than of direct competitors, don't work very well. So you also have the primary issue of whether the action is a good one in the first place.

- Pay for backward-and-forward integration investments that make the organization more capital intensive.

Such purchases can be very threatening to customers and suppliers, causing friendly relations to be harmed. If you don't perform such new activities much better than customers and suppliers do, you also run the risk of hurting your organization's effectiveness.

What can we conclude? Excess cash cannot be removed from the balance sheet in positive ways without examining many alternatives, making some very careful judgments, picking the right methods, and applying such methods at just the right times. As a result, the wisest decision in some cases will be to avoid building up excess cash.

As you can see, I've opened up a major new topic. In future lessons, we look at how to anticipate, to manage, and to dispose of excess cash so that it does the most good for reducing investments by all stakeholders.

What's the key point about avoiding mistakes in extracting cash from the balance sheet? **Redesign of your company's business models, methods of operating, use of facilities, ownership of facilities, breadth of product line, and offerings to reduce investments by 96 percent for you and your stakeholders can create lots of excess cash, a circumstance with potentially negative consequences. A key issue is how to manage such investment reductions to create the most benefit for all stakeholders.**

Assignments

1. Identify the five most significant ways that you could use excess cash to provide more benefits that customers and suppliers are seeking.

2. Consider how such changes would affect your other stakeholders.

3. Investigate how your company's business models, methods of operating, use of facilities, ownership of facilities, breadth of product line, and offerings could be shifted over time to be even more effective by making it easier for stakeholders and your company to operate with very little investment as a result of how you use excess cash.

Lesson Forty-Eight

Choose More Attractive Ways to Extract Cash from the Balance Sheet

"I am the true vine, and My Father is the vinedresser.
Every branch in Me that does not bear fruit He takes away;
and every branch *that bears fruit He prunes, that it may bear more fruit.*
You are already clean because of the word which I have spoken to you.
Abide in Me, and I in you.
As the branch cannot bear fruit of itself,
unless it abides in the vine, neither can you, unless you abide in Me.
I am the vine, you are *the branches.*
He who abides in Me, and I in him, bears much fruit;
for without Me you can do nothing."

— John 15:1-5 (NKJV)

As described in Lesson Forty-Seven, when you increase an organization's revenues by twenty times, reduce per-unit costs of an offering by 96 percent, and also eliminate 96 percent of all investments per offering, you create an organization that has a very high profit margin, large profits, little need to reinvest, and a lot of cash. Such a cash buildup can have negative consequences, as can misapplying the cash.

To understand the best choices for cash use and how they compare to one another, an organization needs a detailed appreciation for the cost, price, and demand effects on its stakeholders when various actions are taken. Because of the potential value of doing the right thing with the cash, one of the highest potential uses for excess cash is to develop accurate models for estimating cost, price, and demand effects on stakeholders. With the insights that such models provide, your organization can improve and grow much more rapidly by relieving constraints on growth within its value chain.

Here's an analogy for what I'm describing about freeing up the value chain. If a minor automobile accident spills broken glass across all the lanes of traffic in a given direction, drivers slow down when they near the accident to avoid glass shards and to gawk at the accident. Once past the accident, most motorists quickly speed up again.

Until reaching the accident, traffic slows to whatever speed drivers select when in the accident's vicinity. If traffic is backed up for ten miles, drivers can spend a half hour to an hour in a traffic jam (unless they exit the congested road and take some other route that isn't as congested).

If, instead, tow trucks quickly remove the vehicles while someone else takes away any hint of broken glass, the traffic jam's length will be shorter because the average speed will be much higher while traveling through the bottleneck.

While I cannot diagnose what you should do with your cash without examining specific stakeholder effects, I may help narrow down the choices by describing some potential uses for excess cash that can eliminate common bottlenecks that slow down profitable growth.

Before going further, let me introduce you to a business concept that may be new to you: *generating more growth, profit, and cash flow by avoiding a cash buildup.* I call this condition the "cash-equilibrium state." Such a condition is best achieved by applying excess cash to the most constrained parts of the value chain, in addition to removing excess cash on hand by making helpful acquisitions, paying cash dividends when doing so substantially increases shareholder value, and making share purchases when long-term shareholders favor such an action.

Here's a hypothetical example to show how valuable it can be to apply excess cash productively to the value chain. Imagine that a business has sales of $100,000 in the current year, pretax profits are $96,000, cash flow after taxes is $62,000, the balance sheet has $125,000 in excess cash on it, and revenues have been expanding at 100 percent a year. Obviously, this is a very attractive business to be in, just the sort of business this book strives to help you to create and to sustain.

Let's assume the hypothetical business is constrained by some customer-related circumstance that could be eliminated or improved by using the $125,000 in excess cash. (While it doesn't matter what this circumstance is, for purposes of this illustration let's assume that customers need a redesigned offering that will be much more valuable to them.)

When the $125,000 is properly spent, the business grows revenues at 400 percent for the next year. After this spending has just been completed, in the first year pretax profits become $480,000 instead of $192,000, cash flow after tax grows to $310,000 instead of $124,000, and the business generates an additional $61,000 in cash beyond what it would have had without making the $125,000 investment.

That's a pretty dramatic example, and your business may not have short-term choices that are nearly as attractive. I'm sure you'll agree that you would be happy to apply any excess cash on the balance sheet whenever your business would generate a lot more profit, cash flow, value, and excess cash in a reasonable amount of time.

With such a purpose in mind, let's look at some opportunities to measure and to consider as possible uses for applying your organization's excess cash:

1. Customers

    a. Lower price paid for the offering
    b. Lower price for related offerings
    c. More features
    d. Lower-priced features
    e. More-valuable features
    f. More availability
    g. Easier to use
    h. Less expensive to use
    i. Longer payment terms

2. Customers' Customers

    a. Lower price paid for the customer's offering
    b. Lower price for related offerings

    c. More features
    d. Lower-priced features
    e. More-valuable features
    f. More availability
    g. Easier to use
    h. Less expensive to use
    i. Longer payment terms

3. Suppliers

    a. Higher price for their offerings
    b. Lower cost of inputs for their offerings
    c. More features
    d. Fewer features
    e. Higher-priced features
    f. Lower-cost features
    g. More-valuable features
    h. More availability
    i. Easier to use
    j. Less expensive to use
    k. Redesign to add functionality and to lower cost
    l. Longer payment terms

4. Suppliers' Suppliers

    a. Higher price for their offerings
    b. Lower cost of inputs for their offerings
    c. More features
    d. Fewer features
    e. Higher-priced features
    f. Lower-cost features
    g. More-valuable features
    h. More availability
    i. Easier to use
    j. Less expensive to use
    k. Redesign to add functionality and lower cost
    l. Longer payment terms

5. Distributors (if any)

    a. Lower price for the offering they distribute
    b. Lower price for related offerings
    c. More features
    d. Lower-priced features
    e. More-valuable features
    f. More availability
    g. Easier to use

    h. Less expensive to use

    i. Longer payment terms

6. Partners (if any)

    a. Lower price for the offering they add value to
    b. Lower price of related offerings
    c. More features
    d. Lower-priced features
    e. More-valuable features
    f. More availability
    g. Easier to use
    h. Less expensive to use

7. Employees

    a. Redesign to make work safer, easier, or more pleasant
    b. More desirable career opportunities
    c. Reduced working hours
    d. Added employee benefits
    e. Increased education, training, or tools
    f. Greater recognition
    g. More compensation

8. Communities You Serve

    a. More jobs
    b. Better-paying jobs
    c. Help with local business development
    d. Solving severe local problems unrelated to the business's impacts on the community

What's the key point about extracting cash from the balance sheet in more attractive ways? **Redesign your company's business models, ownership of facilities, use of facilities, methods of operating, breadth of product line, and offerings to reduce investments by 96 percent for you and your stakeholders, and then use the excess cash that is generated to create the most benefits for all stakeholders by considering improvements to the most constrained parts of the value chain.**

Assignments

1. Identify the five most significant ways that you could use excess cash to provide more benefits that customers and suppliers want.

2. Consider how such changes would affect your other stakeholders.

3. Investigate how your company's business models, ownership of facilities, use of facilities, methods of operating, breadth of product line, and offerings could be shifted over time to be even more effective by making it easier for stakeholders and your company to identify and to implement better ways to operate with very little investment as a result of applying your excess cash.

Lesson Forty-Nine

Choose the Optimal Debt Level to Extract Cash from the Balance Sheet

A certain woman of the wives of the sons of the prophets
cried out to Elisha, saying,
"Your servant my husband is dead,
and you know that your servant feared the LORD.
And the creditor is coming to take my two sons to be his slaves."
So Elisha said to her, "What shall I do for you?
Tell me, what do you have in the house?"
And she said, "Your maidservant has nothing in the house
but a jar of oil."
Then he said, "Go, borrow vessels from everywhere,
from all your neighbors — empty vessels;
do not gather just a few.
And when you have come in,
you shall shut the door behind you and your sons;
then pour it into all those vessels,
and set aside the full ones."
So she went from him
and shut the door behind her and her sons,
who brought the vessels to her; and she poured it out.
Now it came to pass, when the vessels were full,
that she said to her son, "Bring me another vessel."
And he said to her, "There is not another vessel."
So the oil ceased.
Then she came and told the man of God.
And he said, "Go, sell the oil and pay your debt;
and you and your sons live on the rest."

— 2 Kings 4:1-7 (NKJV)

What happens when you increase an organization's revenues by twenty times, reduce per-unit costs of an offering by 96 percent, and then eliminate 96 percent of all investments for each offering? As noted in lessons forty-seven and forty-eight, you create an organization that has a very high profit margin, large profits, little need to reinvest, and lots of cash. As also noted, most companies pick poor alternatives for their excess cash. In this lesson, we look at how to quickly and inexpensively understand the optimal debt level while engaging in the most attractive cash-use choices.

Since 1960, most organizations have taken on ever-more debt as a percentage of their total capital. As a result, some organizations are employing as much as hundreds of dollars in debt for every dollar of equity. Naturally, when economic or financial environments suddenly worsen, it is just such organizations that are brought to their knees. (Bear, Stearns and Lehman Brothers in 2008 are well-known examples in the United States, and the same result would have happened to thousands of other highly debt-leveraged enterprises around the world without the benefit of coordinated government bailouts supplying low- or zero-interest loans, equity infusions, and financial guarantees.)

The concept of a debt-to-equity ratio doesn't apply very well to such a highly effective enterprise as we have been studying because such an organization can be healthy and huge while relying on a relatively small equity foundation. Even if a lot of debt relative to equity were added to such an enterprise, the total amount of debt would be modest compared to the organization's ability to cover interest costs and repay principal through its large and rapidly expanding cash flow.

Some financial theorists point to the level of cash flow and its steadiness as better indicators of safe debt levels than the traditional debt-to-equity ratio. In such terms, a 2,000 percent cubed solution enterprise is a debt-carrying, long-haired Samson. Let's consider an example. Assume that an enterprise has $1 million in sales this year, will grow at 40 percent annually, has a 96 percent pretax profit margin as a percentage of sales, and only requires one dollar of net assets for every hundred dollars in revenues. Here are the numbers:

- Pretax profits are $960,000.

- Net assets are only $10,000.

- Annual pretax cash flow is $956,000 before paying any dividends ($960,000 in pretax profits minus $4,000 in net new assets).

Assuming the organization borrows money at an interest cost of 5 percent a year before taxes and wants to have three times more cash flow than it needs to pay the interest costs, the organization's debt capacity is $6.36 million.

After a year, all of these numbers increase by 40 percent as follows:

- Pretax profits are $1.344 million.

- Net assets are only $14,000.

- Pretax cash flow is $1.3384 million ($1.344 million in pretax profits minus $5,600 in net new assets).

Assuming the organization borrows money at 5 percent a year before tax and wants to have three times more cash flow than it needs to pay for the interest costs, the debt capacity expands after one year to $8.92 million, an increase of $2.56 million.

Some financial engineers would go wild with such an opportunity because they could easily use the expanded debt capacity each year to repay all the interest costs incurred. As a result, they might borrow so much that the interest costs would amount to 80 percent of the forecasted cash flow for the following year. With such an approach, debt capacity expands to approximately $30 million.

I don't think it's prudent to use that much debt, but considering the choice does raise an interesting point: The 2,000 percent cubed solution enterprise described in this example during stable circumstances can raise virtually unlimited amounts of debt. How should such an enterprise think about appropriate debt levels?

First, it's clear that the organization should identify and consider investment options way beyond the scale of what its competitors and similar-sized companies normally investigate. For example, in some industries you have to make a large investment to obtain a new customer, such as occurs for those offering outsourced information technology (IT) services. Such IT customers may expect you buy the existing equipment, hire the current employees, and pay for the software that's already been purchased and developed, as well as pay a price premium to the value of what's received in return for a profitable long-term contract to perform what the customer has formerly done for itself. With its amazing debt capacity, cash would not be a limitation for such an enterprise in adding new customers ... the ability to successfully integrate and operate the new operations, however, would be. In such an instance, it would be worthwhile to consider speeding market-share gains by acquiring competitors with the enterprise's unused customer-adding capacity. Normally, such a strategy wouldn't be affordable except for a company paying with an exceptionally high price-to-earnings-ratio stock for acquisitions and customer investments.

Second, the organization may be able to gain cost advantages on a scale that competitors cannot achieve. For instance, organizations are usually unable to afford hedging their costs very far into the future. A 2,000 percent cubed solution organization would be able to afford to take physical possession of vast amounts of commodities and currencies that are expected to appreciate at a rapid rate, allowing costs to be contained near current levels for many years. Such a tactic makes sense only when the rate of cost increase is well above the interest rate for the borrowed money and the costs of storing and safeguarding what is purchased.

Third, the 2,000 percent cubed solution enterprise may be able to support types of investments by suppliers, customers, partners, and other stakeholders that provide enormous advantages that competitors will never be able to consider matching. Imagine such an enterprise being in the vehicle manufacturing business. At a time when vehicle dealerships were being eliminated very rapidly due to economic distress, such an enterprise could expand and improve its dealerships while also providing very attractive financing to its dealers' customers. With such a strategy in such an environment, enormous market-share gains might occur while many competitors were forced by circumstances to retrench.

Fourth, and most importantly, the 2,000 percent cubed solution enterprise could use the information from its proprietary expenditure models to improve stakeholder performance in ways that greatly accelerate industry growth and enhance competitive position that competitors may not understand until after it is too late to respond. Rather than being limited to what cash flow could pay for, such an organization can leap ahead of competitors (even much larger ones) by increasing its stakeholder-improving investments by a vast multiple. As long as operational integrity is maintained during such accelerated spending, the investment will pay off in huge future cash flows and make it very easy to pay the interest and to repay the principal while maintaining cash balances at optimal levels.

To understand this point, imagine that energy prices will increase very rapidly in the next century. Wind turbines are one of the few relatively untapped nonpetrochemical energy sources. There are few windy places with a political will to allow wind farms. A 2,000 percent cubed solution enterprise might grab a huge share of the ultimate market by acquiring long-term leases now on prime locations for wind farms, putting in the most efficient turbines, and very frequently upgrading its technology. After locking-up the best sites, no one else would have an ability to respond.

As you can see, large amounts of debt can be invested where there is great existing and rapidly growing cash flow to create even more resources for tilting the competitive field in your favor, providing more reasons to avoid piling up cash on your balance sheet as you instead apply an appropriately sized mountain of temporary debt for valuable strategic purposes.

What's the key point about choosing the optimal debt level to extract cash from the balance sheet? **Redesign your company's business models, methods of operating, use of facilities, ownership of facilities, breadth of product line, and offerings to reduce investments by 96 percent for you and your stakeholders and to create lots more excess cash flow. Then, increase your potential to provide the most benefit for all stakeholders by learning a lot at little expense about how excess cash might best be applied to the value chain through modeling the effects of added investments. Use such understanding and cash flow to employ reasonable amounts of unused debt capacity to engage in even better strategic options that help avoid harmful future cash buildups in your enterprise.**

Assignments

1. Identify the five most significant investments to which you could apply excess cash and unused debt capacity to provide more benefits that stakeholders want.

2. Consider how such changes would affect your other stakeholders.

3. Investigate how your business models, operating methods, breadth of product line, and offerings could be shifted over time to be even more effective by making it easier for stakeholders and your company to identify and to implement better ways to operate with very little investment as a result of your employment of excess cash and unused debt capacity.

Lesson Fifty

Choose the Ideal Level for Issuing Equity

*But when the morning had now come,
Jesus stood on the shore;
yet the disciples did not know that it was Jesus.
Then Jesus said to them, "Children, have you any food?"
They answered Him, "No."
And He said to them,
"Cast the net on the right side of the boat,
and you will find some."
So they cast, and now they were not able to draw it in
because of the multitude of fish.
Therefore that disciple whom Jesus loved said to Peter,
"It is the Lord!"
Now when Simon Peter heard that it was the Lord,
he put on his outer garment (for he had removed it),
and plunged into the sea.
But the other disciples came in the little boat
(for they were not far from land,
but about two hundred cubits),
dragging the net with fish.
Then, as soon as they had come to land,
they saw a fire of coals there,
and fish laid on it, and bread.
Jesus said to them,
"Bring some of the fish which you have just caught."
Simon Peter went up and dragged the net to land,
full of large fish, one hundred and fifty-three;
and although there were so many,
the net was not broken.
Jesus said to them, "Come and eat breakfast."*

— John 21:4-12 (NKJV)

As lessons forty-seven, forty-eight, and forty-nine point out, most companies that have a very high profit margin, large profits, little need to reinvest, and a lot of cash often pick poor alternatives for handling their cash. In this lesson, we look at how to understand the optimal price levels and amounts of issuing equity in terms of the more attractive investment choices that are not usually considered. This lesson complements Lesson Forty-Nine concerning the optimal debt levels for extracting excess cash from the balance sheet.

A high-margin, rapidly growing enterprise that requires few new investments often sees its equity value explode upward. That's because most equity valuation methods are built around estimating future cash flows for twenty years and discounting them back to the present by using the current interest rate plus a little added premium for the volatility of equity-market values.

Let me demonstrate how such a valuation process works with an example. I begin by describing the organization's annual changes in financial performance as though they would be the same over twenty years:

Sales Growth	Profit Growth	Cash Flow Growth	Sales/ Net Assets	Return on Equity
40%	40%	40%	25	1,000%

	Annual Cash Flow	Annual Discounted Cash Flow	Cumulative Discounted Cash Flow
Year 1	$5,000	$4,650	$4,650
Year 2	7,000	6,054	10,704
Year 3	9,800	7,883	18,587
Year 4	13,720	10,263	28,850
Year 5	19,208	13,363	42,213
Year 6	26,891	17,398	59,611
Year 7	37,647	22,652	82,263
Year 8	52,706	29,493	111,756
Year 9	73,788	38,400	150,156
Year 10	103,303	49,997	200,153
Year 11	144,624	65,096	265,249
Year 12	202,474	84,755	350,004
Year 13	283,464	110,351	460,355
Year 14	396,850	143,677	604,032
Year 15	555,590	187,068	791,100
Year 16	777,826	243,562	1,034,662
Year 17	1,088,956	317,118	1,351,780
Year 18	1,524,538	412,887	1,764,667
Year 19	2,134,353	537,579	2,302,246
Year 20	2,988,094	699,928	3,002,174

A typical way of calculating the equity value also adds a residual value equal to the discounted present value of a normal market multiple of the annual cash flow generated in the twentieth year to the twenty years of cumulative discounted cash flows. With this calculation, the equity value is $10,001,454 (assuming a present value of ten times cash-flow multiple residual value in the twentieth year). If we compare that equity value to our year one cash flow of $5,000, the comparison gives us a valuation multiple of more than 2,000 times the Year 1 cash flow.

Isn't that ridiculous? But that result follows from using the valuation methods of many so-called sophisticated investors. Valuation-sensitive investors who are more conservative simply slow down the rate of future growth, but they still come up with gigantic multiples of today's cash flow. Such "conservative" investors would probably be willing to pay two hundred times the Year 1 cash flow.

To demonstrate the foolishness of such conclusions, look at the ratio from the other perspective: What is the current cash-flow return-on-investment for an investor who pays so much? The current return for paying 2,000 times cash flow in Year 1 is 0.05 percent. That's pretty meager. The return for paying two hundred times Year 1 cash flow in Year 1 is 0.5 percent, also meager.

However, such high valuations create interesting opportunities for companies. If the organization's growth eventually slows down, interest rates and risk levels rise, and returns drop, the equity value of such an enterprise at such a future time might be only a few hundred thousand dollars.

What opportunity does this drop in equity value create? Well, you can repurchase any high-multiple equity you sold at the later fair (and much lower) value. If enough time passes between the two occasions, you can earn in the meantime a great deal of money on the funds you raised by selling equity.

Here's how such a sequence of actions might look. Let's assume that you can sell 10 percent of the equity at an enterprise value of $3,000,000 in the first year (leaving plenty of room for the most optimistic investors to perceive a "bargain" relative to the valuation of $10,001,454), and receive $300,000 less offering expenses of $50,000. You then have use of the money for twenty years. If you earn 5 percent after-tax annually on the money you raised for twenty years, your cumulative earnings after-tax from having the $250,000 will exceed $300,000. If you can then repurchase the stock you originally sold for $300,000 after twenty years at the same price, you keep the more than $300,000 in earnings you gained from investing the equity sale proceeds. Pretty nice!

Let's assume that you have some attractive places to invest the money that will further stimulate the enterprise's growth and profitability while helping all stakeholders by decreasing their investments. You make such investments with the $250,000 in proceeds from an equity sale in Year 1. That investment dramatically increases company earnings and cash flow performance in the future and the enterprise's value over its life. Whenever the enterprise's equity is fairly valued relative to current performance, you can either borrow money to repurchase the shares you had earlier sold or you can use any excess cash you have built up along the way for the same purpose to retire the shares.

What's the benefit of investing to make breakthroughs for your company and all its stakeholders by first using high-priced equity? You don't have to be concerned that a future stumble leaves the enterprise with a fixed obligation that it cannot afford, such as debt does. The more the enterprise's equity value drops in the future, the less money it takes to retire those shares. It's a natural way to reduce risk!

What about the ethics of these actions? I suggest that you not push selling for anything near the maximum equity price. Allow those who purchase the new equity to calculate in their own ways that they are getting a big discount by buying at a lower multiple than you could charge. Taking this approach will provide such equity purchasers with an opportunity to later sell their shares to someone else at a profit. If your organization continues to do well by making a breakthrough investment, each equity purchaser will make money. Applying the funds you receive in an optimal way reduces the risk that any shareholder will not profit from any equity investments they make … whenever such purchases occur.

What's the key point about picking the ideal level for issuing equity? **Redesign your company's business models, methods of operating, use of facilities, ownership of facilities, breadth of product line, and offerings to reduce investments by 96 percent for you and your stakeholders, creating lots of excess cash and benefits for all stakeholders. Then, learn a lot at little expense about how excess cash might best be applied to the value chain through models that consider the effects of several variables on one another as well as on other stakeholders. Use the lessons of your analysis to consider how employing cash raised by selling highly valued equity could make even better strategic options available that would help avoid harmful future cash buildups in your enterprise and reduce the risk of shareholders not earning good returns.**

<u>Assignments</u>

1. **Identify the five most significant effects for applying excess cash in order to provide more benefits that customers and suppliers want.**

2. **Consider how such changes would affect your other stakeholders.**

3. **Investigate how your business models, methods of operating, use of facilities, ownership of facilities, breadth of product line, and offerings could be shifted over time to be even more effective and make it easier for stakeholders and your company to identify better ways to operate with very little investment as a result of your sales of highly valued equity and wise application of the proceeds from the sale and any excess cash that the company produces.**

Lesson Fifty-One

Develop Deeper and Stronger
Relationships with Stakeholders

In God I have put my trust;
I will not be afraid.
What can man do to me?

— Psalm 56:11 (NKJV)

Trust plays a big role in how much investing an organization must do. Let me give you an example based on the experiences I had while hiring a contractor to put a new roof on our family's home.

When you talk to people who have had roofs replaced, they often tell you a number of things:

1. You have to be concerned that the person actually shows up to do the work after you make a down payment, rather than fleeing the state with your money.

2. Many roofers don't have insurance. If one of their employees is hurt while working on your roof, the employee could sue you, the homeowner, as well as the roofing company.

3. Your homeowner's insurance doesn't cover roofers, and you cannot buy a policy that will pay for workers' accidents unless you personally go into the roofing business.

4. Roofs have to be replaced when it's neither too hot nor too cold, or the roof won't cure properly … and will leak.

5. All roofers in our state are required by law to fix faulty roofs for a year at no additional cost … if you can find them and convince them to do the work properly. But if the roofers don't know what they are doing to begin with, such a requirement doesn't help.

6. All roofing material manufacturers guarantee their products for a few years, less any accumulated wear and tear, but the manufacturers won't pay for the labor to replace any faulty material. Since labor represents more than 60 percent of the roof's total cost, such guarantees for materials aren't worth as much as you might think.

7. Since you only need a roofer once every twenty to thirty years, you probably don't have a long-term relationship with someone you can rely on.

8. Your neighbors probably haven't replaced their roofs since they bought their homes, so they don't know who to trust either.

9. To reduce the likelihood of accidents and damage, roofers should use safety gear, put up tarps around the base of the house, and pick up debris with powerful electromagnets to attract all the loose nails.

10. If the roofers are very active, they will cause so much vibration that many items in the house will break. Roofers will not pay to replace what is broken in this way.

11. Vibration will also cause a lot of dust and dirt to fall into the attic, damaging whatever is there, and roofers will not reimburse you for any such losses.

12. An old roof covers a lot of unseen damage. Until the old roof is removed, you won't know about any structural repairs that are needed. You will pay extra for any such repairs.

I could add many more problems that can occur while replacing a roof, but I'm sure you get the idea: A new roof can be hazardous to your wallet and your home's interior, as well as to your peace of mind.

As a consequence of such valid concerns, successful roofers know that they must go to great lengths to make it easier for potential customers to trust them. Roofers may provide hundreds of reference letters from former customers, make it easy for you to check whether any complaints have been filed against them, arrange for their insurance companies to certify that they have valid insurance, promise labor warranties to repair errors that cause leaks, describe elaborate arrangements to reduce accidents and damage, answer endless questions, and ask for payment less aggressively than they would prefer.

To help overcome a lack of trust, roofing companies must make many more investments than are needed just to provide a fine replacement roof. Here are some examples of excess investments that don't serve much (if any) practical purposes in improving the roof that a customer receives:

- The companies typically employ expensive salespeople to present reasons why you can trust their companies. These salespeople mostly answer questions and provide tangible evidence to make purchasers feel safer. The sales process may require eight to ten hours of an expensive person's time. Most roofers will only "win" one job in ten that they quote on, so this approach adds an investment of 80 to 100 hours of effort by salespeople and related sales expenses for each roof they replace. If the total selling cost averages about $30 per hour, the roofer's price has to include $2,400 to $3,000 just to recover the average sales investment. Since the price of replacing most roofs is between $9,000 and $15,000, you can see how significant such investments are.

- For roofs that aren't very high or steep, the chances of someone being seriously hurt are minimal. As a result, the expensive safety insurance and equipment are unnecessary. Yet, such investments have to be made in advance or the company won't attract enough customers.

- Since the people who work on roofs probably wouldn't be able to find a lawyer to handle a lawsuit for them against a homeowner, the fear of a lawsuit is mostly overblown.

- Performing a good cleanup and avoiding damage from leftover materials are mostly a function of having a meticulous cleanup crew. They don't need to use all those tarps and electromagnets.

- If your roof is easy to access, the roofers don't need ladders and expensive gear for doing the job.

- You don't care if the company owns any trucks or cars. If the workers arrived by bus, it would all be the same to you.

- A company that cares about its reputation is going to do the best possible job, or it won't be in business next year. Customers who appreciate that point could be offered a small discount for making a 100 percent advance payment, and most such owners would accept the offer. When customers do this, roofing work turns cash-flow positive on making a sale and it would be a much more attractive business to be in … attracting better talent into the industry.

What could a roofing company do instead of making such investments? Invite potential customers to observe work in progress by the crew that would do their roofs. I was very impressed by the men who did the work. After watching them for about an hour, I knew I was going to have a terrific new roof. It would have been faster and more helpful for me to have watched them for an hour than by doing the checking that I did. If the roofer had then explained all the ways that it didn't want to make investments to do my job, I would have understood and gone along with their recommendations … especially if there had been some price concessions. The lower price would greatly increase their likelihood of getting the job, so the average sales investment would be much less, as well.

The roofing company knew that trust was important, but it didn't go about creating that trust in the least expensive way to reduce its investments. That was a strategic mistake.

I urge you to rethink how you establish trust with new and existing customers. How might you change what you do so that you could reduce investments that aren't doing you or your customers much, if any, good?

This issue of trust carries over to operations that are ongoing. If you trust someone, you can probably reduce your costs and investments of working with them. For example, if the supplier is doing a great quality job over many months, you don't need to recheck the quality of every item that is delivered. As a result, you may not have to own certain kinds of checking equipment and not have to hire people to use that equipment. And on it goes.

Instead, imagine that you worked with your supplier or customer in the same way you would if they were colleagues in your own organization. What investments could all of you eliminate? How can you build and sustain the trust that's necessary to avoid such investments?

What's the key point about developing stronger and deeper relationships with stakeholders? **Redesign your company's business models, methods of operating, use of facilities, ownership of facilities, breadth of product line, and offerings to build trust that allows you to reduce investments by 96 percent for you and your stakeholders and to create lots of excess cash for all.**

Assignments

1. Identify the five most significant investments you could eliminate if stakeholders could completely trust your organization.

2. Consider how you might build the trust needed to eliminate such investments.

3. Examine how such changes would affect your other stakeholders.

4. Investigate how your business models, methods of operating, use of facilities, ownership of facilities, breadth of product line, and offerings could be shifted over time to be even more effective by making it easier for stakeholders and your company to identify better ways to operate with very little investment as a result of your trust-building activities.

Lesson Fifty-Two

Sponsor Online Contests

And finding some disciples he said to them,
"Did you receive the Holy Spirit when you believed?"
So they said to him,
"We have not so much as heard
whether there is a Holy Spirit."
And he said to them,
"Into what then were you baptized?"
So they said, "Into John's baptism."

— Acts 19:1-3 (NKJV)

Online contests are excellent for developing better ways to expand a market by twenty times, to reduce an offering's costs by 96 percent, and to eliminate 96 percent of per-offering investments. Lesson Twenty-Seven includes some references to conducting an online contest for reducing costs. I describe how to develop better solutions by working with strangers in Lesson Thirty-One. In addition, Lesson Thirty-Six describes how to use such online contests to develop superior solutions for sale to and implementation by others. I suggest you reread those three lessons as background for this one.

Let me expand here on what I wrote in those lessons. Many times, the same solution that reduces costs will also reduce investment intensity ... but not necessarily. To gain such a more desirable result, you should employ a more sophisticated online-contest design. I waited to share such an advanced design with you until now so that you could start from a better informed understanding of market expansion, cost reduction, and investment elimination.

The more advanced process for online contests is described in the following steps:

1. Begin by conducting an online contest to find ways to expand the market by at least twenty times while applying the same or less time, money, and effort. Disclose all the better solutions to all current and potential contestants as they are received, and allow contestants to make new entries that are simply improvements on what others have proposed. Publish the winning solution, praise the winner, and provide whatever reward was offered.

2. Conduct a second similarly structured online contest focused on finding ways to reduce per-offering costs by 96 percent while employing the winning market-expansion solution. Again disclose solu-

tions and allow improvements on them as entries. Publish the winning solutions from the first two contests, praise the winner of the second contest, and provide whatever reward was offered.

3. Conduct a third similarly structured online contest to reduce the investment per offering by 96 percent while employing the two winning solutions for market expansion and cost reduction. Again disclose solutions and allow improvements on them as entries. Publish the winning solutions from all three contests, praise the winner of the third contest, and provide whatever reward was offered.

4. Recast, describe, and publish the combined winning solutions from the three contests in the form of a business model and a business plan. Conduct a fourth similarly structured online contest to improve the effectiveness of this published business model and business plan by another twenty times for market expansion, cost reduction, and investment elimination while expending the same or less time, money, and effort. This time, don't let contestants see the other entries. Disclose as little as possible about the winning entry when you recognize the winner and provide the reward.

My suggestion is that you conduct each of these four contests over a relatively brief length of time, such as two to three months. In that way, you will obtain solutions for each of the first three stages pretty rapidly as well as for the final breakthrough business model and business plan. The resulting business model and business plan should be at least a 16,000,000 percent solution (four complementary 2,000 percent solutions). I suspect it will be much more valuable than that, perhaps reaching a 30,000,000 percent solution.

Regardless of the indicated value of the ultimate solution, quickly put the winning model and plan into operation. Otherwise, some new industry entrant or an alert competitor could begin applying the insights before you. Although you should do your best to keep competitors from learning through your contests, much of such learning is bound to slip out. If nothing else, your competitors can follow you in conducting their own online contests. As Carol Coles and I described in *The Ultimate Competitive Advantage*, that's what happened after Goldcorp proved that online contests are the best practice for locating gold in an existing mine.

You may be able to stay further ahead of competitors by paying close attention to what information needs to be developed about customers and other stakeholders to implement the selected solutions. If you begin to acquire and to organize such information while the contests are occurring, you will be able to move into implementation much sooner and more effectively. In addition, if other resources are needed that take time to assemble, start early to acquire and to organize those resources as well.

Choose solutions from the contests that will become more effective if competitors try to duplicate your methods, such as a market-expansion activity involving lots of publicity. In such circumstances, most of the benefit from publicity accrues to the organization that gains attention first. In that way, the online contests can create a new set of irresistible forces to help you based on competitors' desires to copy.

I realize that this is a bare-bones description of what to do, but you also have more detailed instructions for how to conduct each online contest in Lesson Thirty-Six as well as in the description of the Goldcorp experience in *The Ultimate Competitive Advantage*.

What's the key point about sponsoring online contests? **Engage the whole world online to help you develop four complementary 2,000 percent solutions that work in tandem to expand the market by four hundred times, to eliminate almost all per-offering costs, and to reduce investments per offering to near zero to create lots of excess cash for your business and your stakeholders.**

Assignments

1. **Conduct the sequential online contests as described in this lesson.**

2. **Prepare information about customers and other stakeholders that will give you a faster start in implementing what you learn.**

3. **Put needed new resources in place as soon as possible.**

4. **Select a strategic direction that will be helped by competitors copying what you do.**

5. **Implement the combined business model and business plan quickly and effectively!**

Epilogue

Lessons Fifty-Three and Beyond

And Joshua said to the people,
"Sanctify yourselves,
for tomorrow the LORD will do wonders among you."
Then Joshua spoke to the priests, saying,
"Take up the ark of the covenant
and cross over before the people."
So they took up the ark of the covenant
and went before the people.

— Joshua 3:5-6 (NKJV)

While reading and applying this book's fifty-two lessons, you may have developed a taste for making complementary breakthroughs to enhance a business. If so, I want to applaud you and to encourage your continued interest and activity.

By doing the assignments, you have gained skill in developing and implementing breakthroughs that can be applied to many kinds of opportunities. With each repetition of the 2,000 percent solution process for any complementary solutions you've already implemented, you will add another twenty-times expansion in total benefits. Starting from such a substantial base of benefits, any further increases will be astonishingly valuable.

Lesson Fifty-Two contains a process involving online contests that can be extended and repeated to add many more complementary breakthroughs. However, you may not yet understand what breakthroughs are complementary. If that subject is unclear, read Appendix B of *Help Wanted* where I provide a blueprint for adding many more dimensions of complementary benefits.

For-profit businesses will typically increase stakeholder value by twenty times while lowering the organization's cost of capital by 96 percent as the next dimension of complementary 2,000 percent solutions beyond those solutions described here. After that, an organization can encourage competitors to copy and to improve upon what your organization does in ways that will stimulate yet another twenty-times increase in benefits by encouraging your organization to be more innovative as another dimension of complementary improvements. Profiting from solving large social problems can be used as the next complementary dimension. Increasing the productivity of underutilized people is another dimension of complementary benefit breakthroughs. While I have not published my thoughts about any complementary solution dimensions beyond these, you can use the *Help Wanted* blueprint found in Appendix B to identify and to produce other dimensions of complementary benefit breakthroughs.

Keep in mind that the methods I have described for creating and implementing complementary solutions in this and other books are not the only effective ways to achieve such results. You may well have better ideas. If you do, try them out. I would be most grateful if you would share with me what you learn. You may reach me by e-mail at askdonmitchell@yahoo.com.

In *Help Wanted*, I also describe the value of 2,000 percent solution tutors establishing specializations and sharing what they learn with others who are involved with the same specialty. Even if you don't need such a tutor, you may find it valuable to keep track of what such tutors have learned. Some of their knowledge may directly apply to your situation.

If there is no such existing body of practice, consider creating one by becoming a breakthrough tutor or by working with other businesspeople who have successfully applied this book's lessons to their enterprises.

Beyond these suggestions, let me remind you of an important observation: Whatever it is that you want to learn or to accomplish, someone already knows the answer and can easily describe and demonstrate what you need. Seeking out such an answer can be done more and more easily … almost always in ways that take less time, money, and effort than developing your own solution.

Also keep in mind that you have already observed perfection in some other field of individual or group activity that can be applied to your circumstances. The answer is in your mind, but you don't yet realize how you have the answer labeled in your memory so that you can access it. Read the Ideal Practice Identification Blueprint in Appendix B of *2,000 Percent Living* to identify such personal knowledge more rapidly and with less effort.

Finally, don't be satisfied with whatever your organization's best is today. You are only accomplishing a tiny part of a small percentage of your easily attained potential … regardless of how many breakthrough solutions you have already put into place.

Appendix A

Fast-Start Directions

Now a leper came to Him, imploring Him,
kneeling down to Him and saying to Him,
"If You are willing, You can make me clean."
Then Jesus, moved with compassion,
stretched out His *hand and touched him,*
and said to him,
"I am willing; be cleansed."
As soon as He had spoken,
immediately the leprosy left him,
and he was cleansed.

— Mark 1:40-42 (NKJV)

After finishing the Introduction, fifty-two lessons, and the Epilogue, some readers may be unsure about what to do next. Such uncertainty is most likely to occur for those who have yet to start a business. Similarly, while the assignments in each lesson can help readers learn what opportunities they have, some readers may not have yet turned such insights into focused approaches such as business models and strategies ... and effective plans for implementing them. Appendix A is for these readers.

Some other readers may have experienced occasional difficulties while completing the assignments and learned less than they would like. Appendix A will help fill in any gaps for them.

Still other readers may prefer to learn by talking things over rather than by just relying on their own reading and reflections. No book can be a total substitute for a well-informed partner, a top coach, a knowledgeable tutor, an experienced consultant, or an expert in the field. For those working with someone to implement faster, Appendix A is designed to help you accomplish more.

At this point, I assume that you may not yet know what business you will enter. If you do know, feel free to move ahead in this appendix until you reach directions for a stage of decision-making and implementation that you believe can help you.

Let's begin by spelling out a process for starting a successful business through developing and applying the three performance breakthroughs (expanding the market by twenty times, cutting offering-related costs by 96 percent, and reducing the need for per-offering investments by 96 percent for your organization and your stakeholders) described in *Business Basics*.

Follow This Start-Up Process

*Now Moses wrote down the starting points
of their journeys at the command of the LORD.*

— Numbers 33:2 (NKJV)

While not every entrepreneur and business needs each step of the process described in this section, be sure to follow the steps that add to your or your organization's knowledge. Realize that I'm sharing an idealized approach that doesn't custom fit any specific business. If you don't feel comfortable with a particular aspect of the process, ask your personal and professional advisors to adjust that part of the process to better fit your needs. You may also wish to add steps that are particularly helpful to you or your organization.

In the remainder of the section, summaries of the individual steps are printed in *italic*. The text that follows each *italic sentence* explains and expands on the individual step.

Develop personal goals for what you want operating and owning a business to provide for you. Many people start new businesses in which they hate to work. Such a result often follows choosing a business simply because an entrepreneur knows a little about the industry, believes that she or he has relevant skills, or just perceives that such a business will probably deliver "enough" income. Avoid such a mistake. Instead, understand yourself better before you pick a business to develop. Be clear about what you want to accomplish personally that can only be achieved through having a business. Carefully identify your personal motivations to flesh out what is for you an ideal life of serving others through leading a business. Most people find that they benefit from considering as many different dimensions (e.g., personal relationships, spiritual goals, financial needs) of their lives as possible when defining such goals. The more dimensions of desirable living you can spell out, the better your goals will serve you. While developing such personal goals, avoid for the moment defining a specific business opportunity.

Next, set business goals required to achieve your personal goals. Here's an example of what I mean: If a personal goal is to spend more time with your young children or grandchildren, a complementary business goal could be to have the busiest times for leading and working in a business occur outside the hours when these youngsters are awake and at home.

Then, match existing businesses against your business goals. You may find that relatively few businesses will match all of your business goals. Such a limitation can be helpful by reducing how many alternatives you need to investigate. What if you don't know much about what various businesses would require of you and could provide for you? Invite someone who owns and operates a type of businesses that interests you to breakfast or lunch at his or her choice of dining establishment, and during the meal ask about leading and working in the business. Or ask for permission to "shadow" a business owner for a day or two. If neither approach answers your questions, take an internship or a temporary job working in such a business and ask lots of questions while you are there.

After you locate several types of businesses that match your business goals reasonably well, look for differences in meeting your personal goals among the alternatives of developing each type of business from scratch, purchasing an existing business, and becoming a franchisee. For instance, it usually requires the most money to purchase a successful business, but the total work involved is often much less than for the alternatives. Establishing a franchised operation may cost somewhat less and may also involve less work than starting up a novel approach on your own. Depending on your goals, you may favor any one of the options. However, keep in mind that for some types of businesses starting up something unique on your own may be the only viable choice.

Identify and measure the biggest risks of the most attractive alternatives. Here's what I mean by risk: What are the consequences if you don't succeed? For instance, if you invest $1,000 in legal fees to start up a business, you may lose that whole sum if the business doesn't perform. By contrast, buying a successful business that can be easily improved may cost many times more than a part-time startup, but there may not be much financial risk unless you pay too high a purchase price. After improving such a purchased business, its value increases and someone will usually be happy to buy it for more than you paid for the purchase and what you invested afterward.

Evaluate the surviving choices' business models. My suggestion is that you favor businesses where there may be much untapped potential due to weak business models that could be greatly improved. When you make an evaluation, remember that some businesses are very successful despite having bad business models. In the early days of the video rental industry, for instance, most retail outlets applied poor business models and yet almost all made good profits. Other businesses may already have quite good business models and offer fewer improvement opportunities: Discount stock brokerages operated with self-service software are a good example at the time of this writing. For more information on assessing business models, read *The Ultimate Competitive Advantage* and Appendix B of *Business Basics*.

Investigate how the business models could be enhanced. Focus on opportunities for market expansions, cost reductions, and investment eliminations. Find the answers more quickly by scanning industry best practices in these three breakthrough dimensions. You can also use questionnaires and surveys of the sort I describe in the next section to pin down specific opportunities. The wider the gap between the average successful business in the industry and the best performers, the more room there probably is to make still more enhancements. Such gaps suggest opportunities to apply superior combinations of best practices.

Test your interest in the remaining choices by working in them. I recommend working in them at this point in the decision process even if you have previously done so. With an improved understanding of what you want to accomplish and what the alternatives are, you'll make a better assessment of a business and how it can be improved by taking either a first or a fresh look. In most cases, you can learn what you need in two weeks or less. Many people tell me that during such on-the-job examinations of promising opportunities they find something they love to do that they had never considered before.

Select a type of business and a way to test your ideas. Most people don't have the patience to wait this long in the start-up process before testing. If you feel compelled to run a test earlier, go ahead. Just be sure that you don't spend much money or effort on the test. Why? Chances are that you will have opted to test a relatively unattractive business or improvement opportunity. Some people revise what they want to do dozens of times before finding a good opportunity to test. If they have been testing all along, what they ultimately test will often have little or no connection to what they were thinking about in the beginning. As I continually remind people, "Your first business model will be your worst business model. Your second business model will be your next-to-worst business model, etc."

Identify a management team for the test. In few cases will anyone work full-time in a business before or during a test. If your idea is for a one-person business, no one else may even participate in implementing the test. But each person in the management team should be able to contribute helpful ideas, wisdom, or experience that will make your test more successful and useful for deciding what to do next. Seek diversity in experience, age, and perspective to help fill any gaps in what you can appreciate on your own.

Work with your management team to develop a business model, business plan, and operating plan for the option you want to test. Every improvement you can make before the test can potentially save you months of effort and many thousands of dollars. You will probably find that by working with a number of people the business and test will be more fully prepared to succeed. Without such perspectives, it's easy to make mistakes that either waste time during testing or cause unnecessary delays.

Ask people outside your management team to evaluate your business model, business plan, and operating plan for the test. People who enjoy working together or like to agree with others often fall victim to harmful complacency, falsely believing that they've considered all the angles. Such a sense of self-satisfaction can blind someone to seeing obvious holes in a testing plan. Don't limit yourself just to reviews by experts. Share what you have in mind with people known for their common sense and practicality. In addition, talk over your plans with some potential customers and different kinds of stakeholders. If you are fortunate, they will give you an earful of what you need to hear before you test.

Finalize your initial business model, business plan, and operating plan for the test. If you have received helpful suggestions for test improvements, decide how to apply such suggestions. Being clear about what you want others to do takes quite a bit of thinking, writing, checking, and rewriting. Start well before you want to launch the test. Also, be sure to identify how you will measure the test results so that you will be able to accurately appreciate and assess what occurs.

If needed, obtain the funds to conduct your test. You should be able to test quite inexpensively. I try to keep initial testing costs below one hundred dollars for any new businesses or business models. If you are going to spend a lot more than that amount, I encourage you to first ask more people to comment on your test and to focus on how you could learn the same or better answers at much less cost.

Implement the test. While you do, be sure to make plenty of notes. Expect and look for surprises. Much of what you learn will come from noticing what works much better and worse than you expected. Feel free to add more measurements during the test that help you to appreciate why the results differ from what you expected.

Compare your test results to the test plan. If nothing unexpected occurs, be surprised and look carefully at your results. Typically, tests identify lots of incorrect assumptions; poor implementation; and needs for major changes in business models, business plans, and operating plans. In fact, extremely successful and unsuccessful tests may leave you unclear about what all the lessons are. You should focus first on narrowing down what needs to be addressed and what can be safely ignored.

Decide whether to retest with a changed business model, business plan, and operating plan; to move into limited or full implementation; or to test a different alternative in another type of business. Unless your test is a total flop, chances are that you will be retesting after improving some aspects of the business model, business plan, and operating plan. In doing so, avoid retesting in ways that don't build on what you learned in your latest test.

If you decide to retest or to test a different alternative, repeat the preceding steps beginning with selecting a type of business to fully test. I know how tempting it can be to just make a simple change or two to your last test and then to retest. While a desire to act quickly indicates a "take-charge" mentality that's desirable for entrepreneurs, skipping steps while planning tests and retests often leads to making easily avoidable mistakes. Because you were probably quite thorough in the preceding test, it won't take as long and won't be nearly as difficult to repeat the test-development steps. Give yourself a pat on the back every time that you or someone else finds a problem with the planned retest and two pats on the back whenever you find an effective solution for dealing with the newly identified problem.

Continually improve the business model of whatever you fully implement. It's easy to forget that today's successful test creates what will be tomorrow's obsolete business model. Be continually looking to make breakthroughs in whatever you know and provide. Remember that making your current business model more efficient won't improve performance nearly as much as your next improved business model will.

In describing these steps, let me emphasize that tests can be limited or lengthy in duration, broad or narrow in aim for what's to be learned, and rifle-shot or scattershot for gaining perspectives. As an example, you don't need to answer all your questions in a single test. Instead, it may be more efficient and speedy to use a series of tests that deliberately reduce the learning challenges while drastically reducing the total time and money spent on testing. Start with what's most important to understand and go on from there.

The process for selecting and starting a business that I've just described often reveals that there isn't enough customer desire for the intended offerings. Such problems arise most often because an individual doesn't think like most prospective customers or intends to locate where there just aren't enough good prospects and a local presence is critical to success.

In many such cases, I find that a diagnostic survey or series of interviews can be of immense value in identifying the size and potential of an opportunity while also shedding light on how well a business leader understands what needs to be done. Let's look next at how such a survey or series of interviews might be conducted.

Survey the Opportunity

It shall even be as when a hungry man dreams,
And look — he eats;
But he awakes, and his soul is still empty;
Or as when a thirsty man dreams,
And look — he drinks;
But he awakes, and indeed he is *faint,*
And his soul still craves:

— Isaiah 29:8 (NKJV)

Most people who have a business or want to start one don't think about conducting interviews and surveys to learn more about how to succeed in breakthrough market expansions, cost reductions, and eliminating unnecessary investments. That's true, in part, because most businesspeople lack experience in employing such tools for information gathering and drawing conclusions from the perspectives, facts, and reactions received from current and potential customers. Many people also incorrectly think they don't need to do such information development because of overconfidence about how well the market opportunity matches their own experiences and perspectives, a point of view addressed in Lesson One.

Here is some new food for thought: Most businesses have between twenty and three hundred customers. With that many customers, little expense and effort are usually required to learn quite a lot about customers and to adapt to their preferences. Statistical tests tell us that with such relatively small numbers, you need to gain as many answers as you can in order to accurately understand your market's perspectives. Interestingly enough, learning from about three hundred randomly selected people is also a good number for studying a much larger number of prospects.

What if you have no idea about what to do in gathering and analyzing such information? One alternative is to find an undergraduate or graduate business school where marketing students are expected to perform interviews and surveys on behalf of a business for course credit. Chances are that such a student can help you design and conduct an investigation while you only pay for out-of-pocket expenses. If you decide to work with a student, contact schools about six to nine months before you have a need. That timing will probably put you on a waiting list to be matched with such students before the next semester's course assignments are made.

Another alternative is to find help through an organization that provides volunteer services to businesses (such an organization in the United States is SCORE, which can be found at www.score.org). Taking this approach, you will probably be able to locate either free or low-cost assistance for any investigations you want to do.

If these two alternatives don't work out or don't appeal to you, check online for similar businesses to what you plan that are located just far enough away so that they don't and won't compete with yours. See if any of these related businesses would like to share the cost of market research. By sharing the cost, you can probably afford to hire a local research firm or a professor for an amount you can afford.

If you are willing and able to teach yourself something new, the process of gathering such information isn't very difficult. With the information in hand, you can find many people who can help you to draw conclusions from it at little or no cost.

The rest of this section provides a template and directions for how you could gain such information for yourself quickly and at low cost either through individual interviews or by directing respondents to a Web page that displays your questionnaire. Using such directions, some of my students have gathered the needed information in as little as a few hours at a cost of much less than a hundred dollars. Use what I have provided here as a starting point. You will probably be able to obtain better answers by focusing the questions more narrowly on the key elements of your specific opportunity than this template provides. Here is the information to start you off:

[Directions to business owner: Create your own version of this template so that you will have plenty of room for taking notes or letting respondents write in or type their answers. If you use an online survey, consider SurveyMonkey.com as your supplier. If so, plan to purchase inexpensive clicks from Google AdWords (www.google.com/adwords) to more rapidly reach potential respondents whom you can serve. To do so, place a clickable SurveyMonkey.com general reference into the last line of the Google AdWords advertisement. Google will allow you to supply the exact url for your SurveyMonkey.com survey page in a hidden form so that people who click on the general "SurveyMonkey.com" reference can reach your questions. Be sure to limit who sees your Google advertisements geographically (and in other ways, if necessary, such as time of day) to those who are most likely to be good prospects for your offerings.]

[Directions to business owner about interviews if no online questionnaire is used: Contact people who are customers or who you think are good prospects located where the business can serve them. Probe for more details where you don't understand a response. If you have unasked questions left at the end of ten minutes, point out that you've spent ten minutes together and ask if you may please have a few more minutes of the interviewee's time and attention.]

[Introduction] Hello, my name is [fill in your name]. I would like to start a new business [or "I operate a (fill in the type of business) business and would like to improve it."]. Can you help me, please? This won't take longer than ten minutes. Your answers will be kept strictly confidential. I will not try to sell you anything, and I will be glad to answer any questions you have.

1. How often do you purchase [fill in the name of what it is that you want to sell] in the [name of your target location] area?

    [If the purchase rate for an individual or an organization is lower than for your target customer, thank the person for helping you and end the interview or questionnaire right here. Keep going in completing total surveys until you obtain three hundred responses from prospects who purchase frequently enough in the right area to be attractive to you.]

2. When was the last time you purchased [fill in the name of what it is that you want to sell]?

3. Where did you purchase and what did you like about what you purchased?

4. What did you like about the purchasing experience and related services?

5. What could have been improved about what you purchased that you care about?

6. What could have been improved about the purchasing experience and related services that you care about?

7. How important is [fill in the name of what it is that you want to sell] in your life?

8. What would cause you to purchase from a new company that is offering [fill in the name of what it is that you want to sell]?

9. What else would you like me to know about your views and experiences concerning [fill in the name of what it is that you want to sell]?

   Thank you for helping me! I appreciate the great answers you shared. If I would like to learn more about your views and experiences after I think more about your answers, may I get back in touch to find out just a little more?

10. If yes, how would you like me to contact you? _____

If what you learn indicates there is enough demand for your offerings within the potential customer group, you are ready to begin designing a test. If not, you either need to improve your business concept or to find a better opportunity.

Consider it a blessing if your idea flops during any such investigations. Otherwise, you might have spent a lot of time, money, and effort working on developing something with too little demand. Fast, low cost "failures" can speed your progress toward finding and developing an eventual success. Such so-called failures are usually knowledge-gaining successes in disguise.

When you think you have found a better opportunity, conduct a new survey or set of interviews to measure the sales potential of your intended approach. Repeat what you just did to find still another opportunity if your "better opportunity" doesn't work out either.

After completing interviews or a survey that shows plenty of opportunity to quickly attract and to profitably serve enough desirable customers, it's still important to find ways to eliminate unnecessary costs while the business expands. I find that most people who own businesses or plan to start them intend to spend lots of money that won't help their businesses succeed and may even hurt. Let's look next at how to avoid such harmful costs.

Determine What Costs to Avoid

*But those who desire to be rich fall into temptation and a snare,
and into many foolish and harmful lusts
which drown men in destruction and perdition.
For the love of money is a root of all kinds of evil,
for which some have strayed from the faith in their greediness,
and pierced themselves through with many sorrows.*

— 1 Timothy 6:9-10 (NKJV)

Let's be clear about one thing: A typical new or small business will be a high-cost, money-losing operation without carefully trimming unnecessary costs. I find that this difficulty is seldom appreciated by those who want to start a business.

Let's look at an example to see why problems with high costs can occur. Imagine that someone wants to start a typical retail business in a good neighborhood where there are lots of potential customers. I find that most such people intend to work full-time in their businesses. To do so usually means replacing a full-time income plus the benefits that a current employer is providing.

Do you know what it costs to duplicate those benefits? In many cases, benefit costs in the United States are another 40 percent above the pretax income someone has been receiving. Thus, if a person's salary or hourly earnings now add up to $45,000 a year, the total cost to duplicate such an income and benefits in a business will be $63,000 ($45,000 plus 40 percent of $45,000, or $18,000). In the United States, such benefits probably include a family health insurance policy, half of Social Security and Medicare payments, unemployment taxes, any employer contributions paid to a retirement plan, and life insurance. If someone lives outside the United States, the percentage cost of benefits compared to a salary can be higher or lower depending on where the business is located.

If you will need employees, you will have their salaries or hourly earnings to pay plus the related benefit costs. For instance, three full-time employees earning pretax incomes of $28,000 each will probably cost you in total about $117,600 in the United States ($84,000 in earnings plus 40 percent of $84,000, or $33,600). You'll also have the expense of hiring them, which may include advertising and placement fees, plus the time and effort involved. If employees will need training, you will have expenses for that as well.

Unless you can afford to buy a building for your store, you will almost always rent some retail space. In the Boston, Massachusetts, area near where I live, annual prime space rental rates were about $150 per square foot at the time this book was written. Assuming that you want 2,500 square feet, the annual rent will be $375,000. Some rental agreements also require the retailer to pay other costs, such as for heat, electricity, water, sewage treatment, any increases in property taxes, and insurance for any damage done to the landlord's property.

Paying such rent usually just provides you with some empty space. You'll need to decorate the space, purchase fixtures, and add any equipment required for your operations. If you put in such improvements on a shoestring budget by doing much of the work yourself, you may only need to spend $100,000. If you have expensive tastes or needs for your concept and hire others to do the work, you might spend several times that amount.

Bringing in customers often means advertising or conducting special events. It's not unusual for a retailer to spend 3 percent to 8 percent of sales for such expenses. Your annual cost could easily be $15,000 to $80,000, depending on what kind of a retail establishment you operate.

If customers are going to buy merchandise that they will want to carry away with them, you'll have to stock enough inventory so that you can have on hand what they want. Even when paying wholesale prices, sufficient inventory can cost $100,000 to $300,000.

I haven't listed all the potential costs. If you borrow any money, you will usually have to pay interest as well as repay some of the principal each month. There are also insurance premiums to cover the inventory, the improvements you put in place, and injuries to customers. You will need work done by lawyers, accountants, and other professionals. Many local organizations will expect you to donate goods or money to support their activities. Depending on what offerings you intend to provide, you'll find other classes of costs may be involved, including product liability insurance and injury claims. Spending time with owners of similar businesses is very helpful for determining and estimating such other costs. You should also be able to find a book containing a business plan for a reasonably similar business that describes the costs that its owner or owners expected to incur or experienced. Industry associations may also publish the results of surveys on expenses for similar enterprises.

Once the total costs are understood, I find that most people are helped by comparing such costs to a sales level that would provide a break-even operation. For a retail business, such a calculation means looking at typical gross margins. Surveys regularly develop such information and describe how much more retailers charge for their merchandise than they pay for it. Notice that such gross margins are after any price discounts required to sell merchandise that no one will buy at full price. Let's assume that in this type of store gross margins average 40 percent (typical for family clothing retailers).

I'm going to compare the gross margins not to the cash costs (which include outlays that don't show up in a profit-and-loss statement such as buying the initial inventory), but instead just to the more-or-less fixed annual operating costs (which include wages, benefits, rents, advertising, professional fees, insurance, interest, etc.). Let's assume that such operating costs are $900,000 a year. To break even, I need to calculate how many annual sales at a 40 percent gross margin are needed to cover that level of costs. To do this, I divide $900,000 by 0.4. The answer is $2.25 million.

Before looking further at costs, it's important to look at whether a survey and other research indicate whether that level of sales can be reached. If the survey research indicates that I can attract three hundred customers, for instance, each one will need to spend an average of $7,500 a year in the store before I can break even. Unless these are very wealthy people or substantial businesses that need lots of what I provide, that's probably more spending than I will attract. If my survey suggests that total spending by each of the three hundred customers will be $3,000 a year and I can expect to gain $1,000 of that total, I now know that my retail store needs to reduce costs to break even at $300,000 a year in sales. Since that sales level is less than what I intend to pay in rent, I can quickly see that a radically different business model is needed.

After considering such numbers, many potential retailers have quickly concluded that they need more customers *and* a lot fewer costs in order to succeed. Four primary retail business models have emerged that address such circumstances:

1. Offer online-only sales through automated software that simply takes a purchaser's order and directs a wholesale provider to ship the order to the purchaser in the seller's packaging. In such a business model, almost all costs disappear other than developing and maintaining the Web site and marketing to attract enough purchasers. Such an owner could keep a full-time job, spend little time on the business, and gain a regular cash flow after the Web site was established and enough customers were being attracted.

2. Increase gross margins by going into services or unique higher-margin goods that are sold and provided from a retail location.

3. Combine a retail location with an online business operated by automated software that increases business sales and profit contribution at limited cost.

4. Discount prices below competitors in order to make a special trip worthwhile for customers to buy from you, whether in a retail location or online.

As you can see by studying this list, many potential variations on these models exist (such as providing services or unique higher-margin goods at discount prices from an automated online-only Web site).

What costs should you avoid? Spend no money that's unnecessary to providing the offerings that your most passionate potential customers crave.

Let's apply this spending principle to providing some high-margin item. It's rare that visiting a traditional retail store is essential to purchasing the correct offering. Such a visit is most likely to be necessary with sized clothing and shoes where trying on and seeing the apparel makes a difference in customer satisfaction. Even in such circumstances, people just need a place to see and to try on what appeals to them. A convenient location may work just as well for a customer as (or even better than) a traditional retail store in a shopping district. If zoning permits, you could operate out of two rooms in an apartment with stock in one room and apparel on display in the other. People could change their clothes in a neatly and cleanly maintained bathroom with a lock on the door.

If people know exactly what they want (such as with a textbook) and what you offer is new merchandise, they just need to be able to trust that you will deliver what you promise. Providing a credible guarantee of customer satisfaction can be enough to allow you to obtain orders. Without having a retail store, the break-even level may be reduced to as low as zero. That's part of the appeal of direct selling, whether to neighbors, coworkers, and acquaintances ... or through parties hosted by someone the guests know well.

Temporary locations can also work well for items that people want to inspect, such as a rented table at a flea market or a farmer's market. If you pick the right location, traffic may be substantial at the times when you want to work for just a few hours.

Why do some people starting a business insist on providing expensive retail locations for customers? In most cases, it's because the owners don't know what passionate customers most crave and are hoping that the customers' urges to shop will lead to the owners turning a profit.

It's usually more important to provide experiences that people like than to be located in a specific locale. Consider customers for antique furniture. A lot of the fun of acquiring an antique item can be in "finding" something wonderful in an unlikely place. Someone who wants to offer fine Scandinavian antiques in the United States might discover that operating out of a barn in a Scandinavian farming community near a major metropolitan area would provide an excuse for a pleasant outing and a little adventure to those who are looking to buy. If the word about such a barn-based "store" and its offerings is spread by the seller in low-key ways, customers might also gain the joy of feeling that a rare treasure has been found. Or perhaps there could be an occasional one-day auction of rare items held at the Swedish consulate in a major city, with part of the auctions proceeds donated to a Swedish charity.

Notice that such experience-intensive marketing lends itself to inexpensive tests. If you try ten different unusual ways for customers to purchase your high-margin item, at least one of the methods you test is likely to work just fine. If engaging in such methods requires more time than you have, find ways to work with partners or part-time employees who will be glad to work when you can't.

All the researching and thinking in the world isn't a substitute for trying to make sales. Many people who start businesses have ideas that aren't soundly based in how customers think and feel, and what they actually do. Adding a few customers will soon show you what you don't know. Let's look next at how to learn from your first customers.

Start Adding Customers

"And if you sell anything to your neighbor
or buy from your neighbor's hand,
you shall not oppress one another."

— Leviticus 25:14 (NKJV)

There's nothing quite like having a customer to help you find ways to expand the market, to usefully slash operating costs, and to locate beneficial ways to avoid investments that you deem to be "absolutely essential." I have often seen my students make such improvements after understanding what paying customers are willing to pay for.

Consider the fireman who collected and repaired old fire trucks. His wife gave him an ultimatum, "Make a business out of those fire trucks ... or get rid of them." When he arrived in class, the fireman was sure that kids' birthday parties were going to be a big market. But he wasn't doing much business.

I told each student to find a new customer and to report what had been learned from the customer at the next week's class. After being turned down by everyone he spoke to during the following week, the frustrated fireman wandered into an after-hours bar for the first time late the night before the next class and asked if anyone wanted to rent a fire truck. The bar's owners quickly agreed to rent the fire truck for a parade, realizing that an old fire truck would attract attention at low cost. During the parade, lots of kids also saw the fire truck, liked what they saw, and some of their parents saw flyers passed out by his colleagues and booked birthday parties. The fireman now attends any parade he can to see who is involved and to tell watchers about his fire trucks. A great new way of promoting his business was born, and I regularly see one of his fire trucks transporting happy youngsters around town.

My students usually find it is harder to gain a customer than they think it will be. In a large majority of cases, they realize that there isn't going to be a very big demand for what they believe should be their offering. Such a difficult selling experience usually causes a shift into looking for an opportunity that is more appealing to potential customers.

In other cases, a new entrepreneur might find that there's virtually unlimited demand for a product or service ... but serving the strong demand is unpleasant. In such a case, effective entrepreneurs will immediately change business models to get rid of the unpleasant aspects and will go on to make great successes.

On the cost side, I often run into people starting businesses who plan to spend a lot more money than they can afford. Such "big spenders" always have some excuse for why such spending is justified. If, however, they start serving customers while incurring high costs and have to dig deep into their own pockets because they are losing lots of money, a new attitude usually emerges: "How can I make my customer happier while spending a lot less?"

I suspect that such mental shifts occur because to some people calculated numbers are immaterial and intangible, but everyone notices when much more money is going out than is coming in. Since most new entrepreneurs are better endowed with ideas than with money, the unsustainable spending quickly grabs their attention in a practical way.

With investments, considering opportunities to provide for a customer can be sobering. Let's say that your first customer lives at the corner of Main Street and Downtown Boulevard, and you are providing the retail offerings door-to-door ... but intend to open a retail location. You ask the customer how far she would be willing to travel for your offering. She says, "Six blocks." You check out all the available space to buy or rent within six blocks, and you discover that you can't financially qualify to purchase or to lease any of them. There goes any idea of taking local space to serve this customer. Pretty soon, you start thinking about how to continue delivering directly to the customer in a pleasing and low-cost way rather than to operate from local retail space.

What's going on with the business leaders in such cases? Most entrepreneurs have a lot of confidence, and that psychological orientation helps them to stay focused on developing an idea into a business. While such people should believe that they will eventually find the right answer for succeeding, misplaced confidence is often based, instead, on a fervent belief in an approach. Wrong! Working to find a customer or to assist a customer means that such misplaced ideas are quickly shown to require adjustment. Now, that's the beginning of making real progress! Let's consider how to go from having a profitable part-time business to working full time in it.

Spell Out How to Go from a Part-Time Business to a Full-Time One

The heart of him who has understanding seeks knowledge,
But the mouth of fools feeds on foolishness.
All the days of the afflicted are evil,
But he who is of a merry heart has a continual feast.
Better is a little with the fear of the LORD,
Than great treasure with trouble.

— Proverbs 15:14-16 (NKJV)

Leaving a job they dislike is the main reason for many people to start or to expand a business. Since job dissatisfaction is increasingly common, the number of full-time businesses should be much higher. Why don't tens of millions more entrepreneurs make it beyond operating part-time businesses? Well, it's typically not because the entrepreneurs wouldn't like to have more customers and greater income.

I find that most part-time businesses either cannot be profitably expanded or would pay very little for the entrepreneur's increased time and effort. When such limitations occur, part-time entrepreneurs with full-time jobs become stuck in an unfortunate circumstance. They cannot find any way to profitably expand the business they've been developing, and they have little time left to work on finding something better. In such a situation, many people will persist with what they are doing for many years before doing anything different.

How can more people avoid being stuck in an unattractive job while operating a part-time business they cannot profitably expand? Before starting a part-time business, spell out the economics of making the switch from part-time to full-time operations.

In the majority of cases, there is good news: With business-model adjustments, almost all part-time businesses can become attractive, full-time ones. The time to make those adjustments is before much time is being spent operating such a part-time business. In many cases, procrastinators who lack a focus on business model improvement may avoid looking for improvements due to fear that they won't be able to find a solution, and they rationalize, instead, why they should just keep doing more of what they have been doing.

Here's a typical fear: Someone who doesn't like to work very hard doesn't want to be put in a position where lots of work is required just to survive financially in a full-time business. Now, that's an appropriate concern. However, not addressing what to do won't overcome the existing limitations.

In such a circumstance, my advice is to design a business to work in that's so much fun that you would do the work involved for no pay as a preferred pastime. In addition, develop superior profitability and cash flow so that working at the new business just half time provides more income than from your current job combined with part-time work at an existing business. While having such a positive goal to think about, seeking and making improvements can become light and joyful work. Who wouldn't want to make such an improvement?

Some people are still tripped up by shyness, lack of confidence, or some other form of social anxiety. There are answers for them, as well: Develop a business model that doesn't require doing anything they find to be painful. As an example, those who don't like to meet strangers could develop online businesses that don't require pressing any flesh to add or to serve customers. If introverted people don't even like to interact via e-mails and instant messages, such a site could be fully automated. If that's still more human interaction than feels comfortable, the entrepreneur can partner with someone who enjoys making such contacts with customers and other stakeholders and who doesn't require much direction.

What's the point? Determine why you aren't moving forward, whether it's a limitation of the market, your business model, or yourself … and address any limitations in immediate, forthright, optimistic, and relentless ways. When you take charge of overcoming your limitations, you will succeed! Now let's examine how following joyful alternatives can provide good guidance.

When in Doubt, Seize the Righteous Joy

Why did you flee away secretly,
and steal away from me, and not tell me;
for I might have sent you away with joy and songs,
with timbrel and harp?

— Genesis 31:27 (NKJV)

One of my favorite training exercises for new entrepreneurs begins by closing my eyes tight, covering my eyes with my hands, spinning around until I don't know where I am, and asking the entrepreneurs to guide me to some location in such a way that I don't get hurt. It's quiet at first. I eventually begin to receive occasional directions to do something ... and the initial directions often make no sense. I do my best to obey, and I will occasionally hear an exclamation to "Stop!" in response. Sooner or later, I arrive at the intended destination without serious mishaps. Then, I ask the entrepreneurs to do the same exercise with one another, alternating who is unseeing and who is directing.

Many people report feeling a lot of anxiety during the process, even when they are in control. Many who give directions dither and micromanage. Sometimes, I can only move a few inches before receiving new directions.

Realize that I initially provided no rules for conducting this exercise. Someone who wanted to simplify the task could simply come up, take my arm, and lead me. Or someone could stand in front of me and say, "Follow the sound of my voice" and start walking backwards while speaking, singing, or humming. You can probably think of even more effective, fun ways to lead a "blind" person.

When the entrepreneurs pair off with one another, I tell them that they may not touch one another or lead anyone up or down stairs. Those are the only limits I impose. Some groups never come up with any effective ways to provide directions.

Isn't it interesting that given a totally open-ended opportunity, people choose the most difficult and least joyful ways of accomplishing a task? Most people start by assuming that there's only one way to do something ... or establish their own rules that eliminate most alternatives. Such attitudes are very harmful to making a fast start.

I can always tell when entrepreneurs are going to be big successes: They give themselves permission to do what they enjoy while developing and improving their new business ideas.

In many cases when prospective entrepreneurs operate with too many self-imposed limits, I get the sense that these are people who have never fully put themselves in charge of their own lives. They are so used to being directed to do things that they dislike that they cannot remove all the "orders" that they've heard in the past, even when such "orders" make no sense and aren't required. Think of that. People may be operating as though hated bosses were still in charge of them ... even when there's no boss in sight.

Now, I don't mean to suggest that entrepreneurs should do harmful things, break laws, or mistreat people. I mean, instead, that entrepreneurs should engage in what makes starting and developing a business fun and valuable for them and everyone else. Who wouldn't want to engage in more fun and valuable activities? There may be a few people who prefer stewing in angry silence, but hopefully such a preference will eventually thaw out so that they can, instead, focus on gaining joy from being helpful.

If you can't get started with some necessary task, put a smile on your face and just ask yourself, "What would make this fun and valuable for me and for everyone else?" The answer will come to you, and your progress will be much more rapid. If you reach a point where you don't know what to do, pray and ask for help.

Don't Become Stuck — Pray and Ask for Help

I will lift up my eyes to the hills —
From whence comes my help?
My help comes from the LORD,
Who made heaven and earth.
He will not allow your foot to be moved;
He who keeps you will not slumber.

— Psalm 121:1-3 (NKJV)

While teaching new entrepreneurs, I always start by telling them how to contact me with their questions so that I can assist them. With each class and contact, I ask how I can help.

To help them make faster progress, I provide new assignments and suggestions during each interaction. However, when we have weekly classroom sessions, I can count on most new entrepreneurs telling me that they didn't complete the assignments because they couldn't figure out how to perform some aspect of them. In most cases, the problem they encountered is one that I could have solved for them in a few seconds, and I would have been glad to do so prior to class.

Based on my experience, in only about one case in fifty of encountering a problem will an entrepreneur pray for guidance from the Holy Spirit or contact someone who probably knows the solution. It's as though entrepreneurs would rather fail than ask for help.

Some readers may assume this observation mainly applies to men. However, I don't see any difference by gender in the unwillingness of new entrepreneurs to ask for help.

A few new entrepreneurs may be unconsciously sabotaging themselves in order to fulfill their self-images as ineffective people. In most cases, however, I believe that new entrepreneurs simply prefer to procrastinate. As one new entrepreneur told me, he found daydreaming about someday being the leader of a successful large organization to be great fun, and he couldn't keep his fantasies going while actually working on his business.

Someone always knows a better way to accomplish the result you seek than you do, especially when you are stuck. Here's how I see procrastinating entrepreneurs who are stopped by a minor problem: It's as if people were drowning in an inch of water after falling face down because they didn't lift their unhurt noses out of a puddle. What's with that?

I suspect that such helplessness may be a learned behavior based in school experiences. As youngsters, pupils avoid asking for help. Someone who goes to a teacher for help is often teased for seeking to become a teacher's pet. The "smart" person is perceived to be the one who supposedly already knows all the answers without doing any work. The way to gain respect in many parts of secular society is to be seen as "smart" rather than to have accomplished something through hard work.

Well, being "smart" by itself often counts for little in becoming a successful entrepreneur. In fact, most people who want to study how to start up a new business don't realize that many successful entrepreneurs never do any studying ... but just start doing and then quickly adjust what they do based on their results. But through careful study, you can do better than such trial-and-error management. And if you are "smart," that, too, can help.

Let me explain what I mean through an example. As a youngster, I enjoyed a certain maze at an amusement park. You made twists and turns in a large room filled with glass walls. Some people were stymied after awhile and simply retreated along the way they had entered. Most people, however, did eventually reach the end of the maze.

There were two methods normally employed for navigating through the maze. Most people groped with their hands in all four directions in the same sequence until one direction proved to be missing a glass wall.

(An employee walked behind these people wiping off their fingerprints from the glass walls.) That's the trial-and-error approach that the instinctive entrepreneur uses.

The method I preferred was to study the floor. At the base of the glass walls were slots for holding the glass. Where there was no slot for the glass, there was no glass and you could walk right through. With this method, I could complete the maze in one-tenth the time of those who used the trial-and-error approach. I was greatly amused to see the startled reactions of other people when I moved so quickly past them through the maze.

After exiting, people always asked me how I had so quickly found the right route. I would share my method. People would immediately go back through the maze to try the method and would come back filled with joy. Then, they would have even more fun telling others how they had done it.

But notice that both methods for navigating an unknown route work just fine. One approach just happens to be a lot faster and easier. That's what "study" can do for you when you focus on the right things. What doesn't work is to just stand there without trying or learning anything. That's the procrastinator's approach.

For success in any activity, adopt a humble attitude and seek all the help you can find. That same attitude works well while conducting business. If a customer is angry or a supplier cuts you off, you have to do something immediately. Waiting just makes the problem worse, perhaps even preventing a successful resolution.

Oh, by the way, if you do feel stuck, send me an e-mail at askdonmitchell@yahoo.com, and please let me know how I can help. You can do it!

Appendix B

Business Model Blueprints

Develop a New Business by Combining
Three Complementary Benefit Breakthroughs

For you yourselves know how you ought to follow us,
for we were not disorderly among you;
nor did we eat anyone's bread free of charge,
but worked with labor and toil night and day,
that we might not be a burden to any of you,
not because we do not have authority,
but to make ourselves an example of how you should follow us.

— 2 Thessalonians 3:7-9 (NKJV)

Just before completing the final draft of *2,000 Percent Living*, I visited an exhibition of artist Sol LeWitt's wall drawings that are installed at MASS MoCA in North Adams, Massachusetts, and gained many valuable insights from it. In case you are unfamiliar with this aspect of the late artist's work, let me explain a little about his wall drawings. Mr. LeWitt found the process of conceptualizing art to be interesting and worthy apart from producing the art, and he liked to draw. As a result, he worked on helping people to recreate his drawings on a grand scale without his direct participation.

If you would like to see some of these recreated wall drawings, you can find examples at the MASS MoCA Web site, www.massmoca.org. I also encourage you to visit the exhibition, which is planned to continue until 2033.

As I toured the extensive display of recreated wall drawings, I was impressed by examples of the complex plans that Mr. LeWitt provided for those who want to render his wall drawings. The details are so thoroughly developed and easy to understand that virtually anyone who can read English is able to create an excellent wall drawing that will appear as Mr. LeWitt intended and personally produced. These directions also display a witty view of communicating that express his self-effacing and joy-filled personality.

If you are musically inclined, think of his instructions as being similar to a symphony's score. By performing what the composer wrote on period instruments, musicians can recreate the delightful sounds that existed during the composer's lifetime.

A new question occurred to me while I was touring the exhibit: How well would people understand the nuances of how to create and install 2,000 percent solution breakthroughs after the best of the current practitioners are no longer alive? I imagined that many well-meaning people might misinterpret what has been written on the subject and that, consequently, much effort could go into relatively ineffective activities.

As an example of such a problem, I have been struck by how many learners view answering all of the questions posed in the 400 Year Project books as a complete substitute for following the processes described in the texts. Such questions were intended just to start learners' thinking in ways that make it easier for them to use the processes. In an attempt to avoid such confusion among learners, I have omitted from recent 400 Year Project books most of the kinds of questions that earlier project books included.

Having become aware of the humbling issue of how to best serve unborn generations, I immediately began to appreciate that Mr. LeWitt's instructions could be likened to blueprints. With a good blueprint for making something, any reasonably competent person who knows how to use blueprints and has the right tools and materials can create the desired result.

I immediately determined that I would include blueprints for a few of the most important aspects of *2,000 Percent Living* (directions for ideal practice identification, for succeeding in breakthrough leadership, and for accomplishing breakthroughs as a servant) in an appendix to that book. Learners who just want to graze through the concepts of 2,000 percent living will get what they want from the fourteen lessons that compose the main body of the book. Learners who would like to create many breathtaking breakthroughs can use the blueprints in its Appendix B to make faster progress and to accomplish more.

Since providing such blueprints is obviously helpful, you may be wondering why I hadn't done so previously. I certainly toyed with related ideas, but I avoided doing much about them beyond coauthoring *The 2,000 Percent Solution Workbook*.

In choosing to be mostly silent about detailed process instructions, I was primarily concerned that I not stifle anyone's creativity. I believed that what I'd learned and been writing about could be reconceptualized into simpler and better forms. I also hoped that many 2,000 percent solution tutors would soon begin work and that they would develop better blueprints than I could through drawing on their experiences with applying and teaching the process.

Over the first sixteen years of the 400 Year Project (see *Adventures of an Optimist*), I learned something that surprised me: With God's glorious help I can conceptualize and describe improved breakthrough methods much faster than most people become interested in learning how to use them. That circumstance suggests that I need to focus on making it easier for learners to grasp the importance of and the advantages derived from using such breakthrough methods and to appreciate how little time and effort are usually needed to apply the processes to create remarkable solutions. As a result of my continuing concern about the relatively slow growth in the number of people applying breakthrough processes, I decided to make more blueprints available in Appendix B of *Help Wanted* (the blueprints include adding more dimensions of complementary breakthroughs, interesting and inspiring others to make breakthroughs, and teaching others to tutor breakthrough learners).

In thinking about blueprints for making breakthroughs, I realize that my task is a little more complicated than Mr. LeWitt's. What he wanted to enable will still be literally relevant centuries from now. What I am describing should be improved over time as new resources, knowledge, skills, and circumstances emerge. Therefore, I need to write the blueprints to allow for such advances to be easily incorporated into future solutions. I have done my best to project potential advances in methods with the help of the Holy Spirit. I also made this information more relevant for the future by grounding my writing as much as possible in circumstances that are likely to remain relatively similar to today.

For *Business Basics*, I realized that additional blueprints would be helpful to readers. This time I decided to write blueprints that capture business models that are likely to prosper for many decades from now. Such blueprints are more explicit and practical than anything that I have prepared in the past.

As such, please realize that their very specificity makes these blueprints both more and less helpful to you. They are more helpful in that you aren't likely to miss an important point. They are less helpful in that any potential competitor can read and apply the same material.

As a result, I encourage you to think of these blueprints as being like plans for just the foundation of a much more developed and larger business. Add other business model innovations to accomplish even more … and to insulate your business from competitors who can only copy what they read.

These blueprints can also serve as archetypes for aspects of other business models. For example, a business doesn't have to offer only services or only products. It might do both. Creating such a business model for offering both services and products might be accomplished by combining two or more of these blueprints.

In the interests of clarity, I am sharing extremely narrow business models, designed to be applied in currently valuable specializations. These business models can also be broadened where such expansions add strength, rather than diluting effectiveness.

Each business model is briefly described in terms of the familiar business model dimensions (see *The Ultimate Competitive Advantage*):

- *Who?* (the business's stakeholders)

- *What?* (the offerings)

- *When?* (hours of operation and seasonality)

- *Where?* (location of activities)

- *Why?* (reasons why customers and other stakeholders participate)

- *How?* (methods for providing the intended benefits)

- *How Much?* (approach to and level of pricing)

The blueprints that follow consider:

- professional service organizations that teach how to make breakthroughs as well as provide solutions and implementation assistance to clients who don't want to "do it themselves"

- custom manufacturing

- local retailing

- farming

We first consider the blueprint for professional services.

Professional Organizations
Offering Breakthrough Assistance Blueprint

Then God said,
"Let the earth bring forth grass, the herb that yields seed,
and the fruit tree that yields fruit according to its kind,
whose seed is in itself, on the earth"; and it was so.
And the earth brought forth grass,
the herb that yields seed according to its kind, and
the tree that yields fruit, whose seed is in itself according to its kind.
And God saw that it was good.

— Genesis 1:11-12 (NKJV)

Let me remind you that *Help Wanted* focuses on how to become a breakthrough tutor and describes the steps involved in providing such tutoring assistance. If you want to explore a different aspect of a tutoring and professional-services business for making breakthroughs than is presented here, you will probably find at least some of what you need in *Help Wanted*.

Who? Ideal clients are very eager to make breakthroughs. In addition, such clients either have enough time and interest to learn how to do so themselves or would like to hire a professional organization to help. The clients who want more than learning support must have sufficient financial resources to afford such assistance and the ability to apply the solution that the professional organization provides.

Such a professional-service organization must access the most effective practices for teaching, developing, and implementing breakthroughs. To do so may involve external mentors who train and assist the organization's tutors, individuals and colleagues in other organizations who are engaged in similar activities, and those who have worked on making related breakthroughs.

Such a successful business can grow by adding and developing professionals who play specialized roles for clients that are directly related to making breakthroughs (such as trainers, tutors, researchers, developers, and implementers), as well as those who provide important support activities (such as human resources, marketing, sales, finance, and IT systems staffers) for the service organization itself. Prior to reaching a large size, some of such support roles can be effectively performed by external organizations working as outsourced suppliers.

In addition, it may prove attractive to develop partnerships with organizations that have deep expertise in various sorts of implementation specialties, such as IT systems designers and developers. Otherwise, the service organization could bog down in recruiting, training, and developing a large staff group for itself whose expertise wouldn't primarily focus on developing and implementing breakthroughs.

What? There needs to be a high level of shared enthusiasm and interest among clients and the service organization's staff for making the same kinds of breakthroughs. In choosing a specialty, check for breakthroughs that appeal to the organization's founder and ascertain that the potential demand for services is adequate to meet the service entrepreneur's personal goals for himself or herself and the related business goals. Staff and supplier selection should then focus on finding those with the same breakthrough interests.

For best results, the service organization should initially specialize in one type of breakthrough. Superior knowledge will accumulate much more rapidly in this way. There are marketing advantages, too. Although there's little competition among such service providers now, such a favorable circumstance won't always be the case. Having more experience with a certain type of breakthrough will be highly regarded by potential clients whenever competing breakthrough-service providers emerge. In addition, such expertise will reduce marketing costs by helping attract potential clients through the evidence of a credible track record and lots of successful case histories.

However, such breakthrough-service organizations should avoid overspecialization such as by only working on cost reductions in an activity or for an industry where many people have some relevant knowledge. Such a specialized field could potentially become too crowded with service providers. In addition, since many of the best breakthroughs will be complementary ones, it makes more sense to master over time a series of at least three (and ideally more) such related breakthrough types.

When? Such a professional practice lends itself to having a global client base composed of those who are willing to be served solely through telecommunications and Internet contacts. With such a practice, working hours will need to match when distant clients need help. If services aren't designed to be provided in real time, prompt (within twenty-four hours) responses will usually be adequate.

If services are supplied in real time, client preferences for when to communicate will be very important. In selecting clients to serve and professional services to provide, the "when" dimension of the business model will have to be carefully managed to avoid creating difficulties for those working in the professional service organization. Otherwise, some staff members will be on call indefinitely for twenty-four hours a day.

As a professional organization providing such real-time services becomes larger, individuals in the firm with similar interests and expertise can arrange to provide real-time backup for one another to cover all times during the week. Prior to reaching such a size, colleagues in similar noncompeting organizations who share expertise and interests may also choose to cover for one another to provide enough real-time availability when such a practice is acceptable to clients, much as freelance on-call pediatricians handle night and weekend calls for busy pediatric practices.

Where? Many aspects of breakthrough-related services can be done at a distance. That observation is most true for tutoring. From the beginning of the 400 Year Project, people have learned how to make 2,000 percent solution breakthroughs through a combination of reading and e-mails. As a result, the professionals engaged in any activities that work well from a distance can be located just about anywhere.

When it comes to developing or to implementing a breakthrough for a specific organization, the service organization's location becomes very important. If the breakthrough methods need to be well coordinated with other client activities, a fair amount of information-gathering and implementation must occur on the client's premises. As a result, providing such work should be limited to clients located relatively near to that part of the service organization's staff. Otherwise, professional staff members will burn out from too much travel and time away from home. Results suffer for everyone whenever such burnout begins or increases.

Why? This aspect of a business model is almost always the most important part of achieving optimal results. "Why" refers to the motivations for people to become clients or customers of such a service organization, as well as for stakeholders to establish relationships with the organization. I find that many people don't appreciate the power and breadth of potential human motivations and focus, instead, on economic benefits.

Help Wanted teaches that deep emotional commitments to serve others by eradicating the sources of difficulties provide the best motivational foundation for involvement by clients, tutors, and other stake-holders. Be clear that I mean to distinguish between those who literally draw great emotional sustenance from providing for others in worthy traditional ways (such as by ladling food onto plates in a soup kitchen for homeless people) and those who are motivated by a desire to eliminate the sources of the need (such as by providing homeless people with combinations of counseling, training, jobs, medical care, clothing, and places to live that help clear a path toward an independent life).

People who want to apply this business model should be sure to read chapters one through twelve in *Help Wanted* to learn about more needs that can be better supplied by breakthrough-related services. While reading these chapters, concentrate on finding the most powerful "why" motivations that fit the clients you want to serve.

How? This business-model dimension offers the greatest potential for innovative variations. As an example of what I mean, let me provide two contrasting approaches to breakthrough tutoring that reflect having different amounts of knowledge and experience. In the first approach, a new organization might just provide tutoring of the sort that I describe in *Help Wanted*. As an alternative approach, an experienced tutoring organization might examine its knowledge and expertise gained while serving hundreds of learners who succeeded in making a certain type of breakthrough (such as market expansion for catering companies) to create a "cookbook recipe" for identifying even better solutions.

Naturally, the potential breadth of "how"-related activities is immense due to the numerous choices in possible "what" roles to play. In addition to providing tutorials, training, and implementation services, such an organization might also develop expertise and resources for acquiring data needed in all of such "what" roles. As a result, clients could accomplish greater breakthroughs while expending less time, money, and effort.

In selecting "how" tasks, I encourage those applying this business-model blueprint to look first at activities that clients find to be onerous. Based on my experiences with learners and clients, some possible examples of activities that may be perceived as onerous include:

- conducting survey research and interviews with potential customers

- locating future best practices

- identifying the ideal best practice

- repeating the eight-step breakthrough process

- adding a complementary breakthrough

- training people in client organizations to implement identified breakthroughs

How much? I believe that pricing will greatly change over time for organizations that engage in breakthrough-related services. In the early days of expanding 400 Year Project knowledge, few potential clients will accurately anticipate the effectiveness, income, cash flow, and value benefits they will ultimately receive from such services. Consequently, any charge beyond a token amount will discourage many potential clients from hiring the organization. The challenge of being paid for the actual value delivered will be compounded for those breakthrough-service organizations that are just starting out and whose staff members lack track records. It's one of the reasons that I installed the certification option: By choosing certified tutors, potential clients can feel more comfortable that they are choosing individuals who know what they are doing.

If such professional service organizations build their initial business models by providing services that are delivered by part-time people who also have well-paid, full-time jobs, I don't believe that low initial prices will limit the potential success of those organizations. In such a circumstance, low pricing can be a blessing in disguise by allowing new organizations to spend more of their time, money, and effort on providing services rather than on finding and marketing to potential clients. In addition, initial clients who paid little for the services will have more impressive success stories to share because of gaining very high multiples of benefits from their small expenditures. Such clients will also be more happily surprised by their results than later clients will be. In addition, client-directed word-of-mouth testimonials are more likely to follow from those who paid little but reaped much.

After having experienced unanticipated benefits, clients who got quite a bargain the first time around will be more easily persuaded to pay more for future services. As a result, highly satisfied initial clients can become part of a firm foundation for launching more-profitable related services.

There may also be opportunities for receiving contingent compensation tied to client results. A client with little cash who has just started a new business may not realize how easily the business can become quite large and highly profitable. In such a circumstance, a service organization might provide an implementation activity for adding new customers and be paid for its work in terms of how much incremental business volume is obtained. In contrast to the circumstance of receiving lower fees for tutorials, such implementation work may be more richly rewarded than later work when the potential value is better understood by potential clients. Consequently, there's an important ethical responsibility to be sure that clients have a sense of how much they might pay for contingent compensation compared to fixed-price fees.

Keeping this blueprint in mind for breakthrough professional services, let's next consider a business model for manufacturing profitable custom offerings.

Custom Manufacturing Blueprint

"Now take Aaron your brother, and his sons with him,
from among the children of Israel,
that he may minister to Me as priest,
Aaron and Aaron's sons: Nadab, Abihu, Eleazar, and Ithamar.
And you shall make holy garments for Aaron your brother,
for glory and for beauty.
So you shall speak to all who are gifted artisans,
whom I have filled with the spirit of wisdom,
that they may make Aaron's garments,
to consecrate him, that he may minister to Me as priest.
And these are the garments which they shall make:
a breastplate, an ephod, a robe,
a skillfully woven tunic, a turban, and a sash."

— Exodus 28:1-4 (NKJV)

Manufacturing is undergoing fundamental changes that are creating enormous opportunities for new enterprises. It's wonderful that such changes are taking place while this book is being written so that I can bring them to your attention and help you to appreciate the implications. Before focusing on the business model blueprint for manufacturing custom offerings, let me describe what some manufacturing changes are so that you and I will have the same information in mind.

First, regardless of where a custom offering provider is located, it's become very convenient and efficient to produce custom versions of many items in other countries around the world. As an example, most apparel and accessory designers today send electronic files required to make their offerings from wherever they are to manufacturing plants in Asia. Samples are quickly returned by airfreight. As a result, large-scale manufacturing may begin in just a few days after a design and the requisite software are finalized by the designer. If styles or sizes need to be made somewhat different for one country versus another, designs can be quickly and easily adapted electronically and sent to manufacturers to be made in just the needed quantities for each type of item.

Second, manufacturing equipment has been created to lower the cost of short runs, rather than only seeking to make medium and long runs more efficient. As I described earlier in *Business Basics*, the latest electronic printing and binding equipment permits making a single paperback book for the average cost of producing several hundred such books on offset presses and with conventional binding equipment.

Third, companies are finding highly effective ways to gather information about individual users so that more desirable custom versions can be produced at relatively little additional cost. The jeans market was one of the first to provide the alternative of custom fit to consumers, and this measurement approach for custom clothing has proven to be popular with those who want better fitting apparel.

Fourth, technologies are rapidly improving for manufacturing low-cost, high-quality custom versions of many goods. It's expected that before long small manufacturers will be able to produce high-quality, custom versions of many items by using equipment the size of home washing machines in garage-sized factories. For instance, I recently saw such manufacturing equipment used to create a cardboard sculpture of a person that would make an engaging centerpiece at a birthday celebration.

As you read this blueprint, realize that improved capabilities for defining and making custom items may have been added since I wrote it. Let me suggest that you become familiar with the latest custom manufacturing technologies for your industry before developing your business model.

Now let's turn to the business model blueprint.

Who? Ideal customers are companies and individuals that will either pay a lot more than the added cost for making a custom version of an already-expensive item or will purchase large dollar amounts of a particular custom good.

Let me differentiate two types of customizations. In the first instance, a well-known brand allows you to order custom versions of its existing products. Levi jeans are an example. In the second instance, a custom version of something is so desirable that simply having a "no-name" version is highly desirable. A customized perfume that provides a woman with a unique scent that draws the kind of attention she wants is an example of the second type of customization.

While both types of customizations are certainly feasible, it's a lot easier for new and small manufacturers to provide custom no-name versions than to establish brands and then to add custom versions of such branded offerings. Ultimately, I also suspect that the no-name approach will be more successful for many types of offerings because such customization allows customers who want to be more unique to do so. By contrast, defining oneself by the brand labels that others can see may eventually pale for individuals with the awareness, imagination, judgment, time, and money to engage successfully in enhancing their inherent uniqueness. For individuals who can't make such custom-goods judgments successfully, undoubtedly customizing consultants and retailers will become available to help.

Of course, it's also possible that great success with customizing something that hasn't been customized before can provide the initial basis for a new brand. Some of such brands will, no doubt, celebrate individuality as part of their identities.

Let's apply these customer-defining principles by considering a young chef who is beginning her catering business. Let's imagine that she has developed a level of taste and style that will eventually command widespread respect but that currently few people know about her. Such a caterer could create custom décor and service items for each client's event to complement the food and beverages, enabling her clients to receive major upgrades in style and appearance that they could not achieve on their own or by hiring a typical caterer. Those who hire the caterer or attend the events will quickly spread the news of her customizing abilities.

If you don't yet know how to design custom items, you should learn how or develop relationships with people who do. If the process can be automated in any way, find people who can provide appropriate software and other tools, and recommend the right IT hardware and manufacturing equipment.

282

If you don't intend to do the custom manufacturing, you'll also need relationships with organizations that can efficiently produce your customized offerings.

If you don't have the marketing and distribution clout to develop enough customers to be profitable, you'll need to work with those who do have such clout.

What? A great place to start is with an item that's difficult to custom make that people aren't used to being able to purchase. Providing offerings that are highly noticeable and appealing to trendsetters should be considered first. One such customizing possibility is to print large silk scarves that are more complementary to a woman's complexion, cosmetics, body shape, and wardrobe. Software could be developed so that purchasers can participate in the design process. If such involvement occurs, care should be taken to make it a highly enjoyable experience so that purchasers will want to repeat it. The novelty of having such choices will make gaining sales much easier after word-of-mouth referrals from pleased customers commence.

Another potentially valuable approach is to look for items where customization offers great economic benefits; this opportunity will typically occur with items that are regularly consumed by businesses. An example might be providing caterers and takeout restaurants with highly appealing, less-expensive disposable utensils that end users and customers would keep and reuse for years, providing great in-home and at-work advertising for the restaurants.

A third potentially successful approach for selecting an item to customize is providing much needed comfort for which people are quite willing to pay. During a recent search for a new bed, for instance, I was struck that my wife's and my preferences for mattresses were so different that no existing product could have satisfied us both … including the ones that provided individual adjustments for half a mattress. Had some furniture or bedding store offered a custom bed so that we could have had what we each wanted without switching to twin beds, I'm sure we would have been very interested. Those with lots of back pain would probably also be interested in any opportunities for bed customizations that make more comfortable, better sleep possible.

When? Businesses offering custom items that require in-person interaction are primarily open when most people need to be at work. As a result, many people can't easily fit obtaining these custom items into their schedules. For instance, I well remember my frail mother-in-law's frustration with having very expensive custom shoes made due to the difficulties of finding times when my father-in-law was free to drive her to the appointments.

Longer hours would obviously help, but for a new, small firm it may be more important to offer more evening and weekend hours than competitors typically make available … while experimenting with reducing hours during the work week.

If an item can be customized without in-person visits, custom orders can be taken over the telephone, on the Internet, or by fax. Because customers may be located quite a long distance away, continual availability of someone who can help with placing an order will be important.

Where? For custom personal-use items involving individual characteristics (such as sizing and color matches) that are very important, people are going to be more interested in buying after they see samples and gain reassurance through the order process concerning what they will receive. Consider hearing aids. You wouldn't want to order ones that weren't customized to fit your ear, your type of hearing problem, and how conspicuous you want the hearing aids to be. As a result, you start with an audiologist to obtain a custom fitting. Like most businesses that are operated out of retail locations, few people are going to drive past one such operation to go to a different one. If potential purchasers are unsure about wanting a custom item, they also aren't likely to travel very far to investigate the opportunity. With such location-sensitive fitting circumstances, it will be important to have lots of outlets located where potential customers regularly come during operating hours.

For items that businesses consume, it will usually be acceptable to provide samples that are simply shipped back and forth. If such custom goods are inexpensive, you'll need to consider how the freight costs for providing timely delivery affect profits. If the items are high-value enough, you may be able to afford overnight air freight delivery from some distance away. In cases where freight costs are high compared to the item's price, those in the United States should investigate the opportunities to produce next to United Parcel Service ground delivery hubs so that more distance can be covered in one day by truck.

Why? The more urgent and the more reasons why something is sought, the more often that sales can be easily made ... assuming that there's enough income and cash to pay for such custom items. Here's an example of what I mean. Many people suffer from back pain. Without relief such pain can become debilitating, stealing someone's joy and energies. With a well-chosen combination of the right bedding, custom-made foot orthotics (such as shoe inserts for arch support), lower-back supports (for chairs, sofas, and vehicles), and occasionally custom back braces, a lot of back pain can be eliminated. Over time with such support, back muscles may eventually strengthen so that fewer custom appliances and aids are needed. Providing an environment where all such items could be fitted and ordered at one time would probably be quite a blessing to those whose back pain cannot be eliminated by surgery.

Concern for others can also be an important motivator for purchasing custom offerings. Many families will eagerly sacrifice discretionary spending to provide something that's helpful for a child's education or well-being. If the child is at risk for some negative outcome over a lifetime, such motivation may be even greater. For example, the rapid increase in the number of youngsters with various autism disorders provides incentives for such families to seek customized treatments matching their youngster's needs. Yet, I'm not aware of any parallel effort to create educational items that are customized to help each autistic youngster to learn or improve social interaction skills. Such custom educational items would probably be much less expensive to provide than the special educational interventions that are so often sought. Serving such learning needs in customized ways could develop into a large market. A software program might be developed to diagnose what kinds of custom items would work best for an individual and then to design the items that fit the youngster's needs.

How? After choosing the right item to customize for a manufacturing business, in many cases the next most important business model element is to identify a highly accurate, rapid, low-cost method for specifying the most desirable individual adjustments. An offering's credibility will mostly be determined by whether people can have faith that they will receive a custom item that will enhance whatever it is that they want to accomplish. In the process, it will be highly desirable to simulate the end results to reduce mistakes, as optometrists do now by having patients look at eye charts through equipment with lenses that match their new prescriptions. Cosmetic plastic surgeons do something similar by providing simulated computer images of what the results of various procedures will look like on the patient. In addition, money-back guarantees may be helpful in encouraging trial of some of such custom offerings, as many hearing aid makers have chosen to provide.

By comparison, I believe that the manufacturing itself will be relatively less important to business success ... assuming that customers receive items that are exactly as specified. Laser eye surgery is a good example of this observation. Once surgeons learned how to measure what incisions to make, it was relatively simple to design automated equipment to make more precisely located incisions than any surgeon could manually accomplish.

Where possible, think about results achieved in other types of custom manufacturing businesses (such as the ones I have cited) to help appreciate what aspects of a business model can add lots of value for the three complementary breakthroughs: market expansion, cost reduction, and investment avoidance.

In many cases, there will be no models to study for defining the best custom approaches. Production will probably begin after developing some form of measurements that reliably identify ways to improve desired benefits. The organization offering custom items should then seek to find additional measurements and more effective ways to measure that further improve customer and end-user outcomes and enjoyment.

In particular, realize that most custom processes (think of ordering frames for new optical prescriptions) cannot serve certain needs. For instance, if you have severe astigmatism, need trifocals, and want to have stylish small frames for your glasses, you probably won't be able to find a totally satisfying solution. You will have to make a series of compromises instead, and you'll probably be unhappy with most of the alternatives. A practitioner who specifies such custom items needs to learn how to identify when apparent solutions aren't going to work well in order to avoid frustrating customers with bad results and running up extra costs by producing items that customers reject.

Making the right recommendation for custom items is more difficult because people may have higher expectations for benefits from custom offerings. Even when customers are paying quite a low price for the customization involved, they will often want as much service as for a higher-priced standard item. A wise custom manufacturer will price the custom offerings to afford a high-enough level of service to meet most customers' expectations, even when making the item is quite simple and low cost.

How much? Mention customization and many people will just assume that a premium price over the standard version is involved. That's not necessarily the case. Sometimes customization permits taking away enough costs so there may be an opportunity to charge less than for a standard item. That's what Dell has done with its custom-configured personal computers. In the process many costs were avoided, and discount prices were often charged for custom electronic products. Combined with other helpful business-model innovations, Dell gained market share profitably in serving corporations.

How should you decide among the alternatives of charging a premium price, no premium or discount, or a discounted price compared to standard items for your custom-manufactured offerings? While there are a number of potential considerations, the determining factor will usually relate to how much effect pricing has on purchasing.

Lest you automatically assume that more items are always consumed when lower prices are charged, that's not necessarily the case when dealing with people who, when purchasing, are partly motivated to display that they are wealthier than many other people. If natural diamonds were priced lower than manufactured diamonds for jewelry, I suspect that some demand would shift toward manufactured diamonds just because these stones can display fewer flaws than many lower-quality natural diamonds and some wealthy people might enjoy showing off those advantages just as long as no one thought they were trying to save money. That relative pricing shift won't happen, of course, because the global diamond monopoly does an excellent job of keeping prices for natural diamonds used for jewelry much higher than would otherwise occur.

As marketers learned long ago, most people have trouble deciding how much they want to spend when purchasing. When presented with lots of different choices, many people cannot easily pick one. However, put the same customer in front of three items, a higher-priced one with all conceivable features, a medium-priced one with many practical features, and a lower-priced one with no added features, and almost everyone will buy the medium-priced alternative.

Such simple decision making can be enhanced by providing custom offerings. There is, of course, only one item being offered, the one that the customer orders. Customers can in such circumstances select, feature-by-feature, how much they would like to spend on customization. In considering each feature, the customer might select from two options: no feature at one price, or adding the feature and paying a higher price. As a result, regardless of any increased costs involved to make a custom item, customers will tend to pay more than the medium price for a standard item by selecting more of the custom features.

Customization also offers purchasers the potential advantage of being able to afford more of the features that appeal to them by not ordering some features that are often standard but that they do not want. As a consequence, a buyer may be delighted to pay an average price for a custom version while the seller obtains an above-average profit margin. In addition, satisfaction with such a custom item will be higher than for a medium-priced standard item with average features ... allowing the custom manufacturer to gain market share while enjoying improved profit margins.

In many markets, there is price elasticity such that reducing the price causes unit sales to increase at a faster rate. If such price elasticity is high enough, it may make sense to provide discount prices for custom items.

Since 1970, there has been an increasing likelihood that dropping the price of a more expensive item will increase unit sales faster than by reducing the price of a less expensive one. While I have seen no general work on the subject, I suspect this price elasticity difference is due to the people who buy the higher-priced versions being better-educated consumers. Give purchasers more value for the price paid, and they can and will buy more. Someone who buys the undifferentiated, low-priced version probably just needs to accomplish something straightforward not very often. Lower the price further, and the low-price buyer will not purchase any more ... because there is no additional need.

Another factor that often arises in setting prices relates to "how fast" to provide the offering. While many custom manufacturers offer the option to pay extra for faster delivery, fewer makers present the option to also pay for faster production. If all production is fast, of course, such a pricing alternative won't be worth providing. If there is enough of a time difference to affect purchasers' preferences, consider making faster production *and* faster delivery available for a premium price. Such an alternative may add a lot of value for a given purchaser.

Keep this blueprint in mind while we turn our attention next to a business model for local retailing.

Local Retailing Blueprint

> *"And the foolish said to the wise,*
> *'Give us some of your oil, for our lamps are going out.'*
> *But the wise answered, saying,*
> *'No, lest there should not be enough for us and you;*
> *but go rather to those who sell, and buy for yourselves.'*
> *And while they went to buy, the bridegroom came,*
> *and those who were ready went in with him to the wedding;*
> *and the door was shut."*
>
> — Matthew 25:8-10 (NKJV)

Local retailers are experiencing the biggest changes in their industry since everyday discounting became a primary way to compete. Let me mention four of the most important changes and their most obvious implications.

First, customers can access information over the Internet from a number of local retailers about standard goods in a variety of ways including using a computer, a smart cell phone, and various mobile electronic devices. As a result, customers can know which retailers have what items in stock and at what prices before leaving work or home to make a purchase. A retailer that isn't competitive in either availability or price will less often attract and retain customers.

Second, if the item isn't needed right away and also isn't too costly or awkward to ship, customers can consider purchasing from an Internet seller to obtain either a better selection or a lower price. As a result, sales of many bigger ticket items are shifting away from physical retailers to online ones.

Third, some retail offerings (such as books, recorded music, and videos) are becoming available through low-price online downloads. A physical store, then, actually provides fewer potential customer benefits and is a less convenient outlet for purchasers of offerings that are in electronic form.

Fourth, many "standard" offerings can be bought at reasonable prices in custom versions, as I describe in the blueprint for manufacturing custom offerings. Customers who want custom items will more often bypass local stores that only offer standard offerings. In addition, many custom manufacturers will sell direct to end users, bypassing all retailers.

Each of these four changes is consistent with a longer-term trend: The number of distributors and distribution steps between manufacturers and end users is being reduced, and the amount paid for distribution is becoming a smaller percentage of sales. Keep that long-term trend in mind (as well as the four changes) while preparing a business model for the highly competitive local retail environment.

Let's look at such a business model.

Who? Seek customers who have a number of the seven characteristics that I describe here.

One such characteristic is a preference for shopping and purchasing experiences that cannot be provided online. What are some of the reasons purchasers may prefer to shop and purchase in person?

Sometimes ideas for what to purchase are more pleasantly and easily developed by physically inspecting and interacting with the offerings. That's pretty typical for personal items that affect individual appearance and have to be tried on to ensure obtaining the right size. It's also true for picking out gifts in categories that aren't familiar to the purchaser. In addition, if the choices are complex, the purchaser may want assistance from knowledgeable sales staff such as often occurs at an Apple store for those considering any of that firm's more advanced offerings. Finally, with perishable goods such as produce and flowers, quality varies, and savvy customers want to pick out the best of what's available and may not want to purchase at all when quality is temporarily poor.

At luxury goods stores, customers often receive lots of enjoyable personal attention, may find comfortable places to relax while appropriate items are brought for their consideration, and might even sip complimentary vintage champagne. In such instances, retail store customers are seeking experiences and emotional comfort that cannot be provided by shopping and purchasing items in the most economical ways.

A second characteristic of more attractive local retail customers is telling lots of people about new shopping and purchasing experiences that delight them. In fact, it's even better if such enthusiastic customers like to shop with many different friends. For such customers, having such enjoyable experiences at a local retailer provides another advantage because it's fun to share news about such a "find."

A third desirable customer characteristic is trying lots of new offerings. Such an orientation makes it easier to attract a customer, to encourage a customer to return more frequently, and to profitably improve a store's mix of offerings while providing more customer benefits.

A fourth desirable customer characteristic is being forgiving of an occasional bad in-store service experience or problems with an offering. All retail stores will disappoint even their best customers from time to time, and it's a great blessing to be able to retain a customer after such mishaps occur.

A fifth profitable customer characteristic is infrequently returning purchases. Such returns are expensive to handle and can create a lot of friction and unhappiness among customers and retail staffs.

A sixth important customer characteristic is being someone whom the business owner and retail staff enjoy serving. Key causes of poor service and customer turnover are found in mismatched values, attitudes, and behavior standards among customers and store personnel. I'm sure you've had the experience of walking into a store where no one seemed to be interested in helping you while looking at you as though you were something that they had just stepped on in a gutter and could not get off their shoes fast enough. The scene from the movie *Pretty Woman* where Julia Roberts enters a Beverly Hills boutique by herself demonstrates such an experience.

A seventh customer characteristic is making substantial annual purchases of the offerings a local retail store provides. Ideally, such purchasers are in the top 1 percent in annual spenders for such offerings at all retail outlets.

Even more important than attracting the most desirable customers, though, is effective hiring and training of those who assist customers. Research shows that caring, considerate treatment by in-store personnel can increase a retailer's sales by over 40 percent in a short amount of time compared with providing slack, slow, and inconsiderate service.

I'm sure you've had the experience of going into a department store where the merchandise was in a mess, resembling a dump for used goods, and no one was in sight to ring up your purchase. After you covered what seemed like a couple of blocks looking for an employee, you eventually found someone who brusquely declined to help you, indicating that you should just "hang out until someone returns to that department."

What kind of in-store colleagues should you hire? The qualifications depend somewhat on what your offerings are and the type of in-store experiences you aim to provide, but you should always seek people who gain a lot of personal satisfaction from pleasing others and who are good at helping. In addition, in-store associates should be people whom the customers will feel comfortable talking to and receiving assistance from. Rather than having customer-serving colleagues with similar backgrounds, attract a diverse group of in-store personnel so that customers with different expectations and preferences will be attracted and feel more comfortable.

Look for colleagues who are genuinely fascinated by and approve of what you offer. If your colleagues are already knowledgeable about the offerings, that's desirable … but not essential. New employees can always learn what they don't yet know. However, associates should be interested in learning and capable of dispensing the information they learn and advice in tactful, supportive ways.

As individuals, in-store staff members should be neat in personal appearance and prefer that the store be attractively maintained. Otherwise, messiness will repel many potential customers.

Optimal supplier selection is also essential. Work with suppliers who delight in providing unusual value, either in terms of reducing prices or in making something that's much more desirable for customers for nearly the same price. Suppliers should also be able to provide appealing reasons for purchasing and using their offerings. Much of the information that in-store personnel share with retail customers will be drawn from experiences with suppliers where information is gained about their decisions and practices.

Here's an example of what I mean about ideal suppliers and sharing information about them with customers. I often visit local art galleries, but seldom buy anything. I mostly enter galleries when art museums either aren't open or are located far away. Every once in awhile, however, I will enter a small gallery that has very attractive works at what strike me as low prices for their quality.

In some such cases, a dealer or gallery assistant will approach me and start pleasantly discussing the works and their artists. Those salespeople who teach me about how the art is created and provide personal details about the artists quickly engage my attention. As a result, I linger longer.

I may or may not buy that day, but I'm likely to come back at another time to continue the conversation. At some point during one of these visits, I will decide to eventually buy something. With that intention, I begin scouting for what to buy and think about whether to add artwork to my personal collection or to give a different piece as a gift. Notice how receiving interesting information turns my sense of a potential good value into thoughts that lead to purchasing.

Other stakeholders can make a difference, too. Some retail stores support various causes that are related to what they sell. A women's clothing store, for instance, might participate in charities aimed at reducing deaths from breast cancer. When such causes are popular, some customers will seek out the store as a way to show practical support for a cause.

What? While it's certainly desirable to enhance service experiences in local retail stores so much that people are happy to buy standard brands and unbranded items there, the opportunity for providing break-through advantages is much increased where scarce items are available that customers feel they *must* have. Let me explain what I mean.

As an example of retail differentiation based primarily on service, think of Nordstrom's legendary reputation for being considerate. For instance, Nordstrom is known for even taking back items without question or delay that were bought elsewhere. Knowing what a pain it can be to return something to stores that discourage returns, such a reputation quickly attracts customer interest.

Contrast a service-differentiated approach with the offering-based approach of a small, family-owned and -operated clothing store located not too far from my home. It's called Eastern Clothing of Watertown. The name probably doesn't grab you. This retailer is located in an unattractive former mill building on a secondary street that's over a mile from any other clothing stores. I've only been in this store once, and have only driven past it twice (both times by accident) in over forty-five years.

Why am I even aware of the store? It's the only place that I know of within hundreds of miles where very tall and muscular (as well as overweight, formerly muscular) men can find a large selection of off-the-rack suits, sports coats, trousers, and shirts that fit. You can also be measured there for a custom-made suit. The store mostly advertises on football- and basketball-related television and radio shows, which is how I learned about it.

The value of such a specialization for large men is so obvious that the information sticks in my mind, even though I'm a small man. I've often mentioned the store to large, athletic men who were wearing poorly fitting clothes. Without such an unusual product specialization, I suspect that no matter how good its service had been Eastern Clothing of Watertown would no longer be in business.

Let me be clear about the lesson of this clothing example. Offering custom items can be great for drawing customers. Providing unique items can also help. But also consider providing standard items that are difficult for some purchasers to conveniently find … even if such items are mass produced.

Remember that local retail stores have high fixed costs. Higher gross margins and larger profit contributions per sale count for a lot in establishing profitability. Higher purchase frequency by each customer is also a big help unless the value of each sale happens to be quite large.

As a result, also be open to the idea of offering services that relate to the goods that you sell. A clothing store might offer closet-organizing services. If you don't have the necessary skills to provide such services, team with highly effective partners who do and are delighted to work under your store's brand.

The overall need that I'm addressing, of course, is for there to be enough purchasing to make operating a local retail operation financially attractive. A store specializing in custom-made feather dusters probably won't have much competition, but its overall profitability is bound to be iffy.

Contrast the profit potential of a feather-duster store with the watches-only store near a midwestern American city where you can purchase and carry away almost any of the world's most expensive watches. The watch store's clientele is immensely wealthy, and many customers spend more than six figures a year on purchases there. These customers are mostly fascinated by watches and enjoy attracting attention from others who know about watches.

If you are having trouble deciding what to offer, visit other cities to see what offerings are selling well in locally owned specialty stores. Chances are that you will be able to succeed in your locale with a similar specialization, especially if no one else has yet taken that particular specialty approach.

When? There's a simple answer here: Ask your customers. If you have enough desirable customers and in-demand offerings, selling any item will be profitable. The watch store I just described can easily afford to remain open for several weeks in exchange for making just one high-priced sale. In addition to providing hours that fit the convenience of your customers, consider offering extended hours by appointment ... including potentially making home or office visits.

The challenge, of course, is to be sure that you don't create nightmare jobs for you and your colleagues by being too subject to customers' whims. I well remember being asked to present the results of a consulting engagement in the middle of the night to a busy client who suffered from insomnia. It took me almost two days to physically recover from the experience. Making that presentation was one of the reasons why I decided to look for a new job. If flexible hours are attractive to customers, your colleagues should include people who will be happy to work much different hours than you prefer.

Where? Let me emphasize this principle: Be unavoidable for the attractive customers you want to serve. Let's look at how to apply this principle, element by element.

I'll paraphrase an old saying about investing in real estate that many people also apply to local retailing: "Three things count — location, location, and location." Convenient proximity to customers is extremely important in local retailing. For example, the revenue difference can be as much as 25 percent between being located where most people can make a right turn to drive in and park during prime shopping hours compared to where most people must make a left turn without a traffic light across a busy street during such times.

Part of a location's importance also relates to visibility: Out of sight can truly be "out of mind" for retail offerings that don't compel immediate purchases. (If you don't buy gasoline for your vehicle when you are almost out, your car soon won't take you where you want to go ... but does anyone "have" to buy peanut brittle today?)

What you offer also affects the value of visibility. If you frequently see a store that offers appealing items you regularly buy, you'll enter that store a lot more often than a different one that only carries something you need to buy once a year. Increased frequency of visits will also stimulate purchases that customers didn't have in mind when they entered the store.

Location also helps by providing more convenience during regular trips. Let me share a personal example. There's a restaurant offering good salads at low prices located a block away from the supermarket where I usually shop once a week. In between the two locations is a pharmacy. If I am on my way to do my weekly food shopping, I'll usually eat lunch or dinner in the restaurant, consider if I need anything in the pharmacy, and then do my supermarket buying. I choose to eat first so that I'm better able to limit my purchases of "impulse" food items. I think about what I might need at the pharmacy because the prices of most nonfood items there are less than at the supermarket. As a result of this shopping method, I save time, gasoline, and wear and tear on myself, as well as some money. The restaurant and the pharmacy benefit from my habit simply through their convenient locations near the supermarket that regularly attracts me.

When time is of the essence (such as during lunch on a work day), few people are going to buy from anywhere but the closest acceptable outlet. Be located closer to more potential customers who want to save time, and you will do more business when they are in a rush.

Notice that this observation about being unavoidable doesn't mean that you have to compete just based on your store's location. You can also go to the customer. If your offerings are compact and high value enough, it may make sense to become primarily mobile. It's not unusual for a moveable cart to be more accessible than any nearby store because the cart changes its location to take advantage of daily shifts in pedestrian and vehicle traffic.

Sometimes you don't even have to be there personally. You can, instead, place offerings in a vending machine. While it would be far too expensive for most video outlets to open full-scale operations inside supermarkets, Red Box is able to put DVDs containing some of their most popular films into vending machines that fit near the checkout registers of such high-volume stores.

In fact, the more ubiquitous access is to your offerings, the more sales you will gain. Despite that potential, many local retailers make a mistake by only having one outlet, based on their understandable desire to keep costs down and sales up in that outlet. Instead, considerable attention should be paid to finding many low-cost ways to have more outlets.

Here's an example. In many countries, postal deliveries are quite fast and reliable. If postage costs are low enough, those who are willing to wait a few days for their items can simply request that offerings be shipped to them.

Consider the video rental service Netflix. When one of my sons first subscribed, he could literally look up from his mailbox and see the warehouse from which the company's DVDs were mailed. If he ordered online before noon one day, he would have the video in his mailbox after work on the following day. This way of renting DVDs was much more convenient for him than making special trips to pick up and to drop off DVDs at a video store, especially since he worked at odd hours and such stores were usually closed while he was driving to and from work.

Part of the "where" challenge also relates to creating visibility with desirable customers that's separate from a retail location. Many local retailers are finding that the Internet can be an important resource. Why? Well, many potential customers spend more time on the Internet than they do driving around or watching television. How can a local retailer connect to such customers? Advertising a special event or providing a coupon offer online may attract an opportunity to introduce people to the retail location. After capturing an e-mail address, newsletters, surveys, and special offers can be inexpensively shared so that the contact level can remain high enough to make sought-after customers more aware of and interested in the store and its offerings.

Why? My comments in the "Who?" section are also relevant here. With local retailing, it's very important to capture many different elements of "why" a desirable potential customer would choose one outlet rather than some alternative (including Internet ordering).

Of even greater importance than appealing to "why" someone can be attracted when in the vicinity is reaching the point where a local retail shop becomes a destination of choice when a customer is not in the vicinity. Let's look at a few ways to become such a destination of choice to start your thinking.

As *The Ultimate Competitive Advantage* relates in describing the humble beginnings of Wall Drug (see www.walldrug.com), *add a compelling reason for people to immediately become customers*. In that example, Wall Drug wasn't doing well while only serving the small number of people who lived in remote Wall, South Dakota. However, lots of tourists were driving near the town on the highway to and from Mount Rushmore, the American presidential landmark. After putting up signs on the highway offering "Free Ice Water," many Rushmore visitors in the 1930s left their hot, dusty cars and made the side trip for a cold drink and a break from their travels. Once there, such travelers often picked up a few items they needed or enjoyed ice cream cones for more cooling relief.

Even a store that provides many compelling "whys" for purchasing may not make an impression on most of those who walk or travel nearby. Much as Wall Drug prospered by providing the seasonal appeal of free ice water to hot, thirsty travelers, local retailers can use holidays and special occasions to attract customers who might not otherwise visit. Such compelling "why now" reasons can be identified by interviewing potential customers who never visit a given retail outlet, by conducting experiments, and by doing more of whatever works best.

Consider Mother's Day. A husband who hasn't yet obtained an appropriate card for his wife may find a poor last-minute selection on pharmacy and supermarket racks. Concerned about potential backlash, procrastinating husbands that weekend could be drawn into a well-stocked gift store with a prominently displayed sign offering free Mother's Day cards for those who spend $25. Local media outlets are likely to provide news coverage about such an offer, helping to draw even more potential customers to this destination. If the same store has been regularly visited by the wife and her purchases have been recorded, it may be that employees can suggest gifts that will please, rather than annoy, the husband's wife. A wife who is tired of receiving power tools as gifts from her husband might even establish an account and supply a list of "most wanted" items in the store to help her husband choose. Such husbands might return more than once a year after learning that the store also provides beautiful free holiday, birthday, and anniversary cards for those who make $25 purchases at such occasions.

Some powerful "why now" reasons can also relate to rites of passage. For instance, Claire's provides free ear piercing for young teenagers, many of whom become devoted customers for a variety of the inexpensive accessories until "outgrowing" the store's merchandise. During the ear-piercing visit, some other accessories may be purchased in addition to a nice selection of earrings. A young teen is likely to invite friends and family along as well, providing lasting memories for everyone that may turn into word-of-mouth referrals. Feeling pleased with how she looks with the new earrings may encourage such a customer to make another visit to Claire's to begin a style change.

If someone is having a bad day, a pleasant shopping experience can make the world seem a little brighter. One of the most powerful "why" reasons local retailers can provide is respectfully mentioning customers' names, preferences, and interests without being prompted. Almost everyone wants "to be someone." If you can't be recognized in a local retail store, where can you feel respected in public? From such slight beginnings, relationships between customers and staff members can develop. A key requirement is to have very low turnover of in-store staff so that such potential relationships have time to become established and to expand. The "how" part of this business model addresses the opportunity for providing more personal connection, as well.

Other personal connections to a local store can be established through "community-building" events that help people to meet and become acquainted with others who share the same or similar interests. Regularly hold such events at the store, and there's bound to be some shopping done before or after the event. During such activities, those who work in the store can more easily become acquainted with customers and their interests.

In supplying more reasons to visit and to purchase immediately, local retailers should be sure to provide "why now" benefits that are neither a distraction nor an inconvenience for customers with different needs and preferences. A drive-up window for a pharmacy is a good example. A handicapped person who often needs prescriptions refilled may find it difficult and time-consuming to leave a specially equipped vehicle in bad weather to enter a store. If such a customer is driving by for some other reason and sees that no one is waiting at the drive-through window, such availability is almost as good as a personal invitation to stay comfortable in the vehicle while probably enjoying faster service than by going inside. If there is a separate staff for serving drive-through customers from those who help in-store customers, service times might improve for everyone … a "why" that probably appeals to and boosts purchases by all customers.

In other types of retail outlets, some customers may want quicker access while others would like to enjoy several hours of leisurely shopping. A local retailer should seek ways to serve both preferences without negatively affecting anyone.

Here's an example. A store featuring women's clothing might have a comfortable lounge area where personal shoppers are available to assist those who want to take a relaxed look at clothes while chatting with friends. Various special events might be scheduled to make such lengthy visits more enjoyable, such as fashion shows, classes in choosing colors that complement that person's skin tone and hair color, and musical performances.

Customers who know what they want and are in a hurry could be permitted direct access to stocked racks and shelves to help themselves and be encouraged to use self-service kiosks for faster checkouts. Without affecting the service that both types of such in-store customers enjoy, a retail operation could also offer a custom fitting and ordering service at the customer's choice of home, office, or store location.

How? The key principle is providing retailing methods that the most desirable customers crave. Keep checking on what those you serve and want to attract yearn for because their desires and needs will change. In addition, satisfying one craving often increases interest in a different benefit or experience.

Local retailers should start by giving much thought to the store's ambience. While most local retailers aren't going to provide any of the "sizzle" found in a major manufacturer's multistory theme store located in a big city's downtown, it's certainly possible to create looks, sounds, touches, tastes, and aromas that cause customers to enjoy themselves more at relatively little expense. A single distinctive feature can be enough to launch a customer's imagination into full flight, so that what is not physically present is mentally and emotionally fleshed out from an exciting treasury of a customer's memories.

I want to emphasize ambience simply because I have noticed that most local retail stores mostly rely on "sight" for their appeal and that such views are predominately stacks and racks of merchandise little different from what could be seen in many other stores. Contrast such bare bones retailing atmospheres with what one local Oriental rug store owner provided.

The rug store's owner was an older, beautifully dressed, courtly man. Meeting him made you feel as privileged as if you were a guest in a Persian palace during an earlier era. While chatting amiably and becoming acquainted, the owner would politely offer you refreshments including espresso, mint tea, freshly squeezed lemonade, and irresistible cookies that provided mouthwatering aromas and rich flavors. Some Middle Eastern music played in the background. Richly colored, unique, hand-woven rugs were stacked up everywhere, suggesting an endless supply of possibilities for making a home more beautiful and comfortable.

While spending time with the owner, you could easily imagine yourself being a prince or princess inspecting your treasury of rare artifacts. Three or four assistants followed the owner to pull out, unfold, display, fold, and replace rugs. As you inspected the rugs, the owner made sure that you pleasantly touched them as part of the process of determining what you liked.

The owner emphasized in the store's advertising that he traveled all over the world to personally pick out the rugs, often negotiating a transaction for hours over never-ending cups of tea with the father of a rug-weaving family. As you examined a rug, the store's owner might tell you about the rug's weaver or the village from which the rug came. While you shopped, it wasn't hard to imagine that you were present at one of such conversations in a weaver's home.

If you saw a rug you liked, he insisted that you take it home to see how it looked there. These rugs were worth thousands of dollars, yet he sent them off with a minimum of paperwork and delay as his helpers loaded them into your vehicle. In the process, no money was asked for or changed hands. At home, the rugs reminded you of the marvelous shopping experience. What a treasure! The owner told me that few rugs were returned except by someone who was seeking a more appropriate size and color match to an existing décor. In most such cases, a more expensive rug was purchased.

You may be thinking that you could never afford to provide such a rich retail environment. I agree that matching such an approach would be very expensive. However, while your retail store might not be able to afford duplicating such a sensory-rich environment, I suspect that you easily outdo your local retail competitors, who are probably doing next to nothing, at a cost that your store can afford. Let's instead use the Oriental rug dealer as a source of inspiration to suggest some affordable improvements.

If you have a passion for what you sell, you've probably been given gifts or bought items that reveal something that shoppers either don't know or haven't experienced about such offerings. If such an item is attractive or interesting to look at, you could display it near where you meet customers. Pointing to the object, you could then explain how you feel about the offerings that you provide. If the customer is interested in your story, continue to explain. Otherwise, just focus on whatever the customer wants to talk about and to do.

Such objects don't have to be extraordinary or expensive. It's the personal connection that counts most.

Here's a nonretailing example. My primary care physician is the grandson of an architect whose name is known to most people. During my latest physical, my doctor handed me a brick from a building his architect grandfather had designed. It was delightful to heft the brick while look at a photograph of the building when it was new. Seeing and hearing about his family's heritage reminded me that my physician is concerned about doing a good job because maintaining his family's reputation means a lot to him. If no bricks were available, he could have simply used images of old buildings designed by his grandfather to cause a similar reaction by me.

I did something similar during the early days of my consulting firm. My dad sent me a foot-long section of Santa Fe Railway track when a new rail line was put in. The track segment had little inherent value. The postage cost to send it was more than the value of the steel. I kept the memento on my desk where I often pointed to the track and invited people to lift it (it is heavy!) while telling them about how my father had worked for over thirty years at the Santa Fe as I did during summers while in college. I also explained how fortunate and grateful I was that the Santa Fe had sponsored a National Merit scholarship that paid for my college education at Harvard, where I did original research on the attacks against railway tracks and bridges during the French revolutions in 1848. A local model train store owned by a former railway employee could delight customers by using a similar approach.

Background sounds are seldom well managed by local retailers. Yet it's not hard to find music or natural sounds that pleasantly complement a store's offerings. For instance, a store offering "natural" items from equatorial jungles whose owner contributes to efforts to preserve such natural habitats might play muted bird cries from that part of the world, helping to make a pleasant mental connection to the authentic source of the offerings. A store selling spiritual items might arrange for a small water fountain to run continually so that the gentle sounds of water falling could encourage feeling peaceful.

Smells are mostly ignored by local retailers except in stores that sell various scents. In some outlets, it's critical, instead, to avoid introducing scents because they can't easily be removed from the offerings by those who don't care for a certain odor. Think, by contrast, how seeing a few flowers can brighten your outlook while refreshing you with their fragrances. A woman who makes a large purchase might be offered her choice of a lovely sweet-smelling gardenia corsage or some long-stem roses. Alternatively, many people like the scent of leather. Resting on some comfortable leather furniture could happily reinforce the pleasantly appealing fragrances of a store offering leather sports gear.

Taste is easy to provide. Just offer delicious, freshly made snacks while people are shopping. Avoid foods and beverages that can make a mess (such as popcorn). If you have a terrific food supplier or are a good cook, here's another way to customize your offerings to reflect your personality in a customer-pleasing way.

Retailers often fail to provide opportunities to touch offerings. That's a big mistake. Provide pleasant touches and the rest of the person will be delighted.

Many items can provide delightful experiences through feeling them. Having just enjoyed such an experience, a customer is more likely to purchase an item that reminds her or him of the experience while promising more of such enjoyment. People love to touch silk, beautifully burnished woods, and soft, finely woven goods. The fingertips and palms of our hands have an enormous number of nerve endings. Lips and mouths are also sensitive, another reason to provide plenty of great mouth feel for those who eat your great looking, delightfully smelling snacks.

If you decide to add in-store services, consider ones that deliver gentle, relaxing touches. Various kinds of ethical massages are one possibility. A shoe store might provide a ten minute foot massage to anyone who buys a pair of shoes.

It's easy to underestimate how valuable such services involving touch might be to customers. I once attended a seminar where a man told me that no one had given him a hug in over twenty years. Imagine how wonderful he felt when we all made it a habit to hug him. Some women already describe "retail therapy" (going shopping) as one of the ways they make themselves feel better. Why not make such "therapy" even more complete and satisfying?

Of course, ambience is only helpful insofar as a customer feels welcome and pleased by what's happening. Here's where a local store can make a big difference for a customer. Rather than having a bored-looking senior citizen who avoids eye contact greet customers as many chain stores do, have the most personable staff member who is good at remembering names, faces, and personal details pleasantly engage customers as they enter the store. Being welcomed with a warm smile and a pleasant, personal greeting means a lot to most customers.

It's good to follow such a friendly welcome by encouraging customers to select who will assist them. By keeping track of past purchases and taking notes about prior conversations, individual staff members will be able to provide better recommendations while also making the shopping experience more enjoyable. During quiet times, staff members can telephone and send individualized text messages and e-mails to those customers who have asked to be alerted about new merchandise and special offers.

If possible, turn each contact into an opportunity to make a customer feel more appreciated and better understood. One way to do so is by helping customers see themselves in positive terms that may have escaped them. A retailer who has worked with many customers will have a good sense of how each one is a little different. Where such individual customer differences provide potential advantages in purchasing or employing an offering, it's good to point out such differences and their benefits. The customer may gain lasting advantages.

Here's an example of what I mean. When tasting a complex flavor, most people cannot identify more than just a few ingredients. If the person you are helping to design a custom diet cola drink is able to taste the differences among artificial sweeteners, something many people cannot do, you could point out how unusual this is and how other flavors can be used to change such taste experiences if a particular artificial sweetener is preferred for a reason unrelated to its taste (such as health concerns). The customer is going to be flattered and fascinated at the same time by finding out about having an unusually discriminating palate, and you are going to provide a helpful service that is likely to be much appreciated.

Unless the retail experience that your customers desire is always an open-ended leisurely one, I encourage you to organize how you provide service so that people wait no longer than they wish to. There is much research to show that what is perceived as slow service is as likely to drive away customers as is unpleasant, bad service.

Most local retail stores are going to vary between being empty (often near opening time) and overcrowded (perhaps at lunch) during the day. In part that's true because of customer schedules and preferences, but it's also true because of the random fluctuations inherent in having a small store. Schedule your staff to have as many people as you can afford available at the most likely busy times. For instance, don't have your staff go to lunch when the customers who work during the day are going to be flocking in. If you are overwhelmed with customers despite such precautions, have some backup plan that customers know about that will make them feel at least a little better … such as by providing coupons for discounted purchases on the next visit or by hand delivering for free any items ordered by telephone that day. If you can offer ways for customers to provide for their own needs (such as by checking on orders, starting the process of returning an item, or checking themselves out), do so.

How much? In setting prices, many retailers focus solely on reaching a target gross margin (computed as follows: subtract the purchased cost from the retail price, and then divide the remainder by the retail price) for each item. Savvy local retailers know that it's the total dollars of gross margin that they obtain throughout the year that determines the absolute levels of profits and cash flow they receive. As a result of experimentation, many retailers find that their economic performance can be increased by varying gross margins from offering to offering in ways that attract more sales and gross margin dollars.

"Free" is an unusually powerful word for influencing how customers perceive the value of an offer, and companies can attract quite a crowd if they use the word in the right ways. One of my favorite examples involved a Taco Bell promotion. It was widely publicized that any customer would receive a "free" taco between certain afternoon hours on a single day. The regular price of such a taco was less than a dollar. Despite the limited value of the offer, hundreds of people stood outside my local Taco Bell for over an hour (I know this because I was one of them) to receive the bargain. After standing in line so long, many people became hungry and thirsty and bought additional items, including high-margin soft drinks. The bottom line was probably a highly profitable afternoon from the "free" giveaway. Notice that offering a dollar discount (the similar value to the free taco) from a five-dollar purchase probably wouldn't have worked nearly as well.

One inexpensive way for local retailers to attract more interest with pricing is by putting unusually low gross margins on items that most people know the value of, but don't buy very often. Seeing such a "value" price encourages customers to feel more comfortable with the pricing of everything else in a local store. While in the store, such customers mostly buy offerings with normal gross margins.

Here's an example of this pricing strategy. I well remember a wine shop in Europe that carried just a few bottles of expensive champagne at prices that were about a third less than I saw elsewhere. If a very special occasion was coming up, I would buy such a bottle there and carry it home on the plane. Knowing about that "bargain," at times when drinking champagne wasn't a priority, I would instead choose the same shop to buy "normally" priced wines. I'm sure the profits from having me visit more often to buy full-margin items more than made up for the reduced gross profit margin received from my occasional champagne purchases. In addition, a low percentage gross margin on a high-priced item may well translate into more profit contribution than the full gross margin on a low-priced item.

The opposite approach to pricing can work well when a retail store offers a large variety of items, many of which will probably be bought during a visit. By charging lower gross margins on the most price-sensitive offerings, such a store can draw more customers and cause them to shift all of their purchasing.

Such an approach is often used by supermarkets, for instance, by having a few gaudy "specials" on sought-after, top-of-mind items (such as sweet corn just before the Fourth of July barbecues or potted blooming lilies just before Easter) while charging normal gross margins on everything else. These specials can give an aura of low prices that can lead to purchases of over-the-counter drugs and toiletries that can probably be bought for much less at a pharmacy.

Some retailers succeed by seeking higher gross margins where customers don't have much of a sense of what the "right" price is. That's often the case with items that don't precisely equate to what some other retailer is offering. A container of ripe strawberries at peak season that is within two days of spoiling might be priced much lower than a similar container at another store where the berries will remain edible for five days. Yet such a low price on the riper strawberries might actually provide a higher gross margin than the higher price on the longer lasting berries. You'll see the same pricing issue with bakeries, using differentiation in their offerings to increase eye appeal and to make price comparisons with other bakeries more difficult.

Prices may also be set to encourage you to "stock up" by buying more of an offering than you normally would. Rather than cut the price of men's suits by 50 percent, a retailer is much more likely to offer one "free" suit if you buy one at full price. The effect is to sell two suits at half price rather than just one, doubling the gross margin that is received from a customer. Some stores go so far as to mark multiple-unit prices on an item (such as five for $4.00) while being perfectly willing to sell you one unit (at $0.80 in this case). Such offers are often found on canned goods and other items with long shelf lives.

Store layout also plays a role in pricing. Have you noticed how many things are stacked in retail outlets next to where you are probably going to be standing in line to check out? In a clothing store that I frequent, I once counted how many different types of offerings were available along the hundred-foot-long checkout aisle. I discovered that there were ten times more types of offerings in the checkout aisle than in the entire men's clothing section. Most of such "checkout" items were priced at just a few dollars, which seemed like very little after picking out clothing priced at much more per item. Since it was a "discount" store with the amount of the "savings" spelled out on every price tag, some customers might persuade themselves to think that a little treat or two was in order for having "saved" so much money.

In a retail store where personnel busily help shoppers, you may also be asked every so often if you would like to look at categories of items that you haven't mentioned. In a men's clothing store, a visit to buy a pair of slacks is bound, for instance, to elicit inquiries about suits, sports coats, shirts, belts, ties, and shoes. If you don't act interested, the salesperson is likely to mention some sort of "sale" that will save you money. Such suggestive selling often provides more than half the profit in retail outlets where lower-priced items have larger percentage gross margins.

My favorite pharmacy has a helpful pricing practice that keeps me coming back: The store alerts me if there is a sale coming on anything that I'm in the process of buying, and the check-out register automatically adjusts the price downward to reflect the future sale price. If I smile and say something to the clerk such as, "Oh, I wish I had bought more," the person will pleasantly ask if she or he can add to my order. If I say "yes," the clerk will bustle off to bring me as many more items as I want. In the course of a year, such unanticipated savings at that store are very substantial for me. These pleasant surprises are more than enough to keep me out of several competing pharmacies that are located much closer to my home.

Another popular pricing strategy is to give people either price discounts or nonprice rewards based on how much they buy. Retail cooperatives have long done this, paying out a share of their profits to their members based on each individual's annual purchases. As a result, many cooperative members choose to buy as much as possible in order to support the group and to enjoy a larger rebate check. Seeing how much airline and credit card "rewards" points influence spending, some for-profit retailers have begun to do the same thing.

As you can see from this blueprint, retailing provides a wide and deep stage on which to offer differences that make your customers more interested in buying in ways that benefit everyone. As much as I hate to leave this business model, I must stop now or the blueprint will start to become unwieldy. It's also a pleasure for me to move on to the final business model, one for farming.

Farming Blueprint

*See how the farmer waits for the precious fruit of the earth,
waiting patiently for it until it receives the early and latter rain.
You also be patient.*

— James 5:7-8 (NKJV)

Writing about business models for farming presents special challenges not encountered in the prior three blueprints in this appendix. If you are a farmer, such challenges are no surprise.

If you aren't a farmer, but think you might want to become one, you may not yet be aware of all the challenges that you could face. With apologies to any farmers and well-informed prospective farmers who read this blueprint, let me briefly describe some of these special challenges for those who are less familiar with the business of agriculture.

First, farm locations often constrain business-model choices more than in other activities. Any plot of farmland comes with certain kinds of soil, topology, water resources, climate, transportation access, and shipping costs to various markets. The combination of such factors limits planting choices by even more than what a retail store's location does for which offerings to provide. A retail store can do a number of simple, inexpensive things to become a destination for some customers and to provide attractive online ordering for any customers who aren't usually in the neighborhood. Farmers, by contrast, are much more limited by what can be profitably produced on the land available to them. Farmers can consider planting higher yielding seeds, laying down more effective fertilizers, applying powerful pesticides, and irrigating, but such substantial expenditures only make sense if crop prices are expected to be high enough to repay the costs and to provide a reasonable profit.

Second, farming is very capital intensive and usually not very profitable. Consequently, farmers have a harder time financially than does a typical business in affording increased acreages, productive capital investments, and moving to more promising locations.

Third, farmers rarely move to gain business advantages. Active farmers usually live on or very near the land they work, and any shift in what land is farmed may also uproot a farmer's family. In addition, farmers are highly likely to have acquired their land as an inheritance and to have emotional attachments to farming any inherited acres.

Fourth, prices and costs are more outside of a farmer's influence than is true for most businesses. As a result, a farmer could produce a record crop and lose a lot of money unless crop-revenue insurance had been purchased. Such a result can occur when seed and fertilizer costs are high and crop prices are low due to overproduction by many farmers. In such a circumstance, farmers can choose to hold their crops to sell in the future in hopes that there might later be reduced supplies or increased demand, but making such a choice requires a substantial increase in working capital.

Fifth, severe weather can bring unpredictable results that have nothing to do with how well a farmer has planted and nurtured a crop. For example, a hail storm might destroy all the crops in one area. If you operate a farm there, you may not have any revenue that year unless you had bought hail or crop-peril insurance. Conversely, if the destruction spared you, your profits may be higher if enough other farmers have incurred substantial losses.

Sixth, governments may create economic incentives that can feel "unnatural" to a farmer. When that occurs, farmers may not want to participate in what is to their economic advantage. In some nations concerned about food self-sufficiency, crop selling prices may be supported by subsidies that keep marginal producers in business. Or a nation that doesn't want to import too much petroleum may require that domestic fuels include crop-based ethanol, drawing some supplies away from food consumption. When prices for certain crops are continually below many farmers' costs, a government may even pay farmers not to grow such crops.

Seventh, a particular set of farmers and local "experts" may not know much about producing alternative crops that could be much more profitable. As a result, the practicality of switching to more profitable crops may be more limited than the potential economics suggest.

Eighth, in many kinds of farming, there are major cost-reduction opportunities associated with having more land in one place, such as by making it profitable to use more efficient cultivating and harvesting equipment. Farmers who cannot gain such scale may well see their profits shrink due to lower crop prices that follow increasing production by those who do have such lower costs.

Ninth, it's not unusual for a string of bad circumstances and mistakes to lead a farmer to have too much debt, too little capital, and costs that are too high. When such limitations multiply, a farmer's financial ability to engage in any good opportunities may be very limited.

Keeping these nine issues in mind, let's now look at a simple business model for successful farming that might have broad application around the world. Keep in mind that the remainder of this blueprint mostly speaks about planting and harvesting food crops in the soil. Farmers, of course, also engage in producing milk, raise livestock for sale or slaughter, produce fish in ponds, grow nonfood crops such as tobacco and cotton, and raise seed for all kinds of crops. While those alternatives aren't usually addressed in this blueprint, please do keep them in mind.

Who? The farmers who acquire more knowledge, experience, and skill from study, research, experimentation, and cautious expansions will usually improve their profitability the fastest because many farmers should either be producing different crops or applying more effective practices to produce their current harvests. Learning is also important, in part, because many of the most successful farmers have developed substantial income-producing activities that they engage in when farming doesn't require as much of their time and attention. For instance, a farmer with good mechanical skills might repair vehicles in a local garage during winter months. Or a farmer might work at a seasonal manufacturing job during a slow period on the farm. Some farmers even take night jobs year around so that their outdoor time isn't limited, but their incomes are expanded.

In most cases, the farmer's family is also deeply engaged in farming. Sometimes having a family's help with farm work makes the difference between continued success and the family needing to leave farming. A family's desire to continue farming can also be an important business objective. Family members' efforts may also increase learning and expand capacity for applying improved farming practices.

Farmers should seek help from experts with global perspectives who can advise about other crops to consider, explain how to best produce any given crop in light of local conditions and economics, or assist in establishing and improving new sources of nonfarming income. To make such assistance more valuable, some agricultural experts should become tutors in breakthrough practices for improving farming cash flow as well as with establishing successful business models for nonfarming activities.

Except on very small farms, additional workers will be needed at busy times such as during planting and harvesting. In many parts of the world, farm workers would like to change vocations because their work requires migrant living. For their nonfarming activities, farmers should consider adding businesses that can also provide a good living for any seasonal workers who would prefer to remain in the vicinity. One such possibility could be establishing food-processing cooperatives that operate year around. Such workers might also be employed in custom manufacturing that takes advantage of unused space on farms that are located close to customers who want fast production and delivery.

As farming has become more technically sophisticated, suppliers are becoming more important to developing economic advantages. The increasing use of genetically engineered seeds is one important example of such potential for adding value, as are applying more effective and less dangerous pesticides and herbicides.

For farmers who are producing heirloom (or so-called heritage) crops or using organic methods, finding the right suppliers is critical for other reasons … including gaining the expertise needed to succeed with such more challenging crops and farming methods. Customers are also concerned about the authenticity and characteristics of the crops being produced, which can be highly affected by which suppliers are chosen.

Other farmers are important, too. On many occasions, farmers need assistance from one another to succeed. This aid may include helping out with key tasks while someone is ill or injured, or by simply sharing resources that are too expensive for any given farmer to afford for his or her own operations.

Other farmers can also be essential to opening up new markets. For instance, large customers may not want to purchase specialty crops unless a minimum quantity can be obtained from a geographical area. As a result, some farmers will be able to access more desirable markets by agreeing to cooperate with other farmers to shift what crops are grown and the farming methods used.

Specialty customers who have higher or unusual requirements can also provide attractive opportunities for farmers. The organic milk and produce markets are examples where consumers are worried about ingesting potentially harmful chemicals and the effects of environmental degradation. Because farming in such ways is much more expensive and difficult, farmers need customers who care enough about gaining such benefits to be willing and able to pay much higher prices and potentially to purchase foods that don't look as "pretty."

To attract some of such customers may require organizations to monitor and to certify farming practices. If such certifying groups don't exist, customers with specialized requirements and farmers should work together to establish whatever organizational support is required.

Labeling is important to farmers and their customers. Both existing organizations that set standards as well as government organizations that regulate crops and labeling are important stakeholders. In many cases, farmers may need more or different labeling to gain the most advantages from any specialty crops.

Of course, those who consume the crops are also stakeholders. In many cases, consumers' interests in maintaining various forms of farming can also influence other stakeholders to make accommodations that open or close doors to farming viability.

Governments are usually concerned about the security of food supplies for their own people and visitors. For as long as there have been written records, government leaders have risen to and fallen from power based on the price and availability of food for their citizens and subjects. Farmers should expect that actions will be taken by governments to encourage making more local food available at stable prices.

Some farmers use lots of water for irrigation. Where governments provide such water, farming is often subsidized by charging much higher prices to residential and industrial water users. Anyone who draws from or affects the quality of the same aquifers is also a stakeholder.

In some parts of the world, water rights are owned separately from the property where the water is located. If a farmer needs to interact with or buy from the owners of water rights owners, they, too, are stakeholders.

Lenders are important to farmers who need access to low-cost working capital until their crops are sold. Lenders also help finance equipment purchases. In addition, farmers who want to purchase more land will often need mortgages. Farmers who have experienced many years of losses may also need lenders to supply enough working capital to allow them to stay in business.

As I mentioned in the opening section on the special circumstances of being a farmer, insurers can help by providing risk-reducing policies to cover losses from various hazards as well as low crop prices. Governments may also be involved in regulating and subsidizing such insurance programs. Similarly, some farmers may work with commodity brokers to fix prices for their crops so that they can avoid being tied to whatever the market price happens to be at the time of harvest or selling a crop.

Processors can also play a role in increasing prices paid for crops by setting ingredient standards for in-demand branded foods and nonfood items. Such connections are often valuable for farmers who qualify to supply frozen vegetable and fruit brands as well as ketchup and bottled-sauce producers.

Marketing cooperatives can also help to increase demand for certain crops and establish a way for farmers to obtain a share of the profits from branded products that use their crops. Shares in such cooperatives may also represent an important equity valuable for farmers.

Grain-elevator operators often represent a primary storage option for farmers who wish to hold their crops in hopes of obtaining higher prices after the harvest is over. Not having enough space to store a crop can be very harmful to a farmer in a low-price year.

Transportation companies can be critical when crops need rapid shipment to markets before spoilage occurs.

What? As I mentioned earlier, many farmers only grow or raise what they have always grown or raised, with just some occasional shifts among the various crops and livestock they have learned to successfully produce when there is a large price increase or decrease.

In some cases, awareness that producing some crops (such as cotton and tobacco) reduces long-term soil fertility leads farmers to substitute crops that replenish the soil's nutrients. In addition, when weather greatly changes over a number of years (such as by becoming much wetter, drier, hotter, or colder than usual), farmers may seek new crops that do better in different or more variable weather conditions. In other cases, agricultural agents, universities, and cooperatives may bring information about new crops and how to produce them that can lead to successful crop diversifications.

Obtaining the highest potential return from farming efforts, expenses, and investments should include considering how location will change crop choices, affect profitability, and increase insulation from harmful influences. The potential to produce crops more frequently from the same acreage is an important part of any such considerations. For instance, in some parts of the world favorable weather may permit planting and harvesting of three crops a year from the same soil. In other places, it can be challenging simply to plant and harvest a single annual crop. In some cases, local land costs and the prices charged for seed and fertilizer offset such natural location advantages for more frequent plantings and harvests. Or, the cost of transporting the food to customers may be so high that profitability is greatly reduced.

Those who ultimately consume a crop can have a large influence on pricing and farm profitability. While millions of the people who are poised at or near the edge of starvation mostly eat just a few staples such as rice and wheat, other crops may be used mostly by the wealthy.

Consider flowers. Most poor people have no flowers in their homes, pick wild flowers, or grow their own. Some high-income people are interested in having the very nicest flowers at home and seldom choose to supply their own needs (except for the rare orchid hobbyist or devoted greenhouse gardener). If flower prices are high enough, it may be profitable to ship fresh blooms by air to the world's markets from almost anywhere, such as regularly occurs with many of the flowers that are commercially grown in northern Tanzania.

Even for food staples, customer preferences can greatly affect farm pricing and profits. While rice is often perceived by those where little of it is consumed as an undifferentiated commodity, some Japanese people will pay a substantial premium for the highest grade of domestically produced rice. Testing labs can effectively differentiate higher-grade from lower-grade rice, providing a necessary element for obtaining such premium prices.

Consumers who pay the most for specialized crops may have unmet needs that offer still more profitable opportunities. For instance, some people (and I'm one of them) are allergic to various pesticides. To produce more "perfect" flowers, many varieties of glorious blooms are loaded with pesticides that can cause unpleasant reactions among the allergic. As a result my wife is seldom able to have cut flowers at home. If organic versions of such flowers were available, I'm sure I would be a steady customer and my wife would be most pleased.

Because of not being in touch with ultimate purchasers and end users, many farmers may not be alert to their best opportunities. In some cases, agricultural marketing cooperatives can identify such unmet consumer needs that could be profitably served and then develop the markets.

Some farmers must restrict their consideration of alternative crops due to capital limitations. While a subsistence farmer will undoubtedly find it to be too big of a financial stretch to provide hothouse tomatoes during the winter, the higher return from using a treadle pump for irrigation to greatly increase harvests during dry seasons might generate enough cash so that drip irrigation could gradually be afforded and eventually permit raising high-priced specialty crops that require more continual moisture.

While an impoverished farmer might not be able to afford a treadle pump, several such farmers might have enough funds to join in a lending group so that one of them could make the investment and be able to make better crop choices. When the borrowed funds are repaid from the increased profits, the money received could then be lent to a second farmer … and so on … until a whole farming community could complete a desirable equipment investment. Then, the process could begin again with a further round of investments for a still more expensive technology or farming practice. During subsequent investing rounds, the farmers who lend could study the investing farmers' experiences to learn how to profit from the new investment before personally borrowing funds.

In addition, many governments have programs to facilitate investments that are intended to increase farmers' productivity and profitability. Many times individual farmers don't have the knowledge and skills to access such government programs. Agricultural cooperatives focused on producing, processing, and storing crops can often help in such circumstances. In some countries (such as India), government grant, lending, and subsidy programs are mostly available through such cooperatives. In addition, breakthrough tutors could develop programs to help farmers learn how to access such government programs.

I also encourage farmers to understand more about the relative potential advantages and disadvantages of their locales and farms in the context of world agriculture and consumption. Once farmers understand what to optimize and to minimize about their farms, it becomes much easier to consider what to raise or to grow. Here's an example. Farmers in many lesser-developed countries know that they have disadvantages due to too little or too much water, poor farming infrastructures, and expensive shipping, as well as limited financial abilities to afford hybrid seeds, manufactured fertilizers, and the most effective pesticides and herbicides. Such apparent disadvantages may, however, turn out to be major advantages for producing, say, low-cost organic honey, a highly valued food that's increasingly difficult to acquire in advanced economic countries where organic farming is limited.

In thinking about what crops to offer, it's important to consider where higher-priced markets are located. Many southern hemisphere farmers can earn quite good livings with labor-intensive crops that are in demand during the winter months in populous high-income parts of the northern hemisphere. If there are also good southern hemisphere markets for harvests during their spring and fall months, such crops can take these farmers to higher levels of prosperity.

Having started to look at timing of crops by making this observation about seasonality across the hemispheres, let's now shift to "when" the crops are produced.

When? For those farmers who are in or could shift to operating in locales where multiple annual crops are feasible (including by using hothouse methods), the timing of when to grow which crops becomes very important. Deliver fresh strawberries when almost everyone else does, and prices will be low. Produce the same strawberries at a time when few other good berries are available, and prices will be much higher.

Such a focus on timing can seem counterproductive to a farmer who is anxious to maximize production. In most locales, the right timing for the biggest harvest is important to gaining more good growing weather and access to seasonal agricultural laborers. Yet taking reasonable production risks can pay off handsomely in terms of economic value by making it possible to deliver a different crop at another time, instead of harvesting greater quantities of the usual crops when most others do.

Since most farmers should seek substantial nonfarming sources of income, there's also the question of how best to optimize when such income is earned. While many farmers will automatically assume that the timing should only be when agricultural prospects are minimal, it may turn out to be that nonfarming income prospects are much brighter than for farming opportunities during the usual peak periods to plant, to cultivate, and to harvest.

Here's a hypothetical example. Let's imagine that the family leads wining and dining trips around the world to observe the best ways to farm and to enjoy remarkable meals made from outstanding fruits, vegetables, and meats, and the family's nonfarming business is much more profitable than farming. If the time when such trips are of most interest to tourists is when a farmer's local planting or harvesting might normally occur, such a farmer might choose to shift what crops are grown and their timing to plant, instead, whatever requires the least time and attention during the prime touring season. For instance, a farmer who provides such foreign tourist trips might become an apple grower and convert the family's local farm activities to focus on educational visits during which students and tourists harvest the apples rather than relying on family and agricultural workers. A major source of added income from growing fruit could be turning the apples that students and tourists pick into baked goods (such as pies and turnovers) during cooking classes conducted at or near the ranch.

In New England where I live, many farmers do something even more entertaining by transforming their farms into temporary theme parks during fall evenings and weekends when farming activity is light. On such entertaining occasions, many lunches, dinners, and snacks are served, some of which might come direct from the farm's harvest. Such activities could easily be extended into providing "winter wonderland" experiences during the colder times of the year for city dwellers and suburbanites who want to be outdoors but aren't active as skiers and skaters.

If people develop enough of a "taste" for the special foods available during entertainment visits, the farm family could begin offering processed foods from its harvests year-round to visitors who take the foods home. If that works well, the family could also let customers purchase online, by mail order, and in local stores. I'm told that Knott's Berry Farm (now primarily a theme park) in Buena Park, California (not far from Disneyland), got such a start in branded foods during the Depression by providing its highly regarded boysenberry jams, jellies, preserves, and related baked goods along with tasty chicken dinners to the farm's visitors.

Where? As you can imagine from the "When?" discussion, thinking about seasonality and opportunities for harvesting multiple crops annually from the same soil should also lead to considering how staying in one location and optimizing the farming and nonfarming income opportunities there compare to what can be accomplished in higher-potential locations elsewhere. During the early days of the United States, for instance, it wasn't unusual for a farmer to begin with infertile soil in a poor growing climate and then to move on after hearing about free or inexpensive land with better soil in a more favorable climate. Such a process led my farming ancestors, for instance, to move westward in small stages over more than 200 years from Delaware until they reached the more fertile Illinois plains. I well remember how my paternal grand-father and my father would speculate about how much more could be accomplished by obtaining more fertile land. To their minds, the search for a better location should never end. Despite such sensitivities, most farmers will only consider choices within the same locale. Yet the best opportunities for them are almost always hundreds, or even thousands, of miles away.

In making such comparisons between operating in one location or another, farmers should consider the likely changes in the value of farm land. Farms are normally located in rural areas because it's often easier and cheaper to operate there. In geographical areas where the population is rapidly expanding, what was once low-priced agricultural land may eventually develop a valuation based on potential commercial uses (such as for shopping centers, manufacturing plants, stand-alone retail outlets, and warehouses) and residences (for single-family houses and apartment buildings). That financially favorable result may be due, in part, to an advantaged climate that can make farming more profitable and attract people who will pay a great deal to live in such weather.

As a result, locating where such population expansions are likely to occur will often be much more valuable than simply looking for the most fertile and desirable land. This observation isn't meant to suggest that potential land appreciation should solely determine the ultimate decision, but simply that such appreciation should be considered as one element of such decisions. While some farmers might fear that this approach would lead them to leave farming, such a farmland sale could also finance a farmer to purchase and to farm even more land than would otherwise be affordable in a still more desirable location for farming.

I also encourage farmers to consider the long-term effects of a region's population growth when choosing a location, even if there is no apparent potential for converting land from farming to a use that will increase its value. That's because some other quality of the land may provide benefits that will increase due to population growth. In arid regions, access to pure water to sell can be such a benefit. In areas near cities with poor quality air, winds that drive out pollution that would otherwise stunt crops and annoy people may be a valuable resource for maintaining land value. If there is mineral or hydrocarbon extraction nearby, farmers should consider what mineral and hydrocarbon rights they can obtain by owning farmland in a given location. Yesterday's "worthless" land in some mineral- and hydrocarbon-rich areas can become immensely valuable whenever technology develops that makes extraction financially attractive. *The 2,000 Percent Solution* describes an example of how buying low-cost oil and gas rights in ponds and lakes surrounded by producing wells in Louisiana became a way to create enormous wealth. After drillers learned how to extract oil and gas located under bodies of water, immense hydrocarbon production fields were opened up.

Population growth can also affect the types of farming that are most desirable. Until consumer interest in visiting vineyards and wineries made it financially attractive to plant vines and build wine-making facilities in many fertile parts of northern California, much of such land was once used for little other than cattle grazing. In other areas, population expansion can increase demand for fresh-picked garden vegetables, herbs, and fruits. In such cases, farmers may be able to use their own farm stands to sell the bulk of their harvests to consumers who travel or live nearby.

In other areas, open spaces may not be very available. To make living in densely populated areas more appealing, local residents or towns may be willing to pay premium prices to purchase farmland that can be turned into arboretums and parks. In some cases, families leaving farming have been able to sell their farms to consumer cooperatives that continued farming to serve local residents.

Why? In seeking what to produce, farmers can greatly benefit from understanding more about why end users and consumers are attracted to or repelled by what farmers could grow or provide. Such knowledge is important because both with food and aesthetic (such as flowers and pumpkins for carving) crops, preferences are more complex than how much something costs and what practical benefits (such as nutrition or amount of color) are provided. Deeper insights into motivations can provide greater advance warning about what crops should be reduced or eliminated, and what crops should be investigated and potentially produced.

Let me provide a few examples of such subtle influences. Let's start at the chicken coop to see how industry practices and consumer perceptions can shift opportunities. Many people don't realize that eating chicken was once an occasional treat, partially because chicken was so expensive compared to other meats unless you raised your own. As a result, a fried chicken dinner on Sunday was much treasured in the United States, something that provided a lot of satisfaction for those who cooked and ate it.

Let's fast forward to the 1970s. By then, it was cheaper on a pound-for-pound basis to produce and to process a chicken than it was a steer. As a result, many chicken producers expected an enormous expansion in their markets as this "traditionally preferred" food became much less expensive.

While chicken consumption certainly grew, it did so at a much slower rate than most chicken producers expected. Why? Chicken became less expensive in part due to the rapidly increasing productivity of so-called factory farms and more automated processing plants. The resulting chickens didn't taste the same as the ones that had made such great fried chicken, and people were also more likely to experience illnesses from eating chicken due to crowded conditions for growing chickens and declines in processing hygiene. Chicken increasingly became perceived as relatively tasteless "cheap animal protein" rather than as a delicious, highly regarded treat with pleasant family connotations. A helpful offset to chicken's declining perception was the growing awareness that broiled skinless chickens contained little fat and were low in calories relative to how much protein was provided.

A farmer or chicken processor who understood these consumer perception shifts during the 1970s might have looked into providing premium-priced traditional chickens for those who craved better flavor and less health risk. Instead, the farming and processing focus remained on producing ever more bland chickens at still lower costs.

Since then, some consumers have also grown concerned about the extensive use of antibiotics in chicken houses and the ethical appropriateness of such growing conditions. These concerns led to the "free-range" chicken alternative that allowed some consumers to feel a little better about what they were eating. From there, consumer interest in organically grown chickens also increased.

Let's look at a different trend to see how shifts in the tastes can influence demand. American food has traditionally been relatively plain and bland. Think of a New England boiled dinner (often comprising corned beef, cabbage, and peeled potatoes) as an example. With the arrival of many immigrants whose traditional dishes were more complex, flavorful, and highly spiced (such as are found in Italian, Greek, and Mexican cuisines), alternative cooking styles became well established by the end of the twentieth century. Many people tried different cuisines and liked what they ate. A yearning grew to try even more of the flavorful alternatives that hadn't yet been experienced.

Perhaps the best indicator of this trend towards experimenting with nontraditional American cuisines was found in the popularity of Julia Child's French cooking television show and the huge sales of her cookbook dating back to the 1960s. Farmers who paid attention could have interpreted this interest as being part of a trend that would reward those who provided higher-quality fresh ingredients for various ethnic cuisines. Since those who were buying, preparing, and eating such foods were highly educated, well-paid people, the profit potential from serving such an emerging preference was going to be very good.

Chiles are a good example. American production was initially focused on supplying canners who sold to ethnic restaurants that mostly served people for whom these spicy treats were traditional family favorites. Prices were low, and growing was focused onto the season when the canners operated. But those who wanted to prepare Diana Kennedy's intriguing "authentic" Mexican recipes from *The Cuisines of Mexico* (Harper & Row, 1972) needed to have more kinds of chiles and wanted them be fresh. Obviously, such ingredients were going to be required year-round, and places where chiles could be grown continually (as with strawberries in milder climates) could add another premium-priced harvest, especially for crops produced well before the canning season.

Here's an educationally driven trend that might have been discounted by some farmers: the growing interest in so-called superfoods that provide unusually high quantities of newer, sought-after nutritional qualities. An example can be found in wild blueberries. Those who harvest this small crop argue in favor of eating wild blueberries because of documentation that these berries have about 50 percent more antioxidants (thought by some to help prevent cancer and to retard aging) than the plumper, more visually appealing, cultivated blueberries.

In many cases, such superfoods aren't commercially grown (as with blueberries), but are just harvested in the wild. Various wild algae products provide another intriguing example. At one time such "food" was thought to be only pond scum. Now people pay as much as $100 for a bottle of this freeze-dried food, which is thought by some to provide superior trace mineral absorption due by binding more of such minerals with proteins.

As a result of such nutritional interests, farmers might find that by locating in some places versus others they might acquire access to extremely high-valued crops requiring little work other than harvesting and processing. In many cases, consumers are as concerned about the processing methods for such foods as they are about the raw material's purity. Consequently, wise farmers should either process and market their own, join farmer-owned and -directed processing cooperatives, or supply highly regarded branded processors.

To find opportunities, emerging trends that are being encouraged by processors and branded food providers should also be considered. After Perdue Farms began branding its chickens, CEO Frank Perdue decided to add marigold petals to his chickens' feed. Although most people cannot discern a taste difference from this ingredient, adding the petals caused the chickens to have a differentiated yellow color that many consumers preferred. As a result, farmers located near Perdue chicken houses gained opportunities to grow marigolds on their farms.

A newer processor trend is developing foods that can improve health. While many families have traditionally served homemade chicken soup in the belief that it overcomes a cold or the flu, there's solid research demonstrating that a wider variety of foods can help avoid some sicknesses and diseases. When such foods become popular, farmers would do well to consider how they can become preferred providers.

In other cases, food processors are missing major opportunities due to how they conduct business. In some of such instances, farmers may be able to develop more profitable businesses. Consider vegetables. Many vegetables are either canned or frozen. Except during the height of the harvest, fresh vegetables usually sell for a lot more than preserved ones. Focus on providing fresh "out-of-season" crops from low-cost locations near to consumers during the rest of the year, and good profits will follow.

Here's a different example of shifting what needs to be done in order to fulfill consumer desires. If you purchase a cup of high-quality black coffee at a fine emporium, you might pay two to five dollars for it. Yet, you could probably purchase a pound of the beans to make a very similar cup of coffee for ten dollars and produce from those beans forty to sixty cups of coffee at a cost of $0.25 to $0.38 each. Of that much lower cost, coffee farmers might only receive $0.02 to $0.03 per cup. What's with that?

Well, many consumers of any crop are willing to pay a lot more for the ultimate food preparation and the surroundings where they consume the resulting item than they are for just the raw materials that help make the item desirable. Understanding why consumers spend as they do should cause coffee farmers to cooperate with one another, with cooperatives, and with partners to go into the business of also providing highly preferred preparation methods in desirable surroundings.

While there are many other potential lessons relating to "why" virtually any crop is purchased, space does not permit more examples. With the Internet many farmers can learn enough about purchasing and consumption practices in other parts of the world to spot unusual behaviors that can greatly help or hurt their farming profitability. I don't want to turn this blueprint into a detailed description of how to conduct so-called root-cause analysis, but I do suggest that those who want to develop better answers learn such skills. In the meantime, those who don't yet know how to identify root causes can simply rely on persistence by continually asking "why" seemingly anomalous behaviors occur until a kernel of continuing insight can be gained. As an example of such continual asking, consider the discussion of the shift from bland traditional American foods to spicier ethnic cuisines in this part of the business model blueprint.

How? Few people are aware of all the best practices that can be successfully applied to various aspects any given task. By simply searching out what has worked for other farmers producing the same or similar crops in comparable conditions and testing what is uncovered, farmers who combine more excellent practices than anyone else has can establish a breakthrough future best practice.

Any such investigations should focus on activities with the most potential to increase value added (the price received minus the total cost of all purchased inputs). Shifting farmers' attention to the biggest value-added opportunities will provide the greatest benefits for those who are now focusing solely on increasing crop yields and reducing costs.

Let me explain more about what I mean by increasing value added. Most farmers who grow corn choose seeds that will produce either lots of human food (sweet corn) or animal feed. Neither form of corn usually provides a high income. What can be done instead? Relatively few such corn farmers will consider growing colorful heritage corn suitable for being lacquered and used in decorations as a value-added opportunity. Yet a farmer who grows such decorative corn could also expand into making such decorations and selling them locally and over the Internet. Such a successful commercial activity could increase a corn farmer's value added per acre by more than ten times.

Even more can be accomplished when farmers learn how to develop 2,000 percent solutions rather than simply engaging in traditional improvement analysis. One of my students, Dr. Donald Kamdonyo, showed the potential of such training in his work with chicken producers in Malawi. I suspect that similar benefits will often be found from applying the 2,000 percent solution process to other forms of agricultural production.

Such breakthrough learning methods can provide two substantial benefits:

1. Farmers can identify and emulate ideal practices that no one else is considering. (For more information about identifying ideal practices, please read the blueprint on this subject in Appendix B of *2,000 Percent Living*.)

2. Farmers can build advantaged business models in new markets and improve existing business models while also greatly reducing investments to create and to operate businesses.

Another of my students, Dr. Burra Ramulu, demonstrated that community-wide agricultural cooperatives can use 2,000 percent solution training to greatly increase farming incomes as well as how much land is farmed while substantially reducing debt burdens. (You can read an overview of his experiences in the Introduction to *2,000 Percent Living*.)

A third student, Dr. Ikandilo Kushoka, created a methodology in his doctoral dissertation for developing the farming information needed to identify and implement agricultural 2,000 percent solutions on a regional or national basis. Farming cooperatives, various nongovernmental organizations seeking to improve agricultural practices, and governments can facilitate such learning by following Dr. Kushoka's process. (If you would like to learn more, please contact me at askdonmitchell@yahoo.com and I will introduce you to Dr. Kushoka.)

Reading and applying the lessons of *Business Basics* can also help with identifying improved "how" methods. Combining farming with Internet-based nonfarming businesses appears to have especially great potential. Such a combination works well because farming success can often be enhanced by relocating, and Internet businesses can typically be operated from almost anywhere without being affected. Internet-based businesses can also provide an economic cushion for farmers while they are making substantial business-model shifts that might otherwise be too financially risky to take.

How much? Although this section is about pricing, I found that addressing the topic also dovetails with the just completed "how" section. Please read this pricing material, in part, as an extension of "how" to farm and engage in complementary nonfarming activities.

Focusing on receiving a higher price is another way to help farmers locate better value-added opportunities. Providing differentiated products that deliver highly valued consumer benefits often works well for gaining a higher price.

Corn on the cob provides a helpful example. American families traditionally cooked and served whole ears of corn. This approach can create problems. If you don't shuck the outer leaves at the store, you could find you had bought moldy ears. Many of the kernels near the ends of "good" ears usually aren't as nice looking, tasty, and juicy as those kernels in the middle. Some of the end kernels might even taste a little "off." If a whole ear of corn was too much for someone to eat, an ear would be sliced in half. In that case, someone might receive a portion that mostly contained unappetizing kernels. Children would often "graze" randomly on an ear, leaving most of the kernels uneaten.

The leaders of Bird's Eye® frozen vegetables realized that such difficulties presented opportunities. The organization responded by packaging its frozen Sweet Mini Corn on the Cob in clear plastic bags so that purchasers could easily see all the kernels. The company also packaged just the most prime kernels in smaller lengths that were cut from the center of the cobs. These mini ears provided both portion control and a predictable calorie count. The result was to deliver the best possible frozen corn on the cob.

The Bird's Eye® brand charged a premium price for this product that made it more profitable to sell frozen mini ears than full ears. To provide this superior product at a low-enough cost, Bird's Eye® engaged agricultural experts who taught farmers how to grow ears that could be profitably processed into mini ears. The extra effort involved was worth it for farmers because they, too, received a higher profit margin from growing corn for mini ears.

Notice that even if Bird's Eye® had not created this product, individual farmers who lived close to densely populated areas could have processed their own fresh corn to deliver mini ears with similar advantages and sold them at their own farm stands. Seeing the benefit for making a farm stand more successful, a farming family could have also learned from that experience to look for other higher-priced specialties to sell, regardless of whether such specialties were grown on that farm.

If such an expanded farm stand succeeded with selling specialties, it would be natural to look next at how to extend the farm stand's selling season by attracting customers when no locally grown or produced foods and decorations were available. Such year-round farm stand success might lead next to a search for unique specialties that were always available. If such offerings were desirable enough, it would be natural to begin providing the specialties through direct sales activities via catalogs, mailings, faxes, telephone calls, and the Internet. To help draw more customers outside of the normal growing and harvesting months, seasonal activities could be offered such as tapping maple trees to make syrup in the spring and sleigh rides during the winter. Such a price-enhancing business-model-improvement path could ultimately lead to creating an agriculturally based retail enterprise not unlike what Wall Drug did for nonfood items in the 1990s.

By listening to and serving the farm stand's customers, a farmer could discover the benefits of producing other specialties, perhaps beginning by simply stocking processed versions of such specialties to determine the demand. While purchases were building for a new offering, a farm could begin to shift its crops to produce some specialties for the farm stand, while still providing commodity versions for the wholesale market.

If a farm stand develops enough business, the volume of retail customers could grow to the point that other items could be offered on a seasonal basis. For instance, a farmer in a nation where there are many

Christians could grow Christmas trees on some inexpensive forest land. In December, such trees could be harvested weekly and brought to the farm stand. The farming family could also construct uniquely beautiful wreaths, table decorations, and outdoor décor for those who wanted a more festive look at home or at work. By making such items fresh every day, customers could use the decorations to enjoy more vibrant and appealing holiday celebrations.

Near my home, the Audubon Society operates a small working farm that families can visit to learn more about agriculture. In many metropolitan areas, there are no such learning opportunities. A farming family that enjoyed having visitors could dedicate a portion of a farm to hosting such visits. A modest fee could be charged for tours or the farming family could simply seek enough visitor purchases to cover the costs.

Most children like to ride ponies but have relatively few opportunities to do so. Such a farm could consider keeping a few ponies for this purpose and providing a short trail where parents, guardians, and grandparents could lead ponies for their little cowgirls and cowboys. If enough children enjoyed this opportunity, the farming family could eventually start a small stable and offer trail rides and riding lessons. From there, the family could begin providing stables for horses owned by those with no place to care for them.

Many youngsters like to fish, but often lack convenient places to do so. A farm pond could be stocked with fish so that youngsters could catch fish and take them home to eat. Poles and bait could be provided, and families could simply be charged for the fish they catch based on their weight.

Families lacking appropriate ground for their own gardens might welcome opportunities to rent a patch to grow a few vegetables and fruits. In this way, some youngsters could discover the joys of planting, tending to plants, and enjoying a harvest.

I'm sure you get the idea. In just one to three generations, ties between most people and farms have been lost in many economically developed countries. Families that remain in farming can provide new links to the beneficial experiences that farming formerly provided for almost everyone. Making such connections today just takes desire and being reasonably close to some "city folks" who want to get back in touch with their ancestors' roots.

I would be guilty of great thoughtlessness if I didn't address how to improve the prices received by subsistence farmers wherever they happen to be in the world. The traditional approach for many of these farmers has been to harvest a crop when the crop seemed to be most appealing in the farmer's eyes, to load it up the next day, and to immediately take it to market for sale. Such farmers often had no idea what the price would be when they went to sell, and many could not afford to return home with the harvest if the price was temporarily too low.

In most countries today, cellular telephone service has become inexpensive and available enough that even poor farmers can usually make a call to check on prices. That's important because a farmer might be able to substantially increase income by selling into a peaking market and by avoiding a falling one.

A greater problem for the subsistence farmer has often been the expense of high-interest-rate loans taken out to purchase seed, fertilizer, and tools. Because of these high interest rates, many subsistence farmers cannot afford to wait for a better price than they can receive by selling immediately. Here's where access to lower-cost credit can make a big difference, either through microloans such as the Grameen Bank provides in Bangladesh or through cooperative-based loans such as the Indian government encourages.

Of even greater significance to many subsistence farmers is gaining access to agricultural information over the Internet. From studying such information, subsistence farmers can understand more about why prices are high or low for their crops and how such prices are most likely to trend in future years. In addition, such farmers can use the Internet to identify new nonfarming sources of income and to learn how to conduct such activities.

I also see potential for farmers to work with small specialty retailers in other parts of the world to identify opportunities to sell agricultural specialties that cannot be economically produced in the retailers' own nations. Perhaps Web sites will be established to make such connections between farmers and specialty retailers, performing much in the way that eBay does now in gathering and connecting buyers and sellers of unique items.

I would also be remiss if I didn't point out that there's another entry point for farming: having a high-income "day" job that makes it financially feasible to purchase and operate a farm, orchard, or ranch. In my roles as a graduate school professor and consultant, I've had the pleasure of meeting a number of top professionals whose passions involved farming, ranching, and horse breeding. These highly intelligent and well-educated people saw agricultural activities as ways to advance a state of the art they cared about while enjoying a lifestyle that provided them with more fundamental satisfactions than did their professional work as entrepreneurs, executives, consultants, and educators.

By bringing tremendous knowledge, skills, and resources to agriculture, such farming aficionados have benefited from attracting customers who pay extremely high prices for what they produce and for any training and education that they receive concerning such advanced practices. In many cases, the income opportunities from sharing the state-of-the-art agriculture greatly exceeded what could be earned from solely practicing that same art on the scale of a family operation.

****

While there's always more to observe and to share, the time has come to bring this appendix to a close. Before doing so let me briefly summarize four important lessons that I hope you noticed while reading the four blueprints.

1. With specialization in "what" is offered and "how" such specialties are provided, the small, new business or farm can actually gain pricing advantages that more than offset the cost-based disadvantages of its relatively small size, lack of awareness, and limited distribution.

2. By developing a superior business model and learning how to describe it to others, a business or farm owner can increase the income and cash flow earned from a business model breakthrough by hundreds of times relative to just growing its existing operations.

3. Building from a foundation of seeking to benefit all stakeholders provides a valuable guiding principle to avoid making major mistakes and to gain cooperation that facilitates exponential improvements that would otherwise be impossible.

4. Although ostensibly aiming at different industries with much different stakeholder needs, the natural evolution of all four blueprints will lead to someone engaged in any one of these business activities also becoming involved in some aspects of the other activities. While I spelled out that point most explicitly in the farming blueprint, I'm sure you can also see the potential opportunities to expand from any of the other three blueprints into a different one.

In addition, let me remind you that there are many more complementary dimensions of business breakthroughs that can be added should you feel too limited by working on the three breakthroughs (growing the market by twenty times, cutting costs by 96 percent, and eliminating 96 percent of investments) that have been featured in this book. While I'm unlikely to write future books to spell out those additional dimensions in detail, you can work with certified tutors who are knowledgeable in such other dimensions to help you. If you would like to be referred to one of these tutors, please contact me at askdonmitchell@yahoo.com/.